THE GYRFALCON

THE GYRFALCON

EUGENE POTAPOV

AND

RICHARD SALE

Published 2005 in the United Kingdom by T & AD Poyser, an imprint of A&C Black Publishers Ltd., and in the United States by Yale University Press.

ISBN 0-300-10778-1 (cloth: alk. paper)
Library of Congress Control Number: 2004114869

Typeset and designed by Laburnum Technologies
Printed and bound in China

A catalogue record for this book is available from the British Library.
The paper in this book meets the guidelines for permanence and durability of the Committee on Production Guidelines for Book Longevity of the Council on Library Resources.

10 9 8 7 6 5 4 3 2 1

Contents

Preface

In Reykjavik's old town, close to the harbour, stands the Fálkahúsið (Falcon House). One might assume that the name is merely a quaint one, perhaps given to the building because of the delightful carved falcons that adorn the roof. In fact, the name reflects a long association a fabled creature of the Arctic.

Until the middle of the twentieth century Iceland was under the rule of Denmark, and the two countries share a common heritage, the Norse settlers of Iceland being of the same stock as the folk who inhabited Norway, southern Sweden and Denmark. In medieval Europe falconry was the sport of kings and the bird which was the most prized was the largest falcon of them all. That falcon, the Gyr, was paler than its Peregrine cousin, but the most coveted of all its forms was the snowy white bird. Later, white Gyrs would be found in Greenland and Canada, but at that time the only place where the white bird could be found, and then only occasionally, was Iceland. The gift of a white bird was a gift without equal – and it was a gift whose source was jealously guarded by the Danish kings. Gyrfalcons caught in Iceland would be held in the Falcon House awaiting a ship bound for Denmark, the birds living in conditions that much of the Icelandic population could only dream of.

The Governor-General of Iceland issued trapping permits to a few selected subjects of the Danish crown, usually local dignitaries or officials. The permit holders, of course, hired locals to do the actual work. The Gyrfalcons were trapped at the nest (though these would have been grey-phase birds as Iceland does not have any resident white birds) or during winter, when the sought-after white birds had arrived from Greenland's east coast (Pordarson 1957). The trapping season started in March, birds being caught using bow-nets baited with domestic pigeons or chickens, or with captured Ptarmigan. The Gyrfalcons were delivered to the Royal Falconer at Sessastorir in south-west Iceland at first but, after 1763, the birds were taken to Reykjavik. The Royal Falconer chose those birds that were suitable to be shipped to Copenhagen, sick birds being killed and those unsuitable for falconry being released. Trappers were not paid for birds in these categories.

Almost 5,000 Gyrfalcons were exported from Iceland to Denmark between 1731 and 1793 (Nielsen and Petursson 1995). Of these, the majority were Icelandic birds, but 315 were white and a further 156 were 'half-white'. Not until the 1760s, when falconry as a sport was declining in Europe, did the supply of Icelandic Gyrfalcons begin to exceed demand. In 1766 an annual limit of 100 birds was set for export to Denmark. By the early 1770s this had been lowered to 60, and by 1785 the limit stood at 30. In 1803 only three birds were exported. The last Gyrfalcon shipment was made in 1806.

Neither of us can remember the exact details of our first meeting, in the early 1990s, but we have convinced ourselves that it was at a conference entitled 'Britain in the Arctic'. Then, or perhaps later, we discussed, among many other things, the fact that there was no book on the most beautiful of Arctic raptors. By 1994 we were discussing producing our own book. A little later we involved Dr Andy Richford, of Academic Press, in our discussions. These led to sample writings and, eventually, to a contract for a Poyser book in 1998.

But nothing is easy in the world of ornithological writing. Work commitments, in the UK and elsewhere, meant that the book kept being pushed a little further back. Then the Poyser imprint was taken over, leading to a period of uncertainty about the title. Finally everything, the time, the commitment, slotted into place.

This book is the result of that happy coincidence.

The Gyrfalcon is not an easy bird to study, its habitat being among the most difficult to visit and live in. Yngvar Hagen, the well-known Norwegian ornithologist, was fascinated by raptors from the 1930s, but only on 30 June 1949 did he finally stand on the nesting ledge of a Gyrfalcon. His work on the species was published in the early 1950s. He later made a significant contribution to the understanding of the predator–prey relationship, introducing the 'threshold-to-settle' and 'threshold-to-breed' parameters in describing fluctuating raptor populations.

Alexander Kishinskiy was an outstanding Arctic ornithologist. His studies in the Arctic began in 1954–57 on the Kola Peninsula (in north-western Russia) where he studied Gyrfalcons as part of his Master's degree thesis. Later he studied the fauna of Kolyma and the Koryak mountains. He was working on the analysis of the Eurasian ornithofauna as part of his DSc thesis when he died: the unfinished work was published (Kishinskiy 1988) by his friends and supporters.

Professor Tom Cade pioneered modern field studies of Alaskan Gyrfalcons. His first paper (1960) was based on observations of 86 Gyrfalcon nests (including 31 that he found himself). This was the first direct study of the Gyr which was extrapolatable for number estimates and for general comparison with other populations.

We are grateful for the work of these pioneers, on whose shoulders we have stood to observe Gyrfalcons more carefully.

We would also like to thank the many people who have helped us along the way, both in the field and with studies closer to home.

We thank Professor I.M. Kerzhner who, as a member of International Trust for Zoological Nomenclature, has made exceptionally valuable comments on the strict lines of the Code of Zoological Nomenclature (2000), and Professors M.A. Kozlov and R.L. Potapov (all three at the Zoological Institute, St Petersburg) for valuable comments on systematics and nomenclature. We thank the staff of the Library of the Linnean Society for their assistance. Invaluable information was kept at the

Alexander Library, Edward Grey Institute, Oxford and we thank the librarian Linda Birch, and Mike Wilson for their assistance. We thank staff and curators of the collections noted in the list below, and personally would like to thank Pavel Tomkovich, Vladimir Loskot, Per Ericson, Storrs Olson and Jon Fjeldså for their kind assistance and help. Apart from curatorial help, support by Robert Prys-Jones and the Tring branch of the BMNH was instrumental in the UV reflectance spectrometry studies.

We thank Olga Potapova for her very considerable help with the section of the book dealing with the palaeobiogeography of the Gyrfalcon. We thank Jevgeni Shergalin, Pertti Koskimies, Phil Shempf, Roald Potapov, Maria Gavrilo, Yakov Kokorev, Georgiy Simakov, Johan Ekenstedt, Yuriy Artukhin and Jesper Nyström for their help with rare publications and also for their advice. We are grateful to Ólafur Nielsen and Ulla Falkdalen for the time and effort they provided in the Gyrfalcon habitats in Iceland and Sweden. Research in north-east Siberia was funded by the Institute of the Biological Problems of the North, Russian Academy of Sciences, whose logistics were important for field work. Initial drafts of the book were written at the Department of Zoology, Uppsala University. We are grateful to the department and to Professor S. Ulfstrand for supporting one of the authors. We are grateful to Nick Fox for his support and advice during the final stages of the preparation of the book. The research visit to Copenhagen Museum would not have been possible without the tremendous help of Tom Cade. We thank Andy Bennett and the UV Group of the University of Bristol for their help and support: they were instrumental in the Gyr coloration studies. We thank Andy Richford, and Nigel Redman, Jim Martin, Marianne Taylor, Guy Kirwan and Hugh Brazier at A&C Black/Christopher Helm for their patience and perseverance. We thank Per Michelsen for use of his photographs. The remaining photographs were taken by the authors in Iceland, Russia and Canada. We also thank our families for their help, support and understanding.

Earlier in this preface we suggested that the production of the book has been a happy one. That is true, but the pleasure in preparing the book has been tempered by the need to be extremely careful with some information about the Gyrfalcon. The world population of the bird is relatively small. The bird is protected throughout its range, but the protection offered has to compete with the rewards available from unscrupulous bird trappers (and even egg collectors). There have been occasions when too much information on nest location has led to nest sites being robbed. We have therefore had to be very careful not to expose nest locations and even the concentrations of breeding pairs. This care has necessarily extended to photographs where the need to protect sites has meant that some excellent shots have been excluded or cropped.

The Gyrfalcon is a very special bird – the largest true falcon, the earliest breeding raptor, and one of the earliest breeding birds of the Arctic and sub-Arctic, a bird with a narrow ecological niche, a 'nest parasite', and a bird which is stenophagous in spring. We have attempted to provide as full an insight into this magnificent bird as possible.

Throughout the book we have converted the various units of references (feet, acres, Swedish miles etc.) into metric values. We have used the following abbreviations for the major collections we have referenced:

RMNH	Reykjavik Museum of Natural History, Iceland
BMNH	Natural History Museum, Tring, UK
CMNH	Copenhagen Museum of Natural History, Denmark
ZIN	Zoological Institute, Russian Academy of Sciences, St Petersburg, Russia
MZM	Moscow Zoological Museum, Russia
AMNH	American Museum of Natural History, New York, USA
SI	Smithsonian Institution

Within the text the use of certain scientific words and phrases has been inevitable. Where possible these have been defined at first occurrence. For those where the definition is lengthy, they have been included in a Glossary, which details not only scientific terms but also those from falconry.

In deference to our Mongolian colleagues we have used the spellings Chinghis and Kubilai for the Khans more normally rendered as Genghis and Kublai in English.

CHAPTER 1

Palaeobiogeography and Systematics

THE PALAEOBIOGEOGRAPHY OF THE GYRFALCON

About 10,000 years ago, at the end of the last great Ice Age, the plains of Siberia and much of western and northern Europe formed a single ecological unit, one which extended as far south as Mongolia and Kazakhstan, north to the edge of the Arctic Ocean and across Beringia (the Bering land bridge) into North America. This single ecological entity has been named the tundra–steppe (Yurtsev 1981). On it roamed large mammals, many of them now extinct. The names of some of these are not well known to the lay reader, but the most famous, an animal which has given its name to the whole assemblage, is the Mammoth. The Mammoth Fauna also included Woolly Rhinoceros, Reindeer, Moose, Bison, Saiga Antelope and Cherskiy/Przewalski's Horse.

(This section was prepared by Olga Potapova, Eugene Potapov and Richard Sale)

The landscape of the period has been reconstructed by several researchers (e.g. Yurtsev 1981, Sher 1997 and references therein). It was a rolling steppe of grass species with patches of shrubs and areas of deciduous forest (*Betula, Salix, Alnus* spp. and *Pinus pimula*). A similar landscape can be seen today in parts of Alaska, northern Canada and Siberia north of the timberline, and also in some areas of Iceland. In botanical terms, there are now many small refugia, where the ancient landscapes have survived. These remnant landscapes are mostly located on exposed southern slopes, but can also be found within areas of dense taiga forest (Yurtsev 1981) or in present day tundra. Between 15,000 and 13,000 years ago the sea level was 50–60m lower than the present level (Sher 1997).

In northern Asia glaciation covered only a few elevated places and there was no glaciation at all on the vast Asian plains (Sher 1997). In the absence of a continuous forest belt, the whole landscape formed a single 'hyperzonal' pasture, ideal for grazing and browsing animals. Larch, which now forms the backbone of existing Asian taiga forests, was present, but had yet to form any substantial forested areas (Yurtsev 1966) and the flora of the steppe was fully analogous to present-day communities. By contrast, the forest communities were different (as well as much smaller in size), being present only as forest stands surrounded by shrub and grass communities. Such habitat was ideal for Gyrfalcons as it provided perches and lookout posts as well as being ideal for grouse.

Willow Grouse and Ptarmigan inhabited these tundra–steppes together with Siberian and Collared Lemmings (Abramson 1993), which were the prey of the Snowy Owl (Potapova 2001). The ranges of Willow Grouse, and especially of Ptarmigan, during much of the Pleistocene era significantly exceeded their current ranges (Tyrberg 1995, Stewart 1999). Indeed, the remains of grouse in various sites across Eurasia are so numerous that it has been necessary to carry out studies to differentiate the remains of birds eaten by Gyrfalcons from those eaten by humans and owls (Mourer-Chauviré 1983, Bochenski *et al.* 1998). From these it is clear that there were falcons living close to the caves inhabited by Palaeolithic hunter–gatherers. In addition, there are excavated fossils of Gyrfalcons from the middle (Czech Republic) and late (Germany, Croatia, Slovakia, France, Hungary, Romania, Italy and Spain) Pleistocene periods (Janossy 1972, Mourer-Chauviré 1975).

In the Czech Republic, at the Stranska Skala Cave, remains of both Gyrfalcons (*Falco* aff. *rusticolus*) and Willow Grouse were found in the same strata (Janossy 1972). Similar findings have been recorded in Magdalenian deposits (*i.e.* late Pleistocene period) in France at Pierre-Chatel, a cave (occupied until Roman times) on the river Rhône between Geneva and Lyon where the earliest recorded Gyrfalcon is dated at 13,000 BP (before present) (Desbrosse and Mourer-Chauviré 1973). It is possible that the remains of the falcon and the grouse were brought into the cave by an Eagle Owl (*Bubo bubo*) as the owls are known to feed on both.

In Figure 1.1 (see colour section) we suggest an ancestry of Gyrfalcons and related falcon species. An earlier European falcon, known as *Falco antiquus*

(Mourer-Chauviré 1975), combined features of both the Gyrfalcon and the Saker Falcon (*Falco cherrug*) and was probably the common ancestor of these species. It is known from the Riss glaciation of the late middle Pleistocene in France (Mourer-Chauviré 1975). The earliest record of a true (or, to be more correct, a proto-) Gyrfalcon (*Falco* aff. *cherrug*) is from the Late Villafranchian (Tyrberg 1995) at the Betfia Cave in Romania. The Betfian falcon (dated to 1.8–1.3 million years BP) had many of the distinctive features of the modern Gyrfalcon (e.g. notched beak, massive tarsi); these were probably an adaptation for the hunting of Pleistocene Willow Grouse and Ptarmigan, each of which were both larger and heavier than present-day birds (Stewart 1999). However, as there has been little scientific revision of work on ancient falcons since the work of Mourer-Chauviré (1975), we cannot rule out the possibility that the Betfian falcon, along with the many other remains recovered from Europe's early–middle Pleistocene era, could be classified as *Falco antiquus* – and therefore the same as the falcons from Stranska Skala in the Czech Republic and Horvolgy in Hungary (Janossy 1986). Interestingly there are only a few palaeontological records of large falcons of the *cherrug–rusticolus–altaicus–antiquus* group in the late Pleistocene of Asia. One large falcon – with a much stronger tibiotarsus – has been described from the early middle Pleistocene. It was discovered at the Choukoutien Cave (locality 10), a site famous as the home of Peking man. The bird was named after the person who described it – *Falco chowi* (Hou 1993). The remains of Saker Falcons replaced those of *Falco chowi* in this locality only in the late Pleistocene. However, once again no comparisons were made between *Falco chowi* (aff. *rusticolus*) and *Falco antiquus* (aff. *rusticolus*), so the systematic relationship of the two is not clear. It is possible that they are in fact the same species.

In southern Siberia remains of the Saker Falcon, together with the remains of five species of tetranoid birds (including *Lagopus*) have been found in the Tonnelnaya Cave, close to the Birusa River – a tributary of the Chuna River – some 200km north-east of Krasnoyarsk, and dated to 13,500 BP. Similar finds have been made in the Dvuglazka Cave in the upper Yenisey region (Ovodov and Martynovich 1992, 2000). In the Strashnaya (Horrible) Cave in Altai remains of a proto-falcon (determined as *Falco altaicus*) accompanied by both species of *Lagopus* have been found and dated to 45,000–25,000 years BP (Burchak-Abramovich and Burchak 1998). The falcon very much resembles modern Saker Falcons.

Remains of Pleistocene proto-falcons have also been found in North America, in the asphalt levels of the McKittrick site in California. The remains have been named *Falco swarthi* (Miller 1927) and are larger than both Peregrine and Prairie Falcons from the same site. *Falco swarthi* was comparable in size to the Gyrfalcon, but somewhat different in shape. The remains of Prairie and Peregrine Falcons considerably outnumber those of *Falco swarthi*, suggesting that the bird was rather rare at the site. The tarsi of *Falco swarthi* appear to be about the same size as those of modern Gyrfalcons, but, Miller considered, had relatively greater lifting power.

Again this is likely to have been a necessary adaptation because of the size of the Pleistocene grouse species in comparison to their modern descendants.

A Gyrfalcon was identified from late Pleistocene strata at Bell Cave in the Laramie Range of Albany County, Wyoming (Emslie 1985). The bone found was a tarsometatarsus. Emslie (1985) compared the bone to the extinct species *F. swarthi* from McKittrick, California. *Falco swarthi* is considered to be inseparable from *F. rusticolus* and is synonymised with that species.

In France it has been shown that the percentage of *Lagopus* remains from excavated avifauna steadily declines from almost 100% at *c.* 15,000 years BP to 70% at 10,000–6,000 years BP, and then to about 50% by the period 5,000–1,000 years BP (Tyrberg 1995). This suggests that the avifauna was both changing rapidly and becoming more diverse. In general, the palaeorecords for both *Lagopus* species and proto-falcons suggest that during the Pleistocene the species were evolving in southern and western Europe and southern Siberia, and that in the late Pleistocene/Holocene the birds advanced towards north-east Siberia and into North America. In fact, a similar general trend is also described for the entire Mammoth Fauna assemblage (Sher 1997). There is no doubt that the tundra–steppe animals were migratory, with herds of Saiga Antelope, Cherskiy/Przewalski's Horse, Reindeer, Moose – and also Woolly Rhinoceros and Mammoths themselves – migrating seasonally across western and eastern Siberia. These herds were accompanied by Pleistocene grouse species and, therefore, by falcons. Recent studies of Mammoth tusks excavated on the Taimyr Peninsula have confirmed that Mammoths in the northern parts of their distribution had a complicated pattern of seasonal migrations (Fisher and Beld 2002).

Interestingly Gyrfalcons have preserved the migration patterns of the Pleistocene. Alaskan birds do not migrate south-east with the flocks of Snow Geese (*Anser caerulescens*) and Sandhill Cranes (*Grus canadensis*), but south-west, across the Bering Strait to the Shantar Islands, south-west of the Sea of Okhotsk (see Chapter 7 on migration). Equally interesting is the fact that a parallel migration route is still followed by the Saiga Antelopes of Kazakhstan.

Eventually the larch evolved and spread. Larch is a unique tree, the only species which can thrive in conditions of continuous permafrost, and the tree's spread changed forever the landscapes of the tundra–steppe. As the larch spread, only those animals which were capable of living in, or were able to migrate through, the forests survived. These species were the Reindeer and Moose, though horses and the Saiga Antelope survived on the southern steppe, well outside the taiga zone. Mammoth, Bison and Musk Ox became extinct in northern Asia during a period when the larch forest advanced to the shores of the Arctic Ocean. Bison and Musk Ox survived in North America and Greenland, to which they were able to retreat, but Mammoths were squeezed to their last Holocene refuge on Wrangel Island (Vartanyan *et al.* 1993) where the last member of this relict dwarf form died only about 3,700 years BP.

Species surviving on both sides of the taiga belt became completely separated by the larch, evolving northern and southern forms, the taiga zone acting as an ecological barrier in the speciation process. One species showing this process clearly is the Narrow-skulled Vole (*Microtus gregalis*). Today, the rodent has a disjointed range; the northern population inhabits the tundras of northern Asia and the southern population lives on the steppes of Kazakhstan, Mongolia and Transbaikalia. Pleistocene remains of a common ancestor have been discovered between these two populations (Markova *et al.* 1995).

Something very similar happened to the proto-falcon, with two distinct species evolving – the Gyrfalcon in northern Asia and circumpolar from northern Asia, and the Saker Falcon on the steppes to the south of the taiga, the two species being very similar genetically (see the section dealing with genetics in this chapter). It is the considered view of the authors that future, more sensitive genetic methodologies will show that the Gyrfalcon is actually a younger species than the Saker Falcon.

The *Lagopus* species which form the primary prey of both the Gyrfalcon and the Saker survived not only in both the northern and southern parts of the proto-falcon range, but also in the taiga zone itself, where the birds breed in marshes and wide river valleys. On open tundra *Lagopus* are distributed evenly, but in the forest zone the range of the birds is very patchy. From an assumed common ancestor three *Lagopus* species evolved: the Willow Grouse or Willow Ptarmigan and its subspecies the Red Grouse; the Ptarmigan or Rock Ptarmigan; and the White-tailed Ptarmigan. Almost the entire range of these three species is overlapped by the breeding range of the Gyrfalcon; the roaming range of the Gyr is slightly more extensive than that of *Lagopus* spp.

We conclude that from Pleistocene times the Gyrfalcon (or the species which was its immediate ancestor) lived in close relationships with Willow Grouse and Ptarmigan. We further conclude that the range of the proto-falcon lay within the ecological boundaries of the Mammoth megafauna, and was not limited to either the Arctic or the sub-Arctic. Later the range was split by the taiga belt, an event which (not surprisingly) coincided with the Mammoth Fauna extinction. The Nearctic Gyrfalcon population then became geographically isolated due to the disappearance of Beringia, which was caused by rising sea levels as temperatures rose and the ice melted. In the southern part of the proto-falcon's North American range, the Prairie Falcon (*Falco mexicanus*, a 'recent' raptor species) evolved through isolation as a result of the Laurentide glacier. However, to the north of the Laurentide glacier, in Alaska, the Canadian archipelago and also in Greenland, the Gyrfalcon evolved. Similarly, two species emerged in Asia, in this case separated not by ice but by the expanding larch forest of the taiga. To the north was the Gyrfalcon, an essentially circumpolar species still undergoing gene flow throughout its entire range, from North America though Asia and Europe. To the south of the forest belt the proto-falcon evolved into the Saker Falcon.

THE SYSTEMATIC POSITION OF THE GYRFALCON

Todd and Friedmann (1947) wrote that 'Gyrfalcons have probably given more trouble to taxonomists then any other group of Arctic birds'. This sentence would be an excellent epigraph to this chapter.

SPECIES LEVEL: TRADITION RESTORED

For those not interested in systematics the message is clear: Gyrfalcon (*Falco gyrfalco nomen validum* Linnaeus 1758, *F. lanarius nomen oblitum* Linnaeus 1758, *F. rusticolus nomen dubium* Linnaeus 1758) is a monotypic species. However for those interested in systematics the story behind the species nomenclature is exciting.

Up to the present time the Gyrfalcon has been referred to in the literature by two synonymous names – *Falco gyrfalco* and *Falco rusticolus*. Both names (in addition to several other synonyms) were first introduced by the celebrated biologist Karl von Linné (Linnaeus 1707–78) in his *Systema Naturae* (1758). *Falco rusticolus* was used because Linnaeus mentioned, as a reference for *Falco gyrfalco*, a painting of a Goshawk by Olof Rüdbeck Jr (1660–1740), his teacher at Uppsala University. This interesting discovery was made by the Head of the Zoology Department of the Swedish Museum of Natural History, Einar Lönnberg (1865–1942) (Lönnberg 1930, 1931), who examined Rüdbeck's 1693–1710 collection of plates. Because of this discovery, which made the name *F. gyrfalco* dubious, some researchers have moved to the name *Falco rusticolus* simply because it has page priority. This statement about the page priority is no longer valid (Code of Zoological Nomenclature 2000). To be rejected, in accordance with Article 23.9.1.1(the senior synonym or homonym), it would need to be shown that *F. gyrfalco* has not been used as a valid name after 1899. But the name *Falco gyrfalco* did indeed continue to be used, e.g. by Dementiev (1951) who vigorously defended the traditional Gyrfalcon name and treated *F. rusticolus* as a doubtful appellation. Kozlova (1969) and Ivanov (1976) supported the view of Dementiev, but before we come to any conclusions in the matter of nomenclature we need to look again at the original works of Linnaeus and those of contemporary scientists. In doing so we hope to be able to sort out the mess.

The species name of the Gyrfalcon – Gyrfalcon, Gerfalke, Gerfaut, Jerfalcon, Giervalk – as well as its approximate distribution has been known (in Latin-educated countries) since the famous treatise by Frederick II of Hohenstaufen (1194–1250), which dates from about 1250 (Wood and Fyfe 1943). Shortly after publication of this work Marco Polo (Polo 1324) repeated the observations of Frederick II (without referring to the original – a custom in those days) while extending (disputably) the range of the Gyrfalcon into Asia. Willughby (1676) – written as Willinghby, Francis in Linnaeus (1746) but given as Willingby, Franciscus in Linnaeus/Gmelin (1788) – also left a good description of the Gyrfalcon in Latin. Do these names have priority? The answer is not really, from the point of view of the Code of Zoological Nomenclature. Article 3.2 states that no name or nomenclatural act published before 1 January 1758 enters zoological nomenclature. But can we use this reference to validate Linnaeus's original description? The answer this time is yes: the same Article 3.2 postulates that information (such as descriptions or illustrations) published before 1758 may be used.

It is true that despite these early observations the scientific systematics of the Gyrfalcon (as with many other species) starts in 1758, the year in which Linnaeus published the tenth edition of *Systema Naturae*, in which he introduced binomial nomenclature for the first time. In this edition of his work many species names were born, or reborn. One of these species was the Gyrfalcon, but during its rebirth complications arose that led to systematic disputes which have never been successfully resolved. Linnaeus does not refer to the manuscript of Frederick II, from which it may be deduced that he did not have the work available to him. He does refer, many times, to his own book *Fauna Svecica* (Linnaeus 1746), which he prepared after his trip to the Swedish province of Dalarna in 1734 (Linnaeus 1953: this is a facsimile edition of Linnaeus's diary which had never previously been published – the original diary is kept in the Uppsala University Library).

So is the use of Rüdbeck's plates of 1693–1710 appropriate in the revision of the Gyrfalcon's name? The Code of Zoological Nomenclature (2000) gives the definite answer – no. For a start, the code has a strict rule that authors must base their descriptions on "published material". And the Code also dictates (Article 8) what a publication is. Rüdbeck's plates do not fit this definition because they violate all three criteria for nomenclature publication:

Article 8.1.1   The publication must be issued for the purpose of providing a public and permanent scientific record. Rüdbeck's plates were used not for scientific records, but for lectures.

Article 8.1.2   It must be obtainable, when first issued, free of charge or by purchase. Rüdbeck's plates were not for sale: Uppsala University had to make a huge effort to repossess them from the Rüdbeck family.

Article 8.1.3   It must have been produced in an edition containing simultaneously obtainable copies by a method that assures numerous identical and durable copies. Only two, non-identical sets are known and none was available for the general public for a very long time.

In addition, Article 9 of the Code defines what does not constitute published work:

Article 9.1   After 1930 handwriting reproduced in facsimile by any purpose. This applies to all Rüdbeck pictures reproduced by Lönnberg (1931) and to facsimiles of the original watercolours produced in 1986.

Articles 9.2   (photographs), 9.3 (proof sheets), 9.4 (microfilms), 9.5 (acoustic records as such made by any method), 9.6 (labels of specimens) are not applicable to this case.

Article 9.7   Copies obtained on demand of unpublished work (Article 8) even if previously deposited in a library or other archive. The Rüdbeck originals of 1693–1710 fit this definition perfectly.

Article 9.8   Text or illustrations distributed by means of electronic signals (e.g. by means of the internet). This is clearly not applicable to this case.

Article 9.9   Abstracts of articles, papers, posters, texts of lectures and similar material when issued primarily to participants at meeting, symposia, colloquia or congress. Rüdbeck's originals (1693–1710) also fit this definition as they were material prepared for lectures.

Linnaeus's book *Fauna Svecica*, written in Latin, includes accurate accounts of the Gyrfalcon, as well as accounts of the Goshawk (*Accipiter gentilis*), Lanner (*Falco biarmicus*), Saker and other falcons, with clear descriptions of the species, all of them more or less consistent with the work of Frederick II. Some of these forms were missed in the 10th edition of *Systema Naturae*, while some were treated as synonyms. In Chapter 41 of the 10th edition Linnaeus describes the forms of the genus *Falco* (pp. 88–92), and mentions the Gyrfalcon several times. All the species in the edition were given numbers. Linnaeus divided the genus *Falco* into two parts: birds with yellow cere (*cera lutea*) and birds with dark cere (*cera obscura*). A footnote to the relevant page notes that there are also eagles and large falcons with unfeathered feet.

For each of the species in the book a short note (nowadays called a diagnosis) was given after the species name. The important section of the 10th edition is given in Box 1.1, together with a translation from the Latin of the relevant sections.

From Box 1.1 it appears that the Gyrfalcon is mentioned under the names *canadensis*, and also perhaps under *rusticolus* and *lanarius*, as well as under *gyrfalco*. The Goshawk was mentioned as *gentilis* and *palumbarius*. As Lönnberg (1930, 1931) correctly pointed out, Linnaeus referred to the *Falco gyrfalco* account number 62 in *Fauna Svecica* (Linnaeus 1746), which in turn referred to a picture by Olof Rüdbeck depicting a Goshawk. This, in the view of Lönnberg (1931), means that the name *F. gyrfalco* is not valid. However, before considering that question we need to look at all the material referenced in the 10th edition and also to consider the position relative to the Code of Zoological Nomenclature. The questions that need to be considered are: What did Linnaeus mean when he referred to the Gyrfalcon?

Box 1.1. Extracts from the 10th edition of *Systema Naturae* (Linnaeus 1758)

p. 88

4. Canadensis – cere yellow, feet feathered, body dark, tail white.

Aquila cauda alba

Habitat Canada. Breast white with scattered triangular dots.

[A clear description of a Gyrfalcon – there can be no confusion whatsoever]

5. Rusticolus. F. Cere yellow waxy, feet yellow, body ash-grey with undulate stripes, with white neck.

Habitat Sweden.

[Appears to be a description of a Peregrine rather than a Gyr]

p. 89

12. Gentilis. F. Cere and feet yellow, body ash-grey with brown spots, tail with four blackish stripes. Fauna Svecica 60, Will. Ornithol. 46.

Falco gentilis

Falco montanus

Habitat in mountains. Eats grouse species.

Used in arts of falconry as very good at hunting pigeons and shrikes, as well as gazelles, herons, small passerines.

[The hunting of gazelles is clearly from the manuscript of Marco Polo, a work which was known to Linnaeus. In this part Marco Polo was describing a hunt of Kubilai Khan, son of Chinghis, with 10,000 (!) Gyrfalcons]

p. 91

20. Lanarius. F. Cere yellow, feet blue, underbody with long streaks. Fauna Svecica 61, Will. Ornithol. 48.

Habitat: Europe. Migratory.

22. Gyrfalco. Cere blue, feet yellow (luteis) [more yellow than the yellow in Goshawk which had flavis feet], below with ash-grey streaks, side rectrices white. [A clear Gyrfalcon trait: apart from the white Goshawk of Kamchatka, out of reach in Linnean times, there is no Goshawk with white lateral rectrices]

Fauna Svecica 62, Will. Ornithol. 44.

Habitat Europe. Feeds on pigeons.

25. Palumbarius. Cere marginally black, feet yellow, body dark, rectrices with pale bars, eyebrow white.

Accipiter palumbarius.

Habitat: Europe.

Feeds on grouse.

Underbody with black and white streaks. Rectrices with white ends.

What is the species name of the Goshawk in view of the fact that the 'type painting' was used for another species? What bird did Linnaeus mean under the name *rusticolus*; where is the Peregrine in 10th edition? And, after all the above questions have been considered, which name of the Gyrfalcon has priority?

We begin by considering the relevant sections of *Fauna Svecica* (Linnaeus 1746). These are shown in Box 1.2, again with relevant translations from the Latin. (Note that some species accounts have been truncated to save space.) The Goshawk is described under the names *F. gentilis* and perhaps *F. gyrfalco*, while the Gyrfalcon is described under the name *F. lanarius* and perhaps also *F. gyrfalco*, and there is no mention of the name *F. peregrinus*. Does this mean that on his Dalarna trip Linnaeus did not see a specimen of *F. peregrinus*, or that he was confused with the morphs and age forms of birds of prey? The answer to this question we find in the next edition of *Fauna Svecica* (Linnaeus 1761). In this (Box 1.3), Linnaeus gives more details on *F. rusticolus* than in the 10th edition, but there is nothing suggesting that this is a Gyrfalcon.

What we have instead is a fine (but unfortunately not complete) diagnosis of a Peregrine. Indeed, what is being described is the Arctic Peregrine, the bird now known as *F. peregrinus calidus* (or known, in some early descriptions, as the White-cheeked Peregrine, *F. p. leycogenuys*). Shorter beak and immaculately white throat, together with a neck almost encircled by a white collar – this description was repeated almost exactly in the 1788 edition of *Systema Naturae*. The latter volume, edited by J.F. Gmelin, includes many more forms which refer to the Gyrfalcon. Here are the relevant names, in the order of the original: *canadensis, obsoletus, rusticolus, arcticus, islandus, sacer* (only from Hudson Bay), *gyrfalco, canadicans, islandicus* and *lanarius*. The book also mentions the Peregrine (species 88, p. 272) – "cere and feet yellow, upper body with black streaks, underbody rufous-white, with black stripes, tail with white spots" – which undoubtedly refers to the European subspecies of the Peregrine, which indeed is rusty coloured on the breast.

From the above, we conclude that the name of the Gyrfalcon, if it is to be based on Lönnberg's logic (1930, 1931) (page priority – no longer used in the Code), should be *Falco canadensis* L. 1758 – a potentially valid name (and the senior synonym). The description given by Linnaeus refers to a whitish Gyrfalcon and cannot be mistaken for any other falcon. The very accurate description was even expanded in the later editions of *Systema Naturae* (Linnaeus/Gmelin 1788). In this account of *F. canadensis* there is a reference to the notes of Marco Polo and the hunts of Tatar tribes with *canadensis* on 'hares, antelopes, foxes, wolves'. In the 10th edition similar hunts were mentioned in the account of *gentilis* (see Box 1.1). In the Marco Polo original (Polo 1324) we find similar passages on Gyrfalcons. The name *Falco rusticolus* should be rejected as *nomen dubium* because it is impossible to form a satisfactory identification of the species Linnaeus was referring to based on his description, and there is no type specimen now in existence. It could more likely be a Peregrine than a Gyrfalcon.

Box 1.2. Extracts from the 1746 edition of *Fauna Svecica* (Linnaeus 1746)

---

60. Falco with yellow legs, body ash-coloured, spots dark, tail with four bands.

 Will. orn. 46. Falco gentilis i.e. noble name

      45. Falco montanus

 Raj. av. 13. Falco gentilis i.e. noble name

Falco montanus

 Swedish: Falck.

Habitat: abundant in mountains of Dalarna, where it is captured by Germans every year.

Description: Size of a crow or a chicken. Feet, cere and iris are yellow. Whole body is ash-coloured with dark spots. Tail ash-coloured with four bands across tail.

61. Falco with blue feet, black and white streaks.

 Gesn. av. 76. Lanarius

Habitat: forests.

Description: Back and wings brownish, head and under body white-grey with black streaks, tail feathers with opposite white spots. Tarsi feathered more than a half. Feet blue. Beak blue. Very distinct from Italian Lanario [The Lanner Falcon, Falco biarmicus].

62. Falco with black beak, yellow legs, upper and under body whitish-grey with spots across the body.

 Rudb. Pict. Falco whitish-grey with yellow iris and feet.

[Here Linnaeus has made his famous misspelling: viridis, pedibus luteus. In the original work of Rüdbeck it is iris, pedibus luteus (Bruzewitz 1986)].

 Will. orn. 44. Gyrfalco

 Raj. av. 12. n.3. Gyrfalco

Habitat: rare in settlements.

Description: Back black-greyish, belly white-greyish with horizontally distributed spots, feet yellow, feeds of grouse.

Box 1.3. Extract from the 1761 edition of *Fauna Svecica* (Linnaeus 1761)

---

56. Falco rusticolus. Cere and eyelid and feet yellow, body greyish and with white undulate stripes, collar white.

Habitat: Sweden.

Description: size of chicken. Beak blunt, throat immaculate white, upper body ash-grey, under body white, neck nearly encircled by white. Under body white, with dark distinct spots. Tail roundish with 12 or 13 white spots. Talons black.

The name appears to be based on the Rüdbeck painting, and the latter can be treated as based on a "type" (*sensu* Lönnberg 1931) depiction of *Falco lanarius*. However, as this name has not been used at any later date, it should be marked as *nomen oblitum*, as it fulfils those requirements of the Code of Zoological Nomenclature (2000), *i.e.* it has not been used as a valid name since 1899 (Article 23.9.1.1). In addition the name is based on a Latin and old-French name of the Lanner Falcon and thus could cause confusion, and so violates the general principle of the nomenclature ("to preserve stability and universality").

The name *gyrfalco* has however been applied to the species since at least the 13th century – by Frederick II, where the bird is described in a near-scientific manner with appropriate description (diagnosis) and in a publication, thus fulfilling the requirement of the Code (Article 8) for a valid "publication" – and there is no doubt that Gyrfalcons have been known as such by many falconers and scientists in Europe since that time. In addition, the reference by Linnaeus in his *F. gyrfalco* account (Willughby 1676) is valid, as it, too, is a legitimate "publication", has a picture of a Gyrfalcon, and includes reasonable descriptions of the Gyrfalcon, as well as the Peregrine Falcon, which was perhaps behind the name of the mysterious *F. rusticolus*. Dementiev (1951) wrote of *F. rusticolus* that it was "certainly a different species".

The systematic act of Lönnberg (1931) is, according to the Code, an act of the "First Reviser" (Article 24.2.1). However, it was based on a misunderstanding of the diagnosis of *F. rusticolus*, which refers to the wrong species, if judged on diagnosis. He rejected *F. gyrfalco* based on unpublished material (Rüdbeck's plates), ignored a legitimate reference with published diagnoses and a picture (e.g. Willughby 1676) and no neotypes were referred to. In addition, Lönnberg did not, of course, comply with Code Article 23.9.1, which states that prevailing usage must be maintained when the following two conditions are both met (he fails in one of the two): 23.9.1.1 – the senior synonym or homonym (*i.e. F. gyrfalco*) has not been used as a valid name after 1899 (on this criterion Lönnberg fails); and 23.9.1.2 – the junior synonym or homonym (*i.e. F. rusticolus*) has been used for a particular taxon, and its presumed valid name, in at least 25 works, published by at least ten authors in the immediately preceding 50 years and encompassing a span of not less than ten years (this criterion has been met).

In addition, Lönnberg (1931), as the "First Reviser", acted contrary to Recommendation 24A of the Code: "In acting as First Reviser in the meaning of this Article, an author should select the name, spelling or nomenclature act that will best preserve stability and universality of nomenclature". So, Lönnberg's revision of the name of the Gyrfalcon fails to comply with the Code on nine counts. The Code of Zoological Nomenclature has a special rule for such cases, Article 24.2.5, with a definite verdict: the nomenclature action of Lönnberg (1931) as the First Reviser has to be nullified. It is possible that Linnaeus confused adult Goshawks with Gyrfalcons and described ages, plumages and morphs of the latter as separate species. Nevertheless the Code has specific rules for making zoological names stable and understandable, even in the case of problems relating to the book which introduced the binomial system itself – the celebrated 10th edition (Linnaeus 1758). Therefore the name *F. gyrfalco* L.1758 is still valid. If, for some reason unknown to us, *F. gyrfalco* is considered invalid, the name *F. canadensis* would have priority as senior synonym.

So our conclusion is that *Falco gyrfalco* should remain the valid name. *F. rusticolus* is dubious and should be rejected, and *F. canadensis* is the name that should be restored if, for some as yet unknown reason, *F. gyrfalco* is rejected or considered to be invalid.

SUBSPECIES

At present there is a consensus that the Gyrfalcon is a monotypic species. In other words, there are no subspecific divisions. Nevertheless, here we give a short synopsis of subspecies as noted in old literature. This will provide a basis for discussing the confusion which has arisen with colour morphs and variants, and in the evolution of understanding of the species.

Cade (1960) was the first to express the view that the Gyrfalcon is a monotypic but highly polymorphic species, with the realisation that the colour phases occur in different proportions in various regions. Before him, and even after his paper, some people were still using definitions of subspecies based not on series of specimens but on obscure literature sources and old definitions. Most subspecific names were given at a time when they were believed to form separate species (mostly from the Gmelin edition of the *Systema Naturae* (Linnaeus 1788) and Linnaeus' original work. These names include *F. candicans, F. obsoletus* and *F. islandus*.

In total, 40 races of Gyrfalcons have been described (Snow 1974). Vaurie (1961) reviewed the taxonomy of the Gyrfalcon and concluded that subspecific designations were inaccurate and unnecessary. Cade *et al.* (1998) quite rightly state that although formerly treated as a trimorphic species (white, grey and dark) the Gyrfalcon has complete gradation rendering the term "morph" inappropriate. Each variation occurs in most parts of the range (Vaurie 1961), thus making geographical criteria to substantiate the division of the subspecies impossible to apply. Nevertheless, some subspecies names show exceptional resilience.

Peters (1931) divided Gyrfalcons into five subspecies. Friedmann (1950) considered the Asiatic race *F. r. uralensis* as breeding in western and northern Alaska. He also considered that *F. r. uralensis* was different from *F. r. obsoletus* as its seventh primary (P7) is equal to or longer than the outermost (tenth) primary (P10). In *F. r. obsoletus* P7 is shorter than P10 (here the names of the feathers have been converted into modern terminology). Cade (1960) disagreed with such divisions and stated that there is a huge variation of that trait within both races, and so it cannot be used as a basis for separation of these forms. Todd (1963) revised the systematic position of the Labrador Gyrfalcons and considered that the Gyr there are all of the *F. r. obsoletus* (Gmelin) subspecies. He also noted that "both light and dark birds had been taken from the same nest (in Southern Greenland)."

Dementiev (1951) divided Eurasian Gyrs alone into four populations (one being the Altai Falcon) and synonymised *F. r. uralensis* under the name *F. r. intermedius* as breeding from the Urals to the Lena. According to him a race *F. r. grebentiskii* inhabits eastern Siberia from the Lena to Kamchatka and the Commander Islands. In Dementiev's definition *F. g. gyrfalco* lives in Europe and intergrades with *F. g. intermedius* at the Bolshezemelskaya tundra and the Urals. Portenko (1972) considered that there were three subspecies of Gyrfalcon in Eurasia: *F. g. gyrfalco, F. g. uralensis* and *F. g. grebenitszkiy*, the latter having a predominantly white or light appearance. Godfrey (1986) recognised *F. r. obsoletus* as the breeding subspecies across Canada, and *F. r. uralensis* as a visitor to British Columbia.

RELATIONSHIPS WITH OTHER SPECIES AND NOTES ON THE ALTAI FALCON

As a member of the genus *Falco*, the Gyrfalcon is closely related to what is known as the 'large falcons' or 'desert falcons' group. The group includes Lagger (*Falco jugger*), Saker, Prairie and Lanner Falcons. Gyrs can form hybrids with the members of this group. Gyrfalcon hybrids which are known to have resulted from artificial insemination are Gyr × Peregrine, Peregrine × Gyr, Gyr × Prairie, Gyr × Merlin (*Falco columbarius*), Gyr × ¾ Prairie + ¼ Red-footed Falcon (*Falco vespertinus*) and Gyr x Barbary Falcon (*Falco pelegrinoides*) (Palmer 1988). Gyr × Saker hybrids are fertile in the first generation. In the wild Gyrfalcons have paired up with Peregrine (female–female pair – a homosexual interspecific pairing, see Chapter 11) (Gjershaug *et al.* 1998) and with male Peregrine (Lindberg 1999a, 1999b). In both cases eggs were produced, but in the first case (six eggs in one year, five the following year) without any offspring.

The Altai Gyrfalcon (or Altai Saker or Altai Falcon) has been treated as a separate species (Dementiev 1951), and has been given the status of a subspecies of Saker (Dementiev and Shagdarsuren 1964), a position which is now accepted by most researchers and supported by the authors. Ferguson-Lees and Christie (2001) treated the Altai Falcon as a separate species (*Falco altaicus*). Academician Menzbier was first to describe it as a separate species in 1891. He based this on a specimen from "Yenisey District (gubernia)". This area is a wintering area of both Gyrs and the nomadic Sakers. In the Altai Mountains Sushkin (1925) treated the falcon (mentioned as the Altai Gyrfalcon) as a breeding bird and the Gyrfalcon only as a wintering species. The Saker was placed in the Altai region as a breeding bird which also sometimes stays in winter. In his most complete book on the birds of the

Russian Altai Sushkin (1938) treated the Altai Falcon and the Saker separately. During his expedition to Altai in 1914, Sushkin (1925, 1938) collected five chicks (all females) and shot the adult male (the father of the chicks) from a nest at the Kuskhonuur River, close to the Russian-Mongolian border. Several birds of the brood resemble Menzbier's specimen, and until now this brood represent the 'type' specimens of this elusive form. Sushkin raised the chicks in captivity at his home in Kharkov (Ukraine) in order to monitor the plumage succession. One of the brood was sacrificed the same year (1914); another died, allegedly of tuberculosis, in 1915 having already moulted into second plumage; one chick died during the end of her fifth moult in 1918; and the remaining two had to be killed in 1919 due to the impossibility of providing food. In his account of the Altai Falcon in his book of 1938 Sushkin did not mention the hardships he had to endure in Kharkov during the time of the Revolution and his survival during the infamous famine in Ukraine at the time. All the skins of his brood are preserved in the collections of the Zoological Institute, Russian Academy of Sciences, St Petersburg.

Our opinion on the Altai Falcon is as follows. In the wild there are Sakers which are intermediate in form and colour between dark Gyrfalcons and *milvipes* Sakers. They were described by Dementiev and Shagdarsuren (1964), and have been seen by one of us (Fox and Potapov 2001). Birds in the higher parts of the Altai mountain system can include a range of colours, as if the local falcon is a natural hybrid incorporating varying proportions of Gyr and Saker in its ancestry, or as if the species has not sufficiently distanced itself due to its short period of isolation in the recent geological epoch (see section above on palaeobiogeography). As with the Gyrfalcon, the Saker Falcon has pale and dark colour variants scattered across its range, and these forms are not limited to the Altai Mountains. These variants sometimes occur in individuals within a brood of intermediate or 'normal' coloured birds. Such coloration is not limited to the Altai Mountains, being also seen in central Mongolia. Breeding between natural pairs of North American black Gyrfalcons and *milvipes* Sakers has produced hybrids of ¾, ⅝, ½, ¼ Gyr, with corresponding Saker input, all of which birds are fertile to at least the third generation. These birds closely resemble the Altai types (*sensu* Sushkin 1938) in colour and size.

It also appears that there can be no genetic barriers: nominate Sakers breed all over the Altai mountains and pair up with birds of the Altai type. The carrying capacity of the total alpine zone area suitable for falcons – estimated using Geographical Information System (GIS) covers – is approximately 125,000km^2 (62,660km^2 in Mongolia), sufficient for at best 228 pairs of falcons (extrapolating the high density of Sakers from the Mongolian steppe – the real figure could be five to ten times lower), which is not enough for a minimum self-sustaining population (taken, at given conditions of breeding rate, as 300 successful pairs). Potapov *et al.* (2002) documented, using satellite telemetry, that this area can be crossed by a Saker in a single flight. The elevated alpine habitat in Altai is routinely used by lowland Tuva Sakers. Potapov *et al.* (2002) found Altai-type individual falcons in lowland steppe areas outside the Altai region of Mongolia and *milvipes*-type falcons in the alpine zone at elevations supposedly reported for the Altai Falcon (Sushkin 1938). Potapov *et al.* (2002) found a pair of falcons nesting in the alpine zone, the male of which was of Altai type, the female being *milvipes* type (See Plates 1 and 2). It is possible that from time to time Gyrfalcons remain to pair and breed with Sakers in the Altai Mountains, infusing Gyrfalcon blood into the Saker population and creating hybrids of varying proportions. However, due to the lack of genetic isolation and the small area of habitat, it seems unlikely that the Altai Falcon is an emerging species in its own right.

It was suggested (Fox and Potapov 2001) that the Altai Falcon is a natural hybrid of first or subsequent generations between Gyr and Saker, with Saker pre-dominating. However, after our analysis of Gyrfalcon coloration, we consider that the Altai Falcon is a mere "brand name" used by falcon traders, who would use the name to describe any bird of unusual coloration. Genetic tests would probably confirm that the Altai Falcon, the Saker Falcon and the Gyrfalcon are closely related forms, not genetically separated (as the hybridisation and variation of coloration in the wild shows). However, if breeding attempts of the Gyrs and Sakers between the tundra and forest zone are documented in the future, the question that will arise is more fundamental – whether the Gyrfalcon and the Saker are separate species. This question, in turn, will raise many conservation issues. If the Saker is listed in CITES Appendix II, and the Gyrfalcon enjoys Appendix I listing, to which taxon will the lumped form belong? And in which Appendix will the species be placed?

Nevertheless, the systematic position of the Altai Falcon highlights the problem of closely related species, such as the "large falcon" group. In order to explain their relationships Kleinschmidt (1901) brought forward his idea of *Formenkreis* (form circle), a new taxonomic rank which he thought better suited the large falcons, the Gyrfalcon, Altai Falcon and Saker Falcon amongst them. Otto Kleinschmidt (1870–1954) was a very active German ornithologist (Baumgart 2001). Although falcons were his hobby, his main occupation involved the respectable duties of Protestant pastor. By "form circles" Kleinschmidt (1901) meant self-contained stable (*i.e.* without transition) units of a hidden nature (essence or real meaning) with variable external features such as colour or shape. Though it was not understood at the time, the term Kleinschmidt coined is one of the oldest analogues of "phenotype", used well before geneticists had defined that term. The "form circles" were also very similar to the "factors" of another Austrian monk, Gregor Mendel.

For Kleinschmidt the unchanging unit was body proportions. All geographic representatives of a certain 'type' of body proportions might have significant variations in plumage colour and patterns. Kleinschmidt united into one *Formenkreis*, which he named *Falco hierfalco*, all known forms of Saker, Gyrfalcon (represented in the forms of *F. h. islandus, F. h. gyrfalco* and *F. h. uralensis*), Prairie (*F. h. mexicanus*), Lanner (in the forms of *F. h. tanypterus, F. h. erlangeri* and *F. h. biarmicus*) and Laggar (*F. h. jugger*). Later he added to this 'form circle' *F. h. altaicus* (Kleinschmidt 1923–1937) which he thought was an important link between Saker and Gyrfalcon. Having been formulated by a theologist, a Creationist, the "form circle" theory was considered to be anti-evolutionary, as at the time it was not possible to determine the hidden nature (genes, as we now term it) which control the variable external features such as the colour or shape of birds. The original papers by Kleinschmidt (1901, 1923–1937) are rarely cited, and are now largely forgotten, but it appears that in his works he outlined the modern genetic approach to the understanding of the systematics of large falcons. The name *Hierfalco* has also survived, used to describe either the subgenus *hierfalco*, which includes all the members of the Hierfalco form circle, or a superspecies which includes the Hierfalco form circle members as subspecies.

But the ideas of Kleinschmidt were very close to the theories of a celebrated follower of Darwin, the Moscow professor Alexander Fedorovich Kots (1880–1964). Kots's collection, which he started in 1907, has now grown into the Darwin Museum (Moscow), which is still open and actively pursues the goal of spreading the knowledge of evolution. Kots's deep interest in Gyrfalcons led him to amass a good collection of Gyr skins which he bought, exchanged or otherwise obtained from hunters. The collection also includes some specimens from the famous collection of G.P. Dementiev (1898–1969). The systematic position of Gyrfalcons, Sakers and the enigmatic Altai Falcon occupied Kots's mind from 1930 and his views on both the systematics and the origin of the group were published in 1948. The paper was published in a semi-popular magazine *Priroda* (Nature) and is rarely cited, but nevertheless has several conclusions which were ahead of the time.

The logic of Kots (1948) is as follows: white Gyrfalcons, Icelandic Gyrs and all forms of Eurasian Gyrs are one species, *Falco gyrfalco*. All Saker subspecies and forms are treated as one species. The Altai Falcon, described from a brood and an adult male by Sushkin, demonstrated that the young moulted into plumage resembling Norwegian Gyrs, though one moulted into the plumage of the *milvipes* type of Saker. The origin of the dualism in coloration of the Altai brood can be explained in one of three ways:

1. species dichromatism
2. parallel variability
3. hybridisation.

The dichromatism hypothesis, Kots argues, cannot be totally supported as there is no information about the female. Parallel variability was known long ago: distantly related taxa sometimes show similar patterns in coloration. However Kots ruled out parallel variability between Altai Falcons and Gyrfalcons simply because the number of Altai Falcons in the museums is about a hundred, but Altai-looking Gyrfalcons number about ten. As regards the hybridisation hypothesis, the arguments of Kots were as follows: the breeding of Sakers in the range of Altai Falcons is well known, but there is no evidence of the breeding of Gyrfalcons in the Altai Falcon range. Taking into account the wide range of Gyrfalcons it is, however, possible, and thus there is a possibility of hybridisation between the Saker and Gyrfalcon. The dichromatism of the original Sushkin specimens supports the idea that these forms are hybrids. The difference between the dichromatic and hybrid theories depends on whether the Altai Falcon is a well-established form (with the described colour variation) or whether it has to be produced from hybridisation events. The origin of the Altai form as a dichromatic aberration of the Saker or from a hybridisation process, according to the view of Kots, determines the height of the systematic rank of the form. And at this stage Kots formulated his famous Gyrfalcon syllogism:

> Both types of plumage of the Altai Falcon (as seen in the brood of Sushkin) are colour morphs; and
> Both types of coloration in the Altai Falcon could be treated as separate forms of Saker and Gyrfalcon: therefore

> The plumages of Saker Falcons and Gyrfalcons are colour morphs.

As a result Kots (1948) suggested that all Gyrfalcons are colour morphs of one species, the Gyrfalcon, thus bringing the suggestions of Kleinschmidt (1901, 1923–1937) in line with Linnaean binomial systematics. There is no need for a 'form circle' under the name *Falco hierfalco*, just subspecies of one species. The idea that *F. hierfalco* is in fact one species was also expressed by Meinertzhagen (1954). However the idea of *F. hierfalco* survived, and now lives on in the name of a superspecies, or subgenus taxonomic rank, which includes *F. mexicanus, F. jugger, F. biarmicus, F. cherrug* and *F. rusticolus*. The superspecies (or subgenus) is group of closely related species with, to a large extent, an allopatric distribution. This division of the so-called 'desert falcons' has been recognised since the 1980s (Cade 1982, White *et al.* 1994, Eastham 1999, 2000). Eastham (2000) gives the members of the *hierfalco* group the rank of allospecies within a superspecies.

   Eastham (2000), on the basis of an analysis of biomorphological data, showed that there are grounds to support the idea that the Altai Falcon is a Saker-Gyr hybrid. Gyrfalcon. The idea of hybridisation was addressed earlier (Phander 1994, Ellis 1995, Eastham 2000). Eastham (2000) even suggests that the Altai Falcon is a result of hybridisation between local Sakers and the Gyrfalcons which may have been lost by hunts of Kubilai Khan in the 13th century.

MOLECULAR SYSTEMATICS

Traditional systematics have been challenged, reinvestigated and amplified with the birth of genetic methods. As a result the traditional evolution trees have been updated, sometimes with spectacular changes. The first approach was by Sibley and Ahlquist (1990), who analysed avian systematics with the help of DNA–DNA hybridisation. Later geneticists switched to the sequencing of mitochondrial DNA (mtDNA), coding the cytochrome *b* (cyt *b*) enzyme. The cyt *b* gene is useful in resolving phylogenetic events which took place during the last 20 million years (Helbig *et al.* 1994, Wink *et al.* 1998 and references therein). Mitochondrial genomes of all vertebrate animals analysed so far have the same 37 genes, whose arrangement in the circular DNA molecule varies only in the relative position of a few genes (Mindell *et al.* 1998).

Subsequently, methods with more genetic resolution arrived. These included analysis of microsatellite DNA (see Glossary for explanation of micro- and mini-satellite DNA). In both methods (cyt *b* and microsatellites) scientists determine a sequence in the genome large enough to have some variability within the taxon under question. This sequence is used as a genetic marker to allow various diagrams of genetic relationships to be built. Amongst the genetic methods used, mtDNA (cyt *b*) analysis (Helbig *et al.* 1994, Wink 1998) has produced most of the results to date.

Wink *et al.* (1998) analysed 22 taxa of falcons based on 1,026 base pairs of the cyt *b* gene, and used domestic chickens as an outgroup in the maximum parsimony method (MP) with subsequent use of cladistic computer programs. Wink found a high degree of relatedness amongst the *hierfalco* group (the members of Kleinschmidt's 'form circle'). The group included *F. rusticolus, F. biarmicus, F. jugger* and *F. cherrug*. On the other hand, in contrast to Kleinschmidt's classification, it was very surprising to see a high degree of relatedness between Saker and Peregrine, and Prairie and Peregrine, *i.e.* the Prairie Falcon fell off the *hierfalco* group. The story of the Saker is different: it appears that Sakers might have a hybrid origin. The study showed that Sakers might have a genome of three haplotypes, but one Saker phenotype. Type I is related to the Peregrine and thus implies an old hybridisation between a Saker male and a female Peregrine. Type II is closely related to the Gyrfalcon and might be a hybrid between a female Gyrfalcon and a male Saker. Only type III is believed to be a true Saker genotype. Out of 21 birds studied, 9 belonged to type I, 7 to type II and 5 to type III. The tree without Sakers and Laggars shows close proximity of Gyrfalcons and Lanners. It also has to be noted that the Gyrfalcon group (*F. rusticolus, F. cherrug, F. biarmicus* and *F. jugger*) are the closest living relatives of the ancestral falcon (Helbig *et al.* 1994).

Micro- and minisatellite DNA analysis can be useful for analysing genetic diversity, parenthood, or genetic stress in some species. For example Lifjeld *et al.* (2002) demonstrated that the Peregrine population in south-east Norway shows signs of inbreeding. DNA fingerprinting showed an index of 38.3% compared to 22.5% in Merlins from the same region, and 12.5% in Hobbies from the same region. This suggested that the Peregrines were significantly more similar to each other genetically than were broods of either Merlins or Hobbies. The high similarity in minisatellite DNA between broods indicates a loss of genetic variation in the Peregrines caused by a genetic 'bottleneck' during the second half of the 20th century (the Peregrine was almost extinct in southeast Norway in the 1970s). Negro and Torres (1999) showed that mean band-sharing in the Bearded Vulture (*Gypaetus barbatus*) in Spain, which suffered a population crash were above 0.5, whereas in the fairly common Lesser Kestrel (*Falco naumanni*) the band sharing values were 0.21 (Negro *et al.* 1996, Negro and Torres 1999).

Minisatellite DNA in Canadian Gyrfalcons was studied by Parkin and May (1993). They found that the band sharing index in wild nestlings was 25.9 ± 2.52%. The maximum band sharing between unrelated comparisons was 55.6%, a value approaching the mean expected value for full siblings. This was noted as an exception since the two nests were 1,200km apart. A pair from Richardson Mountains demonstrated a DNA fingerprint pattern that strongly suggested that the siblings were unrelated to each other. This points the finger at egg dumping – intraspecific brood parasitism. Given the size and spatial distribution of Gyrfalcon territories it seems unlikely that a potential egg-dumping female will find a temporarily unattended, but nonetheless active, nest in which to deposit her egg. A more plausible explanation might therefore be that a successful EPC (extrapair copulation) has occurred, resulting in half-siblings with fingerprint patterns more dissimilar than the average. Of three nestlings from the Hope Bay nest site two would appear to be full siblings whilst the third bird is probably a half-sibling. However the analysis is not powerful enough to confirm this beyond doubt.

For the Gyrfalcon the odds against a chance occurrence of identical minisatellite patterns are 300,000 to 1, whilst in the House Sparrow they are as great as 1,014 to 1 (Parkin and May 1993). In Peregrines the probability of identical genotypes in two unrelated Peregrine individuals was 3×10^{-8} compared with 4×10^{-5} in Gyrfalcons with the markers developed by Nesje and coauthors (Nesje *et al.* 2000). The most loci were suitable for analysing were for Gyrfalcons, as well as Merlins, Hobbies and Kestrels. The sample for Gyrfalcons contained 20 individuals from 13 locations.

Nesje and Røed (2000) developed microsatellite DNA markers for sex determination in Peregrines and Gyrfalcons, and thus it has become possible to tell the sex of young nestlings at any age. Eight loci of microsatellite DNA showed enough polymorphism in the tested blood and feather samples of Gyrfalcons. These microsatellites are used as a forensic tool. A similar technique was previously developed by Griffiths *et al.* (1998) on different genes. Griffiths (1999) compared several approaches to the classification of birds of prey, falcons included, using analysis of bones, syrinx and cyt *b* sequences. Although there were no samples of Gyrs or Sakers available for her analysis, it appears that the sensitivity of such an approach is not the most accurate as American Kestrel (*Falco sparverius*), Peregrine and Lanner were exceptionally close in the cladogram tree with no apparent differences. An oligonucleotide probe called GTG 5 was described by Rychlik *et al.* (1994) which was found to have high polymorphic DNA regions in large falcons (*F. peregrinus, F. rusticolus, F. cherrug* and their hybrids). The results of this study indicated that DNA fingerprinting with GTG 5 as a probe could be a powerful method for differentiating closely related falcons.

Some studies have provided more information relevant to the understanding of the systematic position of Gyrfalcons. Helbig *et al.* (1994) stated that the Prairie Falcon is different from the *hierfalco* falcons (Saker, Lanner, Laggar and Gyrfalcon). Cade *et al.* (1998) argued that the Gyrfalcon is most closely related to the Saker, and may be conspecific with it. Hybridisation in nature is unknown, unless the Altai Falcon represents an interbred population of Gyrfalcon and Saker (Kots 1948, Phander 1994, Ellis 1995).

In captivity back-cross and out-cross hybrids were produced mostly via artificial insemination with Peregrines, Barbary Falcons (*Falco pelegrinoides*), Merlin, Eurasian Kestrel (*Falco tinnunculus*) and various multiple hybrids. However the first generation is not viable (Cade *et al.* 1998), except with Gyrfalcon × Saker hybrids which are fully fertile for at least two to three generations (Heidenreich *et al.* 1993, Heidenreich 1997). Sakers and Gyrfalcons breed in captivity without artificial insemination (Fox and Potapov 2001), forming what is known to breeders as a 'natural pair'.

GYRFALCON STATISTICS

GYRFALCONS IN THE WORLD'S COLLECTIONS

We have studied Gyrfalcon skins in the collections of the Copenhagen Museum of Natural History, Denmark; the University of Copenhagen, Denmark; the Moscow Zoological Museum, Russia; the Zoological Institute of the Russian Academy of Sciences, St Petersburg, Russia; the State Museum, Stockholm, Sweden; the Smithsonian Institution, Washington DC, USA; the Reykjavik Museum of Natural History, Iceland; the Natural History Museum, Tring, UK; and the American Museum of Natural History, New York, USA. In addition a small number of skins were studied at the Institute of Biological Problems of the North, Magadan, Russia and at the Academy of Natural Sciences, Philadelphia, USA. The total number of skins used in the following analysis is 1,865. This figure includes 14 birds whose colour patterns have been determined by direct observation in the field (note that

Table 1.1. Gyrfalcon skins studied in museum collections.

Collection	Skins
Copenhagen, Denmark	625
RMNH, Reykjavik, Iceland	258
BMNH, Tring, UK	257
AMNH, New York, USA	203
ZIN, St Petersburg, Russia	167
SI, Washington DC, USA	124
MZM, Moscow, Russia	102
Swedish Naturhistoriska Riksmuseet, Sweden	97
Institute of Biological Problems of the North, Magadan, Russia	2
Academy of Natural Sciences, Philadelphia, USA	16
Field observations	14
Total	1,865

there are no measurements for these birds). The number of skins by collection is given in Table 1.1. The collections include skins from all countries of the Gyrfalcon's current range. These are Canada, Denmark (*i.e.* Greenland), Finland, Iceland, Norway, Russia, Sweden and the USA. In addition there were a number of skins from countries where Gyrfalcons do not breed, but occur sporadically while wintering or on migration, and some birds obtained on vessels in the open sea.

The number of skins by origin is given in Table 1.2. A total of 59 skins were not labelled well enough for the country of origin to be identified with certainty. For simplicity the Gyrfalcon world has been divided into 19 regions, and the total number of skins from each of these regions is presented in Table 1.3. Seventy-four of the preserved skins were not labelled well enough to determine the region of procurement.

The geographical coordinates of the locations were taken from GIS97 digital maps, for Russian locations, and from the *Atlas of the World* (OUP 2002). The coordinates were used to plot the locations of the procurement of the individuals using DIVA-GIS and Arcview (ESRI, Redland, CA, USA) software for the production of range maps. Dates as well as colour pattern codes were entered into the database together with the coordinates of the locations. The data were subsequently analysed using the SAS statistical package (SAS Inc.,Gary, NC, USA) and Canoco (ter Braak and Šmilauer 1998). Only 606 individuals of the examined 1,865 had reliable identification of sex, some of these by dissection. There were many obvious mistakes in sex determination, and in such cases we treated the individual as 'not sexed'. In total we have a reliable identification for 418 female and 281 male Gyrfalcons. However, by using the SAS computer program and statistical estimates of the fitted curves, it was possible to sex 1,851 specimens with a degree of statistical confidence. The sex ratio was 863 males (46.08%) to 998 females (53.9%). This sex estimation was used to check whether coloration patterns differ between the sexes. The sample was verified on the sub-sample of reliably sexed specimens. Only reliably sexed specimens were used to calculate morphometric measurements on a 'by-sex' basis.

Some of the birds exhibited clear indications of breeding (such as brood patches and sometimes there was some indication on the label of the specimen, e.g. 'shot on clutch'). These specimens were treated as breeding birds. In some analyses we assumed that birds of a known location procured between April and August were breeding, or were at least potential breeding birds. The number of such birds, both certain breeders and those collected during the breeding season, was 402.

Table 1.2. Country of origin of Gyrfalcon skins.

Country	Frequency	Percentage
Greenland	868	48.06
Iceland	428	23.70
Russia	241	13.34
Canada	75	4.15
USA	68	3.77
Norway	56	3.10
Sweden	55	3.05
Finland	5	0.28
Open Sea	4	0.22
UK	3	0.17
China	1	0.06
Ireland	1	0.06
Kazakhstan	1	0.06
Total	1,806	100

Table 1.3. Region of procurement of Gyrfalcon skins.

Region	Number of specimens (% of total)
1 Alaska including Aleutians	53 (2.96%)
2 Canada from the Alaskan border to 120°W and south to the border with the USA	6 (0.34%)
3 Canada from 120°W to 90°W and south to the border with the USA	9 (0.50%)
4 Canada from 90°W to the Atlantic in the east and south to the border with the USA, including Labrador and Ungava	37 (2.07%)
5 The Canadian archipelago	23 (1.28%)
6 All lower 48 states in the USA	15 (0.84%)
7 Greenland	874 (48.80%)
8 Iceland	422 (23.56%)
9 The Scandinavian peninsula up to the Russian border (c. 30°E)	119 (6.64%)
10 Russia from the Finnish–Norwegian border (c. 30°E) to 75°E and south to 60°N, including the Yamal Peninsula	61 (3.41%)
11 Russia from 75°E to 120°E and south to 60°N, including Taimyr, Yenisey, and the area up to Ust-Olenek settlement on the Arctic coast	18 (1.01%)
12 Russia from 120°E to the Kolyma delta (c. 160°E) to the east (near Severo-evensk at the southern corner) and south to 60°N, including the Yana, Alaseya and Lena deltas	17 (0.95%)
13 Russian Chukotka from the Kolyma delta (c. 160°E) in the west to the Bering Strait to the east, and south to 60°N	14 (0.78%)
14 Russian Kamchatka, including all of the Kamchatka Peninsula and the Commander Islands	45 (2.51%)
15 Russia from 160°E to 120°E and south from 60°N, including Primorye, Shantar and the Kuril Islands, and Sakhalin	6 (0.34%)
16 Russia from 120°E to 75°E and south from 60°N, including Baikal and the Irkutsk district up to Kyrgyzstan	21 (1.17%)
17 From 75°E to 30°E and south from 60°N, which includes Kazakhstan from Almatata, Beshkek (Frunze), Omsk, Tobolsk, all of the Ukraine to Kiev and Russia to Moscow and the Novgorod districts	45 (2.51%)
18 All Western Europe, the Baltic States, Moldova and the Crimea	1 (0.06%)
19 The open sea far offshore	5 (0.28%)
Total	1,791 (100%)

MORPHOLOGICAL MEASUREMENTS

Wing length

Out of 1,865 skins the flattened wing length was measurable in 1,761 individuals, of which 63 were juveniles with feathers which had not fully grown. They were omitted from the analysis. The distribution of wing length of 1,698 individuals is given in Figure 1.2. The graphs were obtained using spline smoothing of the frequencies of the wing length in all individuals combined.

The distribution shows two local maxima at 370mm and 410mm. The analysis of the distribution of wing lengths of reliably sexed individuals is also given in the figure. A total of 362 females and 243 males were used. The peaks demonstrate good correspondence with the two peaks of the wing length distribution in the top graphs.

A t-test comparison between the means of male and female wing length returned statistically significant differences between the sexes ($t = 34.25$, $P < 0.0001$). This means that if the wing length is less than 380mm the specimen is most probably a male, and if the wing is longer than 390.2mm, it is probably a female. Individuals with wing lengths between 380mm and 390.2mm have an equal probability of being male or female, and wing length in such cases is not a reliable indicator of sex.

The wing length of male Gyrfalcons is 368.2mm ± 12.64mm (SD), $n = 243$, and positive both for skewness (0.76) and kurtosis (2.00). The wing length in female Gyrfalcons is 403.9mm ± 12.44mm (SD), $n = 362$, with negative skewness (−1.09) and positive kurtosis (1.83).

The wing length of Iceland female Gyrs is 419mm ± 15mm ($n = 23$, range 403–480mm) and of males is 373mm ± 8mm ($n = 4$, range 362–381mm) (Cade *et al.* 1998). In the museums of Helsinki and Copenhagen the average female wing length is 391mm ($n = 11$, range 380–406mm), and in males it is 348mm (range 342–360mm) (Forsman 1993, 1999). For Eurasia Stepanyan (1975, 1990) stated that Gyrfalcon wing length increases from west to east. His data are summarised in Table 1.4 below.

Table 1.4 Wing length distribution in Eurasian Russia.

Region	Males		Females	
	Average	Range	Average	Range
European Russia	358	342–372	396	380–407
Mid and Western Siberia	360	343–372	397	381–415
Eastern Siberia and Kamchatka	370	360–382	410	390–418

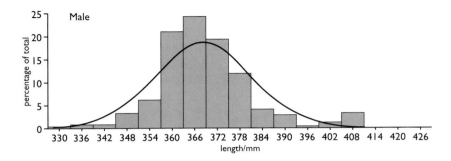

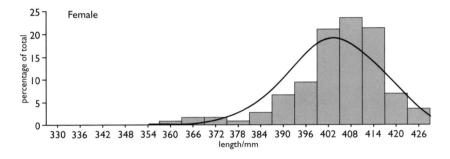

Figure 1.2 *Wing length distribution in male (top) and female (bottom) Gyrfalcons. The wings of the females are significantly longer than those of the male birds.*

For North America the wing length in male Gyrs is 367mm (*n* = 20, range 345–390mm), and in females it is 393mm (*n* = 38, range 345–410mm) (Clum and Cade 1994). Another estimate for North America gives a wing length for male Gyrs of 364.3mm (*n* = 42, range 340–378mm) and for females of 400.5mm (*n* = 63, range 368–423mm) (Todd and Friedmann 1947, Palmer 1988). Clark and Yosef (1998) considered individuals with wing lengths less than 380mm to be males and those with wing lengths equal to or greater than 382mm as females. These data are close to our own measurements, though we consider a more reliable estimate for females to be 392mm in length. Godfrey (1986) gives wing length for Canadian male Gyrs as 364.1mm (range 355–373mm) and for females as 384.4mm (range 361–407mm). After a study in Greenland Mattox (1970) gave wing lengths in males as 378mm (range 370–386mm), and in females as 414mm (range 404–420mm).

Tail length

Tail length was measurable in 198 females and 120 males of our sample. A *t*-test revealed a difference between the average tail length in females (215mm) and males (193mm). This difference between the means was statistically significant ($t = 13.11$, $P < 0.0001$). Nevertheless, if we plot all data available from all skins we obtain one bell-shaped curve with only one peak. This suggests that tail length is not a reliable estimator of sex. For example a tail length of 204mm means that the Gyr has an equal probability of being male or female. The average tail length in males is 193mm ± 14.98mm (SD), $n = 120$. The shape of the distribution has negative skewness (–0.343) and positive kurtosis (4.44). The average tail length in females was 215mm ± 14.18mm (SD), $n = 198$, with negative skewness (–1.42) and positive kurtosis (10.42). The data are plotted in Figure 1.3.

For the Nearctic, Clum and Cade (1994) give the male Gyr tail length as 313mm ($n = 11$, range 195–245mm) and for females as 227mm ($n = 38$, range 210–290mm). Clark and Yosef (1998) consider all birds with tail lengths less

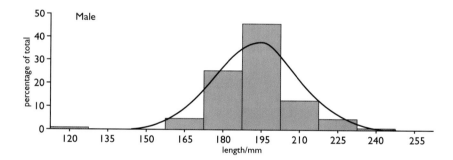

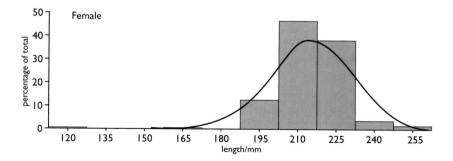

Figure 1.3 *Tail length distribution in male (top) and female (bottom) Gyrfalcons.*

than 206mm as males and those greater than 207mm as females. For Canada the tail length was given as 201.7mm (range 190–206mm) for female Gyrs (Godfrey 1986).

Tarsus length

There was a marginal but significant difference between the diagonal tarsus lengths in the males and females of our sample (t = 2.90, P = 0.0046). The average tarsus length in male Gyrfalcons was 61.1mm ± 6.27mm (n = 48) with both positive skewness (1.01) and positive kurtosis (0.24). For female Gyrfalcons the average tarsus length was 64.7mm ± 6.75mm (n = 73) with positive skewness (0.73) but negative kurtosis (–0.3725). These data are plotted in Figure 1.4 below.

For North America the length of the tarsus was given as 60.9mm (n = 21, range 52.1–68.7mm) for male Gyrs and 62.3mm (n = 38, range 48.9–74.6mm) for

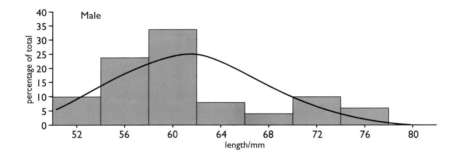

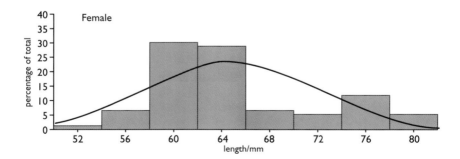

Figure 1.4 *Tarsus length distribution in male (top) and female (bottom) Gyrfalcons.*

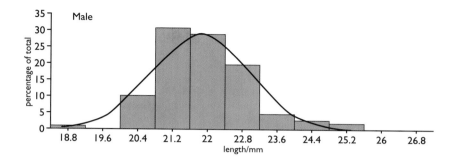

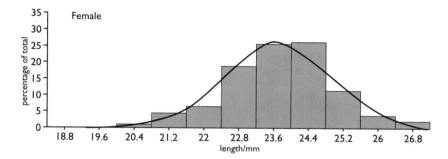

Figure 1.5 *Beak length distribution in male (top) and female (bottom) Gyrfalcons.*

females (Clum and Cade 1994). For Canada the male's tarsus length was given as 61.2mm (range 60.5–63.0mm) (Godfrey 1986).

Beak length

Interestingly, there was a significant difference between beak lengths (measured from the nostril) in males and females (t = 13.74, P < 0.0001). The average beak length in male Gyrs was 21.8mm ± 1.07mm (n = 107) with both positive skewness (0.44) and kurtosis (0.44). For females the average beak length was 23.7mm ± 1.22mm (n = 183) with negative skewness (–0.06) but positive kurtosis (0.32). However the distribution curves are very close. To separate the sexes on the basis of beak length with confidence one has to assume that if beak length is less than 22.5mm the individual is most probably male, and if the beak is longer than 24mm the individual is most probably female. Individuals with beak lengths from

22.5mm to 24mm have an equal probability of being male or female. The data are plotted in Figure 1.5. An estimate of beak lengths for North America (Todd and Friedmann 1947, Palmer 1988) gives an average beak length (from cere) in male Gyrs of 22.8mm (n = 42, range 20–25mm), and in females of 25.2mm (n = 63, range 23–27.9mm).

Middle toe length

It was impossible to measure the middle toe on many specimens, so we did not attempt to measure this parameter. North American male Gyrs were found to have an average middle toe of 55.3mm (n = 13, range 51.0–61.3mm) and females of 61.0mm (n = 22, range 51.9–66.1mm) by Clum and Cade (1994).

Body weight

Data on body weight taken from collection labels gave an average body weight for male Gyrs of 1,107g (n = 9, range 769–1,448g) and for females of 1,491g (n = 19, range 1,250–1,800g). This does not include one individual collected on 5 January 1955 on Medniy Island (one of the Commander Islands) which was labelled as a 2,000g bird. This bird, from the collection of Moscow University Museum, was perhaps the basis of the maximum body weight given by Dementiev (1960), a figure which was later repeated many times in the literature. However, we think that this bird was not weighed correctly (perhaps because it had full crop), as with its wing length of 400mm the Gyr would have had too high a wing loading for a normal life.

Nielsen (1991) reported weights of 1,300–1,450g for male Gyrs (average 1,355g ± 53.4g (SD), n = 5) and 1,675–2,020g for females (average 1,830g ± 102.7g (SD), n = 28) in northern Iceland. The body weight of the females seemed to decrease from the onset of laying. However three females caught by Nielsen before the nesting period (1,675–1,725g), and one caught seven weeks before laying (1,750g) were light compared with females measured during the incubation period. The weights of young Gyrs at inland territories in northern Iceland were: males 1,235g ± 101g (n = 36), and females 1,589g ± 129g (n = 32). For coastal birds the data were: males 1,355g ± 60g (n = 5, range 1,300–1,450g), females 1,831g ± 106g, (n = 27, range 1,675–2,020g) (Nielsen 1986, cited by Cade *et al.* 1998).

In Norway 31 females gave a weight range of 1,200–2150g (Cade *et al.* 1998). Dementiev and Gladkov (1951) give the weight range of 6 female Gyrs as 1,400–1,980g, and the range of 26 males as 960–1,300g (average 1,154g). For Siberia Dementiev (1951, 1960) gives an average of 1,614g for females, with a range of 1,315–2,100g.

For North America Palmer (1988) gave male Gyr weights of 800–1,300g, average 1,140g, and female weights of 1,130–1,980g, average 1,585g. Globally Brown and Amadon (1968) give average weights for male Gyrs of 1,170g (n = 7, range 960–1,304g) and for females of 1,752g (n = 12, range 1,396–2,000g). The body weight of an immature female Gyr caught in November 1971 in Illinois, USA was 1,679.6g (Burr 1975). Wintering females in Washington weighed 1,554g, 1,588g and 1,819g (Dobler 1989).

In Greenland Mattox (1970) measured 10 female Gyrs and obtained an average weight of 1,470g (range 1,262–1,687g), and 4 juvenile males for an average of 1,112g (range 1,021–1,219g).

CHAPTER 2

Identification and Colours

THE IDENTIFICATION OF GYRFALCONS

In most cases the identification of Gyrfalcons is straightforward (this is particularly true in the Arctic), but in many places it can be rather confusing. Confusion usually occurs in regions visited by Gyrfalcons during migration. In the New World identification is reasonably straightforward, even in the places where migrating individuals are mixed with Prairie Falcons, northern Goshawks or Peregrine Falcons, females of which can occasionally be larger than male Gyrs. In the Old World the main confusion occurs in the region where migrating Gyrs mix with Saker Falcons, namely in Kazakhstan, Kyrgyzstan, Tuva, southern Siberia and Mongolia. Here it is necessary to look at the wings, which are broader in the Gyr than in the Saker. However, as the experienced ornithologist E. Kozlova (1969) once wrote, 'immature Sakers and Gyrfalcons are in most cases impossible to tell apart'.

In eastern Siberia and on the Kamchatka Peninsula there is a danger of confusing Gyrs with Goshawks, a confusion which exists with both the 'nominate' and the white Goshawk, which in some larch or willow forests might coincide in one place. Confusion with Goshawks is not rare. A journalist in the former USSR has published a series of articles (with photographs) in a major illustrated magazine entitled 'In search of the Gyrfalcon'. Amongst the photos there was not a single Gyr, all of the illustrated birds being Goshawks. Eventually the journalist did manage to see the nest of a Gyrfalcon. The view of the bird made him so excited that he later published a book called *In Search of a White Gyrfalcon*. A joke common at the time was that if he had seen a second nest he would have produced an encyclopaedia. However, in fairness, confusion between these species of raptors is not uncommon in the murky polar light of autumn and early spring, even among experienced birders. One has to look for the roundish wings of the Goshawk in flight and its bright yellow-orange eyes to avoid such confusion. In the Gyrfalcon the iris is dark brown, in contrast to *Accipiter* hawks. In many cases the colour of the iris is the best identification characteristic in the field.

The Gyrfalcon's wing is somewhat rounded distally, not pointed as in the other falcons, and it is relatively wider near the body. The wing action is decidedly heavier and slower than in other falcons, with motion appearing to concentrate distally (Palmer 1988). In both Peregrines and Gyrfalcons the underwing usually has a fairly broken dark/light pattern. The Prairie Falcon has a paler lining to the underwing with a contrasting dark patch. The Gyrfalcon's head may be mostly dark in dark-grey specimens (and in Peregrines), but it can vary to almost all white, even in the darkest specimens. A white Gyr might be confused momentarily with an albino Red-tailed Hawk (Palmer 1988), the darkest ones with Rough-legged Buzzards and possibly with dark Red-tailed Hawks (Palmer 1988), but the differences in proportion and flight characteristics are significant.

The Gyr is the largest falcon, and in size exceeds, in some cases marginally, the accipiters. The body length is 48–61cm, the wingspan 130–160cm (Cramp and Simmons 1980, Clum and Cade 1994). The bird looks heavy and flies in a 'heavy falcon' style; it is remarkably fast compared to its rather slow wing beat. Its wide wings do make it sometimes look like a Goshawk, but the wing beats are a good key to identification at a distance, just as the Peregrine, with its swift-like wing beats, can be easily distinguished. In addition, the 'barrel-shaped' body (Forsman 1999) helps to identify the species.

Identification in most handbooks is based on the apparent trichromatism in the general coloration of Gyrs. Here we give a compilation of identification tips drawn from our experience and from various handbooks (Cramp and Simmons 1980, Palmer 1988, Johnsgard 1990, Forsman 1999) in the traditional trichromatic way.

White birds

These birds are pure white, except for dark wingtips, or white with some spots. The legs and feet are yellow or blue. Birds with a white background but excessive numbers of spots are treated in this study as a form of the grey morph (irregular barred type – see the section below on colour patterns). The white back may have a variable amount of brownish to blackish markings, varying from streaking to tear-shaped or pendant-shaped when few, and to barring if many. The tail is white with either all-white feathers with white or dark shafts, or with one or more dark bars extending into the vanes, but not reaching their edges. These bars can be slightly offset, or offset at the feather shaft, or can join to form continuous lines.

The front vane of the primaries is white with dark tips. There are one or more dark bars across the front vane, but no bars on the rear vane. Primary shafts are coloured or white. If the tail has dark markings (usually only on the central rectrices), these tend to be located centrally within both vanes if symmetrical, or touching the shafts if irregular. The primaries are dark at the distal tip. The top of the head sometimes has fine and delicate streaks along the shafts. Sometimes the underparts have a few spots in the shape of fine bars, arrowheads or hearts. When spread the wings have a remarkably regular pattern.

Immatures of this form have a streaked crown. If there is a dark pattern, most of the feathers on the back, mantle and wing-coverts have wide white edges. The underbody and flanks are streaked. The general look of immatures, compared to adults, is darker. The feet are bluish to slightly yellowish.

Grey birds

The background colour of these birds varies from grey to white. They have ashy-grey upperparts with darker, slate-grey barring. The tail is pale grey with dense, fine dark barring (usually 9–10 bars) or grey-brown with symmetrical or asymmetrical ovals on both vanes. The underparts are creamy white with dark spots on the breast and wide bars on the flanks. The head pattern varies from a dark, slate-grey full hood (resembling some Peregrines, but not black and lacking the Peregrine's contrastingly pale cheeks) to the very pale head of some old males, which have a narrow, ill-defined dark moustachial and eye-stripe, and a conspicuous white cheek and supercilium. On the head one can often see dark streaks along the feather shafts, contrasting with the pale or grey vanes of the feathers. Pale individuals have the pale markings of the upperparts more pronounced, the pale tail barring is more conspicuous, and the streaking of the underparts and the head pattern is finer. The darkest pale individuals can be almost uniform greyish-brown above. They have only narrow creamy-white margins to the tips of the upperparts of the feathers, a dark head with a pale chin, streaked cheeks and a boldly streaked breast, and thus can approach the appearance of the dark morph. The cere and feet are yellow (but blue in the young, hence the Scandinavian name of the Gyr – *Blåfoten*, bluefoot).

The darkest (melanistic) individuals vary to almost entirely sooty brownish, or have feathers showing somewhat paler margins. The head and entire upperparts are uniformly dark slate-grey, and even the underparts may be largely dark slate-grey except for a paler chin. If there is any light on the head, the 'moustache' mark may form a patch, but individuals vary from having the head overall dark to nearly white. In the underparts the feathers may be entirely dark or bicoloured (with somewhat lighter areas). The tail may be either fairly dark with even darker barring, or uniformly dark, the tip pale brown.

Hatchling Gyrfalcons of all colour phases are covered with creamy-tinged white down. The eye is blackish and the feet and cere are pale yellow.

IDENTIFICATION IN THE HAND

The combination of circular nostrils, a wing length of at least 300mm, and the tenth (outermost) primary being about the same length as the eighth (the ninth is the longest) are characteristic. White-phase birds are unmistakeable. In the typical Gyrfalcon plumage (grey phase) the upper part of the body and upperwing-coverts are crossed by wide whitish or brownish stripes. There are no rusty colours in the plumage. At the throat, thin dark feather-shafts dominate, whereas on the breast and belly there are dark, rounded spots on the whitish background. On the inner vanes of the primaries the borders of white oval spots contrast significantly in some individuals, but are rather diffused in others. The rectrices are greyish with dark perpendicular stripes (Kozlova 1969). Dark-phase birds are usually distinguished by the lighter feather margins, but may need more specific diagnostics - the tarsi are feathered for two-thirds of their length, in contrast to those of the Saker Falcon (where feathers cover one-half of the tarsus). The third toe is relatively longer in Gyrs than in Sakers.

IDENTIFICATION IN THE FIELD

When perched, the large size and rather massive bodily proportions of the Gyrfalcon help to distinguish it from smaller falcons. In addition a Gyr tends to be paler than a Peregrine, and lacks the dark crown and characteristic 'hooded' aspect of that species. The wings are relatively short, the primaries extending only slightly beyond the mid-point of the tail, rather than nearly reaching the tip as in Peregrines. The upperparts are highly variable in darkness, ranging from nearly pure white to almost sooty grey. The underparts are comparably variable, but tend to have some dark breast and abdominal streaking (rather than the dark spotting or barring more common in Peregrines). At a distance Peregrines appear darker than Gyrfalcons. However, as the latter are sometimes of a lighter coloration, they blend into the landscape with remarkable ease. While shadowing Gyrs from a helicopter in Canada's Yukon Territory White and Nelson (1991) mentioned that it was extremely easy to lose sight of the birds. If the helicopter was lagging too far behind, the Gyr could disappear against a dark talus or vegetation, and if the Gyr stooped it became invisible when it passed below the horizon.

In autumn or winter young Gyrfalcons are most likely to be seen as 'grey' morphs. However, the young have a streaked belly, whereas the adults most often have a barred vent. In addition, there are some adults with a 'streaked' belly. These birds have narrower streaks along the shafts, whereas the juveniles have wider ones. The dark streaks reach along the shaft to the base of the feather in the young, but rarely in adults. If that happens, the streaks have a water-drop shape in adults, whereas in the young they are the shape of a cone (Kleinschmidt 1901).

COLOURS

There are few species in the world that show such high variability in coloration and patterns as the Gyrfalcon. One species which does is the Rough-legged Buzzard, which, as with the Gyr, is a bird of northern tundra. There are no two identically coloured Rough-legged Buzzards. Gyrfalcons, on the other hand, can sometimes look similar, even though it is probable that on closer inspection they are very different. Such variation is known as polymorphism. However, there is a big difference between the enormous variation in Rough-legged Buzzards and Gyrfalcons, the latter varying in a more discrete fashion. Raptor specialists prefer the terms dimorphism (white and dark forms), trimorphism (white, grey and dark forms) or more complicated approaches for the description of the colours of Gyrs, these terms also being used for the systematics of the species.

For a long period there was much discussion over the number of Gyrfalcon subspecies, and even over the names of the colour morphs (Flann 2003). The current consensus on the past 'split-ups' and 'lump-ups' is that there are no subspecies taxa within the species. As regards colour morphs, there is no consensus at the moment, so we need to look at the data in detail. After Frederick II (Wood and Fyfe 1943), most authors recognise three colour morphs — dark (or black) morph, white morph and the intermediate or grey morph (Brown and Amadon 1968, Cramp and Simmons 1980, Cade 1982, Palmer 1988, Johnsgard 1990). This traditional approach of colour morph classification is best described by Forsman (1993, 1999) and can be summarised as follows. Most Gyrfalcons are grey; however the colour ranges from nearly white to very dark, almost slate-coloured; some Gyrfalcons also have shades of brown and grey in their feathers, and worn plumage may be tan-brown; Gyrs may or may not have a barred tail and moustachial stripes.

The three colour phases have been traditionally described as grey, white and dark (Kozlova 1969, Snow 1974). However, this classification is understood in several ways, discrepancies being due to the fact that some authors classify the birds on the basis of their background colour (Cade *et al.* 1998). Grey form can then be a bird with grey colour in the background or a bird with a white background but with a lot of dark grey or brown streaks, spots or bars. The degree of the coverage of these spots can then divide the white and grey morphs. As a consequence, it is often difficult to classify Gyrs with excessive numbers of spots and a true white background. Undoubtedly the field notes of different observers would place such a bird in different categories.

Some authors divide the colour morphs into a larger numbers of categories. Ellis *et al.* (1992) used 'light grey' and 'white grey' categories in addition to the traditional ones. In contrast Palmer (1988) considered that the division of the Gyrfalcons 'into two or three colour morphs (phases, races, variants varieties and so on) is misleading', and 'any attempt to categorise Gyrs is subjective', 'because of variations from nearly (entirely?) white to almost or entirely black.' Flann (2003) suggested that the Gyrfalcon has 'continuous polymorphism' and so does not have morphs. However, the presence of asymmetrical birds (see section on asymmetry below) and the results of our multivariate analysis show that there are indeed stable and discrete forms.

Generally the traditional approach of describing the variation of Gyrfalcons confuses several colours. Every Gyr has some dark colour spots (even the whitest birds), and a background colour. The colour of the spots varies from light brown to very dark. The colour of the background varies from pure white to grey and dark brown, almost black. The dimensions of dark spots and the area of background varies significantly in different birds, so on the one hand we can have a bird with white background and no spots, or a small number of spots, while on the other hand we might have a bird with extremely large dark spots reducing the area of background to a few white spots.

Another process is the coloration of the background, which may perhaps be independent of, but is parallel with, the variation in coloration and size of dark spots. So, technically speaking, we have two axes of variation. One is the colour as such, including both the colour of the background and the colour of dark spots. The second axis is the size and pattern of the dark/light spots. Interestingly, there have been no attempts to analyse this two-dimensional variation using objective criteria. In the following section we make an attempt to measure Gyrfalcon colours using a new approach.

THE TRUE COLOUR OF GYRFALCONS

Until recently, studies of animal coloration assumed that animals see colours as humans do. Scientists used general terms to describe the colours, and sometimes tried to use colour tables in order to give the descriptions of animals in general, and Gyrfalcons in particular, a more objective basis (as in Todd and Friedmann (1947) for example). This assumption is flawed. Experiments Bennett has conducted at Bristol University, UK (Bennett *et al.* 1997) show that some birds use ultraviolet (UV) wavelengths (300–400nm, to which humans are blind) when they are hunting for prey, and when they are choosing mates. Furthermore, the Bristol group has demonstrated previously unnoticed avian sexual dimorphism when considering the birds' appearance in UV light (Hunt *et al.* 1999). The ability to see UV is assumed to be universal in birds, with the exception of owls (e.g. Bennett and Cuthill 1994, Cuthill *et al.* 2000 and references therein). Some bird species have a distinct UV reflection which has been proved to be important for sexual selection and mate choice (e.g. Bennett *et al.* 1997, Hunt *et al.* 1999). Birds of prey, in particular those that prey on rodents, such as Eurasian Kestrels and buzzards, have the ability to see at UV wavelengths (Vitala *et al.* 1995). There is a suggestion that birds of prey do not show any specific UV reflectance peak, probably in order to avoid being conspicuous to rodents (Rowe 1999).

Gyrfalcons, whose plumage variation spreads from white to almost black, are interesting in many respects. Firstly, the colour of the white morph could be an adaptation to the snowy background of the Arctic winter (in the form of plumage that appears white to humans), but such a coloration is a handicap in summer. Similarly, black coloration could be an adaptation to offer camouflage against the black background of, say, a cliff, but again this would be a handicap for snowy backgrounds. The grey morph is well adapted to mosaic backgrounds, but would be too conspicuous against snowy backgrounds. In terms of recognition of conspecifics there are no problems for white individuals mating with 'grey' ones. However there is little knowledge about black and white Gyr pairs due mostly to the rarity of both forms. Despite the fact that raptors in particular provide paradigmatic examples of reverse sexual dimorphism in size, there is no evidence for colour-based sexual dimorphism, despite the tremendous variation in coloration. There appears to be no assortative mating based on coloration. Our aim here is to reassess the coloration of various morphs of the Gyrfalcon by considering not only the visible spectrum to which humans are limited, but UV wavelengths as well. In this study we describe the coloration of the white, black and grey morphs using reflectance spectrophotometry and look to see whether there is any hidden sexual dimorphism in coloration, as well as comparing the plumage coloration in both the visual (for humans) and UV parts of the spectrum.

There is a strong case for completely reassessing the coloration of birds, and indeed other animals, using methods that are independent of human colour vision, incorporating UV wavelengths. How does a white Gyrfalcon look against a white background through the eyes of, say, an Arctic Fox or a Ptarmigan? White Arctic animals, and the Gyrfalcon in particular, are interesting because, surprisingly, there has been very little systematic and objective study of their coloration. This has arisen, presumably, because historically it seemed obvious why they appear white – it renders these animals camouflaged against a white snow background (e.g. Hamilton 1990). Such conclusions, however, assume that birds and other predators see colours as humans do. Not only is this assumption unjustified, but recent work by Koon (1998) shows that the white fur of Polar Bears is highly UV absorbing, and so will be conspicuous to UV-sensitive animals. This finding confirms unpublished work by Professor Burkhardt of Regensburg, Germany, one of the pioneers of work on UV sensitivity in birds. Burkhardt not only found such effects in Polar Bears, but in the white plumages of various bird species. Taken together, these results indicate that it is erroneous to assume that plumage that appears white to humans will necessarily offer camouflage to Arctic animals. Rather, some white plumage and fur can be UV absorbing and thus conspicuous, and may play a special role in sexual signalling or as warning coloration.

Modern scientific instruments were used to assess the colours objectively. These were spectrophotometers of two types: one was a Zeiss MCS 501 Diode Array spectrophotometer, the other a Zeiss CLX 500 light source located at Bristol University, U.K. (Bennett *et al.* 1997). This instrumentation was building-bound and so delivery of the Gyr skins from the Natural History Museum, Tring had to be carefully orchestrated as most of the skins of this Red Data Book species are irreplaceable. With the arrival of a new generation of spectrophotometers, such as Ocean Optics S2000, we were able to make measurements in remote field locations, even of distant objects. The cosine adapter of the Ocean Optics S2000 spectrophotometer allowed measurements of sky emissions. Coloration was assessed using reflectance spectra which incorporate the near UV, visual and near infrared (300–800nm). Reflectance spectra are specific for an invariantly coloured object and are therefore an ideal way of measuring colour. The light of a Zeiss CLXIII Xenon bulb was beamed at 45° on to the section of feather and the reflecting light was captured with a sensor at 90° to normal. Measurements were taken from a 2-mm diameter area, recorded in 1-nm steps from 300nm to 700nm, and expressed relative to a Spectralon 99% white reflection standard (Labsphere, Congleton). Each spectrum consisted of 400 reflectance measurements for every 1-nm step. Individual feathers were placed on black velvet during spectroradiometry to eliminate stray reflection from the background. Dark current and white standard reference measurements were taken immediately before measuring each piece to minimise any error associated with drift of the light source or sensor. The location of the measurement was chosen at random, as was the order in which the parts of the feathers from individuals were measured. We measured plumage of males and females separately, sampling nine regions of their plumage for white, grey and black morphs. These regions were: the head (at the top), the back, primaries, rectrices, tail-coverts, wing-coverts, and the neck. In addition we had to measure background and dark spots separately (Potapov and Bennett 1999).

In all a total of 1,080 spectral measurements were taken from the three colour morphs of Gyrfalcons (ten males and ten females for each morph), measured in nine regions with ten replications for every region and made separately for each sex. The resulting spectra were averaged compiling ten spectra taken for black and white spots for every plumage region. This massive dataset was then subjected to a number-crunching session. The resulting spectra are given in Figure 2.1.

The first striking result of this study is that the white patches of the Gyrfalcon, and the white background, are not white at all. The more-or-less-white or close-to-white lines can be seen only from wavelengths of 450 to 500nm, *i.e.* in the red, near-green and green parts of the spectrum. All three studied colour morphs do not reflect in the UV and near-UV part of the spectrum. Secondly, all three colour morphs have similar reflecting curves for dark spots. The dark spots do not reflect UV, but peak in the near-infrared part of the spectrum (*c.* 1,050nm). The latter peak is not shown in the graphs, but there is some evidence that it is very similar in other 'brown' looking birds of prey such as buzzards and Black Vultures. Thirdly, there is no sex difference in the reflecting patterns of black spots across all three morphs. The only sex difference was found in the reflection of white patches or white backgrounds of the primaries and, in some morphs, in the reflection of the rectrices. From above the female's primaries were more reflecting than male ones, but the opposite trend was seen on the primaries from below. Similarly the rectrices of females were more reflecting from above than from underneath. However this trend is not seen in white birds. The white-morph females showed somewhat more reflectance in wing-coverts – a trend which is not seen in grey and dark forms. However, the most important conclusion is that Gyrfalcons are of similar, or close, coloration if viewed in the UV part of the spectrum – the zone which was demonstrated to be extremely important for mate choice in birds (Bennett and Cuthill 1994, Bennett *et al.* 1997).

Clearly, if Gyrfalcons use only UV cues for conspecific recognition then the colour morphs, so interesting for humans, would be less important for them. Obviously, the raptors cannot use UV parts of the spectrum to advertise their qualities as such an advertisement would jeopardise their camouflage and they would become visible to rodents known to see in the near UV (Jacobs *et al.* 2001 and references therein). Rats, for example, have two classes of cones in the eye, one of which contains a UV-sensitive photopigment. Interestingly, birds of prey are able to see in UV, and as we now know that white Gyrfalcons are not white in the UV part of the spectrum, they are extremely conspicuous to any other UV-sensitive bird (including Ptarmigan and other Gyrs) against a background of snow. This suggests that the white colour of Gyrs is not an adaptation to camouflage the bird against white snow backgrounds. It may be an attempt to save the energy required for pigment synthesis, minimising energy expenditure during moult. In the Arctic in summer, the colour of a predator does not matter significantly if the vegetation is not high enough to provide cover for potential prey: the prey simply does not have a place to hide, even if it sees the predator. The situation is different in forested environments. There, a white bird appears extremely conspicuous against the generally green and brown background of trees. Hence the grey and dark Gyr forms have to use energy on pigment since camouflage is a paramount priority in their habitat. By contrast white Gyrs can afford to live without camouflage, relying on their speed, but only in areas of very high grouse densities.

THE COLOUR OF SNOW

It is, of course, common knowledge that snow is white or, in strictly scientific terms, reflects evenly in the UV, visual and near-infrared zones of the spectrum. In the infrared, snow reflection decreases, with some sort of peak in the 1,800–2,000nm range. The differences in snow reflection have been measured in detail in many studies as they are of use in remote sensing (Casacchia *et al.* 2001). In Casacchia's study it was noted that fresh snow has the highest reflection values, followed by so-called equilibrium snow (with rounded crystals) and drifted snow (*i.e.* particles of snow deposited or altered by the wind). All reflectance spectra within the visual and UV parts of the spectrum fall within 85–98%. However in more realistic measurements of snow of different kinds, and including some dust particles, the reflection of snow varied between 65% and 97% and was the lowest for thin snow cover (about 60%) (Winther 1993).

PREY COLOURS

The main food of the Gyrs in winter is Ptarmigan and Willow Grouse. These species (apart from the Red Grouse, a subspecies of the Willow Grouse) are white in winter, but change into plumage that helps camouflage them among the tundra vegetation in summer. In addition, Willow Grouse males have a distinct display plumage in spring. Recently an example of adaptive colouring was described, male Willow Grouse applying dirt to their remnant winter (white) plumage in spring to become more cryptic (Montgomery *et al.* 2001). Within a pair, the onset of soiling was synchronised with the date of the female Ptarmigan laying her clutch. Montgomery *et al.* (2001) argue that the male soiling is best explained by sexual selection and that plumage soiling is an adaptation that reduces predation risk by increasing camouflage prior to the moult into summer plumage.

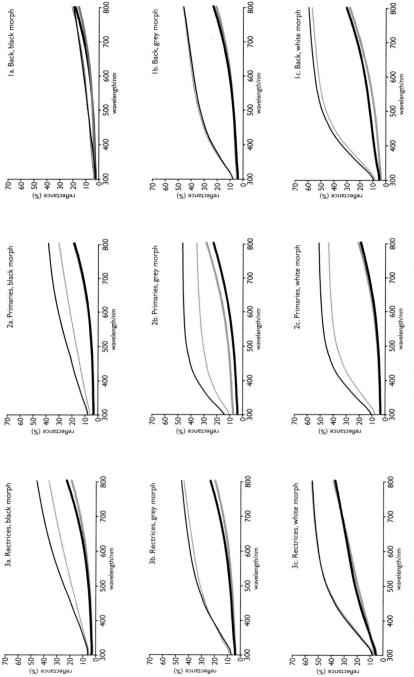

Figure 2.1 *Reflectance spectra of various plumage regions of black (left column), grey (middle column) and white (right column) Gyrfalcons. Reflectance of snow is given in the bottom row.*

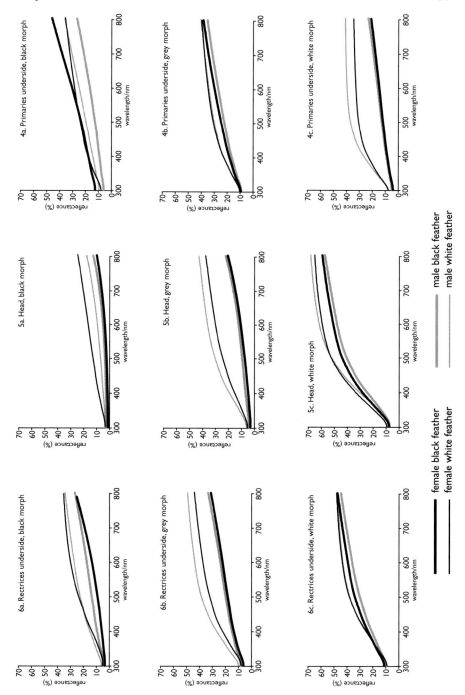

4a. Primaries underside, black morph

4b. Primaries underside, grey morph

4c. Primaries underside, white morph

5a. Head, black morph

5b. Head, grey morph

5c. Head, white morph

6a. Rectrices underside, black morph

6b. Rectrices underside, grey morph

6c. Rectrices underside, white morph

female black feather
female white feather

male black feather
male white feather

COLOUR PATTERNS

After measuring Gyr coloration using objective methods and having begun to understand the importance of colour and its ecological implications, we must analyse the Gyr's colour patterns. Gyrfalcons, in contrast with other polymorphic species such as Rough-legged Buzzards, have only a limited number of variations. This means that they can be separated into objectively described categories and analysed using statistical methods. It is possible to quantify the colour variations and to analyse them using multivariate statistics. Such procedures enable us to:

1. describe variations of patterns in objective ways (for instance to determine whether the suggestion that there are white, grey and black morphs is valid, or if there are any other general morphs, or if there is a continuum of intermediate forms)
2. determine whether the coloration patterns are different between the sexes
3. determine whether various 'colour morphs' are associated with certain geographical areas, or have any regular associations with latitude or longitude.

In Plates 3–7 (see colour section) we present the major types of colour patterns of various parts of the body with relative proportion of its occurrence. Every colour pattern is given a code. This code system was worked out after analysing the 1,865 skins from museums across the world, as detailed in Chapter 1. However, for this analysis we have omitted immature birds, thus making our sample size 1,310 skins. Using the data in these photographs it is possible to describe every skin in museum collections as a series of pattern codes. This technique is equally applicable in the field, if the observer has sufficient time, patience and the luck to watch the bird using appropriate optics. Even photographs taken in the field are sometimes good enough to allow the classification of the bird. However, it must be kept in mind that the pattern codes describe not the Gyr's actual colour, but only the pattern. Wing primary patterns are described only for the three outermost primaries (these are numbers 10, 9 and 8). Every code was then lumped up into a broader category. For the outer and central rectrices we used the same pattern codes, but analysed the two traits separately. However it seems that the coloration patterns in both the outer and central rectrices are closely correlated: they always appeared together on ordination plots.

Odd patterns (those representing less than 3% of the total number of observations) were lumped together with categories consisting of the most similar patterns to accommodate them within the 'rule of at least five cases (sample units) for each observed value' (Tabachnik and Fidell 1989). The latter samples were subjected to principal components analysis (PCA), an ordination technique carried out with Canoco software package (ter Braak and Šmilauer 1998). Ordination is the term given to the arranging of recorded patterns along axes on the basis of data on individual description of the discrete patterns we have selected. The term 'ordination' derives from early attempts to order a group of objects, for example in time or along an environmental gradient. Nowadays the term is used more generally and refers to an 'ordering' in any number of dimensions (though preferably just a few) that approximates some pattern of response of the set of objects. In our case it is used to generate hypotheses about the relationship between colour pattern variants of the Gyrfalcon and the geographical distribution of these forms.

PCA identifies the most important gradients in the dataset, or reduces the number of variables and detects structure in the relationships between variables. Our task is to determine whether there are hidden factors or components (or in our case, coloration patterns) along which our samples vary with respect to geographical distribution.

Our PCA has reduced all forms of the Gyrs in the collections into three groups of synthetic variables that represent most of the information in the original data set. Figure 2.2 shows the three groups of Gyrfalcon patterns. The first PCA axis reflects the greatest variability in the colour patterns and explains 28.7% of the variation. In our case it is the white-to-barred coloration gradient, which can be described as the general proportion of the pattern against the background colours – the greater the fraction covered with pattern, the darker is the general appearance of the bird. On the part of the graph to the right there are two groups of light birds: pure whites and birds with irregular patterns. On the left side of the graph the birds with an intensive barred pattern have grouped. Pure white plain patterns are located on the extreme right side of the first axis. Plain dark birds are positioned in the centre of both the first two axes. The traits such as spotted or barred tail, or plain dark, or intensively dark coloration were closely intercorrelated, and thus represent one continuous gradient. If the first axis separates dark and light birds, the second separates different types of barring. The second axis explains 19% of the variation. On the maximum extent of the second axis (the *y* axis in the top graph of Figure 2.2 and the *x* axis in the bottom graph of Figure 2.2) the patterns have the form of oval spots surrounded by wide dark bars. At the lower part of the axis are grouped patterns with bars which are not wide enough to cover white spots. The latter form light bars comparable in size with the dark bars.

The third axis, explaining 8.6% of the variation, separates plain-coloured birds from barred patterns (the *y* axis in the bottom picture of Figure 2.2). Thus, instead of the three colour morphs generally used used to describe Gyrs, we have found four: pure white, melanistic and two groups of barred (regularly and irregularly barred). The pure white form in the PCA grouping has the following patterns: upperbody A, tail A, breast A, head A and beak A (see Plates 3–7 and Table 2.1 for definition of groups). The most likely irregularly barred type would have upperbody D, tail D, breast D and beak D. This group is rather close to the

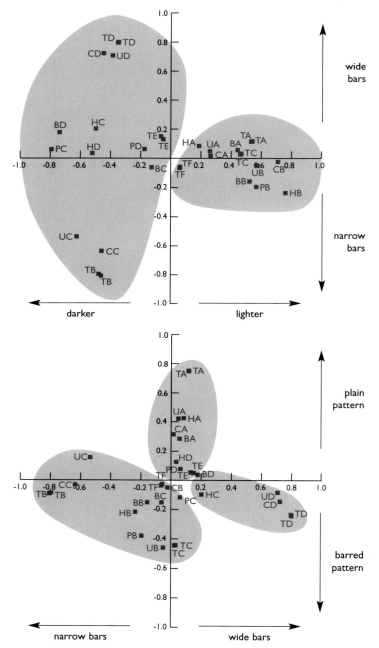

Figure 2.2 *PCA of adult Gyrfalcons (n = 1,310). Above: axes one and two. Below: axes two and three. An explanation of the codes is given in Table 2.1.*

Table 2.1 Identification of codes in Figure 2.2 with colour patterns shown in Plates 3–7. Note that in Figure 2.2 PA is not listed as it overlaps with TA.

Type	Primaries	Upper body	Tail	Underparts	Head	Beak
A	PA	CA	TA	UA	HA	BA
B	PB	CB	TB	UB	HB	BB
C	PC	CC	TC	UC	HC	BC
D	PD	CD	TD	UD	HD	BD
E			TE			
F			TF			

melanistic group: primaries D, tail E, beak D, and head C or D. The regularly barred group would have upperbody C, tail B, breast C, head B or D. This grouping is based upon the intercorrelation of coloration patterns, and suggests that there are indeed consistent coloration patterns on various parts of the body which form clusters. This suggests that the existence of continuous variation in Gyrfalcons is probably not correct. If the latter was true, we would get no groupings of the traits and all of our points would have little ordination. However it is possible

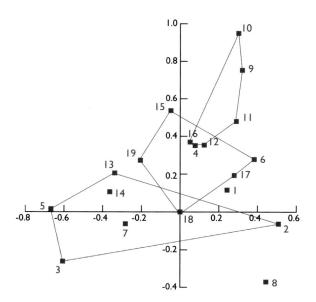

Figure 2.3 *RDA shows grouping of regions of the Gyrfalcon's range and ordination of patterns. An explanation of the geographical codes is given in Table 1.3.*

to say that there is probably a continuum of intergradation from white to black (of white to dark background of feathers, or absent to high-intensity pigmentation of the pattern), but it works on the individual axes of the three-dimensional plot of patterns that we have generated, and thus results in the discrete patterns we see in Gyrfalcons. When we calculated the relative proportion of each type of pattern for males and females we found no difference in the relative occurrences of the patterns amongst males and females.

We then used a Redundancy Discriminate Analysis (RDA) to study the geographical distribution of the colour patterns (Figure 2.3). Geographical regions, used as constraining variables in this analysis, are listed in Table 1.3. The results of the RDA show that the geographical regions form three major groups (the envelopes in Figure 2.3) based on the similarity of Gyrfalcon coloration patterns. The first envelope contains regions 4 (northern Canada), 9 and 10 (north of Russian Europe and Yamal), 11 (north-central Siberia) and 12 (Yakutia): this region has predominantly barred (grey in the literature) morphs. The second envelope represents regions with a mixture of forms, but all at similar occurrence; all these regions are non-breeding areas: 6 (lower 48 states of the USA), 15 (Kuril Islands, Japan), 18 (southern part of western Europe), and 19 (open sea). The third envelope bounds regions 2 (Canadian Yukon), 3 (central Northwest Territories, Canada), 5 (Canadian Arctic), 7 (Greenland), 13 (Chukotka) and 14 (Kamchatka), *i.e.* regions with the largest proportion of the white, melanistic and irregularly barred forms.

We illustrate the geographical distribution of the forms in Figure 2.4. The distribution of irregularly and regularly barred morphs has no clear geographical pattern. The probability of seeing these forms is equal all around the range. However it seems that in the European part of the range there is a lower chance of seeing an irregularly barred bird (e.g. one with, say, a tail pattern C: see Plate 5) than a bird with regularly spaced bars (tail pattern B). The distribution of pure white Gyrs clearly shows concentrations in the regions where the latitudinal extent of the range is maximal: Chukotka–Kamchatka and the Canadian Arctic–Labrador–Greenland systems.

Several researchers have studied the relative proportions of various colour morphs in different regions. Nielsen and Petursson (1995) reported interesting observations from Iceland. They compared historic records of the exported numbers of Gyrfalcons of various colour morphs from Iceland with those of Ptarmigan exports. The data series for white and half-white birds was significantly correlated, whereas the data series for local grey birds and white birds, and grey and half-white birds showed no correlation. It appears that the white (Canadian as locals refer to them) and half-white birds fluctuated irregularly. Grey morph and Ptarmigan showed regular fluctuations. Mattox (1970), while trapping Gyrfalcons for ringing in Greenland, reported 8 white Gyrfalcons, 4 grey, and 2 dark–white.

Stepanyan (1975, 1990) wrote that in the western region of Russia's Gyrfalcon range, the light morph accounted for 2–4% of the population whereas in the

Regularly and irregularly barred morphs

'Plain' morph

Figure 2.4 *Morph distributions around the world. The top map shows the distribution of regularly and irregularly barred Gyrs. The bottom map shows the distribution of 'plain' Gyrs. There are clear concentrations in the same regions as predicted by Figure 2.3. Note that on both maps darker circles indicate individuals collected at breeding times, while pale circles represent those collected during wintering and migratory periods.*

eastern region (north-east Siberia and Kamchatka) the fraction rose to 50%. Very similar data for Eurasia, based on a sample from two major collections, was reported later by Ellis *et al.* (1992).

Kishinskiy (1980), studying Gyrfalcons in the Koryak Mountains of north Kamchatka, found the distribution of morphs as follows: March to mid June – 13 adults, all white; second half of July to August – 21 white and 11 grey; September – 3 white and 7 grey. In general, 70% of the population were white Gyrs. On the other hand, Kishinskiy noted that white birds are easier to spot, so that the proportion of grey birds in the population was probably higher than he recorded.

Lobkov (2000) examined 173 Gyrfalcons from Kamchatka and found that the proportion of white individuals declined from 39.3% to 20% between 1981–90 and 1991–99. Gorovenko (2002) gives the following figures, based on the observation of 44 adult Gyrs in the Koryak District, Kamchatka: 31.8% grey birds, 20.6% light birds (probably silver in other definitions) and 43.1% white birds, and, in addition, 4.5% of a light rusty coloration (or light-sandy coloration in his words). Kessel (1989) examined 55 adult Gyrs from Alaska's Seward Peninsula in 1968: 12.7% were dark grey, 56.4% were grey, 16.4% were light grey, 5.5% straw (cream tone with grey bars) and 9.1% white.

Todd (1963), noting that light and dark birds can originate from the same nest, concluded that the colour differences in Gyrfalcons represent individual, rather than geographical, variation. In this Todd supported Hartert (1915) who denied that dark birds were confined to southern Greenland and light birds to the north of the island. Salomonsen (1950–51) argued that Hartert (1912–1921) was mistaken and considered Gyrfalcons to be trimorphic, with the dark morph being the sub-Arctic bird, the grey phase being from the lower Arctic and the white morph being the high-Arctic form. Todd (1963) considered that the relative frequency of the colour phases is geographically variable. The latter statement is supported by our statistical analysis.

It is interesting to note a likely function of black spots on the white coloration. The dark tips of the white primaries serve a purpose – they reinforce the barbule structure and reduce wear and tear of the feathers. Similar coloring is seen on many gulls, which face similar problems. However, the presence of various arrowheads and 'hearts' is difficult to explain. In the Barn Owl (*Tyto alba*), for example, female birds have more and larger black spots than the males. In addition, successive females mated with one male are similarly spotted. It is shown in the study of Roulin *et al.* (2000) that males prefer to mate with females with a large number of spots. As the 'good gene hypothesis' of sexual selection postulates, the ornamentation signals a superior genetic quality to potential mates. Roulin studied genetic variations in specific antibody production against a non-pathologic antigen among cross-fostered Barn Owl nestlings and assessed its covariation with the plumage spottiness of genetic parents. The magnitude of the antibody response was positively correlated with the plumage spottiness of the genetic mother, but not the genetic father.

This study provides some experimental support for the hypothesis that female ornamentation signals genetic quality. In addition, spottiness signals parasite resistance (Roulin *et al.* 2001). It is difficult, however, to expect a similar role for the spots in Gyrfalcons simply because of its larger variation in plumage when compared to Barn Owls. Nevertheless there is clearly room for further studies. In his experiments Roulin (1999) cut off small pieces of feathers with black spots from female plumage before breeding and observed the male response. It appears that male owls mated with females with reduced plumage spottiness fed their brood at a lower level cadency and achieved lower reproductive success than other males.

ASYMMETRY

Otto Kleinschmidt (1901) was the first to report that the patterns on Gyrfalcon feathers could be asymmetrical. This was later confirmed by Dementiev (1935a) who pointed out that in some collections there are Gyrfalcons with asymmetrical colour patterns: from one direction the bird appears to be a white morph, but from another a dark or intermediate morph. Such birds can be found in the collections of ZIN, MZM, the Philadelphia Academy of Natural Sciences, BMNH and AMNH (see Plates 9 amd 10). In a picture in Eastham, 2000 (p. 10) one bird shows white feathers on the tertiary wing-coverts whereas the overall colour is brownish ('Sakerish', one might say). Another photograph of a bird with asymmetric coloration is shown in Ford, 1999 (p. 22). The photograph was taken at Kuujjuaq (Fort Chimo) in northern Quebec, Canada. Several types of coloration pattern appear in asymmetric individuals. Most noticeable are the ones that mix contrasting colorations, such as tail patterns A and D (codes as given in Table 2.1) as in the bird in Plate 10 (see colour section).

We have documented occurrences of the following mixtures of asymmetrical patterns within one specimen: primaries A2 and C2; primaries A4 and C2; upperbody A1 and D2; upperbody C2 and D3; upperbody A2 and D2; tail C2 and B1; tail A1 and B3; tail A2 and D2; tail A3 and B1.

It is possible that such asymmetry also occurs in uniformly grey individuals, but remains undetected. What it is possible to conclude from these details of asymmetry is that the Gyrfalcon genome contains a variety of plumage genes, and that they can be expressed in one individual at the same time. This also means that the genome of a single Gyrfalcon may contain several sets of genes relating to plumage pattern. Potentially, this means that a population of Gyrs might shift prevailing colours in response to sudden climatic change within a few generations. This could mean, for instance, that a sudden global warming-induced ice age could result in grey European Gyrs changing into white "Canadian" type Gyrs. Clearly this is a simplification of an extremely complex process, but similar examples have been known. The Red Grouse of Scotland differs from the nominate subspecies in the lack of white winter plumage. It remains rufous-brown throughout the winter, camouflaging itself with the colours of its heath habitat. Nevertheless, every year several 'white' Red Grouse appear in bags from Scottish moors (P. Hudson, pers. comm). This means that if there was a climate change and Scotland become covered by snow in winter on a regular basis, the Red Grouse population has the capacity to shift back to its ancestral white winter plumage to blend into the snow background. Gyrfalcons are no different from the grouse in this respect.

Black and white are the dominant colours of bird species in open spaces (Zahavi and Zahavi 1997), black and white both being used for long-distance advertisements. Each colour has its benefits and drawbacks.

The advantages and disadvantages of white and black coloration have been described by Zahavi and Zahavi in the following words:

> The white surface is seen from longer distances, but the edge of a white body looks somewhat blurred. The black object appears bolder, thus it can be seen more clearly, but from shorter distances. Large birds such as swans or egrets are large enough so that a minor blurring of their outer lines is insignificant. White is especially effective in advertising movement. The light reflected from various parts of the body can reveal speed, wing movement and other factors. If a bird has two colours, it is mostly aiming at nearby observers: the zebra's stripes, which can accentuate bodily features, merge into a cryptic grey at a distance.

Uspenskiy (1984) stated that the degree of oxidisation of the dark pigment melanin decreases along with body weight in Arctic species in the Palaearctic, with the maximum being in north-east Siberia (especially Chukotka), and from there gradually decreasing towards the south-west. Thus in Eurasia the largest and whitest animals are found in Chukotka, the size and whiteness of the species decreasing in the direction of Europe and Central Asia. The longitudinal trend of the Uspenskiy phenomenon is not that obvious in the Nearctic. However it probably does exist in the north–south latitudinal distribution of the Gyrfalcon, as we have demonstrated in Figure 2.4.

INTERACTIONS BETWEEN 'MORPHS' AND THE HERITABILITY OF COLOURS

The various morphs of the Gyrfalcon may interbreed. There are numerous observations of white birds pairing up with 'grey' individuals. The resulting offspring are usually grey. In addition there are data that show that a brood may contain young of different 'morphs'. D. Bird (in Gauthier and Aubry 1996) mentioned a nest on the Payne River, Ungava Bay, Quebec, Canada with one white, one grey and one dark brown chick. Unfortunately no photos were taken (D. Bird, pers. comm.). Pictures of a brood with chicks of different morphs can be seen in Ford (1999, p. 16): one bird has a pure white tail and is whitish, another bird has a pure black tail and is uniformly melanistic. A third bird is not properly seen, but appears to be intermediate. Gorovenko (2003) reported two white chicks and one silver in a brood in the Koryak District of Kamchatka. Gladkov and Zaletaev (1962) reported two chicks in a nest at the Anabar River, western Yakutia: one was almost white, another was dark. Very similar variations within broods were described for Altai Falcon (Sushkin 1938). One of us (Sale) was told of (but did not observe) a Gyr nest in northern Quebec which had a brood consisting of three chicks, one white, one grey and one described as orange. In the Lower Kolyma one of us (Potapov) found that white chicks occur in eyries with both white parents, whereas if one parent is grey, all the chicks in the brood are grey.

Kishinskiy (1980) found a Gyr pair in the Koryak Mountains, in which both parents were white (with some black spots), but the chicks were grey. Another pair had an absolutely white male and a white female with a barred tail, and a streaked breast and nape. To of the four chicks of this pair were grey, the others white. One of the white birds had many stripes, whereas another had a smaller number of stripes. Yet another pair at the Khatyrka River had a grey male and a white female, their nest having one grey chick.

According to Palmer (1988) pure 'white' is monozygous recessive (with multiple alleles probably involved), off-white to dark brown are heterozygous, and 'black' is monozygous dominant. True 'blacks' are not known to produce anything but 'black', while dark browns can have variably grey to off-white young. However it is our belief, based on our PCA, that it is possible that at least three sets of genes regulate the pattern: one determines the amount of pigments, another sets the width of the bars, and another sets the characteristics of the pattern as such (plain colour pattern vs. barred).

MOULT AND PLUMAGE SUCCESSION

Stabler (1942) observed the moulting of a Greenlandic Gyrfalcon in captivity together with four Peregrines and one Prairie Falcon. He reported the duration of the first Gyr moult as being as long as 131 days for the primaries. The order in which the feathers dropped was 7, 6, 5, 8, 4, 9, 3, 2, 10, 1, where 1 is the outermost primary. The primary-coverts moulted in 109 days in the following order: 8, 7, 6, 9, 5, 4, 10, 3, 1, 2. The alula feathers moulted for 112 days, and were replaced in the following order: 3, 2, 4, 1. The rectrices moulted for 102 days and were replaced in the following order: 1, 2, 6, 3, 4, 5 (1 is the central feather, 6 is the outermost feather on each side).

Cramp and Simmons (1980) stated that the moult sequence of primaries is 4, 5, 6, 3, 7, 2, 8, 9, 1, 10 with a duration of 98–127 days. However, in captive Gyrfalcons the complete moult duration is not less than 150 days according to Clum and Cade (1994).

The moult begins somewhat later in males (Palmer 1988). The following sequence is known from captive birds (Seifert 1982, Palmer 1988): wing and tail begin first and the body follows soon, the entire process requiring about five months, but whether there is a slowing down or pause in the wild when the duties of feeding the brood are heaviest is unknown. Wing moult starts with P4 and goes in both directions (*i.e.* it is centrifugal). In the secondaries the four outermost moult outwardly, the others inwardly. The tertials moult outwardly.

The alula starts in the middle and moults centrifugally. Some upper coverts in the wing are occasionally retained until the next annual moult. There is early renewal of body down, probably related to the brooding of young in cold climates. Moulting down may be shed or plucked in hot weather, a process perhaps related to thermoregulation. In the tail, the central pairs of feathers (R1 and R2) drop first, some adjoining ones (the order varies somewhat) second, the outermost pair (R6) third. When the new outermost feathers are about fully grown, the adjoining pair (R5) drop last. Thus the bird always has lateral tail feathers, which are of significant aerodynamic importance.

The complete moult in adult Gyrs takes place between April–May and October–November. The female starts to moult during incubation, the male two weeks later (Cade *et al.* 1998). The female restarts moulting when her brood begins to acquire its second down. Contour moult is preceded by down moult in late winter to early spring and overlapped by the second down moult in autumn. It is still unknown whether Gyrs have a complete or partial moult (Cade *et al.* 1998).

The post-juvenile moult starts earlier than that of the adults, in February–March (Dementiev 1951). Some juvenile wing-coverts may be retained for the next moult, as they are in Peregrines.

The following moulting changes in pattern have been documented on museum specimens: breast D1 moulting into breast C1; upperbody D2 into C3; tail D2 into B1; tail C1 into the same pattern; tail D2 into B1. During the moult there were changes from immature plumage to a sometimes lighter variation. However cases where a bird with a barred tail moulted into a bird with a pure white tail are unknown. It appears (and is actually suggested by our PCA – see Figure 2.2) that the tail patterns in most cases act as the most extreme variable along several axes. This suggests that it can act as a marker for colour patterns in other parts of the body. In other words – show me your tail and I'll tell you who you are. The importance of tail pattern was spotted long ago. Todd and Friedmann (1947) and later Friedmann (1950) separated plain-tailed and bar-tailed 'varieties' occurring both in juvenile and adult Gyr plumages. These characteristics were independent of 'conventional' morphs. However the earlier paper mentioned a 'plain-tailed' juvenile which moulted into a 'bar-tailed' plumage. Two tail 'varieties', one with spots and another spot-free, were known to Frederick II in the 13th century (Wood and Fyfe 1943, p. 121 of 1990 edition). Another example of independent variation is the head coloration in melanistic Gyrs: they are usually dark headed, but sometimes have an almost white head (Palmer 1988).

SEXUAL DIMORPHISM

Gyrfalcons have a very pronounced reversed sexual dimorphism in size: females are 40% larger than males on average. In plumage, dimorphism was detected only in

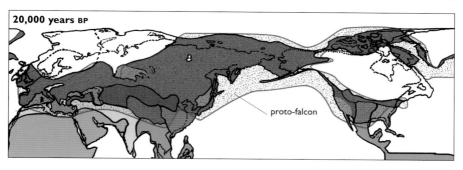

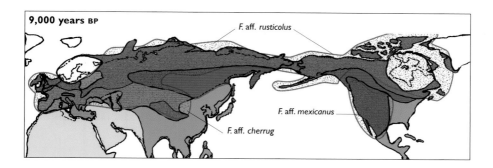

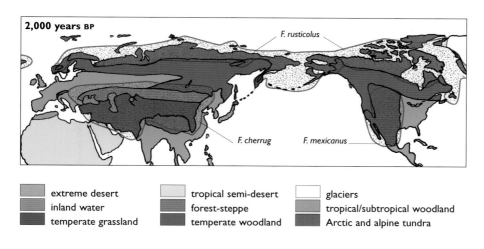

extreme desert | tropical semi-desert | glaciers
inland water | forest-steppe | tropical/subtropical woodland
temperate grassland | temperate woodland | Arctic and alpine tundra

Figure 1.1 *A reconstruction of the biological zones of the northern hemisphere at 20,000, 9,000 and 2,000 years before present (BP). In the top map the hatched distribution is that of the proto-falcon. In the middle map the distribution of* Falco aff. mexicanus *has become marginally detached from that of* F. aff. rusticolus *and* F. aff. cherrug. *In the lower map the distributions of the three species* F. rusticolus, F. cherrug *and* F. mexicanus *are completely separate.*

Plate 1. *A male Altai Falcon on the ground. This photograph was taken at an elevation of about 2,800 m.*

Plate 2. *A female Altai Falcon provides food for her chicks. This photograph was taken at an elevation of about 2,800 m.*

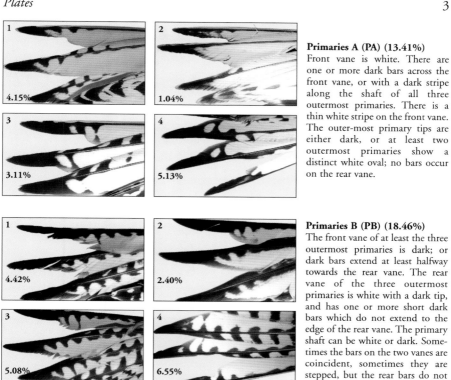

Primaries A (PA) (13.41%)
Front vane is white. There are one or more dark bars across the front vane, or with a dark stripe along the shaft of all three outermost primaries. There is a thin white stripe on the front vane. The outer-most primary tips are either dark, or at least two outermost primaries show a distinct white oval; no bars occur on the rear vane.

Primaries B (PB) (18.46%)
The front vane of at least the three outermost primaries is dark; or dark bars extend at least halfway towards the rear vane. The rear vane of the three outermost primaries is white with a dark tip, and has one or more short dark bars which do not extend to the edge of the rear vane. The primary shaft can be white or dark. Sometimes the bars on the two vanes are coincident, sometimes they are stepped, but the rear bars do not extend to the edge of the vane.

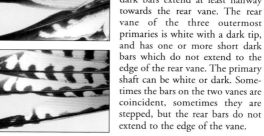

Primaries C (PC) (63.79%)
Significant numbers of dark bars extend from front to rear vane. The front vane has one or more white bars, or is dark, or has whitish oval patches. The dark bars at the rear edge of the rear vane may lose focus, the rear edge becoming a mottled pattern of dark on white, but the bars touch the rear edges of the vane.

Primaries D (PD) (4.34%)
The dark bars at the rear edge of the rear vane lose focus, the rear edge becoming a mottled pattern of dark on white that covers most of the rear vane; or the rear vane is entirely dark with white speckles.

Plate 3. Primary feather types. Figures on these (and all subsequent) feather close-ups represent the percentage of each pattern among all Gyrs. An explanation of feather codes can be found in Table 2.1.

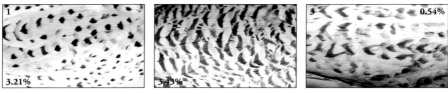

Upper body A (CA) (7.07%)
Bars are short, sometimes in the form of hearts or arrowheads. The ends of the bars do not touch the edges of the feathers. The bars in the centre of the feathers are more or less symmetrical.

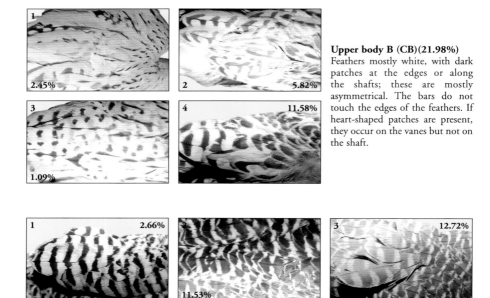

Upper body B (CB)(21.98%)
Feathers mostly white, with dark patches at the edges or along the shafts; these are mostly asymmetrical. The bars do not touch the edges of the feathers. If heart-shaped patches are present, they occur on the vanes but not on the shaft.

Upper body C (CC) (27.75%)
Bars touch the edges of the feathers. White areas touch the shafts.

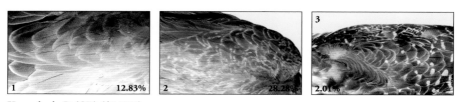

Upper body D (CD) (43.20%)
All feathers uniformly dark, or wih some white spots at the edge of the vanes, or with white areas between the bars that touch the edges of the vane, but do not touch the shafts.

Plate 4. Upper body feather types. See Table 2.1 for an explanation of the feather codes.

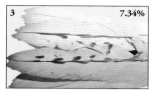

Tail A (TA) (12.95% central rectrices, 13.22% outer rectrices)
Feathers all white; feather shafts white or dark, or dark in some parts. One or more dark asymmetrical patches extend into the vanes, where they touch the shafts.

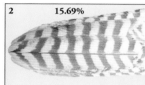
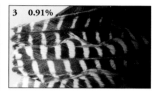

Tail B (TB) (33.04% central rectrices, 32.95% outer rectrices)
Barred tail; the bars touch the edges of the vane and the shafts. White patches are sometimes asymmetrical.

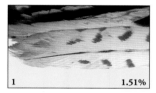

Tail C (TC) (10.51% central rectrices, 10.14% outer rectrices).
Feather shafts dark or white, or like a dashed line. Several dark asymmetrical bars extend from the edges of the vanes towards the shaft. The bars can be slightly offset, completely co-linear, or offset at the feather-shaft.

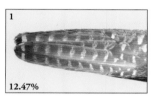

Tail D (TD) (39.98% central rectrices, 40.38% outer rectrices)
Dark bars become wider and encircle the white bars, which are mottled by dark flecks. The white bars may be co-linear or offset.

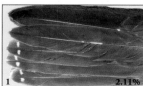

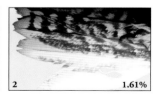

Tail E (TE) (1.84% cr, 1.68% or)
Black tail. Sometimes one or two white spots at the end of the tail.

Tail F (TF) (1.68% cr, 1.63% or)
Streaked tail. If present, bars are broken into lines of mottled dark flecks. The pattern is asymmetrical and possibly random as well.

Plate 5. Tail feather types. See Table 2.1 for an explanation of the feather codes.

Underparts A (UA) (6.33%)
Breast entirely white or with a very small number of small dark spots, coverage by which is barely discernible. Flanks are white.

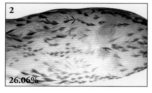

Underparts B (UB) (30.70%)
Breast white with small but significant number of dark markings. These are arrow-shaped and point towards the head; or have a greater density of markings so the breast looks distinctly mottled. The shape of the dark spots could be less arrowlike and more oval – intermediate between the arrow and heart-shaped markings.

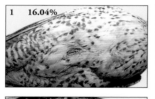
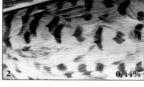
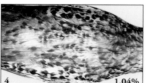

Underparts C (UC) (20.27%)
Markings are heart-shaped on the side of the breast and flanks. The difference between types 1 and 2 is the size of the individual markings. On the lower abdomen the mark-ings on individual feathers may merge to form distinct bars across the bird. Individual breast feathers may have linear patterns along the shafts with tetragonal or triangular shapes at the ends. Dark markings touch the shaft. Bars on the flanks might touch the edge of the vanes.

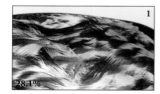

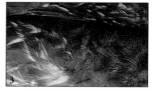

Underparts D (UD) (42.71%)
Dark markings occupy a large proportion of the feather area. Residual white areas are confined to the edges of the feathers, though some feathers may remain predominantly white. Pattern D3 makes up 0.71% of the total.

Plate 6. *Underpart feather types. See Table 2.1 for an explanation of the feather codes.*

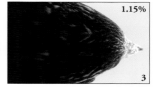

Head A (HA) (3.48%)
Head of the Gyrfalcon is entirely white.

Head B (HB) (40.74%)
Individual feathers have dark stripes along their shafts. The area of each dark stripe makes up less than 50% of the vane.

Head C (HC) (34.44%)
Individual feathers have dark stripes along their shaft. These dark areas occupy more than 50% of the vane.

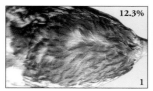

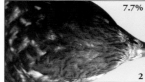

Head D (HD) (21.35 %)
Darker stripes run along the shaft on top of the dark vanes. The white parts of the feathers are not exposed.

Beak A (BA) (10.47%)
Uniformly whitish.

Beak B (BB) (25.44%)
Whitish with a dark tip.

Beak C (BC) (14.84%)
Upper part predominantly dark, with darker tip.

Beak D (BD) (49.34%)
Uniformly dark.

Plate 7. *Head feather and beak types. See Table 2.1 for an explanation of the codes.*

Plate 8. *The wooden falcon on top of the*
Fálkahúsid in Reykjavik.

Plate 9. *Gyr with asymmetric tail and primary*
coloration, from the BMNH.

Plate 10. *Gyr with asymmetric barring on the tail feathers. This specimen is from the American*
Museum of Natural History.

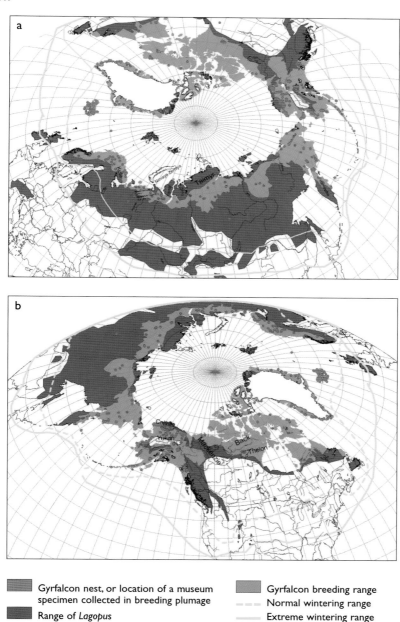

Gyrfalcon nest, or location of a museum specimen collected in breeding plumage

Range of *Lagopus*

Gyrfalcon breeding range

Normal wintering range

Extreme wintering range

Figure 3.1 *The palearctic (**a**) and nearctic (**b**) breeding and wintering distributions of the Gyrfalcon. The range of the Gyr's main prey,* Lagopus *grouse, is also given.*

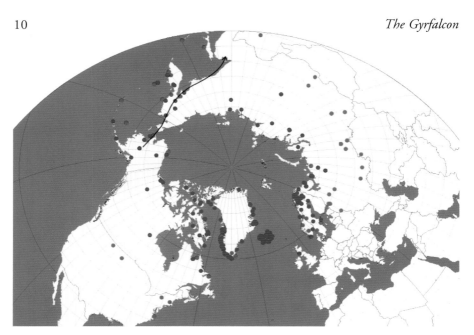

Figure 8.1 *Breeding (blue dots) and wintering (red dots) locations of Gyrs, as revealed by museum specimens. The arrow shows movement of a satellite-tracked immature bird tagged in Denali, Alaska.*

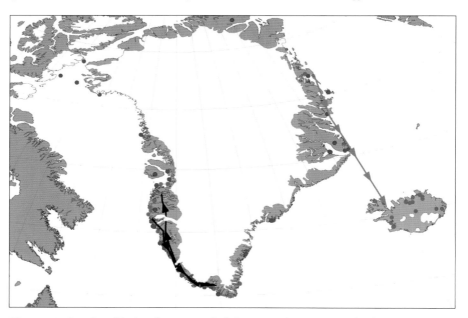

Figure 8.2 *Breeding (blue) and wintering (red) locations of Gyrs in Greenland and Iceland from museum specimens. The black arrow shows the route of a bird tracked by the Peregrine Fund (Burnham 2001). The grey arrow shows a hypothetical migration route between Greenland and Iceland.*

Plate 11. *Gyr nest site on Bylot Island, Canada. The nest is in a cave above the whitewash streaks.*

Plate 12. *Gyr nest site on Bylot Island, Canada. The female is just visible on her eggs.*

Plate 13. *A prey plucking site on Bylot Island, above the nest on plates 11 and 12,*

Plate 14. *A white female Gyr feeds her grey chicks at a nest in north-east Siberia.*

Plate 15. *Eggs in a Gyr scrape-nest in north-east Siberia. The cliff overlooks tundra near the delta of the Kolyma River.*

Plate 16. *A female on eggs at a nest in Iceland peers quizzically at the photographer.*

Plate 17. *A single chick at the nest site seen in Plate 16.*

Plate 18. *A chick exercises its wings. There were two chicks in this Icelandic nest.*

Plate 19. *A female Gyr in northern Canada feeds her chicks (photo: Per Michelsen).*

Plate 20. *Gyrfalcon in flight above the snows of Iceland. The bird was above a volcanic rift and appeared to be working the air, allowing it to sweep up a steep cliff.*

Plate 21. *Two juvenile Gyrfalcons, Norway. The parent birds were rather pale in colour, but their young were dark or very dark (photo: Per Michelsen).*

Plate 22. *Female Gyr with its Arctic Ground Squirrel prey. The Gyr's nest was in one of the coldest places in northern Canada, yet both parent birds were grey (photo: Per Michelsen).*

Plate 23. *An unfriendly interaction between a Gyrfalcon (left) and a Peregrine. The two birds were nesting in the same river canyon in northern Canada (photo: Per Michelsen).*

Plate 24. *Most Icelandic Gyrs are grey, but this female is much paler than usual.*

Plate 25. *A very dark juvenile from a nest in southern Norway (photo: Per Michelsen).*

Plates 26 and 27. *White Gyrs from northern Canada. Gyrs usually decapitate their prey immediately after capturing it; the bird on the right has just completed this behaviour.*

Plate 28. *A Gyr in flight – an unforgettable sight. This bird was photographed in Southern Norway. Note the fanning of the tail, primaries and alula (photo: Per Michelsen).*

the reflection properties of the upper and underwing (males are more reflecting from underneath the wing, females from above). However these reflection differences are not that pronounced in the melanistic form.

Cade (1960) first expressed his concern that many museum workers fail to recognise that the sexes are dimorphic in colour and pattern. The standard references state categorically that the plumages of males and females are alike. According to him, at least in the grey phase, males tend to be paler than females:

> This difference is especially noticeable on the head and the venter where the dark shaft marks and feather bars are often much reduced in males, but pigmentation saturation of the plumage, in general, is less in males than in females. These differences are not absolute, for some males are as dark as some females and vice versa, but in the field they are conspicuous enough to have independently caught the attention of several observers.

Generally male Gyrs tend to be paler than females, a trend which is also seen in Rough-legged Buzzards (Cade 1955a) and Snowy Owls (Witherby *et al.* 1943). Our reflective spectrometry measurements (Figure 2.1) show that in 'background' coloration females are more 'reflective' than males in primaries, wing- and tail-coverts (in all morphs) and in rectrices (dark and grey morphs only); and less reflective than males in underside vanes of primaries (dark and white morphs) and underside vanes of rectrices in grey morphs.

CHAPTER 3

Distribution

The Gyrfalcon is generally considered to be a typical example of an Arctic bird species. Indeed, for many decades (if not centuries) the Gyr was assumed to be the most northerly species of falcon and was thought to be confined to the high Arctic. It is now known that the first assumption is only partially true. The details of the falcon's true distribution also reveal a somewhat different picture from the prevailing Arctic-only assumption.

The Gyrfalcon has a circumpolar range, occupying mountain and forest-tundra, and even plain tundra if this lies close to the timberline or if there are rock outcrops for nesting. Kalyakin (1989) considers that the optimum area for Gyrfalcon breeding (at least in the Yamal Peninsula region of north-west Siberia) lies in southern, typical tundra and forest-tundra regions. Generally the breeding range lies within the range of the main prey species, grouse of the genus *Lagopus*. These grouse are also circumpolar, with the most populated parts of the range lying north of the Arctic Circle, though in Asia grouse spread south into the range of the Saker

Falcon. The presence of *Lagopus* at relatively southern latitudes, together with the grouse's cyclical fluctuations – which are not synchronous throughout the range – mean that the Gyrfalcon roams in response to the cycle, these movements sometimes bringing it into the realm of the Saker. The Saker is sometimes difficult to distinguish from the Gyr, so the overlapping ranges can create confusion.

As noted by Morozov (2000), Gyrfalcons start to breed when food such as Willow Grouse and Ptarmigan becomes available. In these periods the Gyrs are, strictly speaking, stenophagous, *i.e.* they specialise on one species of prey, and thus their distribution is limited to areas where there are enough Ptarmigan or Willow Grouse in spring. There are some exceptions, such as breeding areas located close to seabird colonies, and a few in the high Arctic where Gyrs specialise in preying on ducks and consequently breed almost a month later (E. Potapov pers. obs. in northeast Siberia).

The northern limit of Willow Grouse on plain tundras during winter and early spring, when the Gyrfalcons start to breed, is determined by the height of the local willow trees. If the trees are tall enough to stand above the snow in significant quantities, there will be enough food for grouse in most years (Andreev 1988). In mountainous regions Ptarmigan follow the same pattern, but rely on smaller, shorter vegetation, and therefore are more likely to be found in wind-blown, snow-free areas. The northern limits of the distribution of Gyrfalcons were pencilled on the map by Kishinskiy (1988) in his posthumous book, but the general conclusion was not written, despite the fact that his idea regarding distribution is clear from his illustrative figures. Gyrfalcons are limited by the spring distribution of Willow Grouse/Ptarmigan, and by the distribution of colonies of alcids and gulls, where the timing of Gyr breeding is governed by the arrival and breeding cycle of these birds. In addition, local geography and the availability of nest sites play their role.

Traditionally the Gyrfalcon was believed to be an Arctic (and occasionally sub-Arctic) species, distributed across the northern tundras in the Arctic–Alpine zone, mainly above the timberline (Cramp and Simmons 1980). Grossman and Hamlet (1964) simply describe the falcon's distribution as the 'high Arctic'. This perception was derived from old books whose evidence was anecdotal, based on information from bird traders bringing birds to Western Europe during the Middle Ages. The remarkable treatise of Frederick II (*De Arte Venandi cum Avibus*, dated to about 1250 and translated by Wood and Fyfe 1943) used Idrisi's classification of geographical zones. Idrisi (Abu Abdallah Mohammed Idrisi, *c.* 1099–1154) was an Arab geographer at the court of Roger II of Palermo and author of *Al Raojori*, or *The Going out of a Curious Man to Explore the Regions of the Globe, its Provinces, Islands, Cities and Their Dimensions and Citations.* The manuscript is kept at the Bodleian Library, Oxford.) Idrisi divided the Earth into seven latitudinal zones (between the equator and the point where the earth becomes uninhabitable) and 11 longitudinal zones (from the westernmost point of Africa to the easternmost point of Asia). Frederick noted the Gyrfalcon as breeding in or near the most distant parts of the seventh latitudinal zone: "some of them are brooded on the high cliffs of the Hyperborean territory, particularly on certain islands between Norway and Greenland, called in Teutonic speech, Iceland".

One result of the Gyr's range being almost exclusively the extreme north was that it was – and in many cases still is – believed that the Gyr is the most northerly breeding falcon (e.g. Vaughan 1992). This is not true: the record for the northern-most breeding of a falcon is actually held by the Peregrine (Peregrine Fund Report 1999). The southernmost confirmed breeding location for the Gyrfalcon in Eurasia is the Kamchatka Peninsula, where a specimen with brood patches was obtained from the Tatyana River (54°35'N 161°07'E) in the Kronotskiy Reserve. The southernmost nest in North America was found on Long Island, in Hudson Bay, off the western Quebec coast, at 54°53'N 80°30'W (Brodeur *et al.* 1995).

Since the publication of Frederick II's work there have been major updates on the Gyrfalcon's range, mostly connected with the discoveries of the New World and new Arctic territories. The latest updated series of the *Birds of Western Palearctic* (Cade *et al.* 1998) gives an in-depth analysis of the Gyr's current distribution in Europe. Clum and Cade (1994) present a detailed note on the distribution of the species in the New World. A number of publications deal with the global range of the species, these ranging from wide-audience books to specialist publications (e.g. Dementiev 1951, Dementiev and Gladkov 1951, Dementiev 1960, Cade 1982). Data on the distribution of Gyrfalcons in eastern Europe and northern Asia have been obtained from various sources, including personal experiences, personal communications with local biologists and the study of museum collections. The Nearctic and Palaearctic Gyrfalcon ranges are shown on Figure 3.1 (see colour section).

In Europe the Gyrfalcon breeds in Iceland, Norway, Sweden, Finland and Russia; in Asia it breeds only in Russia; in the New World it breeds in the USA (Alaska), Canada and Greenland (Denmark). These countries are dealt with individually below.

ICELAND

Gyrfalcons breed in all parts of the island (Wayre and Jolly 1958, Bengtson 1971, 1972, Suetens and Groenendael 1976, Woodin 1980, Nielsen 1986, Nielsen and Cade 1990a, 1990b, Cade *et al.* 1998), but the distribution of birds is not uniform. The densest population is in the northern part of the island, around Dalasýsla, Vestfirðir, Hunavatnssýsla, Skagafjörður, Eyjafjörður, Þingeyjarsýsla and Múlasýsla. The Gyr is rare in the centre of the island, most nest locations being recorded at the edge of the central highlands. Only a few pairs breed in the central highlands proper. Several museums (RMNH, MZM, CMNH, AMNH) have specimens of birds obtained from the northern part of the island during the breeding season.

NORWAY

The Gyrfalcon breeds in most parts of the country from elevated parts of the south (starting from Sirdalsheiene) to the north (the Pasvik River valley). The southern sites are all above 1,450m, an alpine tundra zone specific to Scandinavian mountain birch forests. On the western and northern coasts Gyrs breed on cliffs, sometimes close to large seabird colonies. In northern Norway breeding has been recorded in Finnmark (this is the stronghold of the Norwegian population: Haftorn 1971, Frantzen *et al.* 1991, Cade *et al.* 1998), Nordland, Trøndelag, Romsdal (including traditional sites in Dovrefjell), Oppland and Hordaland (Hagen 1952a, 1952b, Hagen and Barth 1952, Langvatn 1977, Langvatn and Moksnes 1979, Tømmeraas 1989a, 1990).

The skin of a female Gyrfalcon taken at Christiania Sound (Oslofjord) during the breeding season is in the collection of the Copenhagen Museum of Natural History. This would potentially represent a southern breeding record, but the bird does not bear indications of breeding.

SWEDEN

The Gyrfalcon breeds in the northern part of Dalarna, the western part of Jämtland, Härjedalen and Lapland, and in the northern part of Norrbotten. The breeding range is almost exclusively associated with alpine tundra, but occasionally includes the timberline border. This border country includes string bogs on the gentler slopes and patches of birch trees on the mountain slopes. There are rumours that Gyrs breed as far south as *c.* 62°N in north-west Dalarna, from Idre to the Norwegian border (U. Falkdalen, pers. comm.). The total number of Gyrfalcons breeding in Sweden is estimated at 100–200 pairs, two-thirds of which breed in Norrbotten. WWF Sweden is currently sponsoring *Jaktfalk* (Gyrfalcon) a project intended to determine the current status of the bird in the country.

FINLAND

Gyrfalcons breed exclusively in the northern part of the country in the provinces of Enotekiö, Inari, Utsjoki and northern Savukoski (Mikkola and Sulkava 1972, Hyytiä *et al.* 1983, Koskimies 1989, Huhtala *et al.* 1996, Väisäinen *et al.* 1998, Cade *et al.* 1998). The stronghold of the Finnish Gyrfalcon is believed to be the country around Inari and Utsjoki in the far north of the country (Koskimies 1995). In Finland the Gyrfalcon's range is the northern taiga/forest-tundra where there are a few hills, though there are also some breeding records from the forest zone (Pulliainen *et al.* 1973, Pulliainen 1975, Koskimies 1995, Cade *et al.* 1998).

RUSSIA

To the present time the distribution of Gyrfalcons in Russia has been poorly studied. Only some individual breeding sites are known, and the reports in the literature are not really adequate (Kolosov 1983). Moreover, professional ornithologists remain reluctant to publish material on breeding sites, and justifiably so as these localities would be likely to be raided by bird traders.

The breeding distribution of the Gyrfalcon in Russia was first presented by Dementiev (1951), later modified by Dementiev and Gladkov (1951). In the west the 1951 distribution curve is known as 'Dementiev's line' (Ellis *et al.* 1992). However, this line was drawn on the basis of specimen collections and academic speculation: it is also not a true range as there is no northern limit. The line also has a curious extension in the centre of northern Siberia created to accommodate two young Gyr specimens, both in the collection of ZIN. This curve has been repeated in subsequent publications (Dementiev and Gladkov 1951, Cade 1982, Ellis *et al.* 1992,) and in view of its importance (since it indicates a southern expansion of the breeding range) the specimens on which it is based deserve close scrutiny. Both specimens were collected 'during the breeding season in the mid-flow of the Nizhnaya (Lower) Tunguska River in the north of the Irkutsk District (Oblast)' (Tkachenko 1937) and were from the collections of Academician Sushkin, the former Curator of Birds at the Imperial Zoological Museum, St Petersburg. They have original tags (from Sushkin) with dates of 17 July 1918 for both (presumably supplied by Tkachenko). The tags describe the place where the specimens were obtained as a 'place called Ukshil', Lower Tunguska, 30km *upstream* from the estuary of the Lower Kachoma River. The river name on the recent maps is the Lower (Nizhnaya) Kochemo River, and the coordinates of the place where the specimens were procured is 62°09'14.9''N, 108°36'18.4''E. Dementiev (1951) gave the location as 30km *downstream* from the confluence of the Lower Kachoma rivers (though the difference between an upstream and a downstream location is minimal: due to river meanders the difference between these two points is a mere 20km). The place name Ukshil identifies the mistake in Dementiev's text.

Interestingly, Dementiev (1951) did not refer to the authorship of the finding and did not specify the source of the information. However, Tkachenko (1937) described the place where he shot the birds: "The river flows in a valley some 5 to 10km wide with many oxbow lakes and marshes along the banks". The specimens were described as "*Falco rusticolus uralensis* ... a pair of young shot during the breeding period in the mid-stream part of the river". The river flows very slowly and is sometimes completely covered with vegetation. The misunderstanding over the origin of these birds stems from the fact that at the time the birds were collected there was a civil war in Russia and a breakdown of local authority. The Lower Tunguska River was controlled by General Kolchak, a distinguished polar explorer, geographer and hydrographer, and an arch-enemy of the Red Army. His headquarters were at Tumen, but he later moved to Irkutsk where he established the University. Tkachenko either did not stress the importance of his finding, or simply corrected Irkutsk Gubernia (Governed Territory) into Irkutsk District. In reality the mid-stream of the Nizhnaya Tunguska is close to the Viluy plateau, which is an obvious falcon habitat. The part of the river where the specimens were collected is at about 64°N, in the Middle Siberian Highlands.

Ellis *et al.* (1992) also mentioned one juvenile Gyrfalcon (ZIN 168211) as having been collected, on 16 July 1956, 'in the upper drainage of the Yana river'. This specimen led Ellis and coauthors to extend the breeding range of Gyrs south of the Arctic Circle. The finding was also mentioned in a number of other publications (for instance Vorobiev 1963 and Solomonov 1987). However, the tag on the bird clearly states that it was collected on the Adycha River. The Adycha is an upper tributary of the Yana, covering an area which extends from 65°N to 67°30'N. The bird was collected by Egorov (1958) on the Adycha plateau close to its confluence with the Nelgese (also occasionally spelt Nelgehe) River (66°42'N 136°31'E). In this place the river cuts through ridges of the Cherskiy range to the east, and the Yana plateau to the west, and it is likely that the juvenile bird was moving through the mountains from elsewhere. The nearest nest site known in this area is close to the source of the Tykakh river (*c.* 68°09'N 133°15'E), between the Yana and Bytyntay rivers, some 215km to the north-west (Vorobiev 1963).

A more balanced line was published by Kozlova (1969, 1975) who omitted the southernmost breeding record at the Lower Tunguska River and included a northern limit. In this book we have merged Kozlova's line with more recent data. The Gyrfalcon breeds in most parts of the southern tundra zone, following the timberline. Breeding in open flat tundra is associated with islands of forests. Gyrs often breed on mountains within the tundra zone, as well as in the deltas and pre-delta areas of large Siberian rivers. In Kamchatka, Gyrs penetrate further south, following mountain ridges covered with a mixture of tundra vegetation and birch forests to about 55°N.

The longest monitored breeding location in Russia is on the Sem' Ostrovov Islands, off the Kola Peninsula (Dementiev and Gortchakovskaya 1945, Dementiev 1951, Shklyarevich and Krasnov 1980), currently part of the Kandalaksha Nature Reserve. Breeding was reported from the islands, which do not have a large density of Willow Grouse but have significant shorebird colonies. Breeding was also reported at Bolshoi Lytziy Island, and possibly on Kharlov and Bolshoi Kuvshin islands. Breeding observations at this site started in the late 1930s (Dementiev and Gortchakovskaya 1945, Dementiev 1951), but the observations were doubted by later researchers (Shklyarevich and Krasnov 1980), who reported breeding at Bolshoi Lidskiy Island. A breeding bird was collected from Kharlov Island in 1947 by the famous Russian ornithologist N. Kartashev (MZM). At present as many as three pairs of Gyrs breed within 20km (along the coast) of the Seven Islands Nature

Reserve. One pair still has a territory which includes the Seven Islands archipelago, but from 1991 the pair had moved to a mainland site close to the archipelago. From that time it is thought that the island site was not occupied for several years, though it still lay within the range of hunting birds. However, it is now possible that the site has been reoccupied (Yu. Krasnov pers. comm.).

Other breeding records from Kola include Kildin Island and the Gavrilovskie Islands (Shklyarevich and Krasnov 1980, Yu. Krasnov pers. comm.),while inland breeding has been observed at the both forested and tundra zones of the Ponoy river valley (Ganusevich 1983, 1988, 1991), at the Lumbovka and Kachkovka rivers (Shklyarevich and Krasnov 1980), at the Iokanga River and in the Lapland Reserve (Vladimirskaya 1948, Dementiev 1951). Kola nests are located either in trees close to the timberline or on the bluffs of the Khibiny Mountains above the tree line (Chun tundra and Nyavka tundra). Pearson (1899) noted a nest at Iokanga River, upstream from Lake Iokanga (Lake Ukanskoe in his transcription), while Kishinskiy (1958) found three nests along the Teriberka, Voronya and Muchka rivers, within 30km of the sea coast, some 80–100km east of Murmansk. The breeding range also includes the south-west coasts of Mezen' Guba Bay, the Kanin Peninsula and the Kanin Kaman' Mountains, and includes bush tundra along the timberline in the Malozemelskaya and Bolshezemelskaya tundra areas. In the Timan tundra breeding has not been recorded in the coastal plains, but it does occur at the timberline (Mikheev 1941, Morozov 2000). It is likely that Gyrs also breed along the timberline in the Timan Kryazh Mountains. Breeding on the Bolshezemelskaya tundra was recorded along the More-Yu and Bolshaya Rogovaya rivers (Voronin 1983, 1986, 1987, Voronin *et al.* 1983). In the Malozemelskaya tundra breeding was recorded south from Lake Urdyzhskoe (Voronin and Kochanov 1989).

In the Pechora Delta there are breeding records mentioned for Lovetskiy Island (Voronin and Kochanov 1989, Mineyev 1994, Rogacheva *et al.* 1995, Morozov 2000), but there are none for the Kolguev and Vaygach islands (Trevor-Battye 1895, Tolmachev 1928 and references therein, Morozov 2000). According to Uspenskiy (cited in Dementiev 1951) Gyrfalcons breed from the Gusinaya Zemlya to the Kara Gate Strait (Karaskie Vorota Strait) on the southern island of the Novaya Zemlya islands. However almost all thorough ornithological surveys of Arctic Russia have shown that the records of Savva Uspenskiy are extremely unreliable: it is likely that the record Dementiev (1951) referred to was imagination. Kalyakin (1993) mentioned the Gyrfalcon in his checklist only as a vagrant bird: Morozov (2000) also states that Gyrs do not breed on Novaya Zemlya.

In the north Urals the southernmost breeding record is at 66°N at the Ust-Usa River (Brandt 1853). There are at least two recent breeding records along the Usa (Morozov 1991). A population of Gyrs was found between the Yugor Peninsula and the Polar Urals (Morozov 1991), with 10–15 breeding pairs discovered in a study area between Bolshaya and Malaya Oyu. Breeding certainly occurs in the Pay-Khoy range to the north of the Urals. In the southern Yamal, Gyrs are known to breed in significant numbers (Kalyakin and Vinogradov 1981, Danilov *et al.* 1984, Ryabtsev 1986, Rupasov 2001) along the northern border of the forests, but no breeding has been recorded north of 70°N. The most significant site in the Yamal is the Shuchya River, at 67°04'N 68°10'E (Mishenko 1981, Ryabtsev 1986, Kalyakin 1989). A section of the lower Ob River, and also the lower Taz River and the Tazovskiy Peninsula, were mentioned as breeding grounds by Dementiev (1951).His conclusion was based on two specimens in the collection of the Moscow Zoological Museum, one collected by Johansen in 1931 with a tag reading 'killed at the nest' and another from the lower Ob, but with no date. In Gydan, Gyrs are not found in the northern parts of the peninsula (Chernichenko *et al.* 1994), but occur in the southern part close to the timberline.

Dementiev (1951) included the entire Taimyr Peninsula in the Gyrfalcon range, even though, at the time, there was no direct evidence of breeding (though there had been observations of non-breeding birds). No breeding Gyrs were found on the tundra zone of the Taimyr during 16 years of continuous research (Dorogov 1985, Dorogov *et al.* 1988). However, it is suspected that Gyrfalcons breed in the Byrranga Mountains (Rogacheva 1988). Rogacheva also mentions an unverified record of breeding in the upper reaches of the Verkhnaya Taymira/Upper Taimyr River by A.A. Vinokurov. The northernmost nest record on Taimyr is at the Lukunskaya River, a tributary of the Khatanga River at 72°31'N 105°04'E, which is at the northern limit of the taiga (Litvinov and Chupin 1983, Dorogov *et al.* 1988). In eastern Taimyr, Gyrs breed on both sides of the Khatanga valley, and also along the timberline in the Siberian Lowlands. However, no Gyrs were found in the northern Taimyr at the Lenivaya river and Vosnesenisiy Bay (75°23'N 89°25'E) despite a thorough study (Tomkovich and Vronskiy 1988, 1994).

Gyrfalcons were known to breed near Duduinka on the Yamnaya River – some 37km away, at 70°08'N 83°12'E – and also along the Kureika river which runs from the Putorana plateau (Dementiev 1951). They also bred at the Khaduttey River at 67°N (Dementiev 1941) and near the Tolstiy Nos settlement of the Eyenisey delta (Rogacheva 1988). There are also breeding records for the forest-tundra of the left bank of the Yenisey and near the Lukunskaya River (Litvinov and Chupin 1983, Dorogov *et al.* 1988). The latter is currently considered to be the northernmost-known regular breeding site in Taimyr (72°31'N). One specimen obtained in March 1897 at the Sysim River, Lower Yenisey, is held at ZIN. In the middle section of the Yenisey (around 64°N), well south in the taiga belt, Gyrs were recorded only once in 17 years of observations (Shaparev 1998).

Gyrs breed in the centre and on the southern slopes of the Putorana plateau (Dorogov *et al.* 1988), in the upper reaches of the Kotuy River and in the Kheta River valley. While working along the Kotuy River Volkov (1988) saw Gyrs during the breeding season (27 June) at the Changada River estuary, Upper Kotuy River (67°55'N 102°17'E), but was unable to locate a nest. Nests and sightings of newly fledged young were noted at the Kotuy River by Litvinov and Chupin (1983). Over a 16-year period Dorogov *et al.* (1988) found 24 nests, mostly on the Putorana plateau. In 1997 Volkov *et al.* (1998) surveyed a total of 600km^2 of the Ayan River and its tributaries during the period 24 June to 4 July and found only one active nest, at the Maliy Honnamakit River valley.

Gyrfalcons were also breeding in the Anabar River valley (Solomonov 1987) and its upper tributaries (the Bolshaya and Malaya Kuonamka) and the Anabar plateau (S. Vitkauskas, pers. comm.). There, the falcons breed on the riverside cliffs in the (mostly forested) highlands. In 1961 Gladkov found a Gyr nest on the right bank of the Anabar River at the timberline, some 7km downstream from the Saskylakh settlement, at 72°00–59'N 114°01–21'E (Vorobiev 1963). On the Lena River breeding was noted in 1882 (collected by Bunge at Sagastir village, ZIN 1893), but no recent records have been reported. In the Yana River basin Gyrs were noted at the Adycha river, close to the Adycha plateau (Egorov 1958). There are no direct records of Gyrs breeding at Verkhoyansk, on the Upper Yana River, a town that is regarded as the coldest place in the Northern Hemisphere. Recent observations in the upper reaches of the Adycha River have also yielded no evidence of breeding Gyrfalcons, though Yu. Labutin collected a breeding bird (12 June 1957, *i.e.* during the Gyr breeding season) at the Tochkah River in northern Yakutia (now held in ZIN).

Further east, the Gyrfalcon breeds in the Yana–Kolyma lowlands along the timberline (Solomonov 1987), on the Lower Kolyma river close to the timberline, and in the delta section of the river (observations by the authors and Krechmar *et al.* 1991). The southernmost record in Kolyma is at the Musovka (Mysovaya) River some 110km downstream from Srednekolymsk, 67°34'N 156°20'E (Ivanov 1976). Gyrs also breed in the Chukotka Autonomous Republic, in practically every river valley with suitable nesting sites. In Chukotka Gyrs rarely breed on the coastal plain tundras (maps in Kishinskiy 1988) following instead the northern limits of the Raven's range (Ravens are the major nest provider for Gyrfalcons – see Chapter 9). Coastal nests were reported at Cape Shalaurova Izba (Stishov and Marukhnich 1990), at a seabird colony at Seyshan, western Chukotka and in Providenya Bay (Portenko 1972).

To the south the range is limited by the forested mountains of the Upper Kolyma and the wide, forested valleys of the Kolyma River and its tributaries. No breeding has been recorded from the Kolyma Mountains (Kishinskiy 1968), though there is unverified information by V.G. Krivosheev on breeding on the Kulu River (Upper Kolyma) (Krechmar and Nazarenko 1989) and on the Bakhapcha River (M. Zasipkin and E. Dubinin, pers. comm.). There is some indirect indication of breeding on the Gizhiga River (Allen 1905).

In Magadan District the most likely breeding sites are on the Taigonos Peninsula (A. V. Krechmar, pers. comm.). Allen (1905) reported one Gyrfalcon specimen from the Gashing River, close to Taigonos. Rumours that the Gyrfalcon breeds at the sea coast close to Magadan, which have become widespread among falcon trappers since 1990, are not based on solid facts.

Dementiev (1951) included the entire Kamchatka Peninsula within the Gyrfalcon's breeding range. Since that report, the peninsula has been widely believed to be the southernmost breeding ground of the falcon, a mistake which was replicated in many subsequent publications (Kozlova 1969, 1975, Cade 1980, Burton 1989, Ellis *et al.* 1992, Ferguson-Lees and Christie 2001), though not in all (Ivanov 1976). The initial report was based on anecdotal information from local people who maintained that Gyrs bred on the coastal cliffs close to the Ozernaya (51°29'N 156°33'E) and Kambal'naya rivers (51°09'N 156°43'E) on the south-eastern Kamchatka coast (Dybowski 1883 – note that Dementiev 1951 mis-spelled both names in his book), and on the skin of an adult bird with an exceptionally white chest which was shot in June 1892 in the Avacha River valley by Slynin (Menzbier 1900). The skin is in the collection of ZIN. Although June is considered to be the Gyr breeding season, neither Slynin nor Menzbier suggest that the shot bird was a breeding adult. The major source of Dementiev's (1951) information was Yu. V. Averin who, at the time, was employed at the Kronotskiy State Nature Reserve. The Moscow Zoological Museum has a large female bird with clear brood patches collected near the Tatyana River, on the Kronotskiy Peninsula, on 13 May 1947. Another bird was killed on 1 March 1949 in Olga Bay, also on the Kronotskiy Peninsula. Dementiev (1951) referred to Averin in his statement that the Gyrfalcons bred on the cliffs of Olga Bay, but there is no material to support this statement. Alexander Ivanov (1976), who was working at the Zoological Institute and studied the skins himself, excluded Kamchatka from the breeding range of Gyrs: "breeding in Kamchatka is possible, but not yet proven".

During the 30 years he spent studying the birds of Kamchatka, Lobkov (1986, 2000 and pers. comm.) did not find a single Gyrfalcon nest. However, he does refer to one sighting of a pair of Gyrs 'near a nest' in 1974 on the Kronotskiy Peninsula. The nest was of sticks, presumably built by a Raven. The contents of the nest are unknown, so the sighting does not establish that breeding took place. In subsequent years the birds were not seen at the location. The southern limit of regular breeding can be taken as starting at the river Uka (57°42'N) in the Koryak National District and proceeding north along the Sredinniy mountain range. Breeding south of Uzon Volcano (the Kronotskiy Reserve) is very rare. In the whole of Kamchatka (which covers both the Kamchatka Administrative District and the Koryak National District) there are probably 150–200 pairs of Gyrfalcons, most of these in the Koryak National District (Lobkov 2000).

North of the Kamchatka District, Gyrs breed in the Koryak National District, in the Koryak Mountains (Kishinskiy 1980, Lobkov 1986, 2000, Gorovenko 2002), along the Penzhina River depression (Pererva *et al.* 1987), on the Goven Peninsula (Kozlov 1983) and in Chukotka (Portenko 1972). On Wrangel Island a single nest was reported by O. Lutsuk on the rocky cliff of Pillar Cape, 10km from the seabird colony on Bering Cape (Stishov *et al.* 1991). Wrangel is not, however, a favoured site. The top Russian ornithologists Portenko and Krechmar did not identify any breeding Gyrs, in spite of extensive fieldwork (pers. comm.), though Portenko (1972) did report three sightings by A. Mineev. Stishov *et al.* (1991) also reported several Gyr sightings during summer months. Such sightings indicate breeding attempts, though the results of these attempts are not known.

On the Commander Islands the Gyrfalcon has been noted only as a vagrant and occasional winter visitor (Artukhin 1998). However, historical records of Gyr breeding on the islands do exist. Dementiev (1951) mentioned a bird shot by Stejnger on Bering Island on 5 May 1883. Clearly this was a breeding bird, and its skin is in the Smithsonian (N92722, dated 2 May 1883).

Finally, there is one breeding record of the Gyrfalcon on Matuwa Island (48°04'N 153°12'E), near Simushir Island, Kuril Islands (Yamashina 1931, 1941). According to the record Mr Norishika Oiwa obtained an adult and nestling Gyrfalcon in August 1924. The stuffed adult is kept at the Japanese Agricultural Department, Tokyo (M. Ueta, pers. comm.). This record was doubted in later studies of the birds of the Kuril Islands (Gizenko 1955), but if valid, is the southernmost record of Gyrfalcon breeding.

ALASKA (USA)

The distribution of Gyrfalcons in Alaska is arguably better studied than in any other part of the falcon's range. Studies began in the 1950s and have been almost continuous, thanks to US Government monitoring programs (Cade 1960, Snow 1974, Clum and Cade 1994, Swem *et al.* 1994). From these studies it is known that Gyrs occur on the Aleutian Islands, the Seward Peninsula (e.g. Cade 1953, 1960, Kessel 1989), the northern slope of the Brooks range, the Aleutian and Alaska ranges (the latter including the Denali National Park), and the Chugach and Kuskokwim mountains. Alaskan Gyrs avoid the plain tundras of the northern coastal zone, but have been recorded breeding on the cliffs of the Askinuk Mountains overlooking the coastal marshes of Hooper Bay at the Yukon-Kuskokwim lowlands (White and Springer 1965).

The highest breeding concentrations are in the highlands of the Seward Peninsula, the Denali National Park and in the western De Long mountains (Swem *et al.* 1994). Kessel (1989) estimates that as many as 70 pairs breed on the Seward Peninsula. High densities of falcons are also found on the northern slopes of the Brooks Range along the Colville River (White and Cade 1971) and the tributaries that flow northwards into it: the Kuna, Etivluk, Kurupa, Killik, and the upper reaches of the Chandler, Nanushuk and Anaktuvuk. Outside the Colville River system there are good breeding grounds at the upper reaches of the Kuparuk, Toolik and Sagavanirktok rivers (which drain the eastern end of the Brooks, *i.e.* the Endicott and Philip Smith Mountains), in the upper reaches of the rivers which drain from the mountains around Mount Chamberlain – the Canning, Sadlerochit,

Jago and Aichilik – and in the alpine tundras of the British Mountains (which cross the border from Alaska into the Canadian Yukon).

On the southern slopes of the Brooks Range Gyrfalcon distribution is more uneven, most of the breeding locations being concentrated close to the sources of the Koyukuk River. On the Seward Peninsula Gyrs breed along the coast from Moses Point to Cape Prince of Wales and also occupy the mountains at the peninsula's heart – Brooks, York, Bendeleben and Darby mountains. The birds avoid the plain tundra of the north-western coasts and Koyuk-Inglutalic lowlands. Breeding has been recorded in the Kaiyuh Mountains and in the Kuskokwim and Ahklun mountain ranges, as well as in the Yukon–Kuskokwim lowlands, sometimes close to the sea (e.g. close to Cape Romanzof) and on Nunivak Island (Swem *et al.* 1994).

Breeding has also been recorded in the Kenai and Chugach Mountains, and in the Alaska Range. Gyrfalcons are not known to breed in densely forested parts of Alaska, such as the lower reaches of the Tanana River and most of the Yukon River valley, including the Yukon Flats. Gyrs also seem to avoid the flat tundra areas to the south of Point Barrow and the Yukon delta.

Nest sites are known in the Aleutian Range on the Alaska Peninsula, on the Aleutian Islands (Unimak, Unalaska), and on Chirirkov and Tugidak islands. However, Palmer (1988) considered that the Gyrfalcon should be considered a vagrant bird on the Aleutian Islands, perhaps following Cade (1960) who stated that the Aleutians were a blank area for Gyrs.

Museum specimens obtained during the breeding period also include birds from the following locations: Herendeen Bay (East Aleutians 55°46'N 160°41'W) (SI), Kangerok River (exact location is not known due to bad handwriting on the original tag) (SI), and Takotha River (62°32'N, 156°47'W) (AMNH).

CANADA

Gyrfalcons occupy most of the Canadian Arctic archipelago, the Arctic coastal plain and the forest-tundra zone (Godfrey 1986, Poole 1988, Poole and Boag 1988, Palmer 1988, Shank and Poole 1994, Obst 1994, Cotter *et al.* 1992). Breeding has also been recorded in the provinces of British Columbia (Campbell *et al.* 1990), Quebec (the northern part of the province) and Labrador.

In British Columbia nest sites have been recorded in the mountain areas from the Spatsizi Plateau Wilderness Park north-westwards to the St Elias Mountains (Campbell *et al.* 1990), including the Atlin area, and in the Cassiar Mountains.

In the Yukon Territory the breeding range of Gyrs has been studied by Mossop and Hayes (1981, 1994). According to their observations the densest areas of breeding are the northern slopes of the Brooks Range, the coastal region, and the Richardson and Ogilvie mountains. Breeding was also recorded in the Mackenzie

Mountains, at the Fifth River (Clum and Cade 1994) and along the Dempster Highway (White and Nelson 1991). The highest breeding density of Gyrs in Canada is along a 20km-wide strip of the northern mainland coast in the Low Arctic Islands and in the Mackenzie and Richardson mountains, which lie along the border between the Northwest Territories and the Yukon (Shank and Poole 1994). Eastwards, in a part of northern Canada that, formerly, was the Northwest Territories, but is now the combination of that reduced territory and the new territory of Nunavut, Gyrfalcons breed from the coastline to approximately 65°N in the west and about 63°N in the east. The southern limit of breeding follows a line from the Great Slave Lake to Eskimo Point on the west coast of Hudson Bay. Records exist for the Thelon River valley in the forest-tundra zone (Kuyt, 1962, 1980, Norment *et al.* 1999). The southernmost nest on Hudson Bay was recorded at Point Louis XIV (Gauthier and Aubry 1996). On the Arctic archipelago there are records from Banks, Victoria, King William, Somerset, Prince of Wales, Southampton, Baffin, Devon, Bylot, Ellesmere (Muir and Bird 1984), Axel Heiberg, Melville and Prince Patrick islands. However, breeding has not, as yet, been recorded on Cornwallis, Bathurst, Ringnes or Mackenzie King islands. A well-known study area with a number of breeding pairs is located around Windy Lake, at 68°05'N, 106°40'W (now Nunavut) (Cotter *et al.* 1992), which is the centre of the Kilgawik study area used in the study by Poole (1988, Shank and Poole 1994).

In Quebec, Gyr breeding has been recorded on the Ungava Peninsula, along the Ungava Bay coast, in the Torngat Mountains, along the Koksoak and George rivers, near Fort Chimo and at Red Bay, Cape Chidley, Paul Island, Nachvak Bay, Hamilton Inlet and Indian House Lake (Clum and Cade 1994). The Koksoak River and Fort Chimo sites date back to 1917 (Todd 1963). There are also unconfirmed tales of breeding in the southern parts of the province and on Newfoundland. Inland nesting is known to have taken place near the Nastapoka River (Brodeur *et al.* 1995, Gauthier and Aubry 1996). Quebec also has the southernmost record of the breeding range: Brodeur and colleagues (1995) reported four nests at about 55°N with the southernmost nest located at Long Island, at the tip of James Bay, off the west coast of Quebec.

GREENLAND

The Gyrfalcon is distributed all along the coastal parts of the island but it avoids the inner island, which is covered by a permanent ice cap and glaciers (Salomonsen 1950–51, Burnham and Mattox 1984, Clum and Cade 1994). The Gyr was reported as a common bird near Etah at 78°30'N by Salomonsen (1950–51), but this observation was not subsequently confirmed (Salomonsen 1967). Nest locations are within gorges and on crags that punctuate the rolling coastal plains. The Peregrine Fund expedition (Burnham and Mattox 1984, and information from Peregrine Fund Reports 1998–2002) notes breeding at York Peninsula, Cape Atholl, Parker Snow Bay and North Star Bay, all of which are in areas close to the Thule airbase. Some sites were also found in Nødre Strømfjord and Søndre Strømfjord, and in the Kangerlussuaq area of western Greenland, just north of the Arctic Circle. Other noted breeding sites include Cape Hayes, Disko Bay, Stören and Uvkusigssat (Hart 1880, Herdemerten 1939, Mattox 1969). In north-east Greenland Gyrs were noted at the Tunnelelv Gorge (Fletcher and Webby 1977) and near Mestersvig at 72°16'N 22°35'W (Summers and Green 1974). They have also been seen, though no nest site was observed, at Myggbukta (R. G. Sale pers. obs.). Greenland has the northernmost claimed breeding of Gyrfalcons, at 82° (Burnham and Mattox 1984, quoting Salomonsen 1950–51).

The museums (CMNH, AMNH, SI, MZM and BMNH) hold specimens of Gyrfalcons which either exhibit brood patches or were taken during the breeding season at Agto, Arsuk e-bay, Illoqqortoormiut (Scoresby Sound), Kangamius, Maniitsoq (Sukkertoppen), Minesland, Nanortalik, Nuuk (Godthåb), Qaqortoq (Julianehåb) and Uummannaq.

STABILITY OF THE RANGE

There is very limited information on the past distribution of the Gyrfalcon, and the information that does exist is confused by the fact that Eurasian observers often confused Gyrs with Saker Falcons. In areas where the two species overlap, the languages of the indigenous people frequently do not distinguish between them, so historical chronicles are not particularly useful. As an example, Marco Polo refers to Gyrfalcons being kept at the court of Chinghis Khan, but here as elsewhere he could be referring to Saker Falcons. Further information on the Marco Polo records is given in Chapter 10. Confusion between the species has led to problems in more recent times. Dementiev (1951) (repeated by Ellis *et al.* 1992) mentioned the extent of the historical range of Gyrfalcons in the South Urals. Both records are based on the information of Sabaneev (1871, 1874) who wrote:

> [The] Gyrfalcon ... is rare in the Bogoslovskiy Ural, where it comes, according to local gossip, from the western slopes, where it breeds, in autumn. It occurs more frequently in regions around Krasnoufimskiy [a settlement at 56°53'N 60°44'E] and Ufimskiy [a settlement at 56°27'N 58°48'E], especially along the Ufa and Chusovaya rivers. I myself saw it in Ufimskiy. Near Kasli [a settlement at 55°53'N 60°44'E] and Kystym [a settlement at 55°42'N 60°31'E] Gyrfalcons used to breed, but do so no longer ... as the Bashkir people robbed their nests and sold the chicks to the Kirgiz and steppe Bashkir people.

Clearly this passage is actually referring to Sakers rather than the Gyr, so the idea that historically the Gyrfalcon range extended to the South and Middle Urals is not justified. The information of Sabaneev was severely criticised by Professor Portenko of the Zoological Institute (1937) who wrote "I sincerely rule out these unverified observations by Sabaneev about breeding of Gyrfalcons in the Perm district, which, as with many of his observations, created a mess in our understanding of the Ural fauna." This view is supported by the work of Kirikov (1952), who found no evidence of past breeding of Gyrfalcons in the South Urals.

It appears that only in Eurasia has the Gyrfalcon's range altered significantly in the Pleistocene–Holocene era, as a result of the change in distribution of tundra–steppe and a movement of the timberline. In other parts of the world there is no historical range data to indicate a significant retreat or advance. Icelandic studies have not shown any change in the Gyrfalcon range, although there are some local shifts in the population. Local range contraction was reported from the Snæfellsnes Peninsula in western Iceland and from the Reykjanes Peninsula in the south-west. The shrinkage was due to low Ptarmigan numbers and an expansion of the range and numbers of Fulmars (*Fulmarus glacialis*), which foul cliff ledges rendering them unusable as nest sites (Nielsen pers. comm., Cade *et al.* 1998).

Generally there are no historical records of Gyrfalcons in Scandinavia. The first historical attempt to describe the biogeography (amongst other things) of the region was the famous map by Olaus Magnus – the *Carta Marina*, the 1539 original of which is in the Carolina Library of Uppsala University, Sweden. The map, and its accompanying book, have no description of the Gyrfalcon, despite several depictions of other birds of prey. It is generally considered that the breeding range of the Gyrfalcon in Norway has remained the same for at least the past 150 years (Tømmeraas 1993, 1994a). There is some indication of a decline in Gyr numbers in northern Finland (Cade *et al.* 1998), but this does not appear to have any implication for the bird's range.

In the Nearctic the distribution of Gyrs does not seem to be significantly different if compared to the past. Although little historical data exists, the few birds shot during the breeding period in Canada were obtained from places where Gyrs are still reported as breeding. However, more thorough surveys in the northern taiga of North America might alter this view. The Peregrine Fund's High Arctic Research Institute (Peregrine Fund Report 2002) suggests that the Gyrfalcon range in Greenland may have shrunk.

Overall, therefore, there is little evidence that the breeding range of the Gyrfalcon has shrunk or is shrinking (and equally none that the range is expanding). There is, however, a general trend of discovery that Gyrs are breeding in forest zones, though this has come as a surprise only to those who had previously considered the Gyr to be limited to the high Arctic. As a consequence the species was overlooked, particularly as forests at the timberline are usually home to myriad mosquitoes and, hence, are not pleasant study areas.

CHAPTER 4

Population

TOTAL NUMBERS IN DIFFERENT COUNTRIES
AND REGIONS

It is difficult to assess the total number of birds of any species, more so in the case of the Gyrfalcon because much of its range lies outside areas of settled human population. In addition, the range countries have different levels of infrastructure, different economies and different cultural attitudes. All except Russia have some kind of Gyrfalcon monitoring in place. Russia has no government-sponsored monitoring of Gyrfalcon populations at all, though some small-scale projects are carried out by individual researchers. Such researchers are often reluctant to publish any results of their findings, because a simple sentence in a paper to the effect that Gyrfalcon numbers are at a good level could result in local decisions to harvest this 'resource'. Below we give what we consider to be reasonable estimates of the Russian Gyr population, together with current best estimates of Gyr populations in other range countries.

ICELAND

An estimate of 200 pairs was made by Bengtson (1971). Cade (1982) considered this an underestimate and suggested that there were 300–400 breeding pairs. His figure was confirmed in later studies (Cade *et al.* 1998, Nielsen and Cade 1990a).

NORWAY

It is considered that Norway hosts 300–500 breeding pairs (Tømmeraas 1994a, Cade *et al.* 1998, Koskimies 1999).

SWEDEN

The total number of Gyrfalcons in Sweden is estimated at 100–200 pairs (Lindberg 2002). The 1995 estimate was given as 55–138 pairs. Of the present population the majority breed in Norrbotten. A conservative estimate of the Swedish population is 100 pairs (Holmberg and Falkdalen 1996). Other estimates suggest that Sweden accommodates 80–135 pairs (Gärdenfors 2000, Tjernberg 2000).

FINLAND

The most recent estimate of the number of Gyrs in Finland is just 25–30 regularly breeding pairs (Cade *et al.* 1998) with 10 additional pairs breeding in good Willow Grouse years (Koskimies 1995). It is believed that the Finnish Gyrfalcon population was several times larger at the beginning of 20th century (Cade *et al.* 1998, Koskimies 1999).

RUSSIA

The total number of Gyrfalcons was estimated at several hundred pairs by Borodin (1984). This was based on an estimate of the density of Gyrfalcons on tundra (0.01–0.04 pairs per 1,000km^2) together with a number for the large concentrations in the coastal zone (two pairs per 1,000km^2 given for the Komi Republic (Estafiev 1980) and Yamal (Danilov *et al.* 1977, Ryabitsev 1986). However, Borodin's estimate had no worthwhile data for the Siberian Gyr population, and is therefore a significant undercount of the total Russian population.

In the recent edition of the *Red Data Book* (Ganusevich 2001) the number of Gyrfalcons in the Russia was given as 1,000 pairs. This figure derives from the following estimates: 8 pairs for Kola (Ganusevich 1983, 1992); 40–45 breeding pairs on the Yugor Peninsula, the Bolshezemelskaya tundra and the western slope of the Polar Urals; more than 50 pairs in Southern Yamal (with the maximum recorded density for Gyrfalcons, according to Morozov (Morozov 1991), of 12.2 pairs per 1,000km^2); 3 pairs in Khabarovsk district (Roslyakov and Roslyakov 1991 - a dubious record as it is outside the Gyr's range); some breeding pairs in Chukotka; and the largest population of Asian Gyrfalcons in Kamchatka – 140–200 breeding pairs (Lobkov 1997). Lobkov (2000) estimated that 650–700 individual Gyrfalcons live on the Kamchatka Peninsula in winter. Later, based on a sample territory with 14 occupied nests in the Karaginskiy and Olutorskiy regions of Koryak District, north of the Kamchatka Peninsula, Gorovenko (2003) reported a breeding density of 0.7 pairs per 1,000km^2.

However, the *Red Data Book* significantly underestimates Gyr numbers since it omits the following data: the Putorana Plateau population (160–200 pairs; Dorogov 1985, Rogacheva 1988), and the Yakutian population (Solomonov 1987). The total number of pairs in the European part of Russia was estimated as 500–700 (Koskimies 1999). We also estimate that the correct figures for other regions, based on range and Gyr density, should be: western Siberia including Yamal 500–800 pairs; eastern Siberia including the Putorana plateau 600–900 pairs; Yakutia 400–1,100 pairs; Chukotka and the Kamchatka Peninsula 1,100–1,500 pairs.

We calculated the likely range of Gyrfalcons in Russia using GIS (Geographical Information System), which returned 2,685km^2. With an average density of 1.5 pairs per 1,000km^2, this gives an estimate of 4,027 pairs. Keeping in mind fluctuations in numbers it is safe to assume that the number of Gyrfalcons in Russia is somewhere between 3,500 and 5,000 pairs.

ALASKA (USA)

The 1989 survey in the Brooks Range of the Arctic National Wildlife Refuge (Sadlerochit and Shublik Mountains) and the north side of the Franklin, Romanzof and British Mountains located 42 occupied territories in an area of about 7,600km^2, giving an average of 5.5 pairs per 1,000km^2 (Swem *et al.* 1994). Generally Gyrfalcons in northern Alaska breed along major rivers, most notably the Colville (>30 pairs), the Kokolik (11 pairs), the Kukpowruk (12 pairs) and the Utokok River system (8 pairs). Gyrfalcons breed in clusters along some stretches of these rivers: 9 pairs in 38km of the Colville River, 7 pairs in a 40km stretch of the Kokolik River and 9 pairs in 56km of the Kukpowruk River. On the Seward Peninsula the density varies from 1 pair per 1,000km^2 in areas where the cliffs are few to 5.7 pairs per 1,000km^2: the average for the peninsula is 1.6 pairs per 1,000km^2. In the Denali National Park the density of Gyrfalcons is 4.7 pairs per 1,000km^2 (Swem *et al.* 1994). The total estimate of the number of

Gyrfalcons in Alaska is 375–635 pairs (Swem *et al.* 1994). Cade (1982) estimated that there were 300 breeding pairs, with fluctuations to around 500 pairs.

CANADA

In Yukon Territory the total number of Gyrfalcons was estimated as a maximum of 750 pairs (Mossop and Hayes 1994). Autumn numbers fluctuate from 2,490 to 4,180 birds depending on the stage of the Willow Grouse cycle. In the Northwest Territories and Nunavut the breeding population was estimated at 1,300 pairs and the total adult population was around 5,000 individuals (Shank and Poole 1994). CITES (2000) considers Shank and Poole's estimate as too low for a barren, but nest-worthy, 900,000km^2 of what is now Nunavut, where the authors assumed a density of one breeding pair per 1,000km^2. If we recalculate the numbers using 1.5 pairs per 1,000km^2, we arrive at a figure of 1,350 pairs for the 900,000km^2 of Nunavut and a conservative 100 pairs for the Northwest Territories. Quebec and Labrador accommodate an estimated 500 to 1,000 pairs (CITES 2000), although it has to be said that no systematic, long-term studies have been carried out in this region to date. Thus the total estimate for Canada is somewhere between 2,550 and 3,200 pairs. Overall, it is concluded that there is no evidence of long-term decline in Gyr numbers in North America. Indeed, Cade (1982) suggests that numbers may have increased in the decades prior to his work.

GREENLAND

Estimates for this vast and largely uninhabited island are difficult. Mattox (1970) calculated that there were about 855 pairs, while Cade (1982) estimated that there were not less than 500 pairs and possibly as many as 1,000. Recently there have been concerns over a decrease in the Gyrfalcon population in north-eastern Greenland and on the west coast, the decreases occurring at the same time as an increase in the number of Peregrine Falcons (Cade *et al.* 1998). The Peregrine Fund's High Arctic Research Institute (Peregrine Fund Report 2000) gave estimates of 750 Gyr pairs and in 2002 (Peregrine Fund Report 2002) they wrote that there are some data to suggest that the both the range and numbers of Gyrfalcons in Greenland may have decreased.

WORLD TOTAL

Cade (1960, 1982) assumed the range of the Gyr as covering 15–17 millionkm^2 of Arctic and sub-Arctic terrain with an average density of one pair per 1,000km^2. This gave a total of 15,000–17,000 pairs. Our GIS-plotted Gyrfalcon world range returned an area of 7,403,749km². With an average density of 1.5 pairs per 1,000km² this suggests a total of 11,106 Gyrfalcon pairs, an estimate that is not far from that of Cade. An estimate based on by-country estimates provided by experts (Table 4.1) returns the figure 7,880–10,900 – not a bad match with the GIS method.

Table 4.1 Minimum and maximum estimates of Gyrfalcon populations in range countries.

Country	Minimum estimate	Maximum estimate	Source
Iceland	300	400	Cade *et al.* (1998)
Norway	300	500	Koskimies (1999) and references therein
Sweden	80	135	Gärdenfors (2000), Tjernberg (2000)
Finland	25	30	Koskimies (1999)
Russia	3,500	5,000	Present authors
USA (Alaska)	375	675	Swem *et al.* (1994)
Canada	2,550	3,200	Shank and Poole (1994), present authors
Greenland	750	1,000	Cade (1982), Peregrine Fund (Denmark) Report (2000)
Total	7,880	10,990	

FLUCTUATIONS IN NUMBERS

A fundamental question when considering the Gyrfalcon population is whether the number of birds varies with oscillations in prey numbers. The answer to this question provides many clues to understanding the biology of the falcons: it also helps in the conservation of the species. Indeed, if Gyrfalcons are specialised feeders on *Lagopus* grouse (see Chapter 6) which are themselves cyclic species, how do fluctuations in grouse numbers affect the population of Gyrs, and is the population affected by the harvesting of grouse by humans?

Hagen (1952a, Hagen and Barth 1952) were perhaps the first ornithologists to spot the dependence of Gyrfalcons on *Lagopus* grouse. Hagen even emphasised it in his paper: "[the] Gyrfalcon … bases its offspring production exclusively on the stock of adult Ptarmigan and [Willow] Grouse". However Hagen points out that there are actually three things to be considered when examining the reasons for there being non-breeding years in Gyrfalcons:

1. decrease in food supply
2. reactions on the part of the prey species
3. competition between predators.

A very successful breeding season for the Gyrs at Dovrefjell, Norway (Hagen 1952a) coincided with a peak small-mammals year. The assumption was that the abundance of rodents was directly responsible for the Gyr success. In fact, this was not the case: Hagen found that rodents were not important food items for the Gyrs. The reason for the successful Gyr breeding was partly due to reduced predation pressure on the local Willow Grouse, which the study showed to be the primary Gyr prey, from predators which would normally compete with the Gyrs but were able to switch to take advantage of the rodent numbers. Also, the grouse population tends to fluctuate with the microtine-rodent cycle, so the Gyr's main prey is itself more abundant in years of high microtine-rodent population.

Observations by Langvatn and Moksnes (1979) supported Hagen (1952a), the authors also stating that Gyrfalcons are able to breed successfully even in years with low populations of microtine-rodents and grouse, and that the proportion of grouse in the diet appeared to be fairly constant from year to year (89–98% by weight). In their study the Kendall rank correlation between the number of fledged young falcons and an 'index' (indicating relative abundance) of *Lagopus* species in the same year yielded a non-significant result. Hagen (1969) suggested that there are two thresholds in food supply which influence Gyrfalcon breeding decisions: the first results in the decision to settle (*i.e.* occupy a territory), and the second in the decision to breed. If the second threshold is crossed, the Gyrs will breed even at low prey densities. In the study by Ødegaard (1969), who observed Gyrfalcons in northern Norway from 1964 to 1968, it was suggested that the population of *Lagopus* grouse fluctuated, but is generally so high that even bad years are good enough for Gyrfalcons to breed successfully. Langvatn and Moksnes (1979), after a thorough investigation of Norwegian data , concluded that there was little evidence to support the idea that Gyrfalcons actually show breeding success and population variation in parallel with fluctuations in the population of *Lagopus* grouse or other tetraonids.

The parallel fluctuations found between populations of some raptorial birds and microtine rodents (Hagen 1969) have often been generalised to include the Gyrfalcon. However, as Langvatn and Moksnes (1979) note, "It should be mentioned that the concept of cyclic variation in the *Lagopus* populations is based primarily on knowledge of the Willow Grouse. In fact, Scandinavian literature on population fluctuations in Ptarmigan … is very limited". The dependence of Gyrfalcons on Ptarmigan was strongly suggested by Suetens and Groenendael (1976) for both Norway and Iceland.

Kishinskiy (1958) considers that the spatial distribution of Gyrfalcons in the Arctic depends on two factors:

1. the presence of convenient nesting sites
2. the abundance of food in spring.

Non-breeding Gyrs can be seen in many places on the tundra, but in winter, during the polar night, one can see them only in places with plenty of food. Kishinskiy considers that there are two ecological groups of Gyrfalcons:

1. Gyrfalcons breeding at the sea coast close to colonies of seabirds with more or less stable population levels.
2. Gyrfalcons breeding inland in the tundra zone and in forest-tundra. In early spring they feed entirely on grouse and hence follow the fluctuations in the number of prey.

The impact of Gyrfalcons, amongst other species, on the local Ptarmigan population was studied by Cotter *et al.* (1992) at Windy Lake in Canada's Northwest Territories, now Nunavut Province. During their study the numbers of Ptarmigan declined from 5.8 birds/100 ha to 3.5 birds/100 ha in the second year and to 2.8 birds/100 ha in the third year. The authors marked the Ptarmigan with radio-transmitters and were able to determine the impact of raptors on their survival. Eighteen percent of resident Ptarmigan (23 of 128) were found dead, thus making the overall annual mortality 57% (including other causes of death and other predators, projected for the whole year). Falcons were responsible for the deaths of 20 of 23 birds, of which 10 were females and 10 were males. Seventeen of 21 kills occurred during the breeding season, one in autumn, and three occurred between midsummer and winter. The predation rate for all the years combined was 14% and did not change significantly between the years. There was also no difference in the percentage of adults and yearlings killed during the breeding season.

In the Disko Bay region of west Greenland in 1974, when Arctic Hare and Ptarmigan numbers were low, Gyrfalcons were seen at some eyries and freshly moulted feathers were found at some others, but no young were found at 14 visited nests (Burnham and Mattox 1984).

In Alaska there was no correlation found between the number of occupied sites along the Colville River in northern Alaska and the number of young fledged per occupied site (coefficient of regression $r = -0.21$, $P = 0.59$) (Swem *et al.* 1994). The number of young produced per occupied site varied from 1 to 2.3. In Alaska's Denali National Park there was similarly no correlation found between the number of occupied sites and number of chicks per occupied site ($r = -0.31$, $P = 0.60$). Here the number of chicks per nest varied from 0.73 to 1.93 across the five years of the study period (Swem *et al.* 1994).

Nevertheless Cade (1960) described a very interesting situation he observed at the Colville river in 1957, 1958 and 1959. In 1957 only three Gyr pairs raised young due to the low density of grouse (in his study Cade did not separate Willow Grouse and Ptarmigan, only stating that the first-named species was twice as abundant as the second). The year 1958 saw a low in Ptarmigan numbers, and that year the Gyrfalcons did not breed at all. In 1959 a large number of wintering grouse concentrated along the Colville and Etivluk Rivers and at Umiat, yet the numbers of Ptarmigan in June were comparable to those of 1957. Gyrfalcons nevertheless bred successfully in numbers higher that in the previous years, with a total of 10 pairs recorded. Examination of the remains of prey at Gyr nests indicated that the Gyrs preyed heavily on Ptarmigan in winter plumage, and in the course of the summer switched to other prey species. Concurrently the snow melt-off exposed a significant density of microtines, namely Brown Lemming (*Lemmus sibiricus*) and Root Voles (*Microtus oeconomus*). These rodents formed a high proportion of the diet of the Gyrfalcons. The rodents attracted unusual numbers of rodent-eating birds of prey, both owls and raptors, some of which also became prey for the Gyrs.

Willow Grouse dominate the diet of Gyrfalcons in Russia's southern Yamal (the region with the highest recorded density in Russia with up to 12.2 Gyr pairs per 1,000km²), where Gyrs seem to depress the local population of grouse almost to zero and then, in the course of summer, switch to alternative prey species (Kalyakin and Vinogradov 1981). Similar views were expressed in earlier work. Cade (1960) considered it plausible that a pair of Gyrfalcons could virtually annihilate the local grouse population around the Gyr's nest. However, the number of Ptarmigan taken by breeding Gyrfalcons is an insignificant proportion of the total Ptarmigan population.

Two papers (Mindell *et al.* 1987, Mindell and White 1988) deal with the fluctuations of Gyrfalcons in the Arctic. Both deal with one dataset obtained from Colville River surveys (13 surveys during a 27-year period). At the Colville River the numbers of Gyrfalcons fluctuated from 8 to 19 breeding pairs and the number of Rough-legged Buzzards from 26 to 90 (Mindell *et al.* 1987). There were no regular or cyclic fluctuations found in the sample for either Gyrfalcons or Rough-legged Buzzards. In one year (1973), however, both species demonstrated synchronous low numbers. The analysis shows that the dataset is adequate for detecting regular fluctuations (Mindell and White 1988), but there was no clear evidence of regularity in the fluctuations. However the authors emphasised that this finding cannot be extended to different time periods, to sub-populations in the same area or to populations in other regions. The authors wrote that "the issue of regularity in fluctuations of Arctic breeding raptors has received scant attention in the past, with 'conventional wisdom' presuming regularity for Gyrfalcons and Rough-legged Buzzards. The issue is complex and will not be easily resolved."

Shank and Poole (1994) studied the Gyrfalcon populations in Canada's Northwest Territories during the period 1982–1991. They found no trends in breeding numbers or productivity. In fact they estimated the population there was stable. In one particular study area the authors measured the density of Ptarmigan and compared it to the breeding numbers of Gyrfalcons. The number of successfully breeding Gyrfalcons was found to be unaffected by the density of Ptarmigan, their main prey in the region. Interestingly, Shank and Poole (1994) found that the Gyr nests were significantly closer to each other in the areas with high July temperatures and in areas with taller willow trees. They suggested that this is indirect proof that Gyr density is higher in more productive habitats.

In contrast to the findings of Shank and Poole (1994), the study in Canada's Yukon Territory by Mossop and Hayes (1981, 1994) found 10-year cyclicity in the fluctuation of the number of adult Gyrs and, more importantly, in the number of young produced per successful pair. Nest occupancy fluctuated between 60% and 95%, and the breeding success fluctuated from 2.2 to 3.3 young per successful pair. The cyclic pattern was very similar in the southern and northern parts of the region. In the best year about 60% of pairs produced young, whereas in low years only 10% of pairs had chicks. The productivity of the Gyrfalcons followed the pattern of Willow Grouse density.

Huhtala *et al.* (1996) reported that the breeding success of a pair of Gyrfalcons in Salla, north-east Finland, could be quite high in years with a low density of Willow Grouse (1985 and 1990 in his study). There was no significant correlation between the numbers of Willow Grouse and clutch size, brood size or number of chicks fledged by the Gyrfalcons. Woodin (1980) observed variation in the breeding of Gyrfalcons in Iceland in 1967. The previous year had been a peak year for Ptarmigan. The increase in Ptarmigan numbers started in 1961 when there were 1.7 breeding pairs/km^2, rising to 7.4 pairs/km^2 in 1966. In 1967 the numbers started to fall, and Woodin reported that in that year some Gyrfalcons remained in the area but did not breed. In northern Iceland 46% of occupied territories fledged young on average (22–67%). In all years combined, from 804 observation-years for occupied territories 355 (44%) had no sign of breeding, 72 (9%) had failed breeding pairs and 377 (47%) had successful breeding pairs (Cade *et al.* 1998).

Nielsen and Petursson (1995) analysed the numbers of falcons exported from Iceland to Denmark between 1731 and 1793 and the number of Ptarmigan exported to Europe between 1864 and 1919. A total of 4,318 Gyrfalcons and 3,276,815 Ptarmigan were exported in those periods. The authors were looking for a correlation of time series between grey, white and half-white morphs. The study returned interesting results. There was a significant correlation between white and half-white falcons, *i.e.* between the morphs which do not breed in Iceland. This is an indirect indication that the winter occurrence of the white and half-white forms was influenced by some event elsewhere. The native Icelandic Gyrfalcon time-series did not show any correlation with that of the outsiders, indicating that the cyclicity of the native Gyrs was different from that in other regions. The fluctuations of both Ptarmigan and native Icelandic Gyrfalcons showed a distinct 10-year periodicity.

Gudmundsson (1972) studied fluctuations of Gyrfalcons and Ptarmigan on the island of Hrisey off the coast of Iceland. This small island (only 800 ha) was peculiar since no predator other than the Gyrfalcon was present. Despite heavy predation by Gyrfalcons, Gudmundsson concluded that the regular and predictable changes in Ptarmigan numbers could not be attributed to predator–prey oscillations. But as Ptarmigan is the main dietary prey of Gyrfalcon, it is not surprising that Gyrfalcon numbers fluctuate with Ptarmigan numbers and that during years of Ptarmigan scarcity many Gyrs do not nest at all.

A seminal paper dealing with the cyclicity of Gyrfalcon numbers and the interdependence of Gyrs and Ptarmigan was published by Nielsen (1999a). The paper was based on data from north-eastern Iceland and covered a 16-year period from 1981 to 1997. The study area (which was the same as that for Nielsen's doctorate, also on Gyrfalcons: Nielsen 1986, 1991, Nielsen and Cade 1990a, 1990b) covered 5,327km^2 and was large enough to accommodate 82 traditional Gyrfalcon nesting territories. Nielsen sampled Ptarmigan in six plots within the study area and monitored the clutch size and breeding rate of the Gyrfalcons, and the number of occupied territories. The Ptarmigan population demonstrated a five-fold difference in density across the study area, a 4.3-fold difference between the high and low years, and a complete 10-year cycle. The Ptarmigan spring density was the most important factor in determining the composition and variability of the diet of the Gyrs. The estimated total Ptarmigan population in spring available for 82 Gyrfalcon pairs ranged from 14,000 to 60,500 in the different years of the study. The number of occupied Gyrfalcon territories varied between 39 and 63, giving a range of 85–137km^2 per occupied territory, a 1.6-fold difference.

The fluctuation of the Gyrfalcon population was less pronounced than that of the Ptarmigan: a statistical analysis correlating the populations of Ptarmigan and Gyrfalcon gave significant positive coefficients for time-lags of 1 to 4 years, the maximum coefficient being for a 3-year lag. Successful Gyrfalcon pairs did not correlate with Ptarmigan numbers. Interestingly, the average annual brood size did not fluctuate much (2.2–3.2 young per successful pair), and again did not correlate with Ptarmigan numbers. The total young produced in the study area reflected the number of successful pairs and ranged from 22 to 117 young per year. The total number of Gyrfalcons (adults plus fledged young) in autumn varied from 116 to 227. Statistical analysis showed that the total number of autumnal Gyrs lagged Ptarmigan numbers and gave significant positive coefficients for 1- and 2-year lags.

The number of Gyrfalcons per 1,000 Ptarmigan was highest during low Ptarmigan years and then declined logarithmically with increasing Ptarmigan numbers. This means that predation peaked during the decline and the low phase of the Ptarmigan cycle. Gyrfalcons remove, on average, 18% of adult Ptarmigan during the breeding season (ranging from 32% during low Ptarmigan years to 11% in peak years). The decline of predation rate with increased Ptarmigan number was also logarithmic. Thus the Gyrfalcons accelerate the decline of the Ptarmigan, and accentuate the amplitude and affect the length of the low phase of the Ptarmigan. The Gyrfalcons are an essential part of the Ptarmigan cycle. However, there are no data to suggest that the Gyrfalcons initiate the start of the decline. In other words, the Gyrfalcons try to maximise their stability while depending on a fluctuating main resource. As a result they shape and amplify the cycle of the prey.

CHAPTER 5

Habitat and Landscape Preferences

The Gyrfalcon is a bird of open spaces, a bird that does not live in forests or amongst tall bushes. With a few exceptions Gyrs live in the Arctic and sub-Arctic. The Gyr has evolved to be fast rather than manoeuvrable and so has difficulty in coping in 'enclosed' environments. In this chapter we explore aspects of the Gyrfalcon's landscape.

HABITAT PREFERENCES

Cade (1960) stated that the Gyrfalcon was a bird of foothill tundra and alpine areas, as well as being 'coastal'. This generalisation, although at the time based on relatively few known breeding locations in Alaska, still stands. At the time of Cade's statement the biology of Gyrfalcons had not been extensively studied, with research in northern Canada, Greenland and Scandinavia yet to start. By contrast, significant research had been carried out in Russia on general distribution and systematics, but there was little research focusing on the ecology of the bird.

Now the range of the Gyrfalcon is more or less known and it is possible to make certain overview statements on the general habitat preferences of the species within that range. Essentially, over a large part of its range the Gyrfalcon is a bird of the tundra, forest-tundra and timberline, usually preferring the gentler slopes of mountains. Occurrences of Gyrs on truly flat tundra are rare. The Gyr is distributed in the Arctic and sub-Arctic biogeographical zone, or, in more modern terminology, in mountainous or zonal tundras of Arctic and sub-Arctic, as well as along the northern border of the boreal forest. It is also possible to describe the Gyr as primarily a bird of the timberline and gentle mountain slopes. Below we define several ecological subgroups for breeding Gyrfalcons.

Gyrs of the timberline and gentle mountains are the most numerous and widespread. Gyrs of this subgroup range from the mountains of Fennoscandia, the northern Urals, the Putorana plateau and the Anabar hillocks to Chukotka's rolling, hillocky landscape from the Kolyma to the Bering Strait and the Koryak Mountains; from Alaska to the Richardson Mountains in Canada's Northwest Territories, islands of Nunavut, Quebec and Labrador. In Canada's Yukon Territory, the breeding habitat of Gyrs was described as characterised by vegetation within 5km of nests being as follows: treeless tundra dominated (65%), followed by taiga (24%), the remaining 9% being shrub tundra or forest (Mossop and Hayes 1994).

Most breeding locations in Iceland and Greenland belong to the tundra/gentle slopes subgroup, except those Gyrs at coastal cliffs. Gyrfalcons avoid steep or very high mountains, but will breed where steep mountains rise from foothills with tundra or forest-tundra vegetation. The distinct feature of this most numerous subgroup is its major dependence on *Lagopus* grouse, especially at the onset of the breeding season. The Gyrs of this subgroup breed exceptionally early to match chick hatching to the display period of the grouse. Shrubby vegetation is present around most of the breeding locations of the subgroup, stands of arctic willow being characteristic for the Gyrfalcon habitat of the Canadian Arctic archipelago (e.g. Muir and Bird (1984), who studied Gyrs on Ellesmere Island).

A second subgroup is Gyrs breeding on flat tundra. These are rare, unless there are elements of timberline present, or there are human-created structures such as abandoned oil rigs, dredges or triangulation towers, or there are single pinnacles or cliff structures standing above the flat ground. Most breeding occurrences of this ecological subgroup are at the estuaries of large rivers, sometimes without shrub vegetation at all. The breeding time of such pairs might be shifted towards later periods and even coincide with the breeding period of Peregrine Falcons and Rough-legged Buzzards. Dependence on *Lagopus* grouse is much less in such areas, the Gyrs relying on ducks and waders as the main food throughout the breeding season.

A third subgroup is Gyrs that breed in dense forests. These are also rare unless there are open bogs with scarce bushes and plenty of grouse in the area. However, while it is true that Gyrs avoid dense woodland, they will live in a special type of woodland at the northern extremes of boreal forests known as *listvinichnoe redkolesie* – a Russian term used to describe the particular form of habitat which can be found from the Urals to Hudson Bay and which means, literally, 'larch forest with sparse trees'. Gyrs prefer it if patches of such forest are intermixed with sections of tundra, large bogs, and/or slopes with alpine vegetation.

Larch forest is mentioned specifically here because the larch is the only tree at the northern extent of the Asian and North American forests (though the latter also has other conifers, predominantly white and black spruce, at the timberline). There may be other kinds of trees along rivers, such as Korean willow or poplar, the rivers usually being surrounded by permafrost-free soil. This creates a phenomenon known as 'gallery forest', a strip of not-very-dense forest (Kishinskiy 1980). The thickness of the strips varies across climatic zones, and with the relief of a particular region. The vegetation surrounding gallery forest is usually a dense carpet of dwarf willow and dwarf birch shrub. The mountain birch forests of Fennoscandia also fit the definition of gallery forest. In most cases penetration of Gyrfalcons into the taiga zone occurs along large rivers. Kalyakin (1989) considered that the southern part of the tundra and forest-tundra is the optimal habitat for the Gyrfalcon of Russia's southern Yamal.

A fourth ecological subgroup of Gyrfalcons is formed by those birds breeding on coastal cliffs, usually in the proximity of shorebird or seabird colonies. Such breeding places are usually clustered around colonies of Common (*Uria aalge*) and Brünnich's Guillemot (*Uria lomvia*), Kittiwake (*Rissa tridactyla*), Little Auk (*Alle alle*), Glaucous Gull (*Larus hyperboreus*) and Herring Gull (*Larus argentatus*). Breeding success in such locations depends on the arrival of colonial birds unless supplementary prey species such as Arctic Hare or *Lagopus* grouse are available.

Gyrfalcons do not breed on high mountains. No breeding records exist for elevations exceeding 1,700m. At present the highest recorded Gyr breeding site is a nest found at 1,630m in the Brooks Range (Swem *et al.* 1994). In general in Alaska Gyrs tend to decrease in breeding density above 1,000m in the Brooks Range, with nests above 1,400m a rarity. Cade (1960) found his highest nests at an altitude of 1,066m in the Okpilak River valley and said that it was unlikely that Gyrs bred in Alaska at altitudes above 1,219m (but note Swem *et al.* 1994, above). In the southern part of Canada's Yukon Territory Gyrfalcons were found breeding above 1,500m, where the timberline limit was 1,200m (Mossop and Hayes 1994).

In winter Gyrfalcons can be seen almost anywhere at the timberline where there are also wintering flocks of Willow Grouse and Ptarmigan. Many more-southerly breeding locations are occupied throughout the winter (Poole and Bromley 1988a, Tømmeraas 1989a, Nielsen and Cade 1990a). Those Gyrs which migrate outside their breeding range usually stay in open fields or prairies. There are a few records of wintering Gyrfalcons in towns, usually close to grain elevators where the pigeon density is high. Occasional visits to villages to chase domestic fowls are also known, but hardly represent a wintering habitat.

Kishinskiy (1958) considers the Gyrfalcons as nest-site limited. Although there are usually many cliffs available on sea coasts Gyrs are limited to sites close to seabird colonies. On plain tundra Gyrs will be present at cliffs only if these coincide with places of high prey abundance. On plain tundras across Eurasia there are many places with high populations of grouse but without suitable Gyr nest sites.

NEST BUILDING

Gyrfalcons do not build their own nests, but usurp the nests of other species or make a scrape on a cliff ledge. In older literature there are references to Gyrs building their nests, but these sources were usually written without direct observation, or were assumptions made after the nest-building period. Some of these assumptions were copied from book to book in early bird handbooks.

At present there is no documented record of nest-building by Gyrfalcons. Such nesting activities as are seen are usually limited to trampling of the cup of a stick nest, chewing of twigs in an old nest platform and the subsequent scraping of a cup, or the chewing of the remains of soil or vegetation on a ledge into a sand-like substance.

We believe we have traced the origin of the legend that Gyrs build their own nests. Most of the first-hand material was initially cited by Dementiev and Gortchakovskaya (1945). These authors described the nests of Gyrfalcons in a way that suggested that the Gyrs were capable of building them. Dementiev (1951) repeats similar statements but also refers to V. Modestov, who claimed to have seen a male Gyr bringing twigs to a nest on Kharlov Island, off Russia's Kola Peninsula on 8 May 1939. However this is too late a date for nest building: the Gyrs would already be incubating. It has to be noted that at the time the telescope was an unknown piece of equipment to Russian ornithologists, so whether Modestov indeed saw a twig delivery or the intestine of a prey item remains unclear. However, twig delivery was also mentioned in the sexual display section of Dementiev's book. Dementiev describes a male Gyr symbolically bringing twigs for the nest, and notes that this activity was immediately followed by copulation. The Gyr's ability to pick up twigs has been confirmed in later studies. Jenkins (1978) noted that an incubating female Gyr stretched her neck and picked up a twig which she held in her beak. This was repeated several times. However, time-lapse photography of this study does not show any 'nest-building completion' of this behaviour. Voronin (1986) considered that Gyrfalcons do not build their nests, but may refurbish them before the onset of breeding; they refurbish alternative nest sites (see below) as well.

However, Kishinskiy (1958) and Shklyarevich and Krasnov (1980) were convinced that Gyrs were able to make nests themselves. The latter authors claimed that the Gyrs refurbished nests with grass and small twigs, and that one year they built the nest themselves. Such statements were challenged by Morozov (2000) who pointed out that the dates of the observations of these authors (including those of the work of Dementiev and Gortchakovskaya (1945), as given in their papers, could not have allowed them to observe nest building. Kalyakin and Vinogradov (1981) suspected that the Gyrfalcons were builders of one of the 12 nests studied in Russia's southern Yamal. The nest in question was less dense than the nests of Rough-legged Buzzards, the usual builders of the nests used by Gyrfalcons in the area. However, there were no direct observations of the building process.

In Russia's Bolshezemelsakya tundra Voronin (1987) reported that the first snow cleaning of nests was observed on 21 March 1985. There were footprints of the Gyrs in the nest, though the alternative nest of the same pair was still covered by snow. On a second visit to the nest on 31 March Voronin found that the Gyrs had started to prepare both nests. The first nest was decorated inside with delicate, fresh twigs of dwarf birch, whereas the second one was refurbished with small branches of willow. Refurbishment consisted exclusively of willow and dwarf birch twigs. It was not however clear whether the small twigs were delivered by the Gyrs or by another bird. As it is known that Gyrs and other species occasionally compete for nests the species responsible for the delivery of the twigs is unclear. This may seem to be unnecessarily cautious, but in Norway Tømmeraas (1989a) placed a time-lapse cine-camera 2m from a Gyrfalcon nest and recorded all stages of nest 'adjustments' and egg laying. He noted that on 2 March at about 09:00hrs a 'jet-black creature' partially hidden behind an icicle delivered four twigs to the snow-covered nest. This was, perhaps, a Raven. A Gyrfalcon arrived at 12:30hrs on the same day. In the following 20 days the Gyrs spent about 3% of their time on the nesting ledge. As soon as ambient temperature rose sharply, the time spent at the ledge went up to 30%. During this time, between 23 March and 5 April, both male and female Gyrs participated in the formation of a scrape. Loose material and clumps of soil, sticks and twigs were removed with the beak until a clear circular mound had been erected around the cup. During this period the female lay in the nest for long periods of time. Perhaps she was melting the frozen soil to facilitate further scraping.

Platt (1976) studied nest-site selection and the wintering of Gyrfalcons in a study area south of the Beaufort Sea. The study area contained 31 territories in which young Gyrs were reared. In winter the Gyrfalcons used two types of perches close to the nest. One type was situated in an open location, often commanding a view in every direction and always of more than 180°. Scattered excrement and foot tracks, but only occasional pellets, marked these sites. The other perch type was located on the face of the nest cliff, either in a crevice or under a large overhang. The field of vision from these perches was estimated to be between 90° and 130° in all cases. Present at these perches (roosts) were pellets and dozens, and in some cases hundreds, of individual excretions on top of the snow. A roost was found in 13 out of 17 frequented nest cliffs. The Gyrfalcons did not preferentially frequent cliffs with snow-free eyries. In January the Gyrfalcons walked into the three eyries that were snow-free. In late February these eyries continued to show evidence of falcon visits, and a fourth showed evidence of visitation for the first time. None of the eyries showed evidence of the scraping of a cup. At least 18 sightings of Gyrfalcons (both males and females) were made during the winter study (January–February): eight of these were made at nest sites. In February only two pairs of Gyrs were seen at nest sites, all other sightings referring to lone birds. The study showed that the sites which were more frequented in winter were most likely to be occupied in the subsequent season. However, an additional three Gyrfalcon nests were found in the subsequent breeding season. These were not alternative nest sites within the same territories, but rather widely separated different sites.

NESTING HABITAT AND NEST DESCRIPTIONS

The nesting substrates of Gyrfalcon are derived from three fundamentally different categories: nests on cliffs, nests in trees and nests on artificial structures. The nest itself is no different in these categories and is usually a scrape in vegetation, peat, soil or gravel, a hollow in a nest platform of a larger species, or an unaltered, or slightly altered, stick nest.

Gyr nests studied on Russia's Kola Peninsula were up to 35cm high, the branches used for construction being up to 1cm thick. For lining the inside of the nest Gyrs used various mosses (*Aulocomnium, Plueurocaium,* etc.) and lichens (*Cladonia, Alectoria*). Some birds also picked up turf with soil still attached. To some extent the stems of grass such as *Festuca ovina* and *Solidaga virga* and, rarely, *Gnaphalium* sp., are used. All these plants are available in the cracks of cliffs. Kishinskiy (1958) noted that Ravens have virtually the same nest decoration habits.

Of the 50 nests he examined, Morozov (2000) found only one on a ledge (the others being in trees). The ledge nest was in a small niche on a riverine cliff with a cup similar to that of a Peregrine Falcon. The floor of the niche was covered with dry soil dust.

Palmer (1988) considered that Gyrfalcons do not defecate in the nest, and clean it of food remains. This observation is not entirely correct. A nest on Ellesmere Island consisted almost entirely of Arctic Hare bones in a mound 60cm high (McDonald 1976) while in south-west Greenland one nest consisted of a 'layer of excrement over 2m thick' (Burnham and Mattox 1984). A nest in Russia's Lower Kolyma consisted of a layer of Willow Grouse bones and excrement some 45cm high. The whitewash fall under the nest was visible from a distance of several kilometres, although some of the whitewash, which had probably accumulated for decades, was already covered with characteristic orange lichen. (Whitewash is a common euphemism for the white streaks of faeces that occur below Gyr eyries.)

Palaearctic Gyrfalcons use trees as nest sites more frequently than those of the Nearctic. It is also true that in Eurasia Gyrfalcons might use both trees and cliffs as nesting substrates within one area. In Russia's Koryak Mountains. Gyrfalcons bred in trees in only one case, compared to seven nest sites on cliffs (Kishinskiy 1980). Later, Gorovenko (2003) surveyed a similar region and found Gyrfalcons breeding on cliffs and pinnacles in five cases, and on trees in three cases. On one occasion Gyrfalcons were found breeding on a tree only some 800–1,000m from suitable nesting cliffs (on which Gyrs were known to have bred in previous years; in the year of the study that cliff nest was occupied by Ravens). In the Horton River study area in Canada's Northwest Territories in 1987–93 there were 16 tree nesting Gyrfalcons in the area, 22 cliff-nesting and 6 'bank-nesting' Gyrs, a bank nest being one without a substrate on an earth ledge of a high river bank (Obst 1994). In three territories the Gyrfalcons alternated between bank and tree, tree and cliff nests in successive years. Seven out of 18 nests were on trees in the Thelon River area in Canada's Northwest Territories and Nunavut, the rest being on cliffs (Kuyt 1980).

Kalyakin and Vinogradov (1981) studied 12 Gyr nests in Russia's southern Yamal. All except one of these nests was located on larch trees, the exception being on a pinnacle some 60km north of the timberline. Some of the tree nests were located close to suitable nesting cliffs, in one case a significant 5km-long canyon. Such a preference for trees led Kalyakin and Vinogradov to conclude that tree nesting is more characteristic of the Gyrfalcon than breeding on

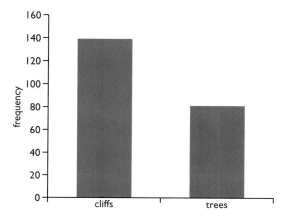

Figure 5.1 Nest substrates in zonal tundras and forest-tundras (n = 220). Nests from Iceland, Greenland and the Canadian Arctic are not included due to the scarcity of trees in these areas.

cliffs, suggesting that cliff breeding only occurs if trees are not present. However, in zonal tundras and forest-tundras the total number of known nests on cliffs outnumbers nests on trees by 63% and 37% (*n* = 220) (Figure 5.1). To derive this ratio we had to exclude samples from treeless zones on large and small islands, most notably the sample from Iceland (Cade *et al.* 1998: *n* = 442). We did, however, include nests in areas that represented a transition from taiga to tundra zones.

It appears that snow conditions at potential nest locations have a decisive effect on the nest choice of the Gyrfalcon. Direct observations have indicated that Gyrs lay more often on snow-free ledges than on those covered by snow (Platt 1977), although they will sometimes make a scrape in a snow-covered nest (Voronin 1987, Platt 1989, Tømmeraas 1989a). However, if a Raven were to start nest construction nearby, the Gyrs would opt for the freshly built nest (if they were able to oust the Ravens). The normally well-exposed nests of Rough-legged Buzzards are often under a thick layer of snow at the start for the breeding period and so are used less frequently by Gyrs. The late arrival of the latter species means that freshly built nests are not available for the early-breeding Gyrfalcon.

NESTS ON CLIFFS

Nests of this type are known from most parts of the Gyrfalcon's range, and are, we suggest, the most widespread nest type. The cliff nest is the only one used on the Canadian Arctic islands, in Iceland and in Greenland where there are no suitable trees.

In Norway, Gyrfalcons were studied on Dovrefjell by Hagen (1952a, Hagen and Barth 1952). The alternative nest sites Hagen observed over a number of years were located above the timberline in the Norwegian mountains. The nests were located between 900m and 1,300m above sea level, surrounded by peaks of up to 2,200m. There was one pair of Gyrfalcons per 2,560km^2 in the study area. In the lowest part there were outposts of pine forest, while birch forest covered the slopes and river valleys up to 1,100m. Above 1,100m there was typical mountain tundra covered with shrubs, mosses and grass. The nest sites Hagen observed were located on cliff ledges in a ravine. The height of the nest from the bottom of the valley was 70–80m in one site and 20m in another.

Suetens and Groenendael (1976) reported six Gyr nests located in cliff niches and three in Ravens' stick nests in Iceland. They noted that the Gyr outlook was normally within 50m of the nest. One nest they observed was located in a small cave on a cliff face and had originally been built by Ravens. The nest was facing a narrow river valley with barren shrub-tundra on both sides.

Also in Iceland, Nielsen recorded a total of 442 nests (Cade *et al.* 1998), of which 52% were stick nests, 25% were on ledges, 22% were in cavities and 1% in other situations including rock pinnacles and at ground level above a cliff. Ravens provide the only stick nests available in northern Iceland. A total of 84 out of 86 studied nests in Iceland were protected by overhangs (Nielsen and Cade 1990a). Langvatn and Moksnes (1979) found six nests in central Norway. All these nests were found in the transition zone between the sub-alpine and the alpine, at about 800–950m. The nests were located on a steep, south-facing mountain cliff with stone scree below. Almost all the nest sites were below overhanging parts of the cliff. The nesting cliffs were approximately 12–15m high, and the eyries were placed some 6–9m from the foot of the cliff. The nests had originally been built by Rough-legged Buzzards and Ravens. On the cliff below the eyries there were large quantities of nitrophile lichens such as *Umbilicaria arctica*, the red-coloured ornithocoprophile *Xantoria candellaria*, and *Ramalina polymorpha*. The habitat surrounding the nests consisted of open river valleys at about 700m above sea level, with wide boggy areas on the valley floor. The mountains on the side of the valley rise to 1,500–1,800m. Some of the mountain tops are peaked, but the majority appear as rounded ridges or plateaux. There are some ravines with small creeks running down gentle hill slopes, as well as a few crags up to 10–15m high. The dominant vegetation types of the area were sub-alpine birch forests, sub-alpine marshes and bogs, low alpine moors with scattered scrub, and a middle alpine heath of sedge and heather. In the habitat surrounding one particular nest the wader population was particular numerous. The dominant bird species were Willow Warbler (*Phylloscopus trochilus*), Brambling (*Fringilla monti-fringilla*) and Fieldfare (*Turdus pilaris*) in the subalpine birch forest, and Meadow Pipit (*Anthus pratensis*) and Willow Tit (*Parus montanus*) in the subalpine bogs and low alpine zone; the total density of passerines varied from 77 to 310 territories per km^2.

In the eastern Hardangervidda Mountains of southern Norway, Gyrfalcons breed exclusively on cliffs. Between 1987 and 1998, 52 breeding attempts were recorded on cliffs, the majority of the cliffs having some form of overhang: 25% of all nests were completely covered by an overhang, 55.8% had at least half of the nest sheltered by an overhang, whereas the remaining 19.2% had less than a half of the nest so covered (Steen 1999b). In northern Finland one nest was located on the ledge of a south-facing cliff, 420m above sea level and 300m from the alpine zone. The eyrie was located some 12m above the foot of the wall and 5–6m from its top. In addition to the alpine and sub-alpine zones of the local fjells, there were typical taiga forests, bogs and a large burned area in the surrounding area. In one year the Gyrfalcons occupied an alternative site 50m from the ledge mentioned above. Both nests were originally built by Ravens (Huhtala *et al.* 1996) The eyrie had been located prior to Huhtala's study (Pulliainen *et al.* 1973, Pulliainen 1975), Gyrfalcons having bred there in 1973, 1974, 1985 and in 1988–91.

In Russia, on the inland Kola Peninsula, Gyrfalcons breed in small niches in the rocks beside rivers (Kishinskiy 1958). The surrounding habitat in this area is of small mountains covered with tundra with patches of stone birch. Kishinskiy reported three pairs of Gyrfalcons in the area, all cliff-nesting. Pearson (1899) also noted a nest on a canyon cliff in Kola (on the Iokanga River).

Kalyakin and Vinogradov (1981) found 12 nests on a territory of 900km^2 in southern Yamal. Here only one nest was located on a cliff type substrate, it being set on top of a pinnacle some 60km north of the timberline. On the Anabar River Gyrfalcons occupied a nest on a 30–35m cliff. The nest was located some 18–20m up the cliff (Gladkov and Zaletaev 1962). Close to the same area three cliff-nesting Gyr pairs were reported on cliffs of a similar height on the Ebelyakh and Kuanamka rivers, tributaries of the Anabar, in 1993–94 (I. Vitkauskas, pers. comm.).

In the Lower Kolyma region six of seven studied Gyr nest sites were on cliffs. The cliffs were 25–40m high, all but one without an overhang. Krechmar mentions several nests on cliffs in the Chukotka Autonomous Region in north-east Siberia (Krechmar *et al.* 1991), while Portenko (1972) mentions Gyrfalcons nesting on a cliff along a river some 20km from the sea coast of Chukotka.

Detailed data on nest sites were given by Kishinskiy (1980) for the Koryak Mountains. Here, of eight nests, seven were on the cliffs at 150–500m above sea level. The height of the bluff on which the nests were situated was usually less than 10m, although it did rise occasionally to 30m. Almost all nests were situated out of easy reach, being located in niches or half-caves with overhangs. Two of these were stick nests built by Ravens. One nest was merely a scratched hollow in a niche, without any bedding material, which is assumed to have been constructed by the Gyrs themselves. One occupied nest was originally built by a Golden Eagle (*Aquila chrysaetos*).

Cade (1960) reported that 18 out of 21 nests of Gyrfalcons along Alaska's Colville River were overhung. It was suggested that since Gyrfalcons, like Ravens, breed before winter's snow has melted the choice of overhung nests is for protection against snow. However, Woodin (1980) argued that an overhang may not always protect a nest from snow, and actually made no difference to the observed snow cover in the nest. High winds, he suggested, were a more important factor in determining snow cover on nest ledges. This does not mean that the snow cover is not a factor in nest-site selection by both Ravens and Gyrs, but does argue for overhung nest sites having as much to do with concealment as avoidance of snow cover.

In Alaska the height of nest sites above a river was an average of 29m (range 7.6–91m), the distance above the base of the cliff averaging 15m (range 1.8–61m). Eleven nests were on shale formations, ten were on sandstone or conglomerate. Seventeen nests were on the ledges of precipices, three in potholes, and one was in a scrape cut at the end of gentle slope on a river bluff where a sharp break occurred (Cade 1960, White and Cade 1971). Kessel (1989) reported a Gyr nest on the top of a tor near the Serpentine Hot Springs on the Seward Peninsula of Alaska.

In the Yukon Territory of Canada Mossop and Hayes (1994) found Gyrfalcons breeding almost exclusively on cliffs. All 259 nesting territories studied were associated with cliffs. However it seems that the Yukon Territory is unique as "virtually all habitats … have cliff faces available within reasonable flight range". In British Columbia, 10 out of 13 Gyr nests were located on cliff ledges. Others were in unused Golden Eagle nests. The nest ledges were up to 24m long and ranged in height from 6m to 25m above the ground or water. All were protected by overhangs. The ledge nests were on bare ground with no material added (Campbell *et al.* 1990).

In the central Canadian Arctic Gyr nests occur on cliffs, with 68% of them having complete overhangs. The orientation of both the Gyrfalcon and Raven nests studied did not differ statistically from an equal distribution among the eight directions examined (Poole and Bromley 1988b). Most of the Gyrfalcon nests (*n* = 34) were built by Ravens (62%) or eagles (23%), 6% were stick nests of uncertain origin and 9% were ledges with no stick substrate (Poole and Bromley 1988b). The nesting cliffs of Gyrfalcons in the central Canadian Arctic had an average height of 24.5 ± 9.8m, with the nest placed at a height of 12.9 ± 6.5m. These parameters were close to those measured for Raven nesting cliffs: 21.2 ± 9.5m and 11.0 ± 6.6m respectively, reinforcing the view that Gyrs often usurp Raven nests (Poole and Bromley 1988b). Poole and Bromley also noted that nests with a northerly orientation had a higher breeding success than those with a southerly orientation.

At the Thelon River study area of the Northwest Territories and Nunavut, the Gyrfalcons were breeding on cliffs in 11 out of 18 sites. The preferred nest sites were on cliffs facing south (4) or west (4), north or east facings being rare (1 and 1). Three of nine cliff nests had overhangs, and the Gyrs clearly favoured stick nests rather than scrapes (Kuyt 1980). In Nunavut (Northwest Territories at the time of the study), in the Melville Peninsula/Wager Bay area, Calef and Heard (1979) reported five nest sites, all on cliffs. Two of the sites had previously been occupied by Pergrines. In Quebec and in the Canadian archipelago (Henderson and Bird 1996, Brodeur *et al.* 1995) Gyrfalcons predominantly breed on cliffs.

A nest studied in north-east Greenland (Fletcher and Webby 1977) was on a cliff and had an overhang. The nest was located on a ledge 15m above the bottom of a gorge which was 40–50m deep. The nest was beneath the overhang and faced almost due south.

NESTS IN TREES

Tree nests, previously unknown in Finland, have recently been discovered in the north (Puntila 2004). In nearby Russia, within the Lapland Nature Reserve, resident Gyrfalcons are known to breed on trees (Vladimirskaya 1948, Semenov-Tyan-Shanskiy and Gilyazov 1991). A nest found in 1938 was placed on a tree 6–7m high in mixed forest close to the shore of Lake Chuneozero, some 1km from the headquarters of the reserve. The nest was 1m in diameter and 1.5m high.

Voronin (1986, 1987) studied a small enclave of Gyrfalcons on the Bolshaya Rogovaya River and on a small island of forest surrounded by tundra along the river More-U. There the Gyrs were found nesting exclusively on trees. A small patch of gallery forest surrounded by tundra covering an area of 100km^2 accommodated four nesting pairs. The nests identified as having been used by Gyrs were located on spruce (8), willow (4) and birch (1). In spruce the nests were located on the southern side, on birch and willow in the forks of large branches. The nests – usually placed about 4m above the ground – averaged 60–75cm in diameter, with a height of 40–42cm (though in one case 95cm). The inside diameter of the nests averaged 24–26cm, and the inside depth was 12–15cm. The thickness of the inside layer was 6–8cm. The diameter of the twigs from which the nest was built varied from 1.8 to 2.8cm.

Danilov *et al.* (1984) reported at least three Gyrfalcon nests in the old nests of White-tailed Eagles (*Haliaeetus albicilla*) placed on larches. One of these nests was known to have been occupied for a number of years (Kucheruk *et al.* 1975, Mishenko 1981). The nest was 150cm in diameter and 90cm high. It was located in a river valley in a group of three larches surrounded by thickets of alder and willow up to 3m high. There was a moss/cotton-grass bog to the north of the nest, and the gentle slopes of the Bolshoy Sopkuy hillock range were nearby. Another tree nest was on the bank of a small river called the Yadayakhodyjakhe, south of the Porsyakha trading post. Here the nest-bearing larch tree was bent by some 70° towards the river due to permafrost melt. This resulted in the loss of one of the eggs which rolled out of the nest and was found, rotten, on the ground below.

Some Gyr nests were reported on the Shuchya River, Yamal, as being located on cliffs. However Rupasov (2001) reported only tree-nesting Gyrfalcons in Yamal. He considered that Gyrfalcons did not inhabit the tundra zone of Yamal outside the timberline. All four nests which Rupasov found were located in patches of larch forest with a minimum size of 0.5ha. In a later study Rupasov reported five nests, four of which were located in river valleys with forest patches of one or more hectare (Rupasov 2003). In a previous study in the same place Kalyakin and Vinogradov (1981) found 12 nests in an area of 900km^2. All the nests except one were located on larch trees in habitats within the forest-tundra subzone.

One nest out of eight in the Koryak Mountains (Kishinskiy 1980) was on a poplar tree on the edge of a patch of forest. The nest had been originally built by a Raven. In the same region Gorovenko (2003) found Gyrfalcons breeding on trees in three cases (out of eight). One of the tree nests had been built and previously occupied by Golden Eagles. Golden Eagles were also the builders of a nest on a tree in the Yana plateau (Vorobiev 1963), as well as of a nest on the Ilirneiveem River in the Anuy basin of western Chukotka (Artukhov 1986).

In Canada the first record of tree-nesting Gyrfalcons was by MacFarlane (1891, cited by Palmer 1988) who recorded 18 nests on the tallest trees, 'generally in pines'. Much later, tree-nesting Gyrfalcons were studied in detail by Obst (1994) at the Horton River study area, Northwest Territories. The nests were situated beside the trunk or in a fork of white spruce. The nests were exposed to all directional aspects and to weather. They were placed 5–8m above the ground and 1–5m from the tops of the trees, which were 6–12m tall. The nesting trees were surrounded by tundra, close to lake shores in forest-tundra on plains. A total of 78% of the 14 identified tree nests were occupied every year during the period of monitoring (1987–1993). One nest on a tree was used for one or two years and then abandoned for four successive years.

On the Seward Peninsula, Alaska a Gyr pair raised its young in an old Raven nest in a large Balsam Poplar (*Populus balsamifera*) along the Pilgrim River in 1966 (Kessel 1989). At the Thelon River, Northwest Territories and Nunavut, a pair of Gyrfalcons was recorded as tree-nesting, the pair apparently having two nests, each located in an old nest of Rough-legged Buzzard. Both nests were on white spruce, in one case on a 'witch's broom' (*i.e.* a disease on a branch of the tree). The landscape around the nests was predominantly patches of white spruce and thick willow (Kuyt 1962). In a later paper Kuyt (1980) mentioned several tree-nesting Gyrfalcons breeding regularly in such places. In total he identified 18 Gyrfalcon nest sites, two or three of which were regularly occupied. Seven out of these 18 nests were on trees.

NESTS ON THE COAST

Of 82 breeding pairs of Gyrfalcons in a study area in northern Iceland (Nielsen and Cade 1990a) six were located on coastal cliffs. Some coastal locations are also known in Greenland.

On Russia's Kola Peninsula Gyrfalcons were reported to breed on sea cliffs by Shklyarevich and Krasnov (1988). Off the Kola coast, on Kharlov Island, part of the Seven Islands archipelago, Gyrfalcons placed their nest on a small (50cm × 50cm) ledge of a high, sea-facing cliff with an overhang (Dementiev and Gorchakovskaya 1945). The nest faced south-west and was a scratched cup in a mere huddle of Dwarf Birch twigs. On the cliff there was a small colony of Shags (*Phalacrocorax aristotelis*) and a larger Herring Gull colony. There were no Willow Grouse and Ptarmigan on the island, but in some years there were significant numbers of Norway Lemmings (*Lemmus lemmus*). The island was also the site of a large number of seabird colonies. Another nest described by Shklyarevich and Krasnov (1980) was also located on a cliff, but in a nest originally built by Ravens.

Portenko (1972) mentioned a Gyrfalcon nest on the coastal cliffs of Provideniya Bay, on the Chukchi Peninsula, and another breeding pair close to a seabird colony at Seyshan. Stishov and Marukhnich (1990) reported a nest on a pinnacle together with six Herring Gull and two Glaucous Gull nests (which, technically, constitutes a small colony) on the Shalaurova Izba Cape of Chukotka. There is also an unconfirmed record of Gyrfalcons breeding at the Taigonos Peninsula in the Sea of Okhotsk, a site said to be close to a large colony of guillemots. In Alaska nests on coastal cliffs are known in the Lisburne Peninsula (Swem *et al.* 1994). Coastal nests are also known from the Canadian Arctic archipelago (e.g. Bylot Island). One observed by one of the authors (Sale) was in a cave in an overhanging section of cliff some 20m from the base.

ARTIFICIAL NESTS AND NESTS ON ARTIFICIAL STRUCTURES

Gyrfalcons are known to use artificial structures for breeding (Voronin and Kochanov 1989, Ritchie 1991, Cade 1982). However, it is necessary to separate nests on artificial structures built by humans for human purposes (e.g. industrial activities) and artificial nests which are built specifically for Gyrfalcons.

Tømmeraas (1978) mentioned a very successful site in Finnmark, Norway, located in a well-protected cave in a cliff. The nest site had a long history, having been first recorded in 1855 (Wolley 1864). The site was rediscovered in 1968 and was then occupied for nine of the next 11 years. The site was restored in 1970 (Tømmeraas 1989a) after it had fallen apart during the breeding season. In the following year the Gyrfalcons bred in the area, but unsuccessfully. The nest was then altered again, effectively becoming an artificial nest. This second restoration was to the liking of the Gyrs, who used it until at least 1987.

Tømmeraas (1993) suspected that poor nest condition could lead to low breeding success, a conjecture that led to the establishment of an artificial nest programme which included the building of nest boxes and the construction of ledges (which occasionally included the blasting of cliffs with explosives) (Tømmeraas 1978, 1993). The project was aimed at the restoration of traditional breeding places, and it was successful, with nesting reported in seven of 13 artificial nests.

Steen (1999b) reported seven subsequent breeding attempts in an artificial nest imitating a Raven nest structure, which was placed on a cliff ledge in East Hardangervidda, southern Norway. Gyrfalcon breeding on a dam has been reported from Sweden (P. Ingesson, pers. comm.).

In European Russia, Gyr breeding has taken place on a wooden triangulation tower on Lovetskiy Island in the Pechora Delta. The tower is located 30m from the sea shore (Voronin and Kochanov 1989). The nest, originally built by White-tailed Eagles, is known to have been occupied from 1986; from 1996 the site was protected as part of the Nenetskiy State Nature Reserve (Glotov 2000). Two nests on triangulation towers are also recorded in north-west Siberia (Kalyakin 1988). This particular finding convinced Kalyakin that Gyrfalcons are nest-site limited and that artificial nest platforms should be provided in order to increase the population.

In Alaska, Gyrfalcons were noted as breeding on the boom of an active gold dredger in Taylor (Ford 1999). Such nests are described in detail by White and Rosenau (1970). One was on an active dredger on the Seward Peninsula, the nest having been originally built by Ravens. The nest (named the Tweet nest after the owner/operator of the dredger) was situated on a platform under the top of the front gantry of the dredger. The nest was occupied by Gyrfalcons every year from 1956 to 1963, except in 1957 when the Ravens reoccupied it. In 1959, 1960, 1961 and 1963 the dredger was operational after about 15 June, but the young Gyrs successfully fledged. Another active nest on an abandoned gold dredger was studied in 1963. It was sited within 25km of the nest described above. Another nest almost certainly occupied by Gyrfalcons was located about 1.6km from the Tweet nest. It was spotted from an aircraft in 1968 and held two chicks. The nest was located on an elevated sluice box. A failed clutch was reported from this nest in 1969.

Interestingly, the building of the Trans-Alaska Pipeline provided new breeding substrates for Gyrs: they have been recorded breeding on above-ground portions of the pipeline some 150km south of Prudhoe Bay (Ritchie 1991).

NEST SITE FIDELITY

There is indirect evidence, based on the individual colour markings of the birds, that Gyrs are faithful to their nest sites (Cade *et al.* 1998, Koskimies 1998). This fact was verified by Nielsen (1991) who ringed adults in Iceland and later recorded them on the same nests. There is no better detailed study of Gyrfalcon nest site fidelity than that of Nielsen. Prior to his work it was generally understood that Gyrs might shift their nest site some distance in consecutive years, but remained more or less faithful to their nesting territories (Dementiev 1951, Palmer 1988). The approach of the Nielsen (1991) study was simple and straightforward: he ringed the birds. Two males ringed as nestlings were four years old when caught as breeding adults (both with broods). It is possible that one of the males was breeding at the same territory in the previous year. The second male was paired with an unringed female in immature plumage. In captivity Gyrfalcons are known to breed at the age of four, so breeding by an immature bird is rare. Indeed, this female is only the second bird to have been observed breeding in immature plumage in 250 successful breeding attempts (Nielsen 1991). The females caught as breeding birds (with successful broods) were two and three years old when captured. The breeding occurred at sites 14km and 25km from the male's natal areas and 53km and 84km from those of the females. All female Gyrs caught more than once were re-caught within their old territories, though some were at different nest sites. Four females bred successfully in all the years in which they were known to occupy their territories: one female was caught in three separate years at the same nest, another had moved 3.7km. The maximum distance between different nest sites on the same territory was 5.9km. One ringed female was found dead two years later just 2km from the nest site. Subsequent to her death her territory was occupied by a successful pair for the following four years.

Following the Nielsen study, it is now generally believed that Gyrfalcons have high fidelity to their nesting territories. It is known that Gyrs move nest sites from time to time, but these relocations are generally minor and reflect the choice of an alternative nesting ledge in the same nesting territory.

Gyrfalcons continue to occupy single territories presumably for their lifespan, with possible gaps in poor food supply years. In Norway Tømmeraas (1994a) stated that one territory was occupied in 10 out of 12 years. Generally, an established breeding pair maintains their territory throughout the year unless food shortages force them to move. On occasion only the male Gyr will stay within the territory during the winter. If the pair move it is usually the male that is the first to appear in the spring. In Canada's Yukon Territory solitary males tend to stay on their cliffs throughout the breeding season, whereas solitary females do not (Platt 1977). Seventeen of 31 breeding territories showed signs of winter use, with six male Gyrs and one female seen in January, and six males and five females in February, at least 60 days before egg laying commenced. Most eyries in Canada's Yukon Territory, being sheltered, are winter loafing sites and/or night roosts (Platt 1977).

ALTERNATIVE NESTS

Stick nests are often destroyed by the young at the end of the breeding season, so the Gyr pair is forced either to use the ruined nest or to go to an alternative location, or to wait for a Raven or Rough-legged Buzzard to build a new nest (Voronin 1987, Burnham and Mattox 1984). Gyrs usually have 2–5 alternative nests in their territory and they often switch nests each year (Poole and Bromley 1988a, Cade *et al.* 1998). In some places pairs breed in one nest for many years: one Norwegian nest was monitored for seven years, producing at least three chicks each year (Steen 1998). However, in Jämtland, Sweden, nest sites are occupied only once every three years (Falkdalen and Holmberg 1997).

Usually alternative nest sites are located within the same territory at a distance of 1–5km from each other. In their study in Iceland Nielsen and Cade (1990a) found an average distance between nests of 1.4km (range 0.03–6.4km, *n* = 15). In Finland and Norway the distance between alternative nests was reported as 10–17km (Cade *et al.* 1998, Steen 1998), whereas in Canada the average distance is 4.8km (Poole and Bromley 1988a).

In Russia, at inland sites on the Kola Peninsula Kishinskiy (1958) studied three pairs of Gyrfalcons and reported that all had at least two alternative nest sites (one pair had three) at a distance of between 60m and 1,200m from the active nests. In Anabar in 1994 at least one Gyr pair out of three had an alternative nest some 150m away. This nest had been the breeding location in the previous year (S.Vitkauskas, pers. comm.). A similar distance was reported by Voronin (1987) for the forest island in the Bolshezemelsakya tundra. Dementiev (1951) states that the distance between main and alternative nest is 0.5km. A.V. Kondratiev (Krechmar *et al.* 1991) found a Gyrfalcon nest in an old nest of White-tailed Eagles along with two alternative sites along the Rauchua River in eastern Chukotka.

There are some data on the occupancy of nest sites in Alaska. Of 34 active nests observed on the Seward Peninsula in 1968, only eight were re-used in 1969, and 77% of 107 nesting sites observed in 1968–70 were used only once by Gyrs (Rosenau 1972, cited by Kessel 1989).

Tree-nesting Gyrfalcons were studied in detail by Obst (1994) in the Horton River study area of Canada's Northwest Territories. Nine nesting Gyrfalcons out of 16 had alternative nest sites (six tree nests, one cliff and one bank nest). These nests were within 25m to 2,350m of a previously used site. Kuyt (1962) reported that one tree-nesting Gyrfalcon shifted to a nest some 100m away the following year.

TERRITORY USE

Kishinskiy (1958) considered that neighbouring pairs of Gyrfalcons were not sharing hunting territories, and that the distances between nests was large enough to maintain such separation. In a contrary view, Woodin (1980) stated that Gyrfalcons breeding close to each other do share hunting territories. However, they would defend the area immediately about the eyrie. In addition Woodin reported that Gyrfalcons share their hunting territory with Ravens.

Nielsen and Cade (1990b) studied Gyrfalcons in northern Iceland. According to their research Gyrfalcons breeding at the coast and in terrain with lots of lakes travelled more than 7.5km to reach areas with good concentrations of waterfowl or seabirds (average 3.4km in winter). Gyrfalcons breeding in heathland had to fly from 13 to 33km (average 12.9km) to reach rich areas of waterfowl and seabirds.

In a winter study in Washington State, USA, Dobler (1989) tail-mounted radio transmitters on two female Gyrfalcons and put a back-mounted transmitter on a third (one immature and two adults) and radio-tracked them between January and March. The immature female lived on a major estuary in Northern Puget Sound. Its home range had a core (most used) area of 136km^2, the total home range (as measured by the Minimum Convex Polygon) being 354km^2. The adult females scored 58km^2 and 731km^2. The first female had a territory in part of Washington's largest area of coulees (deep ravines). The second female was using an agricultural area consisting of irrigated fields with ditches. The cropland included cornfields and wasteways, which provided cat-tail cover, both of which attracted Pheasants.

White and Nelson (1991) studied hunting behaviour of free-living Gyrfalcons followed from a helicopter in the mountain–forest–tundra mixture some 10km from the Dempster Highway in Canada's Yukon Territory. In an unprecedented study – imagine how long it is necessary to stay in the air in order to follow a hunt – White and Nelson managed to observe nine flights of a female Gyr and five flights of a male, totalling 4hr 1min and 3hr 10min respectively (although these figures required a total of 29hr 36min of observations from the ground, due to the fact that it was virtually impossible to predict the timing of a hunt). The noisy Bell 206A Jet Ranger helicopter disturbed the Gyrs, making the observations questionable, but there is really no alternative technique available for observing hunting falcons. White and Nelson found that flying the helicopter upwards 200–300m from the Gyr, and then slowly approaching it horizontally, caused neither attack nor avoidance. Usually they followed the Gyrs from behind at a distance of 30–50m with the bird at the 10:30 to 11 o'clock position. A Gyr would sometimes glance back over its wing, indicating some concern, if the helicopter was directly behind. The authors noted that 'the potential threat of the helicopter-shadowing technique to the lives of the raptors and their broods, and to the lives of the human observers, may be high and must not be taken lightly.' In the study the female Gyr patrolled an area within 3.2km of the eyrie, whereas the male went up to 24km from the eyrie while hunting. One sortie was remarkably long:

> The male flew high, north towards the mountains, passing 8km east of a neighbouring occupied eyrie, then 7.5km east of another eyrie. At that point he curved north-east and eventually arrived over a bank of low cloud which blanketed the mountain ridge. He then flew east for about 5km, over the edge of the mountains and cloud until turning south when 6.5km west of another eyrie. He flapped and glided almost directly south for about 14km, turning south-west when 4.5km from yet another eyrie. After flying about 10km south-west over the tundra plain, he wandered 5km north-west and begun a series of low level hunts. After about 10km of low-level hunting he landed during a rain shower, and eventually we lost him… His total observed travels in just over 3 hours of our flight time encompassed about 280km^2.

In Greenland territory use and home range size of a female Gyr was measured using a 65g satellite-radio transmitter (Klugman *et al.* 1993). The range estimated using the Minimum Convex Polygon procedure was approximately 589km^2.

BREEDING DENSITY AND INTER-NEST DISTANCES

In Iceland the minimum distance between nests was measured as 8km by Wayre and Jolly (1958) and as 5.5km by Woodin (1980). In later studies the nearest-neighbour distance of 82 traditional Gyrfalcon territories was found to be

5.8km (range 0.3–12.5km), or 63km^2 per territory (Nielsen and Cade 1990a), the highest density recorded for a large study area (Cade *et al.* 1998). In the period from 1985 to 1989 the annual variation in distance between settled pairs was 6.2 to 8.1km, or 90 to 135km^2 per occupied territory. Suetens and Groenendael (1976) reported that the individual territories of Icelandic Gyrfalcons were 160, 220 and 490km^2. However it is not clear how they determined the size of the Gyr territories.

Hagen (1952a, and before him Sjölander 1946, both referring to another's finding) appeared to report the maximum Gyrfalcon density ever recorded. In a lemming peak year the Gyr density rose to 10 pairs in some 10 square miles (25.6km^2) at Lulevatn (the Stora Lulevatn lake, near the Sarek National Park in northern Sweden). This figure was repeated by Palmer (1988) and Cade *et al.* (1998). However, what Hagen did not mention in the English edition of his paper (Hagen 1952a) was that Sjölander (1946) probably meant the so-called Swedish mile (1 Swedish mile = 10km); the Norwegian edition of his paper (Hagen 1952b) does not have any indication of the area's size. So the resulting density (10 pairs per 1,000km^2) was not a record high, and is in fact consistent with the current measured density of Swedish Gyrs. In Jämtland, Sweden, the minimum distance between two Gyr pairs was 6km (Falkdalen and Holmberg 1997). In Norrbotten, northern Sweden, the Gyr density was one pair per 200km^2 in 1997 (Tjernberg 1997).

In Norway the average distance between nearest Gyr neighbours varied from 12km to 33km (Tømmeraas 1990). In the Norwegian study of Langvatn and Moksnes (1979) the distance between neighbouring nests was reported as 4.5km in one case. In Finland the overall (extrapolated) density was one Gyr pair per 1,000km^2 (Cade *et al.* 1998).

In Kishinskiy's study of Gyrfalcons on the Kola Peninsula (Kishinskiy 1958), the distance between the active nests was 35 and 12km. Although radio-tracking or helicopter shadowing techniques were not available at the time, some circumstantial evidence, such as kill sites, direct observations and knowledge of the distribution of prey species allowed Kishinskiy to conclude that the Gyrfalcons took their prey at up to 12km from the nest. He estimated the total diameter of the hunting territory to be 10–15km. Interestingly he wrote that the Gyrfalcon does not hunt close to the nest, yet he stated that the closest kill was made at a distance of 300m.

Voronin (1986, 1987) reported that the average distance between occupied Gyrfalcon nests on Russia's Bolshaya Rogovaya River (at Pechoro-Nenetskiy Okrug in European Russia) was 6.5km in 1982, 6.2km in 1983, 12km in 1984 and 7.5km in 1985. The minimum distance between the nesting pairs was 4.8–5.0km. The nests were located in clusters of alternative nests within patches of forest up to 2km long close to a river and surrounded by shrubby tundra with numerous small lakes. One nest cluster consisted of three alternative nest sites located in a patch of willow trees. The total area of the patch was 0.8km². There was dense bush cover under the dominant trees. The patch was sheltered from northerly winds by a high river bank. A second territory was located some 10km south of the first and had two alternative nests, occupied in different years. One nest was located on a spruce tree, the second on a willow. Both nests were built in a narrow strip of spruce trees 300–350m long surrounded by willows. This 'island' of trees stood beside the river. The total area of the tree patch was 0.5–0.8km². This forest patch was occupied for a number of years, but in one year both nests collapsed.

The next territory was located some 5km from the previous one. The two alternative nests here were located in a small (0.1km²) tree patch, one on a spruce, the second on a willow. In one year both nests collapsed. The following year a Rough-legged Buzzard nested there, but in the next year the Gyrs re-occupied the patch. A fourth territory was located some 7km south of the third territory in a large spruce patch. The patch was 2km long and occupied not only the river bank, but also part of the valley. There Voronin found 6–8 nests, which in some years were occupied by Rough-legged Buzzard and Merlin (*Falco columbarius*).

Kalyakin and Vinogradov (1981) reported that the majority of Gyr breeding sites in southern Yamal had one nest. However one site had two nests (*i.e.* one alternative) and one had three nests (two alternatives). It appears that all nests looked refreshed and visited by the birds. Also in Yamal, Rupasov (2001) found Gyrfalcons with a breeding density of 0.10 pairs per 10km of the river valleys. However, this conclusion was based on a survey in early August, so it is possible that some early nests might not have been detected.

At tributaries of the Anabar, Ebelyakh and Bolshaya Kuanamka rivers, inter-nest distances were reported as 24km (I. Vitkauskas, pers. comm.). In the northern Urals the distances between neighbouring nests varied between 7km and 40km in the shrub tundra subzone (average distance 20km, *n* = 18) and between 10km and 20km in the typical tundra subzone (average distance 14.7km, *n* = 6) (Morozov 1991). The minimum distance between occupied Gyrfalcon nests in southern Yamal was 4– 5km (Kalyakin and Vinogradov 1981).

On the Putorana Plateau of the southern Taimyr (Dorogov 1985, Rogacheva 1988) the distance between the nests was 7 to 30km, with a single Gyr territory varying in area between 150km² and 380km² (average 250km²). In the same area Dorogov *et al.* (1988) found that nests were located at distances of 7–30km along the Ayan Lake, at an average of 25km in the Delocha and Kotuy river valleys, and at distances of 40, 45 and 350km along the Kotuy River.

Morozov (1991) gives the following density of Gyrfalcons for the north-eastern part of European Russia: an area of 14,000km² accommodates from 10 to 15 pairs of Gyrfalcons (0.7–11 pairs per 1,000km²). In the shrub-tundra subzone the density drops to 0.4–0.6 pairs per 1,000km². If the area of the Vorkuta industrial zone, where there are no Gyrfalcons, is omitted the average density in 1983–1988 becomes 0.7 pairs per 1,000km². In the typical tundra subzone the density reaches

1–2 pairs per 1,000km². In Chukotka's Koryak Mountains the distance between two neighbouring nests was 18km (Kishinskiy 1980).

In Alaska, White and Cade (1971) reported distances between locations of 3.2 to 17km. Generally in northern Alaska Gyrfalcons breed along major rivers, most notably the Colville River (where there are more than 30 pairs), the Kokolik (11 pairs), the Kukpowruk (12 pairs), and the Utokok river system (eight pairs). The Gyrfalcons were noted breeding in clusters along some stretches of these rivers: nine pairs in 38km of the Colville River, seven pairs on a 40km stretch of the Kokolik Rive, and nine pairs in 56km of the Kukpowruk River. On the Seward Peninsula the Gyr density varies from one pair per 1,000km² in areas where cliffs are few to 5.7 pairs per 1,000km². The average for the peninsula is 1.6 pairs per 1,000km².

A survey carried out in 1989 in the Brooks Range of Alaska's Arctic National Wildlife Refuge (the Sadlerochit and Shublik Mountains) and on the north side of the Franklin, Romanzof and British Mountains located 42 occupied Gyr territories in an area of about 7,600km², making the density 5.5 Gyr pairs per 1,000km² (Swem *et al.* 1994).

In Denali National Park in central Alaska the Gyrfalcon density is 4.7 pairs per 1,000km² (Swem *et al.* 1994). In an 11-year study 40% of territories were occupied for more than six years, 20% only once. The percentage of successful territories (*i.e.* from which young fledged) varied from 33% to 80% (mean 61%).

Shank and Poole (1994) stated that the average distance between nests in Canada's Northwest Territories and Nunavut is smaller in areas with high July temperatures and in areas with tall willows, supporting the view that Gyrfalcons breed more densely in areas of high productivity. However there was no such trend in brood size, meaning that even in more productive areas Gyrfalcons breed at the same rate. The mean distance between active nests varied from 9 to 56km.

In Canada's Yukon Territory (Mossop and Hayes 1994) the nearest-neighbour distance between the nests was rather uniform, varying between 8.1 ± 2.3km and 96.7 ± 14.6km in various regions of the territory. The breeding densities varied from 0.6 to 6.1 pairs per 1,000km². In the Territory's Ogilvie Mountains Gyrs reach a density of 5.7 pairs per 1,000km² (Barichello 1983, cited by Swem *et al.* 1994). Near Hope Bay in Canada's Nunavut Province the mean distance between nests was 10.6km (range 1–20km) in the period from 1982 to 1986, which equates to one territory per 99km², and one occupied territory per 250km² (Poole 1987, Poole and Bromley 1988a). In other parts of the Northwest Territories and Nunavut summer densities ranged from 0.68 to 4.31 pairs per 1,000km² (Poole and Bromley 1988a). In the studies of Shank and Poole (1994) the distance between nests varied between 5 km and 93km.

The minimum recorded distance between active Gyrfalcon nests is km (Poole and Bromley 1988b). The same authors report that breeding success declined significantly when the nearest-neighbour distance was below 5km (Poole and Bromley 1988a). In the Horton River study area of the Northwest Territories the average distance between clusters of nests along the river was 5.3km for tree-nesting Gyrs (*n* = 13) and 5.4km for cliff nests (Obst 1994). In a tree-nest cluster away from the river (20–55km) the average distance between the nests was 16.2km (*n* = 4). Although the density along the river is not surprising, the finding of nest clusters in the forest away from the river led Obst to suggest that the number of Gyrs might have been underestimated as there may have been a significant number of Gyrs breeding in the region's expansive forest-tundra.

In west Greenland the minimum distance between seven studied nests was 7.8km (Burnham 1975). In south-west Greenland the average distance between nests at inland sites was 10.4km for occupied sites, with an average of 12.3km for successful nests. The minimum distance between nests at coastal sites was 15km (Burnham and Mattox 1984). Bertelsen (1932) reported 30 nest locations in the Unamak (now Uummannaq) District of West Greenland, which corresponds to a potential density of a Gyr pair per 400km^2 of ice-free terrain. Jenkins (1978) reported inter-nest distances in Greenland of 4.8km and 19km.

In conclusion, we believe that the available data show that in general Gyrfalcons prefer nests on cliffs, even if trees are available, but that they will also use artificial structures if these allow breeding in favourable areas. Gyrs show high territory fidelity and within their territory will have several alternative nest locations if these are available, occasionally shifting from one site to another. What dominates choice of territory is a combination of food and nest site availability. In areas where both are abundant high nesting densities are accepted.

CHAPTER 6

Food and Feeding Habits

DIET

Research from throughout the Gyrfalcon's range suggests that the birds rely heavily rely on Willow Grouse and Ptarmigan, especially at the initial stages of the breeding period when the breeding grounds are under snow. Exceptions to this rule are usually associated with places with a superabundance of other prey species, such as lemmings or seabirds. It is probably appropriate to say that Gyrfalcons are stenophagous (*i.e.* the birds feed on a limited range of similar prey) during the early stages of breeding. However, as spring progresses and new bird species start to arrive at the Gyrfalcon breeding grounds, and as the melting snow makes small mammals available, our strictly stenophagous bird becomes a very eclectic feeder.

Figure 6.1 shows the 'average' diet of Gyrfalcons based on an analysis of the data from the entire Gyrfalcon range. Prey species making up less than 2% of the total were combined in the 'others' category. These are mostly species which occur in

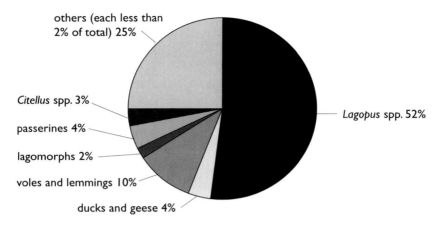

Figure 6.1 *Gyrfalcon diet averaged over all ranges*

one geographical area (and which are therefore absent in other regions), thus making part of the diet of the species geographically variable. *Lagopus* grouse were combined in one category. The other largest categories of prey are small mammals and ducks.

Traditionally, diet studies of Gyrfalcons, as well as those of other birds of prey, rely on the identification of prey remains found in the proximity of nests, at the nest itself and at plucking posts; on pellet analysis; and on direct observations. The latter have sometimes been carried out with the help of sophisticated gadgets such as time-lapse cinematography or video-recording. Sometimes the nest of Gyrfalcons consists of a good layer of bones tramped by chicks into a rather solid platform. Excavation in such nests after the breeding season usually offers considerable diet data.

FOOD PROCESSING

The normally solitary Gyrfalcon plucks and eats its prey on the spot (Cade *et al.* 1998). Grouse delivered to nestlings or mates are usually plucked and decapitated beforehand. Small prey items can be delivered to the nest unplucked, but here too the prey is often decapitated.

Gyrfalcons have a characteristically distinct way of food processing, so for the experienced observer it is almost always possible to tell the Gyrfalcon's work from that of, say, a Raven, Rough-legged Buzzard or other predator. In contrast to Ravens, Gyrs process bones less thoroughly. Tendons and sinews are frequently left; the skeletons are usually rendered muscle-free, but bits of the muscles are occasionally left on the bones. By contrast, bones found at a Raven's nest would be immaculately clean and usually tendon-free as well. The area around a Rough-legged Buzzard nest site tends to be decorated with a large number of pellets. These pellets are larger than those of the Gyrfalcon, and have a greater specific gravity. In addition, Gyrfalcon pellets usually consist of feathers and characteristically crushed bones, the bones sometimes precariously sticking out of the pellets. This is rarely seen in Rough-legged Buzzard pellets.

Bochenski *et al.* (1998) studied bone damage in the pellets of Gyrfalcons, the primary reason for their work being archaeological. The remains of Willow Grouse and Ptarmigan bones are found in many Palaeolithic sites, and archaeologists needed to be able separate bones left by humans from those left by birds of prey or other predators. The 1998 study showed that it is rather easy to recognise Gyrfalcon-processed bones. Firstly, it is rare to find head bones in remains since the falcons remove the heads of grouse before delivering them to the nest site. Secondly, all types of bones are heavily modified by digestion. Traces of digestion were observed on more than 80% of bone ends, nearly 100% of broken surfaces and on some shafts. Only a few bones, most often the coracoideus, carpometacarpus, phalanx digitorum major and tarsometatarsus, were not broken. Other bones were represented exclusively by fragments. Most fragments were unidentifiable shafts (71%). As regards the representativity of the bones, the highest MNI (minimum number of individuals) was for tibiotarsi. The wing bone/leg bone ratio was 56.5%. A total of 59% of fragments of axial skeleton had digestion holes. Long bones in particular were heavily modified by digestion.

Hagen (1952a, Hagen and Barth 1952) noted that the food items Norwegian Gyrs delivered to the nest were mainly breast muscles. The number of sternum bones outnumbered the number of wings by 4 to 1, and the number of legs by 10 to 1. No heads were found on the nest ledges in his study. His studies indicated that the Gyrfalcons normally remove head, legs and intestines before bringing the rest of the prey to the nest. Suetens and Groenendael (1976) reported that Icelandic Gyrs also often removed the heads of Ptarmigan before delivering the prey to the nest, and parts of skulls and beaks were discovered in adult pellets.

Poole and Boag (1988) observed that the mean weight of prey delivered to the nest by male Gyrfalcons was 250g, and was significantly lower than the 330g supplied by females (P = 0.036). The lower mean prey weight of the males reflected the higher proportion (85%) of passerines taken. Males supplied most (95%) of the Ptarmigan taken. Harvesting of Arctic Ground Squirrels (*Citellus* spp.)was divided about equally between the sexes (27% by males and 23% by females). Ptarmigan were brought to the nest eviscerated, always decapitated, and with most of the body feathers removed. Squirrels were decapitated on most occasions, but were not plucked (*i.e.* skinned: the reference material uses 'plucked' to describe the removal of feathers from bird prey and skin from mammal prey). When fed to nestlings, squirrels were eaten from the neck downwards, with the stomach and intestines pulled out and left on the nest. Passerines and microtines were usually eaten without pre-processing, except for occasional plucking of primaries or fur at the nest.

Langvatn (1977) studied the relative occurrences of remnants of prey in Gyr sites in central Norway. According to his results, it is the humerus which is left at the nest sites in most cases (28.3%), together with the sternum and other bones, followed by sternum alone (19%) or with other attached bones (4.1%). The number of other bones was significantly smaller. Most of the feathers of the prey were found at the plucking places near the nests. Small numbers of feathers were found attached to the legs or distal parts of the prey's wing skeleton.

Dementiev and Gortchakovskaya (1945) noted that in Gyrfalcon pellets the skulls had usually had the roof crushed and the brain eaten. The pellets sometimes contained beaks of prey. Wayre and Jolly (1958) wrote that the Gyrfalcons of their study brought mostly cock Ptarmigan to the nest, usually headless, but unplucked and otherwise intact. However on one occasion a male Gyr brought part of a Ptarmigan (leg and thigh), a well-plucked and headless Ptarmigan on another occasion, and an eviscerated, headless cock Ptarmigan on a third occasion.

It has been suggested that both Ravens and Gyrfalcons pluck their prey, but that only Gyrfalcons pluck the primaries. However, Woodin (1980) examined approximately 250 Gyrfalcon kills and only one had not had at least one primary plucked. The number of primaries plucked varied from one or two to almost all. Woodin (1980) also noted some characteristics of Gyr kills. Firstly the head is almost always eaten by the adult at the capture site. The head is apparently bitten off from the back, the mandibles often being found, sometimes with portions of the frontal skull attached. Secondly, the intestines and sometimes the gizzard are removed and discarded. Finally, the Gyr does a neat job – the breast is cleanly stripped of flesh, as, usually, are the legs and wings. The keel of smaller prey may have large bites taken out or be eaten completely.

Woodin (1980) also states that Gyrfalcons remove the remains from the nest vicinity. Diet observations in most cases can be skewed by this fact. However, such removal is highly irregular. In some nests it becomes more frequent after hatching. Some remains were dropped within 100m from the eyrie, but some remains were carried much further away.

In the video study of Booms and Fuller (2003b) Gyrfalcons plucked 96% (207 birds) of the Ptarmigan delivered to the nest sites. By contrast, passerine prey was rarely plucked (<1%). The Gyrfalcons did not pluck most of the captured Arctic Hare leverets (86%, or 122), typically delivering the leverets in pieces. The most common piece was the back half of the hare, a section consisting of lumbar vertebrae, the pelvis and hind legs. Only small leverets were delivered whole, some of these being decapitated. One-third of the Ptarmigan were delivered either partially eaten or dismembered.

In Alaska, White and Springer (1965) observed a male Gyr dropping a food item (a bird) to the ground near the nest. The female Gyr then flew from the nest to the item, and plucked and ate it *in situ*.

DIET: EUROPEAN STUDIES

Hagen (1952a, 1952b, Hagen and Barth 1952) studied the diet of Gyrfalcons in Dovrefjell, Norway. He analysed a total of 214 prey remains and 46 pellets from the breeding territory of a pair of Gyrs he monitored for a number of years. Although Hagen notes that there may be some minor inaccuracy in the diet composition for Gyrs as some of the prey remains he picked up might have been left by Rough-legged Buzzard, the general conclusions of the study are almost certainly correct. The Gyrfalcons of Dovrefjell are *Lagopus* specialists, the proportion of Willow Grouse/Ptarmigan in the diet reaching 96%. The fraction of small rodents in the diet was correspondingly small, despite the study years being relatively high in rodent numbers. The average dimensions of the pellets studied were 61 x 23mm, with length varying from 42mm to 101mm, and diameter from 17mm to 34mm (Hagen 1952a,b, Hagen and Barth 1952).

In the study of Langvatn and Moksnes (1979) in central Norway (Langvatn 1977 refers to the same data subset) a total of 468 prey remains were collected. Willow Grouse and Ptarmigan accounted for 84% (88% in Langvatn 1977) of individual prey numbers, or 91.9% by weight. Apart from two chicks, all the *Lagopus* individuals were adults. Other birds in the diet were pigeons, Hooded Crows (*Corvus corone corvix*) and small passerines. Small rodents comprised 2.3% of the diet, with the Root Vole (*Microtus oeconomus*) predominating. Among the prey species noted in this study were Curlew (*Numenius arquata*) and Woodcock (*Scolopax rusticola*), two unusual species for Gyrs, all the more curious as their breeding grounds were distant from the study eyries.

Huhtala *et al.* (1996) studied the diet of Gyrfalcons in northern Finland. Their study indicated that the Gyrs fed almost exclusively on birds, which accounted for 98–100% of the biomass. Ptarmigan and Willow Grouse were the main prey, constituting 63–86% of the total biomass. In the south-eastern forests of Finland the diet was more diverse, the proportion of *Lagopus* species being lower at 41–71%. Large tetraonids and waders were the main alternative prey in these forests, these groups constituting 10–20% and 6–24% of the biomass respectively.

Mikkola and Sulkava (1972) studied the diet of 10 pairs of Gyrfalcon in northern Finland. In their study the diet consisted of 71.5% *Lagopus* grouse, with another 8.5% consisting of Norway Lemming. Pulliainen (1975) collected food items from an eyrie in Finnish Lapland, two-thirds of the prey species being Willow

Grouse, the most abundant tetraonid in the surrounding area. In the nearby Lapland Reserve in the southern Kola region of Russia, the Gyr diet was studied by Semenov-Tyan-Shanskiy (1959, Semenov-Tyan-Shanskiy and Gilyazov 1991). In these studies the Gyrs also mostly consumed Willow Grouse, though other tetraonids played an important role, together with small rodents.

The diet of Gyrfalcons in the European part of Russia has been described by Voronin (1987), who studied birds from the Bolshaya Rogovaya River basin. Voronin notes finding the remains of six species of birds and four species of mammals, the major part of the diet being Willow Grouse. This is perhaps not a surprise when Voronin states that in the region where the Gyrs were breeding there were noticeable Willow Grouse movements from forest-tundra to the north. During the period from 3 to 22 April 1983 he registered 67 flocks of grouse totalling 3,000 individuals. Interestingly, Voronin noted that the Gyrs preferentially took male birds, influencing the sex ratio of the adult grouse. At the end of breeding season the diversity of prey in the diet increased, with waders and ducks being included, though Willow Grouse still dominated the diet. There were few or no small rodents in the diet, though this is likely to have been because the years of the study period corresponded to a time of very low population density of small mammals.

Kishinskiy (1958) collected a total of 493 prey remains and 317 pellets containing fragments of 702 individual prey animals from three active nests in Russia's Kola Peninsula. The samples he gathered showed an incredible variation of diet. The mammals varied in size from shrew to hare, the birds from pipits and redpolls to Black-throated Divers (*Gavia arctica*). Despite this, Willow Grouse and Ptarmigan (Kishinskiy did not distinguish between the two species as some skeletal elements of the two are very similar) dominated the diet. Mammal prey was chiefly rodents, mostly Norway Lemming. At one nest on the Muchka River there was a large proportion of lemming in the diet, but Kishinskiy also noted a number of dead lemming in the river, indicating a lemming population peak. One interesting feature of the study was that lemmings and voles were found almost exclusively at coastal nests, with inland nest sites having a much lower proportion of the rodents. Apart from rodents the coastal Gyrs consumed a lot of Kittiwakes, but only in June and July. However, despite the relatively high proportion of rodents, Kishinskiy noted that no breeding was recorded at coastal sites if no grouse or Kittiwakes were breeding. In spring, grouse was the main diet as in the inland nests, although there was a significant variation in the proportions of grouse and small rodents in the diet of different birds.

On Kharlov Island (Seven Islands Nature Reserve) off the Kola coast close to Murmansk, the Gyrfalcon diet was studied by Dementiev and Gortchakovskaya (1945). The island is well-known for its seabird colonies, and for 'lemming years' – sharp peaks in the population of Norway Lemmings. However, there are very few Willow Grouse or Ptarmigan. The diet consisted mostly of seabirds and lemming, but also included grouse, suggesting that the Gyrs were willing to fly to the centre of the island in order to include them in their menu. The length of the pellets studied varied from 30mm to 70mm, with an average of 50mm.

DIET: ASIAN STUDIES

In his study of Gyrfalcons in the Koryak Mountains Kishinskiy (1980) noted that their diet comprised almost exclusively of grouse and Arctic Ground Squirrel. Interestingly he noted that wolves would often come to pick up the remains of squirrels from beneath the perches of the falcons.

On Yamal (Danilov *et al.* 1984) the Gyrfalcons were observed to prey on Root Voles and Northern Water Voles (*Arvicola terrestris*) as well as on Willow Grouse. Kalyakin (1989), who also studied the diet of Gyrfalcons on Yamal, confirmed that Northern Water Voles formed part of the diet of local Gyrs, but underlined that the majority of the prey items in samples (up to 80.5%) were Willow Grouse. Kalyakin concluded from his studies that during the spring Willow Grouse is the main, and occasionally even the only, prey of the Gyrfalcon. However the proportion of Willow Grouse in the diet decreases with the arrival of migratory birds, this decrease being maintained until the migrants depart.

In northern Yakutia, at a cliff nest at the Saskylakh River, Vorobiev (1963) found 150 remains of the Siberian Lemming (*Lemmus sibiricus*), together with those of Willow Grouse and Naumann's Thrush (*Turdus naumanni naumanni*). During the winter the Gyrs feed almost exclusively on Willow Grouse, sometimes taking the prey from the snares set by local hunters (van Orden and Paklina 2000). Gladkov and Zaletaev (1962) reported Willow Grouse and Naumann's Thrush in the diet of a pair at the Anabar River, western Yakutia. Some 140 mummified lemmings and bird remains were found nearby. Some 150 mummified Siberian Lemmings were found under the nest.

In the Lower Kolyma (Potapov, unpublished data), the diet of Gyrfalcons (at seven study nests) consisted primarily of Willow Grouse (71%). It was also noted that grey or white/grey mixed pairs of Gyrs had a diet dominated by grouse, while that of pure white Gyrs (with white, spotless tails) was dominated by ducks, followed by waders. However, the white Gyr nest was located in the area away from areas of high grouse population, explaining the difference. In the Commander Islands wintering Gyrs were noted feeding on Red-backed Voles (*Clethrionomys rutilus*) and rats (*Rattus* spp.), as well as ducks and Ptarmigan (Marakov 1965).

Dorogoi (1991) found that Gyrfalcons in north-east Chukotka fed on Arctic Ground Squirrel (79%), Willow Grouse (4%), Long-tailed Duck (*Clangula hyemalis*) (4.2%), Mongolian Plover (*Charadrius mongolus*) (4%) and Pacific Golden Plover (*Pluvialis fulva*) (8%).

DIET: NORTH AMERICAN STUDIES

The winter diet of three female Gyrfalcons was studied by Dobler (1989) in Washington state, USA. The Gyrs were all taking Rock Doves (*Columba livia*), but one bird showed a preference for waterfowl, with American Wigeon (*Anas americana*) and Mallard (*Anas platyrhynchos*) dominating her diet. Another of the three also took some Grey Partridge (*Perdix perdix*), while the third bird specialised on Pheasants, but also took other birds, including raptors – American Kestrels and even a Prairie Falcon. The Gyrs also made successful piracy raids, attacking Red-tailed (*Buteo jamaicensis*) and Rough-legged Hawks (*B. lagopus*) as well as Bald Eagles (*Haliaeetus leucocephalus*).

Dissection of four digestive tracts of Gyrfalcons taken in the Bering Islands in winter contained Red-backed Voles (an introduced species) and a gull (Stejneger 1885, in Palmer 1988). Rats were mentioned as having been found in the stomachs of Gyrs taken at Amchitka Island in the Aleutians (Kenyon, in Palmer 1988), while on the Pribilof Islands the stomachs held rosy finches and Snow Bunting (*Plectrophenax nivalis*) (Palmer 1988). Summer studies of mammal species in Gyr stomachs on mainland Alaska, on the Seward Peninsula, included Arctic Ground Squirrels, Red-backed Voles and Collared Lemmings (*Dicrostonyx* sp.), with bird species including Brent Goose (*Branta bernicla*), redpolls and Short-eared Owl (*Asio flammeus*), as well as *Lagopus*, waterfowl, shorebirds and seabirds. The bird total was dominated by *Lagopus* (876), but there were also 155 Long-tailed Skuas (*Stercorarius longicaudus*), 30 American Golden Plovers and 12 Short-eared Owls (Rosenau 1972, in Palmer 1988).

Muir and Bird (1984) studied the diet of Gyrfalcons on Ellesmere Island in Arctic Canada. They collected and examined 606 pellets as well as observing 72 prey deliveries to the nest at one site. In order to minimise their impact on brood survival Muir and Bird provided food supplements to the young Gyrs (but naturally they did not include these in the diet analysis). Their study revealed that Arctic Hare (given as *Lepus timidus* in the reference) dominated the diet followed by Red Knot (*Calidris canutus*) and Ruddy Turnstone (*Arenaria interpres*). At one nest they observed a female Gyr bringing not only young Arctic Hares, but the hind quarters of larger, adult, hares to the nest. The female was in each case working very hard to carry her heavy load. On one occasion, the authors noted, after delivering the prey the female stood for nearly a minute with drooping wings and a half-opened beak, panting and evidently fatigued. These heavy loads were an exception, as usually even young hares were brought to the nest only as partial carcasses.

Poole and Boag (1988) studied the diet of Gyrfalcons in the Kilgavik area of the central Canadian Arctic. They found that the major prey species was Ptarmigan (with only two Willow Grouse being found) followed by Arctic Ground Squirrel and Arctic Hare. As the authors wrote, Gyrfalcons have to cope not only with fluctuations in their food base during their lengthy breeding season, but also with year-to-year changes in the relative abundance of particular prey. In this study area Ptarmigan migrate from the south-west in large flocks (up to 200 birds), usually between 5 and 10 May, and disperse into their territories within 14 days of arrival. Migration and territoriality appeared to be weather-dependent: both events were delayed by cold, snowy weather. These Ptarmigan formed the major avian proportion of the Gyr diet, virtually all the remains being of adult birds (99.2%). Simplicity in the spring–summer diet of the Gyrfalcons was evident: only three species (Ptarmigan, Arctic Ground Squirrel and Arctic Hare) comprised 81.8% of all prey taken and 96.5% of total prey biomass. In total, 11 species of birds and five species of mammals were identified among the prey.

The study noted that the Gyr diet differed significantly between the two observation years. Ptarmigan represented a smaller proportion of the kills made in July 1985 than they did in July 1986, although in both years the proportion of Ptarmigan in the diet decreased from May to August. In 1985 juvenile squirrels were taken immediately after they emerged, contributing 32% of the total prey biomass in July. There were no adult squirrels in prey remains in 1985. There were no observed differences in Gyr preferences for either male or female Ptarmigan, based on an analysis of the length of humeri in the prey remains: the humeri of male and female Ptarmigan differ in length, although there is a degree of overlap. Only adult Ptarmigan are available as prey for Gyrfalcons during incubation, the hatching of young Gyrs being timed to coincide with the appearance of Arctic Hare leverets and young Arctic Ground Squirrels, as well as with the summer-plumage moult in Ptarmigan males. Female Ptarmigan moult into cryptic plumage almost a month earlier.

Cade (1955b) found that Willow Grouse and Ptarmigan as well as Arctic Ground Squirrel dominate in the diet of Gyrfalcons in Alaska. Also in Alaska, White and Springer (1965) found only Ptarmigan in the diet of the Gyrs prior to brood hatching. Later, other birds such as passerines and waders were added to the diet. White and Cade (1971) reported grouse (mainly Willow Grouse) as a dominant food of Gyrfalcons at the Colville River. Amongst other species Arctic Ground Squirrel, rodents (including Root Voles) and Short-eared Owl were also noted. The proportion of rodents in the diet in the years 1967–69 was up to 48% of bird and mammal food items, excluding Ptarmigan.

Cotter *et al.* (1992) studied the diet of Gyrfalcons, together with other species, in the central Canadian Arctic during a time of decline in Ptarmigan numbers. Despite the decline the diet was still dominated by Ptarmigan. Kuyt (1980) reported the following items in the diet of Gyrfalcons in Canada's Northwest Territories: *Lagopus* grouse, Short-eared Owl, Northern Pintail (*Anas acuta*), Long-tailed Duck, Hudsonian Godwit (*Limosa haemastica*), Savannah Sparrow (*Passerculus sandwichensis*), American Tree Sparrow (*Spizella arborea*), Arctic Hare, Stoat (*Mustela erminea*) and Arctic Ground Squirrel. Poole (1987) showed that the three prey species Ptarmigan, Arctic Ground Squirrel and Arctic Hare accounted for 96.5% of the total prey biomass identified. After 1 July the proportion of squirrels increased; before 1 July Ptarmigan and hares accounted for 98.2% of total biomass identified. As predicted by optimal foraging theory, larger prey items, on average, were brought to the nest as foraging time away from the nest increased.

DIET: ICELAND AND GREENLAND

In the study of Suetens and Groenendael (1976) the diet of Gyrfalcon in Iceland at two nest sites consisted of 90.4% Ptarmigan, 3.8% ducks, 3.8% Golden Plover (*Pluvialis apricaria*) and 1.9% Black-headed Gull (*Larus ridibundus*).

In Iceland Woodin (1980) found that the diet prior to mid-June consisted exclusively of Ptarmigan. In the second half of June the diet was supplemented by ducks. In Iceland, cock Ptarmigan begin to set up breeding territories in April, and for the next two months the Gyrs depended heavily on the males. Then, in June, when the Ptarmigan egg clutches are complete, the cock birds acquire their summer plumage and become much less territorial. Consequently they are less conspicuous. The cocks do continue to display, but mostly at twilight and only into July. For the Gyrfalcons this change of behaviour of the Ptarmigan cocks comes at a pivotal time – one or two weeks after the young Gyrs have hatched, when the requirement for food is at a maximum. At this time there is a marked shift in the diet of the Gyrs. Cade (1960) reported a similar shift to rodents in the middle of June at the Colville River, Alaska.

Icelandic Gyrfalcons may bring small prey (5–350g) from lakes at a distance of 10km from their nest, whereas larger prey from the same lake (over 700g, such as adult ducks and large goslings) were brought up to 22km (Cade *et al.* 1998). Gyrfalcons living in lava fields to the east and north of Myvatn prefer to fly 15–22km to areas of high concentrations of pre-migratory or wintering flocks of waterfowl (Nielsen and Cade 1990b). Puffin (*Fratercula arctica*) remains were found in the nests of Gyrfalcons in north-east Iceland that were 33km from the sea and 57km from the nearest Puffin colony (Cade *et al.* 1998).

In Iceland the diet of the Gyrfalcon was studied in detail by Nielsen (Nielsen 1986, 1999a, Nielsen and Cade 1990b) and by his predecessor Bengtson (1971). From their work it seems that Icelandic Gyrfalcons feed almost exclusively on Ptarmigan during courtship and the early nesting period regardless of the availability of alternative prey. In his study, Bengtson (1971) collected 556 food items over a two-year period from sites close to the Myvatn area, and inland in an area high in Ptarmigan numbers. In all cases the proximity of the lake made it possible for the Gyrs to hunt ducks and other waterfowl, but despite that Ptarmigan again dominated the diet, though in this case waterbirds replaced Wood Mice (*Apodemus sylvaticus*) as a secondary prey. Nielsen's study (1986, 1999a,

Nielsen and Cade 1990b) was carried out in the same area of Iceland. The data were collected between 1981 and 1997, and the sample size was an impressive 28,034 prey items, the largest study of Gyr diet to our knowledge. The results show that again Ptarmigan dominated the diet of the Gyrfalcons in all years (1981–97), averaging 72% of the biomass. Other important groups were waterfowl (19.5% of biomass), alcids (3.8% of biomass) and waders (2.9% of biomass). There was a large difference in diet between coastal nests and the ones located inland (on heathland). On heathland territories Ptarmigan accounted for between 60% and 100% of all prey remains collected, whereas samples from the coastal and lakeland territories contained 8–85% and 13–91% Ptarmigan respectively. These studies (Nielsen 1999a) reveal that the juveniles represent only 0.5% of the Ptarmigan share of the diet.

Changing from Ptarmigan to alternative prey species involved, in most cases, a change of hunting habitat from upland areas to wetland and coastal areas. During the non-breeding season the Gyrfalcons fed on the prey available in their habitat: Ptarmigan and sometimes waders on heathland, waterfowl and Wood Mice in lakeland areas, and waterfowl and waders in coastal territories. Wood Mice, a species brought to Iceland by settlers from Scandinavia, were present in the diets of Gyrfalcons in all habitats in small numbers (up to 5%), but in some years in lakeland areas the role of the mice was somewhat higher (17%). The spring catch of Ptarmigan consisted mostly of male birds.

Summers and Green (1974) and Fletcher and Webby (1977) collected information on the diet of Gyrfalcons in north-east Greenland (*c.* 72°N), their studies noting the preponderance of Snow Bunting, Arctic Hare and Collared Lemming as prey. Their studies also noted that Gyrfalcons could breed in Greenland in years when the lemming population was low. Amongst other prey a Barnacle gosling (*Branta leucopsis*) and Arctic Hare were noted.

Booms and Fuller (2003a, 2003b, 2003c) studied the Gyrfalcon diet in an area near Kangerlussuaq in west Greenland using time-lapse video cameras. They covered four Gyr nests over two seasons of observations and managed to record an impressive 921 food item deliveries of 832 items, identifying 793 items (93%) to order, and 450 (54%) to species. According to their study, the local Gyr diet consisted of Ptarmigan (24%), Lapland Bunting (*Calcarius lapponicus*) and unidentified passerine birds (13% and 24% respectively), together with Arctic Hare (15%) and 'small birds' (17%).

UNUSUAL PREY AND EVIDENCE OF SELECTIVE PRESSURE

Hagen (1952a) mentioned a Gyr pellet recovered in Alvdal, Norway in February which included the feathers of a female Capercaillie (*Tetrao urogallus*). A young Capercaillie was reported as a food item in an October study at a Yenisey River site

(Yudin 1952): a young bird is clearly a much easier target for a Gyr than an adult bird. A Gyr eating a Capercaillie was reported in the Mari Republic, in the central European part of Russia (Baldaev 1983). In Finnmark, besides *Lagopus* grouse, the remains of Whimbrel (*Numenius phaeopus*) and Pintail have been reported. In Sweden the feathers of Snowy Owl have been found in Gyr nests (Rosenius, after Holmbom, in Hagen 1952a). Semenov-Tyan-Shanskiy and Gilyazov (1991) mention both Tengmalm's (*Aegolius funereus*) and Pygmy Owls (*Glaucidium passerinum*) in the diet of a pair of Gyrfalcons breeding in the woods of the Lapland Reserve. Nielsen and Cade (1990b) mentioned geese and Common Eider (*Somateria mollissima*) amongst the prey items of Icelandic Gyrfalcons. Perhaps the strangest prey items of all are fish. Fish were reported in a Gyr nest during a study by Todd (1963), and a Brown Trout (*Salmo trutta*) was found amongst prey remains at a nest site in northern Iceland (Nielsen 1999a).

Dementiev and Gortchakovskaya (1945) noted that Gyrfalcon pellets sometimes contain remains of such prey species as Cod (*Gadus morhua*) and small mollusc fragments (e.g. mussels – *Mytilus edulis*), as well as leaves, crowberries and cloudberries, and, most remarkably, pebbles and sand.

Fish were also reported at a nest site by Todd (1963, p. 239) and a dead Cod was seen being consumed by a group of five Gyrfalcons at the surf-line in north-east Iceland (Stevens 1953, pp.199, 204). Fish is apparently not a bad food for a Gyr: Cade (1953) mentioned that one Gyrfalcon chick taken from a nest at Nuxapaga River, Alaska was initially fed entirely on fish – Grayling (*Thymallus arcticus*) and Pike (*Esox* sp.). Later, the bird refused the diet and was fed on ground squirrels.

As regards the maximum weight of prey, Gyrfalcons can take young Arctic Foxes, Snowy Owls and even swans (Glutz von Blotzheim *et al.* 1971). Semenov-Tyan-Shanskiy and Gilyazov (1991) observed a Gyrfalcon kill and eat an adult male Capercaillie with an estimated weight of 4,000g. Pulliainen (1975) showed that a Gyrfalcon could carry a load of 1,800g (Arctic Hare or a female Capercaillie) and could hunt considerably larger animals. In the study of Booms and Fuller (2003a) the weight of Arctic Hare items delivered to the nest sites varied from 325g to 1,765g, with an average of 890g.

It is not uncommon for Gyrfalcons to feed on carrion, especially in winter. Usually this consists of dead Reindeer (*Rangifer tarandus*), snared grouse or trapped Arctic Foxes. Eating trapped animals usually leads to conflict with local trappers (see Chapter 11). Carrion eating by Gyrfalcons has been summarised by Tømmeraas (1989b). He reported 34 instances of Gyrfalcons taking carrion, these incidents spread more or less evenly across the year. He noted, however, that juveniles were most commonly seen at carrion at the end of the summer and in autumn. Notorious examples of carrion eating include the theft of eyes from the heads of slaughtered sheep put out for drying in Iceland, the consumption of offal, and the eating the strychnine-loaded carcass of Reindeer, causing the Gyr to succumb to the poison. Beebe and Webster (1994, p.203) note that a Gyrfalcon was seen on the carcass of a Polar Bear (*Ursus maritimus*), together with Ravens. Gyrfalcons may sometimes visit built-up areas, especially in autumn and winter. In these areas they can be seen chasing pigeons and even attacking domestic fowl (Tømmeraas 1988). Tømmeraas reported 81 attacks on fowl, 67 of which were successful. More than half of the attacks were recorded in Britain and Norway, with the largest percentage against chickens. Chickens were killed in 42 out of 45 attacks on them. Other attacked species included doves (19%), pheasants (14%), domestic ducks (5%), domestic geese (2%), turkeys (1%) and rabbits (1%).

In fact, the visit of a Gyrfalcon to Uppsala, Sweden on 4 February 1698 led to the first documented scientific name of the species – the disputed scientific name *Falco lanarius* (Linnaeus 1758) – as the incident was painted by Olof Rüdbeck, the date and place being given on the work. Attacks by Gyrs on domestic fowls are not limited to Europe. An incident of an attack on a chicken on 30 October 1961 was recorded at Novoakersandrovsk, Sakhalin (Nechaev 1991).

Kalyakin (1989), who studied the diet of Gyrfalcons on Yamal, considers that the Gyrfalcons might regulate populations of Willow Grouse, but also that the falcons preferentially select wounded individuals. Similar remarks have been made by Nielsen (pers. comm.), who frequently found Ptarmigan with abnormal bones in the prey remains of Gyrfalcons in north Iceland. In this respect the Gyrfalcon is, of course, acting in the same way as all other predators. Gyr activity also limits the spread of invasive species – harriers, crows, gulls and various owls – into the tundra.

SPECIES DIVERSITY

In spring Willow Grouse or Ptarmigan are usually the dominant Gyrfalcon prey. However, the diet becomes more diverse in summer as the falcons hunt those species which arrive after the annual migration. The Shannon-Weaver diversity index (H') calculated for one pair of Gyrfalcons from Salla in north-east Finland (Huhtala *et al.* 1996) varied from 0.49 to 0.90, and its variation was significant across the years. Huhtala *et al.* (1996) compared the diets of three Gyrfalcon pairs from northern Finland and found that the diets of birds from Salla and Inari, and from Salla and Enontekiö, differed significantly, whereas the differences between the diets of the Inari and Enontekiö birds were not significant. No correlation between the diversity index and the density of the main prey, Willow Grouse, was found. The proportion of Willow Grouse in the diet was at a maximum during the period before 15 June. In the Greenland study of Booms and Fuller (2003c) the H' diversity in the prey remains was calculated as 1.28.

On the Bolshezhemelskaya tundra of north-east European Russia, Voronin (1983) noted that in April the proportions of male and female Willow Grouse in the Gyr diet were 54.5% and 45.5% respectively. However, in June–July

Gyrs preferentially took male birds (96.6%), with the more cryptic females making up only 3.4% of kills. Naturally, this significantly affects the sex ratio of the adult grouse. At the end of the breeding season the diversity of prey in the Gyr diet increased, with waders and ducks being included, though Willow Grouse still dominated the diet.

Nielsen (1999a) found that species diversity in the diet of Gyrfalcons in Iceland showed a statistically significant decline compared to the spring Ptarmigan population. This means that if Ptarmigan numbers are high, there is no need for a Gyr to spend time and effort hunting other species. In years of low Ptarmigan density the diet becomes more diverse as the Gyrfalcons switch to other species, mostly waders and ducks.

HUNTING BEHAVIOUR

In general it seems that Gyrfalcons do not hunt in the vicinity of their nests during the breeding season. They instead prefer to hunt at a moderate distance. In studies from a helicopter close to the Dempster Highway in Canada's Yukon Territory, White and Nelson (1991) observed no hunting attacks in the immediate vicinity of the eyrie by either of a pair of Gyrfalcons. Both birds tended to hunt after observation from commanding perches on rocks or high ridges, but never on the eyrie cliff. The female often spent time hunting in a similar way to a harrier, flapping and then gliding slowly along an erratic path 2–20m above the tundra and fine gravel ridges. This behaviour may have been specific to the hunting of Arctic Ground Squirrels: White and Nelson observed one squirrel kill, with the female catching the rodent on a clear patch of earth then gliding a short distance further before swinging back along the ridge to the eyrie with the freshly caught prey. In general the female hunted within 3.2km of the nest, with the longest hunting flight lasting 63 minutes. The male bird also made both short and long hunting sorties, the longest hunt being 67 minutes. In Alaska Gyrs have been observed to travel much further distances while hunting. White and Cade (1971) report distances of 12–15km from the eyrie, the male travelling further than the female as judged by her briefer absences from the nest site.

The observations of White and Nelson are supported by those of Kishinskiy (1958) who, during observations of three breeding pairs on the Kola Peninsula of north-west Russia, saw no hunts near the nest sites. However, such observations have been disputed by some observers. Jenkins (1978) noted that four Ptarmigan were actually killed near an eyrie, although he also noted that it was possible the birds had been killed before nesting began. He also reported an unsuccessful chase by a male near the same eyrie and three hunts which took place within 1.6km of the nest site. Woodin (1980) also reported Gyrfalcons hunting in the area of the eyrie. These observations seem to undermine the idea that there is a 'safe' zone for quarry around the nest (proposed by Dementiev 1960): however, contrary observations seem to relate specifically to the pre-egg laying period, so Dementiev's hypothesis may apply once incubation has begun.

In addition, on Bylot Island off northern Baffin Island one of the authors (Sale) saw a male Gyr, which had been watching over the brooding female from a high perch, attack a Lesser Snow Goose (*Anser caerulescens*) just in front of the nest. It was an opportunistic attack: the goose evaded the first dive, but was hit on the second dive and fell into an open water lead in the sea ice. The Gyr could not feed on the goose or return to the nest with it.

HUNTING TECHNIQUES

While following Gyrs in a helicopter White and Nelson (1991) reported ridge gliding, usually seen only on days with sufficient wind and particularly favoured by the female. With just a few wingbeats she would glide at a height of 3–8m along, and then back over, the windward side of a long high ridge. In the mountains the male bird usually travelled close to low peaks, crossing high over intervening valleys. Several times the male ridge-hopped (crossing very low over a ridge) so that he would appear suddenly above an expanse of tundra in which unsuspecting prey might be spotted. The male also used a forest-slalom hunting method in which, from various heights, he would make a rapid shallow swoop which ended with a twisting race for 50m (and occasionally much more) among the tops, but also the mid-height areas of the scattered spruce trees on the slopes of the tundra plain.

Suetens and Groenendael (1976) reported a harrier-like hunting pattern, with observation from a boulder followed by a fast flight at a low altitude. In their case the prey was Ptarmigan. Jenkins (1978) observed hunting Gyrs using orographic lifts (upcurrents of air which are deflected by hills and cliffs: this technique is also known as slope soaring). Poole and Boag (1988) noted a trend for larger prey to be brought if the hunt time was longer, despite a considerable variation in time within each prey class. All passerines and microtines were brought to the nest after an absence of 90 minutes or less, whereas in 19% of cases when Arctic Ground Squirrels and Ptarmigan were taken, the hunt time exceeded 90 minutes. The relationship between prey size and hunt time was highly significant, but only explained a small proportion of the total variance, implying that other factors were also operative.

Platt (1976) observed wintering Gyrfalcons from a helicopter in Canada's Yukon Territory. On one occasion he saw a Gyrfalcon flying slowly around scattered willow bushes, almost hovering above each bush. Willow Grouse was the most abundant bird in the observation area with a density in willow plots in February reaching 40–571 individuals per hectare. Ptarmigan were also seen in flocks averaging 60 individuals, with a range of 14–400 individuals. Platt (1977) reported that in winter the Gyrfalcons chose Willow Grouse, no evidence of Ptarmigan being found in Gyrfalcon food remains.

Hunting methods were also studied in Iceland by Bengtson (1971). In this case hunts often started from a perch on top of a rock or on a telegraph pole. The Gyr flew about 2m or less above the ground, the bird's speed varying according to the terrain: it could be 'very fast'. Occasionally Gyrs were seen soaring at a considerable height, and also hovering (a very unusual observation). Gyrfalcons were also seen flying over water on many occasions, and even over potential prey (ducklings), but were only once seen attacking in such circumstances: a Gyr attacked a merganser, which dived in response to each of the three quick-succession attacks and escaped. Bengtson (1971) did not observe any prey strike at a height greater than 2m above the ground. Many of the attempted prey observed in this study were waders, mainly young Redshank (*Tringa totanus*). To attack them the falcon increased speed while several hundred metres away. Then, just before reaching the prey, the Gyr gained height in readiness to stoop. However, in all observed cases the waders were too alert for the falcon and flew off, calling loudly. The Gyrs were more successful when attacking Ptarmigan. Attacks on three male Ptarmigan were observed: each time the prey was perched on a lava outcrop. One Ptarmigan was killed instantly, whereas in the two other cases the prey saw the falcon early enough to take off and head for cover of nearby scrub. In one of these attacks the falcon pursued the prey, and, after a short chase gained sufficient height for a stoop: the Ptarmigan was knocked down and taken. In the other case the falcon gave up the attack. On another occasion Bengtson saw a Gyr take a Black-headed Gull which was sitting on top of a lava outcrop. The gull was struck less than one metre above the ground.

As well as quartering flights (*i.e.* flights at a substantial angle to the wind) Gyrfalcons also use dive hunting. Tucker *et al.* (1998) and Tucker (1999) used an optical device to record the three-dimensional paths of 11 dives of a 1,020g-male Gyrfalcon named *Kumpan*, which had been trained as a falconry bird. The dives started at altitudes of up to 500m and inclined at angles of 17–63° from the horizontal. Rather than simply falling from the sky, the bird controlled its speed during the dives, which had three distinct phases. During the first (acceleration) phase, the falcon accelerated to speeds of 47–58m/s (169–208km/hr), as measured in the eight fastest dives. The bird adjusted its profile to minimise drag as the accelerations were close to those theoretically predicted.

The falcon then began a second (constant-speed) phase, increased drag by a factor of 1.3–4.8, while at an altitude of 100–350m. The falcon increased the drag of the wings without increasing lift by keeping the wings in a cupped position while diving (Tucker 1998) allowing speed to be regulated. The constant-speed phase lasted no more than a few seconds and the falcon then began a deceleration phase by further increasing its drag, this time by factors of 1.7–2.3 and so decelerating, with a mean value of *c.* 0.95g (g = gravitational acceleration). During all three phases, the dive angle was almost constant, though it increased during the deceleration phase, and the falcon made no changes to its body shape that could be observed through the tracking device telescope, except to reduce its wingspan as it accelerated. However, the falconer, who was close to the bird at the end of the dive, could see that during the deceleration phase it held its wings in a cupped position, apparently with a high angle of attack and therefore high drag. At the end of the deceleration phase, the falcon dropped its legs, spread its toes and, finally, spread its wings as it approached the falconer.

Although the speeds reported here are the fastest ever measured with known accuracy in animals, the falcon could theoretically have reached more than 72m/s (259km/hr) if it had continued to accelerate with minimum drag until close to the ground. It could pull out of such a dive with an additional vertical drop of 14m (Tucker 1998, 1999) so that even at this very high speed the bird would have had enough altitude to pull out of the dive before crashing into the ground. Several authors have estimated that a diving 'ideal' falcon could reach speeds of more than 70m/s (252km/hr). Wild falcons may reach such speeds when they make long, steep dives on birds flying high in the air. The fastest falcon in the wild was believed to be the Peregrine, which may have reached a speed in excess of 300km/hr in a dive (Cade 1982, Tennesen 1992, Tucker 1998). However, surprisingly, there have been no other accurate measurements of the speeds of the larger falcons except the studies of Alerstam (1987), Tucker (1998, 1999), Peter and Kestenholz (1998) and Tucker *et al.* (1998). Alerstam (1987) used radar to track wild Peregrines in three dives that started 374–1,022m above the ground, with dive angles of 25–64°. The fastest Peregrine reached speeds of up to 39m/s (140.4km/hr): therefore, the Gyrfalcon in the experiments of Tucker *et al.* (1998) is the fastest proven stooper. Clark (1995) also questions whether Peregrines can exceed a speed of 41m/s (147.6km/hr). In his work Clark re-evaluated the origin of the Peregrine myth: most of the speed values came from 1930s and came either from a 'second' party or were measured using inadequate equipment. However, radar was used in the measurements of Peregrine diving speeds (Peter and Kestenholtz 1998), with the top measured speed being 49.6m/s (182km/hr).

When Gyrfalcons are accelerating to top diving speed, the air pressure on the eye must be enormous. As the falcons do not have the human option of protecting their eyes with a pair of goggles, natural selection has delivered a solution: the eyes are turned *c.* 40° to the side of the head, as measured in the Peregrine. The consequence of this is that the falcons must turn their heads *c.* 40° to one side in order to see their prey with maximal acuity of the deep fovea of one eye while stooping. This turning of the head increases their drag by more than a factor of two (Tucker 2000a). Falcons resolve the conflict created by this by diving along a logarithmic spiral path with their head held straight ahead and one eye looking sideways at the prey, rather than following a straight path to the prey with their head turned sideways. The spiral path is longer than the straight one, but calculations predict that the falcon can reach the prey more quickly along the spiral trajectory because the speed advantage of the straight head more than compensates for a longer path (Tucker 2000b).

CHASING OR STOOPING?

Why does a falcon switch between quartering and stooping as a means of hunting? The reason lies in the structure of both the Gyr and its chief prey species, the aerodynamics of falcons and grouse having been studied by Pennycuick *et al.* (1994). They flew several birds of prey, trained in a traditional falconry manner, after Sage Grouse (*Centrocercus urophasianus*) in Idaho, USA. There were four Gyrfalcons in the falcon research flock. The 1994 paper notes that the falcon needs to be capable of prolonged aerobic flight, for hunting and chasing, and also for migration, and that this requirement places a lower limit on its wingspan. But the wings must be long enough for continuous horizontal flight to be economical, which in turn places an upper limit on the minimum power speed. High flapping flight speeds can then only be attained by flying at many times the minimum power speed. To achieve this combination, the flight muscles have to be capable of developing power over a wide range, which raises other problems. The falcon can therefore either overtake its prey by stooping, so converting potential energy into kinetic energy (*i.e.* trading height for speed) which cannot be maintained once height is lost, or it may rely on its capacity for prolonged aerobic flight at a lower speed to tire a bird which does not share this capability.

The grouse is most vulnerable to falcon attack in the first few seconds after take-off, while it is accelerating and has no room, and limited capacity, to manoeuvre. If it can dodge the falcon's initial attack, and accelerate to a speed faster than the falcon can maintain, it may evade further pursuit. The grouse has a speed advantage owing to its very large flight muscles and short wings relative to its body mass (the weight of an adult Sage Grouse is 2,010–3,266g in males and 1,142–1,754g in females.) Once the grouse is ahead of the falcon, it easily outdistances it in level flight, and, indeed, soon changes from continuous flapping to flap-gliding, landing again once it is well clear of its pursuer. But Cade (1982) describes prolonged chases as a typical behaviour of wild Gyrfalcons, and falconers say that Gyrfalcons and large hybrid falcons will sometimes pursue a Sage Grouse, eventually catching it after a chase lasting several kilometres. The explanation is that the falcon is capable of prolonged aerobic flight, while the grouse, although faster in level flight, is not. If the grouse is pursued for long enough, it is eventually forced to land, and the falcon can then strike it on the ground.

If the Gyr misses its prey on the first try, it often loses the advantage, at least momentarily, and is forced to pursue their prey in level flight, or to give up the chase altogether. One Gyrfalcon was observed missing three short stoops at a Rock

Ptarmigan during a 30-second downhill chase, then giving up when the Ptarmigan flew rapidly uphill again (White and Weeden 1966). On another occasion, again after three unsuccessful stoops, a Gyrfalcon landed and screamed loudly, apparently in frustration at losing the advantage and not wishing to be forced to pursue the prey in level flight.

White and Weeden (1966) observed 13 hunting chases of Ptarmigan and Willow Grouse by Gyrfalcons in a treeless area of Alaska. The authors divided the hunting methods of the falcons into three types: firstly by search from high above the ground, secondly by search in low flight, and thirdly by low flight together with observations from temporary perches. The birds used two or all three techniques in relatively quick succession. The authors observed Gyrfalcons flying 150–300m above the ground, the birds then often being hard to see, especially when against the sun. The falcon's progress across the tundra was by soaring in spirals, without gaining or losing much altitude, with bursts of flying in direct flap-and-glide flight for up to 1.6km between soaring periods. This flight pattern closely resembles that of Golden Eagles. Twice the authors saw a Gyrfalcon flying 6–18m above the ground, apparently hoping to surprise and flush the prey ahead of it. Their flight was direct and rapid in most of cases, although once a Gyrfalcon quartered back and forth until it flushed a family of Willow Grouse. A common tactic was for a Gyr to hunt low over one ridge top, passing directly across an intervening valley, and then hunting along the next crest (ridge-hopping, as mentioned above). The Gyrfalcons often landed on rocks, knolls, or small trees in the course of these low flights. At these times it was obvious to the authors that the bird was not merely resting, but was actually searching for prey. This method of hunting is one used frequently by accipiters. The resemblance was especially striking in mid-October 1963 at Eagle Summit, when Weeden observed a Goshawk and a Gyrfalcon hunting Ptarmigan in the same area on four successive days. Both raptors visited one brush-covered slope frequently because Ptarmigan often fed there, and several times Weeden had to look very closely to determine which raptor he was watching.

It was also clear that people walking across the tundra were frequently followed by Gyrfalcons. The authors describe how two Ptarmigan chicks were taken by a Gyr after being (accidentally) flushed by one of them. In both cases the falcon had apparently stooped from a fairly high position, struck and held the young Ptarmigan, and then continued with no detectable pause. An adult male Ptarmigan was struck in the air 100m from where it had been flushed just after a Gyrfalcon had landed in a nearby tree. The falcon began its flight from a point 15m higher than the Ptarmigan, overtook its prey rapidly and hit it from behind and slightly above. The Gyr then carried the Ptarmigan another 15m before landing on the snow with the dead bird in its talons. Similar reports of Gyrfalcons using humans as beaters were given by Palmer (1988). White (in White and Weeden 1966) saw an immature and adult Gyrfalcon coursing low over flat tundra, the young behind the adult. An American Golden Plover was flushed by the lead falcon and was taken (in a sideways grabbing motion) by the second. Both falcons continued in direct flight, then began to circle upward, flying toward distant bluffs. This suggests that the use of human beaters by falcons is not as remarkable as it might at first seem.

Winter hunting behaviour was observed by Garber *et al.* (1993) in Lander, Wyoming, and in Dillon, Montana. The attacks originated from fence posts and involved 'direct pursuit'. On one occasion a Gyrfalcon flew directly from a post to a strip of sagebrush and landed on the snow where it walked in small circles amongst the sagebrush for about a minute searching for prey. The bird was then disturbed by observers and returned to the post. About ten minutes later the Gyrfalcon flew back to the same area and flushed five Sage Grouse from a strip of short sagebrush, and repeatedly made shallow dives at them. It chased one of the grouse, and then a second, but ceased pursuit of both after minimal effort. Ten minutes later the Gyrfalcon flushed another Sage Grouse and chased it vigorously for about 275m until the grouse escaped into a strip of tall sagebrush. On another occasion, when an observer flushed a large flock of Sage Grouse, the Gyrfalcon immediately pursued the flock for about 350m, catching and killing one. Another pursuit of a lone Sage Grouse was observed (again after an observer flushed the prey). The Gyrfalcon quickly caught up with the grouse and, by approaching it from below and slightly ahead, cut if off from the cover into which it was attempting to escape. The falcon then climbed 5m quickly and caught the grouse.

Dekker and Lange (2001) observed 141 hunts by three female Gyrfalcons in Edmonton, Alberta, Canada. They reported details of the capture of 17 Mallard and 15 Rock Doves. In another study (Dekker and Court 2003) the authors reported 16 successful hunts (and four possibly successful) out of a total of 70 observed hunts, a success rate of 22.9% (with the addition of the probable kills this rises to 28.6%). The majority of the hunts in the study of 2003 were pursuits. In two instances they observed a Gyr which was reluctant to attack a duck that refused to flush. The Gyr repeatedly stooped on the duck, but did not grab it. After several attempts the Gyr gave up, but perched nearby. Gyrfalcons are similarly reluctant to attack tethered decoys that refused to flush (Dekker and Lange 2001).

Langvatn and Moksnes (1979) observed one fascinating Gyr hunting chase. First they saw a Willow Grouse approaching at high speed, flying close to the snow-covered ground. Close behind, and a little higher, came a Gyrfalcon, diving at the grouse, which headed for an area of low birch. The Gyr accelerated, dived beneath the grouse and attacked it from below. The grouse made a rapid evading ascent, and then took a steep dive towards the birch trees. The Gyr, having missed with its first attack, regained some altitude and made a new attempt, using the same tactics as before, making a half-roll as it attacked from below. Again the attack failed and the grouse succeeded in escaping into the trees, forcing the falcon to give up the chase. The authors noted that by attacking from below the Gyr was not only attempting a kill, but also forcing the grouse both upwards and away from the trees, so offering the falcon a better chance of capture.

Equally fascinating were the observations of Woodin (1980) in Iceland. On one occasion he observed a 'tail chase': a Ptarmigan flew over his head, pursued by a Gyrfalcon which was only 1.5m behind it and gaining altitude. The Ptarmigan dived into scrub and the falcon turned abruptly and plunged into the scrub after it. Five minutes later the Gyr reappeared from the same spot, having failed to catch the Ptarmigan. Woodin (1980) also occasionally saw Gyrfalcons flying low over scrub. The Ptarmigan along their flight path either froze, and so avoided detection, or were flushed, exposing themselves to pursuit. However Woodin never saw a Gyr strike on any of these occasions. Woodin also noted that if ducks came too close to a perched Gyr they would usually fly away rather than swim, flying being the faster option. Woodin also observed what he calls the 'sneak attack'. In this the Gyr watched from the same advantageous lookout perch, and then flew, dropping almost to the ground and moving with startling speed over the ground and scrub toward an unsuspecting, non-flying prey. Woodin saw this method used against both Ptarmigan and shorebirds. Others have also seen this method of attack. The authors have witnessed it in the wild, and Potapov has also been able to replicate it with a young, trained Gyr.

OPPORTUNISTIC HUNTING

During the summer, Bengtson (1971) observed Icelandic Gyrs taking a variety of prey. A young Golden Plover standing in the middle of a road only 40m in front of Bengtson's car was taken by a Gyr, which plucked it up with one foot. The Gyr flew away with the plover dangling from the same foot. Two successful attacks on ducks were observed in June and August: a female Scaup (*Aythya marila*) idling on the shore was surprised by a low-flying Gyr. When the Scaup tried to take off she was hit and tumbled into the water, apparently dead as her head was hanging submerged. In the other case, a Gyrfalcon was flushed from its perch by the observer and disappeared behind a small hill. When it reappeared just a few seconds later it had a full-grown male Tufted Duck (*Aythya fuligula*) in its talons. The attack was unexpected because the falcon had been disturbed, and because ducks usually avoid approaching low-flying falcons by flying or diving. In this case it would seem that the duck was emerging from a dive at the moment the falcon passed over it.

In the Koryak Mountains Kishinskiy (1980) observed Gyrs sitting perched the ground by the exits of burrows of Arctic Ground Squirrels, waiting for the rodents to emerge. When he flushed the falcon, it took off, went to low-lying ground where there were tussocks and willow shrub, and grabbed a squirrel. Kishinskiy also saw a successful attack by a Gyr on a chick in a Herring Gull colony. He also reported cases when Gyrs followed hunters, attacking young grouse which were flushed. This reinforcement of other observations of Gyrs using humans as beaters demonstrates astonishingly bold behaviour on the part of the falcon.

In the Lower Kolyma one of us (Potapov) observed the attack of a Gyrfalcon on Willow Grouse. The adult male Gyr had been sitting for about 40 minutes on top of a triangulation pole some 2.5km from its nest. It was watching a large brood (or perhaps several broods in a group) of Willow Grouse feeding at a distance of about 400m. The falcon was rather conspicuous on top of the pole, but as soon as the brood, led by at least two adults, went behind a ridge and moved out of view of the falcon, the Gyr took off. It flew at around 1.5m above the ground. It seems that the falcon took an adult bird while it was still on the ground, although the actual moment of impact was obstructed by the slope of the ground. Even if the grouse took off it did not rise more than 0.5m into the air or it would have been visible. The Gyr spent about ten minutes plucking the grouse and then took off into the wind, carrying the prey to its nest.

Gyrfalcons kill their prey through the force with which they strike it, together with the almost instant grasp of the talons. The Gyrfalcon only carries its prey with its feet: no example of prey transport by beak has ever been recorded.

REACTIONS OF THE QUARRY

As might be expected, Ptarmigan are very afraid of Gyrfalcons and always exhibit a strong reaction to the sight of them, even when the falcon is far away. When a falcon is seen high above the ground, Ptarmigan become motionless, either immediately or after walking slowly to an easily reached piece of cover. The Ptarmigan then remains quiet, its head cocked toward the sky until several minutes after the raptor has gone (White and Weeden 1966). If there are other Ptarmigan present, females emit a high, crooning alarm call when they see a Gyrfalcon. Adult males give a prolonged soft rattling or snoring under the same circumstances. Weeden (White and Weeden 1966) imitated both calls, causing Ptarmigan to stop walking long enough to be captured in a net. The authors also noted that the alarm calls of Willow Grouse seemed different from those used at other times, even if a Peregrine was sighted. Ptarmigan also 'freeze' when a Gyrfalcon alights near them. Gyrs were seen perching close to Ptarmigan at least four times, the falcons being unaware of the birds as long as they were motionless, even if the Ptarmigan were not concealed by vegetation or hidden by rocks. As White and Weeden note, 'in this situation, a Ptarmigan that moves has a very short life expectancy'. However, if a Ptarmigan sees a Gyrfalcon hunting low over the ground while the raptor is still far enough away to allow time for escape, the prey bird will often fly ahead of the Gyrfalcon rather than remain hidden. This behaviour is especially common in autumn when Ptarmigan have a tendency to fly more often and further when a falcon is spotted than they do during the summer.

Evasion in Flight

Ptarmigan being pursued downhill by Gyrfalcons usually incline sharply when they get to the foot of the slope, almost 'bouncing' back uphill, in an attempt to throw off the falcon. In level flight, the Ptarmigan observed by White and Weeden (1966) tried to evade the pursuing falcon by twisting and turning, or by dropping abruptly into dense thickets. The general impression gained by White and Weeden was that the falcons and adult Ptarmigan are of almost of equal ability in flight: unless the Gyrfalcon surprises its prey and is relatively close to it, or strikes it on the first stoop, the prey bird has a good chance of escape. They note that 'perhaps hilly terrain helps Ptarmigan to evade Gyrfalcons under some circumstances'.

One important study on prey behaviour was carried out by a Russian team including one of the authors (Potapov). They trained a young male Gyr to fly on Willow Grouse in the Lower Kolyma lowlands. The landscape in this area is uniformly flat, with some river valleys crossing a terrain underlain with permafrost. The river valley chosen for the experiment had deep meanders and tall (up to 1.5m) Arctic willow stands. The remaining tundra was dotted with shorter willows, sometimes following permafrost-formed polygons. The river valley was a prime habitat for numerous Willow Grouse broods. In peak years a territorial cock grouse would be seen about every 100m along the valley. Soon after hatching, the grouse broods occasionally concentrate in one area, usually at a large meander of the river. Each brood is accompanied by both adults. The female grouse usually stays close to the chicks and leads them through the tundra. Like the adult female, Willow Grouse chicks are very well camouflaged. The chicks are also of an extreme precocial type – they are feathered with down and so can thermoregulate from their first day out of the egg, can walk behind their mother, and collect food for themselves. In addition, the chicks can fly, if flushed, at the age of just 1.5 to 2 weeks. The male maintains a position 20–50m away from the female and chicks. The male's position is usually very obvious to the female and brood, as he seeks to use every high tussock as a lookout.

In the experiment, one of the present authors (Potapov) tried to figure out why there were no breeding Gyrfalcons in this typical flat tundra zone. He walked slowly across the river valley in search of Willow Grouse broods, finding that it took very little time to spot a male. As soon as the male grouse spotted the Gyr on Potapov's fist he either called or climbed a tussock to made himself visible. The slipped Gyr would fly fast and direct towards the male grouse, and chase it into tall bushes. By following the Gyr Potapov was able to confirm that, close to where the male had been spotted, there would be a female and brood, now stationary and merging with the tundra vegetation. Meanwhile the Gyr would fly back. The grouse brood was flushed so that the returning Gyr would have a secondary target. The studies showed that in 31 trials the Gyr chased the male grouse on every occasion, but failed to kill it on all 31 chases. In 24 of the trials Potapov managed to flush a single grouse (on all but one occasion a fledgling rather than the female). On 22 of those occasions the Gyr captured the flushed bird (21 chicks and the single female). In the other seven trials more than one chick was flushed, and only one of these chases was successful.

The conclusion was that in this particular landscape the chances of the Gyr killing a grouse are negligible – the male grouse are too fast and their escape routes too well defined, while the females and chicks will not be flushed unless the Gyr has help which, of course, is not available to wild falcons. The consequence of the lack of Gyrs is that Willow Grouse cocks will display at any time of the day in flat tundras, a sharp contrast with, for instance, the mountains of northern Sweden where the cocks only dare display in the poor light of dawn and dusk (E. Potapov pers. obs,).

FOOD CACHES

During the early phase in the nest Jenkins (1978) noted that most food items were large enough for food to remain after both the adults and young had eaten. Food items removed from the eyrie were generally cached. The female Gyr made efforts to place the food items behind grass tufts, presumably in an attempt at concealment. The male Gyr was never seen to cache food. The female Gyr always used one particular part of the nesting cliff for caching, with three or four specific sites being used. Not all cached items were retrieved. One cached Long-tailed Duck was left untouched and became infested with maggots.

Poole and Boag (1988) noted that in their Kilgavik study area of Canada's Northwest Territories, partially consumed prey was usually cached so that food items did not accumulate in nests. Caching was observed 58 times, with 29 deposits and 29 retrievals, the food items being deposited on adjacent cliff faces and, when retrieved, being eaten by the adult birds or fed to the nestlings. No caching of microtines or passerine birds was observed. Female Gyrs performed 93% of the caching, with male birds participating on only four occasions, all of them retrievals rather than deposits. As might be expected, caching behaviour was most frequent when the chicks were young, and decreased as the nestlings grew. No caching was observed after the nestlings reached 29 days of age.

Caching sites were typically small vegetated cliff ledges, the prey item being carefully placed at the back of the ledge or beside a clump of vegetation. Most caching (43 of 49 where the exact location was determined) were within 100m of the nest, the furthest being at a distance of 200m. Re-use of cache sites was infrequent. P. Bente in Palmer (1988) considered food caching as a common Gyr activity during the breeding season. Food items were usually cached out of sight of the eyrie, but within 400m of it, and not always hidden. As most caches were on the nesting cliff, hiding the food items was perhaps not necessary as they were inaccessible to many other predators. Palmer contended that both sexes cache prey, and that female Gyrs cache food both before and after feeding on it. One male Gyr was seen returning from hunting 'empty-handed': it retrieved some cached prey and delivered it to the female. Maximum caching occurred after the young were four weeks old.

FOOD CONSUMPTION

There is little information obtained by direct methods on the food requirements of free-living Gyrfalcons. There are, however, some studies which present data obtained indirectly – by observations of the number of food items brought to the nest and an estimate of the average weight of the prey species. Below we present such data as is currently available on the feeding times of Gyrfalcon young, on the number of prey items delivered to the nest and on the consumption rate of the young.

Poole (1988) set time-lapse movie cameras on two nests at the Kilgavik study area in Canada's Northwest Territories. The feeding rate fluctuated between four and 12 per day in manipulated broods. The time spent feeding varied from 45 to 150 minutes, and was at the maximum when the oldest chick was 10–12 days old. Poole also found that the prey biomass delivered to the nest varied directly with the number of chicks, and the time spent feeding was longer in large broods. However the number of feeding events per day did not vary with the brood size. In Iceland Wayre and Jolly (1958) observed that the Gyrfalcons fed their young three times per day, usually before 07:00hrs, between 11:00 and 13:00hrs, and after 17:00hrs.

Suetens and Groenendael (1976), during a study in Iceland, noted that female Gyrs usually delivered two or three prey items per day, all of them originally hunted, then delivered, by the male. In Norway Gyrfalcons are believed to deliver 2.5 to 3.0 quarry per day (Langvatn and Moksnes 1979). On that basis, during the breeding period the food requirements of a pair of Gyrfalcons and their young would require some 180–200 prey items.

Voronin (1987) observed the hunting behaviour of a pair of tree-nesting Gyrs with a single chick on the River Syatteivis (in the Bolshezemelskaya tundra, in north-east European Russia) from 13 June to 15 July 1982, from a hide and using telescopes (which were rare at the time in Russia). He reported that only the male Gyr was hunting for the family. Usually the male delivered two grouse each day, one in the morning, the second in the evening. The male left the quarry on a ledge of the cliff close to the nest, from where the female retrieved it and delivered it to the nest. There the female ate and fed the chick. Voronin estimated that the consumption of meat reached 190g per bird, which translates to a requirement of 120 grouse for the entire breeding period.

A chick raised by one of us (Potapov) in the Lower Kolyma area of Russia in 1987 was fed at a rate of 270g of bird meat per day, with a variation between 90g and 650g. The chick was fed 'on demand' with no restrictions, *i.e.* it was taking as much as it could eat.

Kishinskiy (1958) observed a pair of Gyrfalcons with two chicks on the coastal plain of Russia's Kola Peninsula over a 12-day period. During this period the pair consumed one shrew, one vole, another small mammal, and 25 birds including Ptarmigan, two Willow Grouse, one unidentified species of grouse, an unidentified species of skua, an Arctic Tern (*Sterna paradisaea*), a Herring Gull, a Glaucous Gull, ten Kittiwakes, two unidentified species of guillemot, a diving duck, an unidentified species of teal, two Golden Plovers and a Snow Bunting. The total weight of the prey was estimated at 13,500g, giving a food consumption of 1,125g of food per day for the family.

Within each year, prey biomass recorded at sites with broods of four was greater than at the sites with broods of two by a ratio of approximately 2:1 (Poole and Boag 1988). The adult female Gyrfalcons fed either at the nest or at the perches where the prey was collected. The prey biomass delivered per day during the nesting period generally peaked in the second and third weeks after hatching, and then declined as the time of fledging approached. The decline is presumably so that the young birds lose weight in order to reduce wing loading. Though there seem to be no direct studies of this in Gyrs, weight decline has been studied in other species (including other falcon species). What is clearly true is that the female Gyr not only deliberately decreases food delivery but will also tease the young by carrying around, but not delivering, prey. On average 1–1.5kg of prey (per nest) was required per day over the 47-day breeding period. Based on the number of Ptarmigan and other larger prey items identified at the nest sites, the equivalent of 120–170 adult Ptarmigan are required to successfully fledge four young Gyrfalcons. Fewer young would obviously require fewer prey items.

However, Kalyakin (1989) estimated that a family of Gyrfalcons with three young consumes 700kg of prey per year, assuming that the young survive until the end of September, and 900kg if the young survive through to December. In June–September such a family consumes 400kg of prey, including up to 200 Willow Grouse (or 1,000 for the year: Kalyakin 1989).

Pulliainen (1975) observed the feeding rate during the last 13 days of the fledging period. The food brought to the eyrie represented about 1,300g of prey per day. The maximum number of feeds in a single day was 12 in the study of Poole and Boag (1988). The mean feeding time was 11.8 minutes, though interestingly there was no relationship between brood size and mean feeding duration (per chick). Neither did the total time spent in daily feeding at each nest bear any relationship to the daily maximum temperature or the precipitation index. The feeding rate bore no relationship to brood size, but total time spent feeding daily was greater for broods of four than for broods of two.

Nielsen (1999a) used a bioenergetic approach to calculate the food requirements of the Gyrfalcon. He estimated that a male Gyrfalcon needs 241g of food per day, a female 301g per day, and a chick, on average, 169g per day. The mean weight of Ptarmigan in Iceland is 537g. The calculated DEB (daily energy budget) at 2.5 BMR (basal metabolic rate) for birds of 1,831g (adult female), 1,355g (adult male), 1,537g (young female) and 1,262g (young male), and the length of the breeding season is 111 days, including 14 days of courtship, 43 days for laying and incubation, 47 days of nestling period and seven days post-fledging period. Based on the relative proportion of the diet he sampled in his study area, Nielsen recalculated the figures as total numbers of individuals consumed and total biomass consumed in his study area (5,327km^2). The calculated biomass consumption for all Gyrfalcons in the monitored area fluctuated between 2,875kg and 4,693kg during the breeding seasons 1981–97. In terms of Ptarmigan (keeping their proportion in mind) this means a variation from 4,039 to 7,170 individuals per year (or 758 to 1,346 Ptarmigan per 1,000km^2 per year). It should be noted that the energy requirements of free-living Gyrfalcons were not measured, but estimated from general bioenergetic equations.

CHAPTER 7

Breeding Cycle

Only the Raven and, perhaps, the Golden Eagle match the Gyrfalcon in its ability to breed in the freezing temperatures of the early Arctic spring. Among falcons the Gyr is certainly unique in this respect. Even the Snowy Owl usually waits for the snow to melt, though this can be viewed as essential since the owl nests on the ground. By contrast Gyrfalcons do not need to wait until the snow melts as they nest on cliff ledges, in caves or in trees. All the Gyr needs is an abundance of Willow Grouse, or, in some cases, Arctic Hare or sea- or shorebirds. In most parts of their range the Gyrfalcons rely on the abundance and, in non-coastal biomes (*i.e.* continuous tundra), on the timing of, the breeding of *Lagopus* grouse. The close association between Gyrfalcons and grouse was first noted by Kishinskiy (1958), and was developed in detail by Cade (1960), on the basis of his observations in Alaska. Cade noted the highest variation in the timing of breeding in the year of a widespread decrease of Ptarmigan numbers. Subsequent authors have concurred with the association between Gyr breeding and grouse abundance (Poole 1987,

Morozov 2000). To such an extent is Gyr breeding associated with grouse availability that sometimes the falcons do not breed even when there is a high density of Arctic Hares as the hares can be difficult to catch in the early spring. In Figure 7.1 we develop Cade's ideas on the basis of more detailed studies of *Lagopus* grouse and on the updated field observations cited in this chapter.

Gyrfalcons breed for the first time at the age of two (*i.e.* the third calendar year of the bird's life) or older (Palmer 1988). Dementiev (1960) stated that both sexes are capable of breeding (with eggs being laid) when they are yearlings, a claim that was later supported by Nielsen (1991) although at the present time there is no hard evidence to confirm this conjecture. However, captive-bred Gyrfalcons breed at four years (Platt 1977, Cade *et al.* 1998).

Most Gyr biologists consider that pair bonding occurs during the winter at the breeding grounds. Such evidence as there is to support this is circumstantial: observations of three Gyrs wintering in Pennsylvania, USA, noted that a white and a grey bird flew close together (1982, *American Birds* 36: 278) apparently in a 'passing-and-leading' display. This was considered either to be pair formation behaviour, or, more likely, was related to bond maintenance while remote from the breeding range. In north-east Greenland a female was shot at a nest on 19 May, and on 14 July another Gyr flew from the site, implying that the male had taken another mate (Manniche 1910, cited by Palmer 1988). This is probably the same observation of a replacement female as that mentioned by Cramp and Simmons in *BWP* (1980).

PRE-LAYING

In general, Gyrfalcons remain on their breeding grounds during the winter (see Chapter 8). Woodin (1980), studying Gyrs in Iceland in March, found the birds already paired. On 10 March a cup had been scraped at a nesting ledge, and when the observers arrived a single bird did not leave the area directly, but circled several times around the nest site. Prior to egg-laying all falcons spend a good deal of time perching, singly or together, in the immediate vicinity of former nest sites. The birds perch together for several hours in the afternoon and evening and also roost near old nests at night. However, hunting at this time still appears to be a solitary activity. At the time when the Gyr pair start to scratch their nest the ambient temperature is well below freezing. Platt (1977) reported temperatures of -40°C at a nest site in Canada's Yukon Territory during incubation.

Gyrfalcons are not renowned for their flight displays, though Woodin (1980) once observed mutual gliding during courtship followed by copulation. One flight display was described: one or both of the pair performed a flight display above the eyrie. The bird would either soar with the eyrie at the flight centre below it, or glide at a lower altitude in a series of circles or arcs that took it back and forth over an area of 400–600m diameter. Woodin writes "I saw one of the mates (once female, once male) go into a stoop in the eyrie area, once right before the eyrie ledge and once a little way off. In both cases stoop was associated with a flight display above the eyrie."

COURTSHIP BEHAVIOUR

Courtship behaviour is an essential part of pair bonding, pair formation, and successful breeding. The fact that female Gyrfalcons are larger than males brings an extra dimension to the perils of mating. Females in the raptor world are a potential hazard to their mates, and social behaviour must counteract inherent strongly aggressive tendencies. If such behaviours fail the male will be killed and often eaten, something which has happened many times in captive-breeding programmes in breeding facilities and zoos around the world.

Courtship behaviour of a number of falcon species, including Gyrs, in captivity has been described in a classic paper by Wrege and Cade (1977). The postures adopted during Gyrfalcon courtship behaviour closely resembled those of Peregrine Falcons. The following postures are typical for both Gyrs and Peregrines: head-low bow display, scraping, food transfer display, ledge display, curved-neck display, copulation solicitation display, threat behaviour, chatter, chupping and copulation. The 'head-low bow display' is widely used during ledge displays and food transfers, but the frequency of 'head-low bow display' is much less than that in Peregrines.

Some additions to the displays observed by Wrege and Cade were made from field observations by Platt (1977), who observed pre-laying behaviour from hides erected near nests in the Yukon Territory, Canada.

Overall, three groups of behaviour can be distinguished amongst the displays:

1. Head-low bow displays; ledge displays; food transfers; copulation solicitation; whine, chup and chatter vocalisations.
2. Male pre-copulatory postures, female copulation solicitation and wail vocalisations: in each of these behaviours there is an aggressive component.
3. The third group is at least partially aggressive; it includes chatter vocalisations, upright and horizontal threat displays.

HEAD-LOW BOW DISPLAY

This display can be performed by either sex in response to the close proximity of the mate. Imprinted birds will display towards humans. This display is non-aggressive. The bird holds the head below the body plane with the beak directed away from the mate (usually towards a substrate), and has a generally sleeked plumage (*i.e.* with all contour feathers pressed close to the body). There are both horizontal and vertical forms of the display. The horizontal head-low bow involves crouching in a horizontal body position, the head bent at almost 90° to the body plane and the beak often contacting the substrate. The vertical head-low bow is a less intense form, with the body in a normal perching position, but with the head depressed. Both forms of display may involve bowing up and down from the head-low position to a normal posture with the head above the body plane. Often the head-low bow is maintained without vigorous bowing, especially when in close proximity of the mate. Vocalisations may accompany this type of display. In contrast to Peregrines, Gyrs do not engage in vigorous bowing.

LEDGE DISPLAY

At the eyrie, numerous behaviour components have been given labels, but ledge display in its various forms is included in most of them. Ledge display begins with a visit to the chosen ledge, either by one or other bird, or both together. Both may be in a horizontal posture, head lowered and 'chupping' rapidly. Either may squat and rock the body, scraping with the head up. Other components may be interwoven, such as the male bringing food to the female, mutual scraping with the beak and so on.

Individual ledge display

This display is given by the male or female alone on a prospective nesting substrate, usually centred on a scrape. According to Platt (1977) individual ledge display is performed more often by male Gyrs than females. According to Platt, the most common form of this activity is a visit: either falcon stands alone in a normal position on the edge or walks into the eyrie and stands upright.

Male ledge display

In this display the scrape is approached in a horizontal head-low posture with a continual *chup* vocalisation. The horizontal head-low posture is initiated during intense activity at the scrape, with repeated *chup* vocalisations. Pauses in the display begin after five to ten seconds: during these the male looks at the female. At any time a movement by the female is likely to elicit renewed intense display. According to Platt (1977) ledge displays occur only at a proposed nest site.

Following the ledge display the male often stands facing out from the nest ledge for two to five minutes. He is generally quiet, but may 'wail'. This type of activity can often be seen before egg-laying.

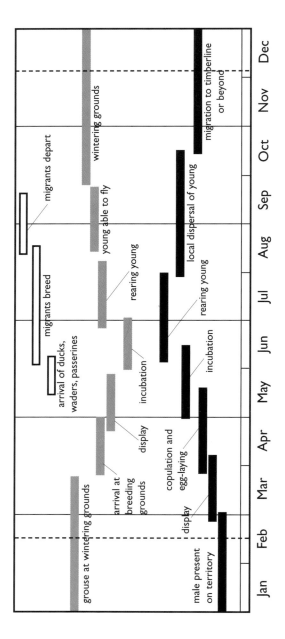

Figure 7.1 *Breeding cycle of Gyrfalcon (black lines, bottom),* Lagopus *grouse (grey lines, middle) and Arctic migrants (white lines, top). The polar night lines marked on the chart are equivalent to a latitude of around 70°N.*

Platt (1977) observed a lone male Gyrfalcon as he defended a nest cliff and attempted to attract a female. The lone male demonstrated 'male ledge display' (see below), 'wail', 'undulatory roll', 'eyrie fly-by' and 'wail-pluck'. The latter two types of behaviour have not been seen in a mated male.

Female ledge display

Female ledge display differs from that of the male in several ways. It is less intense and is sometimes difficult to distinguish from non-display activities. The postures are less distinctive and more variable. The approach is normally horizontal (*i.e.* head, body and tail are all on one plane). The female turns around in the scrape, touching debris on the ledge and scrapes. Pauses are frequent.

Mutual ledge display

Simultaneous activity by both sexes on the nest ledge usually occurs at a scrape. The most intense display occurs when both sexes are at the scrape, each in horizontal head-low posture with beaks close to the substrate, noisily 'chupping'. Billing is often seen during longer mutual ledge displays, and occasionally the birds may perch very close together. Billing involves twisting the head sideways (seen mainly in the female) and nibbling between the beaks. The female's head is usually very low with her beak directed upward, while the male faces downward. If billing occurs during a mutual ledge display, the normally loud *chup* vocalisation tends to diminish to 'peeping' and a quiet female 'chupping'. According to Platt (1977) the mutual ledge display is performed when the female arrives at the nest while the male is performing an individual ledge display. The adults stand facing one another over the scrape in the same horizontal position used in the individual ledge displays, but give a faster series of the same *chup* call.

Scraping

Scraping is exhibited by either sex during solitary activity on a ledge or as part of individual ledge display. During scraping the body is centred forward, with weight on the breast, the beak frequently on the substrate, and with the tail relaxed and sloping towards the ledge. A shallow depression, the 'scrape' (see Chapter 5), is made by vigorous backward pushing with the feet. No vocalisation accompanies this scraping behaviour. According to Platt (1977), scraping usually follows ledge display. It is accomplished by the bird resting the upper portion of its breast on the substrate and thrusting its feet back, pushing away any surface material. This scraping motion forms the scrape inside which the pair's eggs will eventually rest.

FOOD TRANSFER DISPLAY

A common courtship display involves the transfer of food from one mate to the other, usually from the male to the female. Either sex may initiate a transfer. The female uses a wail vocalisation or, rarely, a whine, combined with a vertical head-low posture to solicit transfers when the male does not have food. If the male has food, the wail and chup vocalisations are used roughly equally by the female, often accompanied by the vertical head-low bow display.

Male solicitation, which elicits the female's approach, always occurs when he has food, either spontaneously or initiated by female movements designed to engage in transfer. Transfer from the female to the male is not obviously solicited.

Prior to actual transfer, the male drops the prey item from his beak and stands vertically, head up. The female maintains the head-low posture, often becoming horizontal, and both sexes give complete *chup* vocalisations.

CURVED-NECK DISPLAY

This display is engaged in by both sexes but is especially characteristic of the male throughout the reproductive cycle, developing as sexual motivation reaches its peak. It is consistently given in flight to and from copulation and in male pre-copulatory behaviour. The display can be divided into two forms: flying and standing. During curved-neck flight the wings are held high, with short wingbeats mostly from the wrist. The legs are well forward, and the tail is depressed, resulting in a slow-motion, bouncing flight. Frequently the flight path involves a low approach to the perch with a last-minute bound above and then a standing down on to the perch. No bounce occurs when the male flies to mount for copulation.

Standing curved-neck display occurs for brief to moderately long (two seconds) periods after the male lands on a perch, frequently at the onset of mutual ledge displays. It is always expressed prior to copulation. Most often the body posture is vertical to semi-horizontal, held high on stiff legs. The head is low, and the wings are hitched up high against the body to form a deep, V-shaped depression along the back. Another variation includes a horizontal head-low position, with the legs stiff and the wings hitched. Vigorous bowing, with a side-to-side swing, is a part of this display.

COPULATION SOLICITATION DISPLAY

The female's motivation to copulate is communicated by a series of vertical postures and some vocalisations. It may begin with a whine vocalisation, concurrent with, or just preceding, a head-low bow. Alternatively, the female may approach the male head-on in a horizontal posture, sometimes even threatening the male. Threat behavious can be shown in ledge displays and during copulation solicitation. There are two forms. In the horizontal threat the tail, body, and head are in a horizontal plane, the beak directed at the mate, with the wings slightly extended, the head and neck feathers erect. The upright threat is when the body is vertical with most feathers erect. The wings may be spread to varying degrees and the beak is usually opened.

The female's vertical, head-low posture is usually given while the male is at some distance. Copulation will follow if the male shows a reaction. During solicitation, either following the vertical posture, or independently, the female assumes a horizontal posture. She gives the whine vocalisation, her body is close to horizontal, the tail and tail-undercoverts are slightly raised, and her orientation is usually perpendicular to the male. This phase may continue for up to 30 seconds. When the male shows his intention to mount, the female sleeks her body feathers, crouches and leans forward. As the male lands on her back the female moves her tail up and to the side in preparation for copulation.

Woodin (1980) observed a pair that showed elaborate pre-copulatory behaviour. The behaviour consisted almost entirely of preening movements. The birds faced each other, about 8m apart, on a snow-covered slope. First one bird, and then the other, took the initiative at preening. The movements included lifting and preening under the wings, bending the head back while elevating the tail as though to touch the beak to the preen gland, scratching under the chin, and lowering the head while bobbing the tail. The last movement of the sequence, performed only by the female, was a bending of the tail sideways, while reaching back under it with the head. Such preening episodes occupied about 20 minutes, and were followed by the male taking off and mounting the female, as usual, from the wing. Billing was part of the copulatory behaviour in some of the pairs Woodin observed. Copulation took place every hour or two, usually at one perch after another.

COPULATION

Woodin (1980) observed the first copulation on 4 April. It was accompanied by several vocalisations. During copulation the female bowed her head almost to the ground, while the male balanced on her back, slowly moving his wings. During copulation the female pitches forward, making an angle of about 60° with respect to the perch. The copulation wail is given throughout. The female spreads her wings out at the elbow, about a quarter open. The tail is moved to one side and may be partially raised. The male flaps his wings throughout copulation, maintaining an upright posture with the head bent in a curve. Usually the male gives one or two bursts of vocalisation before, during and just after copulation, and even *chups* occasionally. Towards the end of copulation the male stops his tail movements, pressing his cloaca against the female's. Rapid movements accompany his tail-press. The female may spread her tail partially at this time. After copulation the female flies to a perch with a curved-neck display. Woodin noted, that after copulation the male left the area and had not reappeared almost two hours later. Either sex initiates copulation: it can take place wherever the female happens to be and at any time of day (Palmer 1988). One Gyr pair was observed to copulate at a maximum of six times per hour at 3–4 weeks before egg-laying, and another five times in five hours in the week before laying. Copulation takes place on various perches, but Platt (1989) points out that copulation never happens on the nest ledge. However, Dementiev (1951) claimed that copulation on Kharlov Island, off the Kola Peninsula, happens close to the nest, or at least on the nesting cliff. Before copulation the male might bring some twigs for the nest.

Copulation is known to continue at least until the third egg is laid, though Woodin noted that egg-laying essentially marked the end of copulation. Egg-laying in Iceland ended between 18 and 19 April, and only two copulations were observed later, on 19 and 24 April.

VOCALISATION

Todd (1963) called Gyrfalcons 'silent birds'. However, during the breeding season Gyrs are moderately noisy. 'Chupping' can also occasionally be heard during flight displays in winter. The male Gyr's voice is higher-pitched than the females (Palmer 1988). The vocalisations can be characterised as 'cakking', a guttural, harsh, hoarse call (*kweck-kweck-kweck*) uttered by both sexes and which can be heard in threats, including those against humans. 'Wailing' indicates anxiety by both sexes. It is most commonly heard from females when approached by a male with food, and also if the male lingers after transfer. Wailing is also used by a solitary male to attract a female. The wail is a two-syllable rising call given in an irregular series of three to ten calls spaced by a silence of one to ten minutes. Wailing is usually performed at a perch, but it can be part of the 'eyrie-fly-by' (Platt 1977). Begging nestlings have a mewing call that develops into wailing. The young are also capable of rudimentary 'cakking'.

'Chupping' may be a single syllable or repeated. It is a contact call used by both sexes and is also used during aerial and perched displays. A parent bird 'chups' to announce its arrival with food to nestlings. 'Chuttering' or 'chattering' are repeated, speeded-up versions of 'chupping'. Variants are used by both sexes in particular situations: one variant, for example, is used by male Gyrs during copulation.

A display noted by Platt (1977) and called the 'wail-pluck display' occurs when the male returns to the nest site with a prey item, or occasionally after he has recovered discarded prey remains from a perch. He begins wailing while slowly plucking the item. He often pauses in the plucking to look around, but continues to wail. A male performing this display takes more than 50 minutes to pluck and eat a *Lagopus* grouse. By contrast, incubating female Gyrs can pluck and eat a grouse in less than 30 minutes.

AERIAL DISPLAY

Beginning early in the breeding season, sometimes before a female is present, the male makes himself conspicuous by high-perching. The high perch is normally decorated in whitewash visible for some distance. It is possible that the ultraviolet (UV) reflection of the whitewash is somehow indicative of the male bird's quality (Potapov *et al.* in press). Saker pairs which have a high UV whitewash reflection on the male's high perch tend to be more productive than those with poor reflection perches. The male will begin aerial displays from this perch.

Many of the Gyr's aerial actions are modifications of 'high-circling', in which the bird makes wide circles around, or close to, the nesting site at a height of 30–60m. Another display is the 'undulatory roll' (Platt 1977, 1989), in which the bird makes a sudden steep dive during the circle, then flies high again while rolling the body 20° in one direction, then 180° in the other direction.

These elements are combined in the 'eyrie-fly-by' in which the male Gyr advertises a nest site to the female. The eyrie-fly-by consists of the male flying parallel to the nest cliff at nest level and about 10m from it. After passing the eyrie he turns away from the cliff, and back towards the nest. He sometimes lands in the eyrie, but usually passes it and again banks away from the cliff and turns again towards the nest. The flight therefore forms a figure eight in front of the nest cliff with the central crossing point in front of the eyrie. This pattern is repeated two or three times before the male lands at the nest. Near-constant wailing accompanies this display, and a prey item is often carried. The prey item may be carried to the eyrie, but it is neither plucked nor eaten there (Platt 1977). In 'roll-display' (sometimes called an undulatory roll) the male Gyr's body partially rotates. The male dives steeply and shoots upward again. Usually he makes one or two of these sudden dives.

Another display involves high-soaring in which the male Gyr soars above the breeding site, the soar probably aided by an updraft at cliff sites. There is also mutual soaring in circles or other configurations. This is done silently. Soaring and some other display activities almost certainly also occur above the territory during warm spells in winter if both birds are present (Palmer 1988). It definitely occurs from the onset of territorial advertising until well into the rearing period (Palmer 1988).

In 'passing-and-leading' display the birds are close together. In 'mutual floating' the male, often 'cakking', flies 3m or less above the female. With tails spread, legs lowered and wings partially closed, the pair gradually lose altitude. Variants and combinations of these flight patterns are numerous. A wailing male often carries prey, which stimulates female involvement. He may deliver it to the eyrie, as if inducing her to alight there, then fly off with it. Presumably the female then receives the prey via an aerial food pass. Palmer (1988) suggested that if prey were so scarce that the male could not get any to display with the breeding cycle would be disrupted.

In the Koryak Mountains, Kishinskiy (1980) observed flight displays of Gyrfalcons on 27 April 1960. The display happened during severe weather. The birds were flying at about 100–150m above the ground, turning upside-down and making a noise which was not at all similar to their normal calls – a *tur-tur-tur*, rather like a flute.

LAYING AND HATCHING DATES AND DURATION OF INCUBATION

The production of eggs is an extremely energy-demanding process. The female has to produce a minimum of 23g/day (1.4% of body weight) of 'live protein' (calculated on the basis of a female weight of 1600g and an average egg weight of 67g, with no resorbtion of embryos). Assuming that the embryos are growing simultaneously, the actual production rate (although somewhat recoverable thanks to resorbtion) is higher. A simple linear relationship of this production rate to humans would mean that a human of 75kg would have to produce 1kg/day, and that would have to be repeated 3.5 times on average, all at the temperature of the high Arctic.

On average, Gyrfalcons breed one month earlier than neighbouring Peregrines. As Cade (1960) wrote:

> Its timing need not be so precise as that of the Peregrine: if a clutch is lost Gyrs can lay a second set with a reasonable chance of survival. Being largely resident and preying predominantly upon resident Arctic species of prey are attributes that make possible a longer period of development in Gyrfalcons.

Platt (1976) agrees that a replacement clutch is laid if eggs are lost in the early stages of incubation. Such re-nesting occurred twice in his study area, which accommodated 31 nest territories. Re-laying was reported within 14 days. A replacement clutch was also reported from Canada's Nunavut Province by Poole (1991).

As we have already noted, Gyrs start to breed when prey becomes abundant. Although primarily this observation deals with the abundance of grouse, Gyrs that rely on other prey species exhibit the same timing: pairs relying on seabirds also time egg-laying with the arrival of the prey birds (Dementiev and Gortchakovskaya 1945, Salomonsen 1950–51, Shklyarevich and Krasnov 1980, Cade *et al.* 1998).

The male Gyr's delivery of food to the female usually begins at least ten days before laying (e.g. Platt 1976, 1978), and the female is dependent on him for all her food once she begins to accept it. Thus the pair bond is established or reaffirmed. The male may also begin to wail while he is still a long way off to announce his approach to the nest. The female then flies toward him, beating her wings in a distinctive shallow arc, and the prey is transferred. Very infrequently he actually reaches the eyrie with food. In that case, once the female takes possession of the food, she may face him in a horizontal posture which causes him to depart immediately. The female may then feed at the eyrie, or carry the food to a nearby plucking place. She may cache any uneaten portion close by. After a food pass the male may immediately perform an undulatory flight display before departing.

Laying dates have long been enigmatic for ornithologists. In 1960 Cade wrote that "nothing is known of the time when Gyrfalcons first occupy their nesting cliffs in Alaska". Since then the situation has improved with several studies, most notably by Platt (1977) in Canada and Nielsen (Nielsen and Cade 1990a) in Iceland, which shed light on the problem.

In Iceland Gyrfalcon courtship was observed at an average 17 days before the laying of the first egg with a range of nine to 25 days (Nielsen and Cade 1990a). Nelson and Cade then observed laying dates in more detail. They reported the first (and perhaps the earliest) laying date as 28 March, with most egg-laying starting in the period between 3 and 10 April. The latest laying date was 9 May. Nielsen and Cade also found that during a snowstorm no clutches were initiated. The laying period in Iceland was spread across a 14- to 40-day period in the different years of observation, the difference between laying dates across the years being highly significant statistically. Hatching in Iceland was reported between 10 May and 18 June.

Suetens and Groenendael (1976) observed egg-laying in a nest in Iceland between 5 and 20 April and fledging of young between 20 June and 5 July. The egg-laying of Icelandic Gyrs was also studied by Woodin (1980) who gave the following laying intervals: first egg 11–12 April; third egg 18 April; fourth egg 19 April.

A laying interval of about 59 hours was observed in Norway (Tømmeraas 1989a). It took seven days for the female to produce a clutch of four, the eggs being laid on 5, 7, 9 and 12 April. When the first egg was laid the female spent less than 50% of the time incubating. During the remaining time the female either stood at the nest or was away from it. When the second egg was laid the female incubated the clutch for 70% of the time. The time the eggs were incubated reached more than 90% two days after the third egg was laid (and one day before the fourth egg was laid). In Russia's Kolyma region one of us (Potapov) was never able to observe laying dates, mostly due to snowstorms and near-spring conditions (when the snow starts to melt there is a chance of being cut off from civilisation by the break-up of ice on local rivers). However, one nest visited on 9 May 1987 contained four eggs.

Also in Russia, the first complete clutch was reported by Voronin (1986, 1987) on 11 April (three eggs). In a neighbouring nest a clutch of three eggs was seen on 22 April 1982, and this had increased to four eggs on the next visit on 30 April. At a third nest, visited on 24 April, there was a completed clutch of four eggs. In the next year at the same place on the Bolshaya Rogovaya on 5 April the nest was empty, but cleaned of snow, and the female was sitting there at the time of the visit. There were no eggs in two neighbouring nests on 18 and 22 April respectively. However the females were sitting in the nests at the time of the visit.

In the Koryak Mountains, Kishinskiy (1980) gives estimated laying dates of 20 April to 8 May. Portenko (1972) reported a nest on the sea coast of Chukotka with two hatchlings and two eggs on 29 June. At another nest 20km inland there were apparently two chicks in down on 23 March 1935. This date is almost certainly a mistake: it is probable that the correct date was 23 June. Dorogoi (1991) found a nest with two chicks (one of which was three weeks old) at the Koolen' lake, north-east Chukotka on 11 of July. Fledging of Gyrs in a nest at Anabar River (western Yakutia) was reported after 20 July (Gladkov and Zaletaev 1962).

Obst (1994) reported the dates of egg-laying in cliff nests at the Horton River study area of Canada's Northwest Territories to be slightly earlier than in tree nests. In cliff nests the egg-laying started during the period 23 April to 7 May, whereas in tree nests it was between 29 April and 19 May. Kuyt (1980) reported an estimated hatching date at Lookout Point, Thelon River, in Canada's Northwest Territories, of 30 May. The study-site chicks fledged between 20 July and 9 August in tree nests and between 14 and 28 July in cliff nests.

In British Columbia the onset of laying was estimated as 3 April, but most egg-laying probably takes place in late April and early May (Campbell *et al.* 1990). The laying interval in the central Canadian Arctic is about 60 hours (Poole and Bromley 1988a), Salomonsen (1950–51) states that in the high Arctic of Greenland Gyrfalcons never lay before the end of May, whereas in the low Arctic laying takes place in mid April and through May.

Cade (1960) suggested a 29-day incubation period, with a fledging period of not less than 46 days and no more than 49 days. Cade's figure is consistent with the 28–29 days reported by Manniche (1910). This time was repeated by Dementiev (1951), Dementiev and Gladkov (1951), and later carbon-copied by many authors in the west (e.g. Snow 1974, although she did note that the duration of incubation was not clearly determined) and, especially, in the Russian literature.

The incubation period was directly recorded by Woodin (1980) in Iceland. Having observed, at one nest, the timing of egg-laying (as noted above), Woodin then observed two eggs hatched on 23 May, with a piping third egg on the same date. On 24 May two dry chicks were observed, together with one wet chick and a piping fourth egg. Thus the observed period of incubation was 35–37 days. Platt (1977) gives an incubation period of 35 (34–36) days per egg.

In Norway, Hagen (1952a) extrapolated the onset of laying as the second half of April, fledging (in three different years) on 1, 3 and 5 July. Kishinskiy (1958) noted that if the development period of the chicks is 45–47 days, the extrapolated date of hatching on the Kola Peninsula was 20–22 May. If the incubation period is 34–36 days, that makes the laying date 15–17 April. The fledging date in one nest in the two-year study period was 6 or 7 July. Shklyarevich and Krasnov (1980) reported hatching at Bolshoy Litzkiy Island, part of the Seven Islands Nature Reserve on the Kola Peninsula, on or between 25 May and 27 May in 1976, and on 24, 25 and 27 May in 1978. Two chicks fledged at the age of 44–45 and 48–49 days.

In captivity, in an incubator, the first egg of a four-egg clutch hatched in 33.8 days, the others taking 3–5 days longer (Seifert 1982). Seifert also noted that in captivity the laying interval is 56 hours for a four-egg clutch. The length of incubation was reported to be 31–34 days in an incubator set at 37.2°C with 17% humidity (M. Patterson and D. Durman-Walters, pers. comm.). It is now considered that the incubation period for Gyrfalcon is 34–36 days, with a hatch-to-fledge period of 47–49 days, and that Gyrfalcons have so-called synchronous hatching, *i.e.* the chicks at essentially the same time. In Iceland Suetens and Groenendael (1976) reported fledging on 5 July from an estimated laying date of 5 April.

The fledging date at the Severnaya River nest was 12 and 13 July. At another nest at the Khatyrka River the lone chick left the site on 21 July. In the Lapland Reserve (Vladimirskaya 1948) two chicks fledged on 25 July 1938. In a nest at the Ayan Lake, Taimyr (Dorogov 1985), the young Gyrs hatched on 3–7 June: the laying of this clutch had been completed by the beginning of May.

EGG SIZE

Gyrfalcon eggs are oval with a pale white-yellow base colour, spotted with red. Occasionally the eggs can be whitish, but again with red spots. Icelandic eggs from 19 clutches kept at the BMNH (Tring) have dimensions reported as length 58.89 ± 1.67mm x breadth 46.67 ± 1.08mm (n = 42), with a range of 55.75–62.10mm x 44.45–48.70mm (Cade *et al.* 1998).

A total of 90 eggs reported by Palmer (1988) had lengths from 53.5mm to 64.4mm, and had breadths from 41.4mm to 50.8mm, for an average of 58.7mm x 45.7mm. A second series of 55 eggs gave ranges of 56–63mm x 42–48mm, for an average of 59.4 x 43.5mm. The colour of the eggs in this study was said to be pale reddish cinnamon. There is no precise data on the weight loss of eggs during incubation. The fresh eggs of North American Gyrs weighed about 70g (Palmer 1988). In Norway egg weights were 59g, 61g, 63g and 64g after ten days of incubation (Tømmeraas 1989a).

The average dimensions for eggs measured in Russia's Komi Autonomous Republic (Voronin 1986) were 57.6mm x 44.9mm (n = 8). Voronin considers that the last egg in the clutch has the lowest level of pigmentation and usually does not hatch. In another study the average egg size was 59.4mm x 45.3mm (Bent 1938 in Johnsgard 1990). An estimated egg weight of 67.3g (Johnsgard 1990) corresponded to 3.8% of the weight of the female Gyr. Shklyarevich and

Krasnov (1980) measured three eggs in a nest at Bolshoy Litzkiy Island, off Russia's Kola Peninsula noting dimensions of 57.1mm x 44.8mm, 55.8mm x 45.2mm and 55.5mm x 45.6mm.

CLUTCH SIZE, BROOD SIZE AND BREEDING RATE

In Gyrfalcon nests the clutch size varies from one to five eggs (Figure 7.2a). A maximum clutch size of five eggs was first reported by Dementiev (1951 in Dementiev and Gladkov 1951). This figure was later confirmed in Iceland (Cade *et al.* 1998). To date we know of no confirmed reports of a clutch size exceeding five. However, Bannerman (1956) mentioned that Lord Rothschild had once recorded a clutch of six. Data on Gyrfalcon brood size are presented in Figure 7.2b. The data for the clutch and brood size figures has been derived from that presented below for the various parts of the Gyr's range.

EUROPEAN DATA

The clutch size in Iceland (Woodin 1980) was four in two cases, the brood size in four cases being 1, 3, 4, and 3 (giving a mean of 2.75). Nielsen (Cade *et al.* 1998) observed 157 complete clutches in north-east Iceland. The average clutch size was 3.47 ± 0.75. A clutch of one egg was observed five times, clutches of two were recorded eight times, clutches of three 56 times, clutches of four 86 times and a clutch of five eggs was recorded twice. In northern Iceland the number of young produced per occupied territory was 2.78 (Cade *et al.* 1998). Bengtson (1972) reported an average brood size of 3.4 (n = 6, range 2–5), the average number of chicks fledged being 2.4.

   Hagen (1952a, Hagen and Barth 1952) observed one location during the period 1945–52 in Norway. He reported four chicks fledged in 1948, three chicks in 1947 and 1949, no breeding in 1946 and 1950–52, and a brood of unknown size in 1945. Tømmeraas (1978) reported a site in Norway producing 22 nestlings over a period of six years (3.7 young on average). The number of offspring produced by the pair in the years of successful breeding was 4, 4, 3, 4, 4, 3 (years 1966–77). Also in Norway, the breeding rate is variously reported to be 2.64 young per successful pair (Tømmeraas 1994b), 2.15 per successful pair and 1.91 per breeding attempt (Steen 1998), or about 2 per pair (Sortland 1997).

   In Jämtland, Sweden, the average clutch size was reported as 2.6 (n = 66, range 1–4) (Falkdalen and Holmberg 1997). A clutch size of one was reported in four cases, two in 23, three in 31 and four in 8 cases. In 1999 the Gyrs of Jämtland produced 2.8 chicks per successful nest (n = 25), and 2.5 chicks in 2000 (n = 28) (Lindberg 2002).

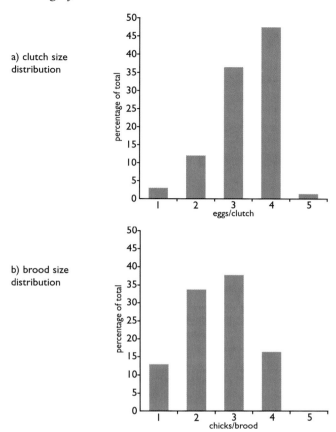

a) clutch size
distribution

b) brood size
distribution

Figure 7.2 Distribution of clutch (a) and brood (b) size. Clutch data is dominated by the sample from Iceland (Cade et al. 1998), whereas brood data is dominated by the sample from Canada's Northwest Territories (Shank and Poole 1994). All other data used are mentioned in the text.

In one exceptional breeding territory in Jämtland, 2.9 chicks per breeding attempt, or 3.1 per successful breeding, was reported (Lind and Nordin 1995).

In Norrbotten, Sweden, the average brood size was reported to be 2.17 chicks out of 2.5–2.6 hatched eggs per successful pair (Linder and Tjernberg 1997). Lindberg (2002) has incorporated the latter data to give the average breeding rate of Gyrfalcons in Norrbotten as 2.5 chicks per pair. In 2002 the breeding rate in Norrbotten was 3.9 chicks per successful pair, very high and probably due to a peak in the numbers of Willow Grouse: in 2003 it was 2.78 (Ekenstedt 2001–03). Also in Sweden one territory had an average 3.9 eggs over 15 years (Lind and Nordin 1995), while in the Alta–Kautokeino river system four pairs produced 103 young in 11 years, an average of 9.4 young Gyrs per year (range 4–13) with the average number of young per pair being 2.45. Huhtala *et al.* (1996) reported that a pair of Gyrfalcons in a location in north-east Finland, not far from the Russian–Finnish border, produced four eggs and four hatchlings in 1973; in 1974 two eggs were laid, but no chicks survived; in 1985 four chicks were produced from four eggs; in 1988 three chicks from four eggs; in 1989 two chicks out of clutch of three; in 1990 three out of four; and in 1991 two chicks out of clutch of four. The average figure for clutch size was 3.6 ± 0.8, for a brood of 3.0 ± 1.4, and for the number of chicks fledged of 2.4 ± 1.3 (*n* = 6). L. von Haartman collected about 60 clutches of Gyrfalcon in Finland, the mean clutch size being 3.53 ± 0.62 (Cade *et al.* 1998).

Kishinskiy (1958) reported two young fledged from one nest in two consecutive years on the Kola Peninsula, with one young fledged from another nest. In the third year of observation no pairs were breeding. In the Lapland Reserve of the Kola Peninsula two chicks fledged on 25 July 1938 (Vladimirskaya 1948). Shklyarevich and Krasnov (1980) reported that a pair of Gyrs breeding at the Seven Islands Reserve, Kola, produced one fledged chick out of clutch of four in 1976, and two fledglings out of clutch of four in 1977 and 1987.

The maximum clutch size reported from Bolshaya Rogovaya on the Bolshez-emelskaya tundra of north-east (European) Russia is four (Voronin 1977, 1983). Morozov (1991) also states that the maximum clutch size is four in northeastern parts of European Russia. The normal variation of clutch sizes there is from two to four. However Morozov suspects the possibility of a clutch size of one in some nests. From a study of four nests Morozov reported one clutch with no success at all, two clutches with total success and three chicks fledged out of clutch of four in one instance. Brood size varied from one to four. In the Bolshezemelskaya tundra Voronin (1986) reported three chicks fledged out of four eggs laid; another pair fledged one chick, with the second found dead close to the nest. Attacks by neighbouring Peregrine Falcons were suspected as cause of the death of the chick. The average breeding success in north-east European Russia is two chicks per pair per year in the shrub tundra subzone (variation from 1.7 to 2.3 chicks per pair). In the Nenetskiy Nature Reserve at the Pechora River the average clutch size for four years at one monitored nest was two, with the average brood size 1.6 (Glotov 2000).

ASIAN DATA

In the northern Urals two young per successful breeding pair was observed by Morozov (1991), while in southern Yamal the figure was 3.67 (*n* = 15) per successful nest (with a variation in clutch size from two to four) (Kalyakin and Vinogradov 1981). At the Anabar River a brood of two chicks close to fledging age was reported by Gladkov and Zaletaev (1962).

Danilov *et al.* (1984) reported clutch sizes of three and four in two nests in the Yamal. In both nests one of the eggs did not hatch. Two, two and three chicks successfully fledged from three locations in the Yamal Peninsula. In 2001 Rupasov (2001) reported an average brood size for Yamal of 2.5 (4 nests). In the area of the Kolyma River and its estuary, in north-east Chukotka, the brood size was 3.14 ± 0.69 (*n* = 7) (Potapov personal data, Krechmar *et al.* 1991). Portenko (1972) reported a nest with two hatchlings and two eggs at a sea-coast site in Chukotka, while Dorogoi (1991) reported a nest with two chicks at Koolen' Lake, north-east Chukotka on 11 July.

Kishinskiy (1980) referred to a report from a Reindeer herder from the Achayvaam River, Chukotka, about a nest with five eggs, but the maximum clutch size he witnessed was four. A similar maximum clutch size was reported by Kalyakin and Vinogradov (1981) for Taimyr. In the Koryak District of north Kamchatka Gorovenko (2003) observed eight clutches and noted that they all contained four eggs. Out of 16 eggs in his sample 11 chicks fledged.

DATA FROM NORTH AMERICA AND GREENLAND

In Alaska out of 133 eggs a total of 82 young were reared (Cade 1960). The average of number of chicks found in nests of Alaska was reported as 2.4 (Cade 1960). White and Roseneau (1970) reported 3, 2, 4 and 1 chicks fledged in 1959–63 from a site at the Tweet dredger, Seward, Alaska, where four eggs were laid every year during the period 1958–63. Another site on an abandoned sluice box had four eggs in the clutch. However, only two eggs were found on 11 June. During subsequent visits on foot the researchers found two cold eggs which were collected for pesticide analysis. Kessel (1989) reported that 16 clutches on the Seward Peninsula in 1968–69 averaged 3.6 ± 0.5 eggs.

In Canada's Yukon Territory Platt (1977) reported a breeding rate of 2.9 to 3.3 young per successful pair in the nests which were undisturbed or subjected to disturbance by humans. During this time Platt was making his study of the influence of disturbance on Gyrs of both humans and a helicopter (see Chapter 6).

Kuyt (1962) reported a brood size of three in two consecutive years on a site at Lookout Point, Thelon River, in Canada's Northwest Territories. All three chicks successfully fledged from this site. In a later paper more detailed data were provided (Kuyt 1980): the Gyrfalcons produced an average 2.9 ± 0.6 chicks per year (*n* = 17). No trend in the occupancy levels was detected.

In the Horton River study area, Northwest Territories, Canada the average clutch size was 3.7 eggs (Obst 1994). The mean brood size was lower for tree (2.1) than cliff nesters (2.86). Obst also found 11 dead nestlings under tree nests with an estimated average age of 20 days ± 6.8 days. Poole (1987) recorded clutch sizes in a 2,000km² study area in Canada's Nunavut Province which accommodated 14–18

Gyrfalcon territories. In the years 1982–86 the mean clutch size was 3.80 ± 0.52, and the mean brood size was 2.53 ± 0.89, with the mean number of chicks fledged 1.50 ± 1.43 per successful pair. Later, Shank and Poole (1994) studied Gyrfalcon populations in 13 study areas across the Northwest Territories and Nunavut, Canada. They observed a total of 316 broods during the period 1982–91. The average brood size was 2.5 ± 0.91. The brood size distribution across the years was far from normal. Although it was more or less symmetrical (skewness 0.03), the kurtosis was –0.79, indicating platykurtic distribution. Skewness in this study fluctuated between –0.51 and +0.51, showing that in some years the brood size distribution could be skewed towards small broods, or towards large broods. Interestingly, brood size in Shank and Poole's study (1994) demonstrated amazing stability over ten years and had no statistically significant differences across subsample territories or across years. Earlier, Salter and coauthors (1980) reported 25 young produced from ten sites in 1973, 13+ young at four sites in 1974, five young at two sites in 1975, and 18 young at six sites in 1976. The mean brood size varied from 2.22 to 2.86 in the years 1983–86 (Poole and Bromley 1988b).

Summers and Green (1974) reported four successfully fledged Gyrs at a nest in north-east Greenland in 1972 at 72°16'N. The fledged young were seen later in the season. In west Greenland (Peregrine Fund Report 1999–2002) it was reported that the breeding rate was 3.28 young per successful pair in 2000 and 2.9 young per successful pair in 2001. Note that these results are preliminary as the study is on-going and the data are not yet fully analysed and published.

Conclusions

Data available from the literature, with a small addition from our data, allows us to calculate the mean clutch size across the range (3.3 ± 0.81, *n* = 308) and brood size (2.6 ± 0.91, *n* = 364). Figure 7.2a demonstrates that the clutch size distribution is not normal but asymmetrical (negative skew coefficient –0.83: this means that the distribution is skewed toward large clutches). Negative kurtosis of the clutch size distribution means a 'peaky' distribution. Brood size is more symmetrical (see Figure 7.2b), although it still has a negative skew (–0.07) and a positive kurtosis (0.29), *i.e.* a 'blunt' bell curve. Hatching success varies from 0 to 100% in some clutches and years, but overall the hatching success rate is of order 80%, with a fledge success rate of order 67%.

White and Cade (1971) have shown that breeding output is dependent on local Ptarmigan density. They recorded 2.2 young per nest when the Ptarmigan population was decreasing, 1.3 when it was reduced, and, in the worst of five years, there was no breeding at all. Along 183 miles of the Colville River, when Ptarmigan and microtine-rodent numbers were low, 12 pairs of Gyrfalcons produced 18 young to fledging.

SEX RATIO IN THE BROOD

In Iceland the sex ratio was documented by Nielsen (Cade *et al.* 1998) as 101 (50.5%) males to 99 (49.5%) females. In Sweden one territory produced 15 males and 16 females in 15 years (Lind and Nordin 1995). In Canada's Nunavut Province, Poole and Bromley (1988a) noted 35 males and 35 females in their study. However, despite these data pointing to the sex ratio in Gyrfalcons being the normal 50–50 distribution, currently there is insufficient data to draw any firm conclusion as it is known that in cyclical populations the sex ratio of young can differ from normal.

DEVELOPMENT OF THE CHICKS

Hatching is usually almost synchronous, all eggs hatching within 72 hours. This figure was reported by Poole and Bromley (1988a) who observed hatching in six nests within 48 hours and in one nest within 72 hours. Immediately after hatching the chick weighs 34.4 g (Shklyarevich and Krasnov 1980).

Chicks were nine days old at two study nests before the female left them alone; thereafter the females were away from the nests for about two hours each day (Platt 1989). Females begin longer foraging trips when the nestlings are 14–25 days old (Jenkins 1978, Poole and Boag 1988, Platt 1989).

The size differences within the brood (which sometimes indicate a spread of up to six days in the estimated age of the chicks) are not always due to asynchronous hatching. It is also possible for such differences to develop as a result of sibling competition for food, or even starvation (Cade *et al.* 1998). However, Kishinskiy (1958) found a nest on the Muchka River on Russia's Kola Peninsula when the chicks were in first down plumage. Of the two chicks one was significantly older.

Young are not usually aggressive towards each other (Fletcher and Webby 1977, Potapov and Sale pers. obs.). Competition for food is, rather, expressed in races along the ledge to reach food delivered by an adult. If it is a male delivering the prey item, it normally does not tear the item into pieces: instead it gives it to the first chick. The latter then moves it towards a corner of the ledge with wings spread, trying (in most cases successfully) to isolate the prey item from other siblings. If the adult female delivers the prey item, it normally tears off small pieces of prey and gives the pieces to the chicks individually. Naturally they swallow the pieces as fast as possible and loudly claim another piece, trying to force themselves as close as possible to the female. Young Gyrs at about 25 to 30 days of age are able to feed themselves, but most often try to swallow the delivered food in one piece.

The development of nestlings was studied in detail by Poole (1989). The aim of his study was to develop a method of determining the age, and therefore to allow a back chronology of breeding. The study showed that determination of the sex of chicks is unreliable below four weeks of age. The study was based on the growth curves of 11 males and nine females from a total of seven nests observed over two years in the Kilgavik study area of Canada's Nunavut Province. The weight gain of Gyr chicks produced an S-shaped curve (Figure 7.3) which is typical of birds. The maximum rate of growth occured between 12 and 23 days. During this period, the average weight gain in female Gyr chicks was 59g per day and in males 50g per day (Poole 1989).

At the age of 25 days the chicks had primaries in pin ('brushes'). On the 30th day rectrices in pin appeared, as did all the flight feathers, primary-coverts, alula, breast feathers and head feathers. Poole (1989) stated that the rectrices were often tattered because of abrasion in the nest. He found that the age of a nestling could

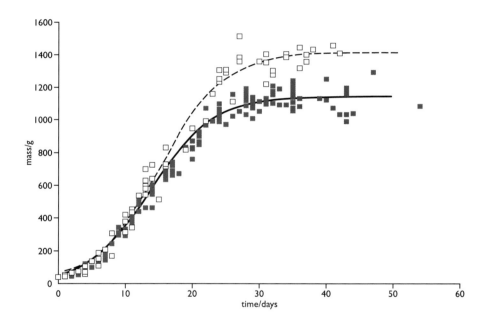

Figure 7.3 *Growth curves of male (lower line) and female (upper line) Gyrfalcons. Data combined from Kola (Shklyarevich and Krasnov 1980), central Canadian Arctic (Poole 1989), and Lower Kolyma, north-east Siberia (Potapov, unpublished data). The curve equation (see Ricklefs 1983 for explanation and Potapov 1993 for fitting technique) is:*

$$Wb = \frac{A}{1 + e^{-k(t - t_i)}}$$

where A = asymptote, k = growth constant, t = age, days, t_i = age at the inflection point. Fitted parameters are: males: A = 1153, k = 0.2119, t_i = 14.6; females: A = 1408, k = 0.2086, t_i = 15.1.

be calculated on the basis of the length of the seventh primary: age (days) = 0.15 primary length + 11.7. This formula was correct if the age of the nestling was more than 11 days. If the nestling was less than 11 days old (*i.e.* prior to the emergence of the primary remiges), then the bird's age was best determined by this formula:

$$\text{age (days)} = -0.000069(\text{weight})^2 + 0.057(\text{weight}) - 1.2$$

The young start to flap their wings at the fourth week (Woodin 1980). Males fledge at the age of 45–50 days (mean 46 days), females 45–50 days (mean 48.3 days) (Cade 1960, Shklyarevich and Krasnov 1980, Poole and Bromley 1988a, Cade *et al.* 1998).

BEHAVIOUR OF THE PARENTS

BROODING BEHAVIOUR

The female sits on the clutch from the laying of the first egg, but she does not sit tightly until some time later, probably from the laying of the third egg (Palmer 1988). At some eyries female Gyrfalcons can be approached very closely before they move off her clutch. Usually the male transfers the food to the female while she is off the eggs and, for the few minutes while she is eating at a perch, the male broods the clutch. On occasion the female might get off the eggs in order to pursue intruders seen from the nest, e.g. Golden Eagles, skuas and foxes (Palmer 1988).

   Most of the work of incubation, brooding and guarding is done by the female Gyrfalcon. The male is the major food provider during incubation and the early brooding period, though he does also incubate and brood the chicks himself. The male most often relieves the female in the morning and the afternoon while she is eating the food he delivers, but will sometimes replace her even without provisioning (Cade *et al.* 1998, Platt 1989, Jenkins 1978). In Canada the proportion of the male's share of incubation was reported as 17–24% (Poole and Bromley 1988a). The average duration of a male incubation shift is also lower, at 140 minutes, compared with 261 minutes for the females (Platt 1989). There is, however, a large variation in the proportions of time shared by the sexes in incubation and brood duties in Gyrfalcons, so that while it is true to say that the female Gyr performs most of the incubation, the male may sit for as much as one-third of daylight hours (Platt 1977). Cade *et al.* (1998) concluded that the chicks were brooded by the female for almost 80% of the time in the first two weeks.

   In Woodin's (1980) study, both sexes made many of the same movements while incubating the eggs. These movements were:

1. an incomplete rotation, which involved a rocking from side to side of the body, a back-and-forth shuffling of the feet, and, later, a downwards bumping of the belly
2. picking up and dropping material in the nest cup with the beak
3. preening
4. snapping at flies.

The time between egg turnings was variable and ranged from over an hour to a few minutes. The function of the female's picking up and dropping of the nest cup material with her beak, if not merely a nervous release, might have been to keep the nest material broken up and soft, thereby creating better insulation for the eggs against the cold. Male Gyrs were not observed manipulating nest material in this way.

The mechanics of nest exchange vary greatly. Female departure seems to be stimulated simply by her awareness of the male's arrival in the vicinity. When the female departs, the male may then either go on to the eggs immediately or may delay doing so, sometimes for up to 30 minutes. Only occasionally does the male Gyr initiate the exchange of incubation duties. In Woodin's study (1980) the male did this by flying to the eyrie ledge and calling angrily until the female surrendered the eggs. His way of surrendering the eggs to her was also variable. Sometimes the mere sight of the returning female was enough to make him depart. At other times he left the eggs only reluctantly and with much urging on the part of the female.

Jenkins (1978) studied Gyrfalcon behaviour at two nests in west-central Greenland using time-lapse photography. According to his observations both females spent almost their entire day (82–84%) at the eyries brooding during the first 15 days of the nestling period. The male's participation in brooding varied somewhat between the nests, but was significantly lower than that of the female (3–11%). Jenkins perhaps assumed that the Gyrfalcon follows the trend of Eurasian Kestrels and Peregrines, and that both sexes avoid being on the nest at the same time (Tinbergen 1940, Enderson *et al.* 1972), but he managed to photograph at least eight instances of the male and female attending the nest together at one nest and numerous instances on the other, and even noted that the two participated in cooperative feeding behaviour.

The time-lapse photography was also able to reveal the nest relief sequence. The male brought food to the cliff and the female flew out to meet him with considerable screaming. She became quiet only after he left or brooded. Usually the male brooded the young while the female ate. After she had eaten, she picked up the rest of the food item, brought it to the nest, and fed the nestlings. As she approached the eyrie, the brooding male quickly slipped off the nest, seldom actually waiting for her to arrive. He usually left the area, but sometimes perched on the nest cliff. Jenkins also observed the cessation of brooding behaviour, and found that it did not occur suddenly. Instead, the young were left unbrooded for increasingly longer periods.

At around ten days, the second nestling down is evident and nestlings have acquired considerable thermoregulatory control. At this time brooding begins to wane. The brooding of 14–20-day-old nestlings took place chiefly during times of (relative) heat and cold, and during precipitation. The last period of any recorded brooding at one eyrie was a two-minute period by the male Gyr when the young were 19 and 20 days of age. Due to the size of the chicks the brooding had probably become physically impossible at this time.

At a second site Jenkins reported that the female did not immediately leave the vicinity of the eyrie when the young were older, but frequently spent time perched within a couple of metres of the nest. Eventually she began to spend increasingly longer periods away from the eyrie, presumably to hunt.

Females, and occasionally males, 'guard' their broods by perching quietly on the nest, or on a nearby ledge or tree. Their main objective seems to be to observe the vicinity of the nest which may not be visible from the nest itself. In the event of the approach of a dangerous animal (human, bear, etc.) the adult Gyr will leave the perch and fly between the dangerous object and the nesting cliff, at the same time alerting the mate and/or the young at the nest and roughly indicating the direction of the danger (Potapov pers. obs.).

FEEDING THE CHICKS

Poole and Boag (1988) stated that in the Kilgavik study area in Canada's Nunavut Province male Gyrs participated in only 5.7% of the direct feedings recorded on time-lapse equipment at five Gyrfalcon nests. In many instances females flew up to 2km to meet the incoming male and receive prey. Thus the predominance of feeding by females recorded on film cannot be interpreted as representing the killing of prey by females. Male Gyrfalcons provided 73% of prey items brought to the nest site (n = 125). Males also provided all the prey for the females during incubation and for the females and chicks during the first 2–3 weeks post-hatch. Females began foraging trips when the chicks were 18–25 days old. Absences covered short periods initially, then increased as the young grew.

In the study of Woodin (1980), the male did all the hunting after the eggs had hatched, though only the female was seen to feed the young. Sometimes she fed herself before bringing food to the chicks. The rate of feeding was erratic, with many feedings on some days and few on others. The ceremony surrounding the exchange of prey between male and female had become quite regular by the time of hatching. In the first weeks after hatching, while the female remained near the young or in the immediate vicinity of the eyrie, prey exchange occurred near the eyrie, as it had during incubation. Sometimes the female made wailing calls after receiving the prey: in the most prolonged (and remarkable) instance the female called continuously for 16 minutes until the male had left the area.

The female is responsible for dissecting the prey and actually feeding small pieces to the young. In general, male Gyrs seem only to deliver prey, either to the female or to the nest, or to a ledge close to the nest. If the female is not on the nest when the male delivers food the prey might lie close to the nest for several hours. The female usually stands on the prey item and pulls out pieces of flesh with her beak, feeding the young beak to beak. Prey intestines are fed equally with muscle tissue (Kishinskiy 1958).

According to Jenkins (1978), feeding of the young took two forms:

1. active feeding by tearing off small pieces of flesh from a carcass and passing them to the young
2. food delivery or the passing of an entire food item to a nestling.

The former was used by both adults (if the male engaged in feeding) when the young were too small to tear morsels from a carcass. After the nestling developed the strength and coordination to tear up its own food, the male began making food delivery visits. The male began this when the young were 23 and 24 days old, and engaged in active feeding only occasionally after that. The female actively fed the young throughout the entire nestling period, never allowing the young once to feed themselves. However, observations at a second eyrie (and personal observations) suggest that this may not be usual Gyr behaviour.

Feeding was recorded for every hour of the day, with a maximum occurring at around 16:00 hrs and a minimum at midnight. There was little regularity or predictability to feedings, the periodicity being linked entirely with hunting success and prey activity cycles. The first recorded feeding of chicks took place on the first and second day of life for the two nestlings observed by Jenkins (1978). Enderson *et al.* (1972) recorded feeding within four to eight hours of hatching for Peregrine chicks.

From the study of Poole and Boag (1988) the feeding frequency showed slight morning and evening peaks (around 08:00 hrs and 18:00 hrs), but the overall pattern was effectively even through the day. The daily feeding rate increases from hatching until the chicks are 10–12 days of age, at which point it reaches a plateau. The rate then slowly decreases after the young reach about 25 days of age. A maximum feed rate of 12 feeds a day has been recorded. Feeding lasts from 1 to 37 minutes, averaging 12 minutes (Poole and Boag 1988, Cade *et al.* 1998). The interval between feeds was reported as 3.1 hours in younger and 4.2 hours in older broods (Platt 1989). However the frequency of feeding varies. In Norway when the chicks were about to fledge it was observed that the rate was three feeds per day (Langvatn and Moksnes 1979). In Kola the chicks were fed from three to six times per day, with an average of four daily feeds (Schklyarevich and Krasnov 1980).

In Greenland the feeding time on a single delivery of a Ptarmigan lasted from one to 30 minutes with an average of 15.9 minutes (Booms and Fuller 2003a).

The same study showed that feeding on a hare leveret lasted from one to ten minutes with an average close to ten minutes. On average the feeding time on any prey item lasted 13.3 minutes. This average was the same across the four nest sites of the study and did not vary with the number of nestlings. Booms and Fuller noted two slight peaks in delivery frequencies: one between 07:00 hrs and 11:00 hrs, the other between 16:00 hrs and 21:00 hrs. There was a substantial decline in deliveries between 21:00 hrs and midnight.

For older nestlings food delivery times are short. Jenkins (1978) reported that after 28 days the adults spent less than 3% of the day at the eyrie. Visits by the male Gyr were of minimal duration, averaging only 9.3 seconds, so short that there was a fear that time-lapse recording had missed many visits. This could be connected with the fact that at 5–7 weeks old the chicks start eating on their own, but could also be connected with the aggressiveness of the hungry young towards their parents. In one incident Jenkins (1978) recorded that when one nestling of a pair received a food item from a parent and carried it to a corner of the eyrie, the other nestling continued to beg from the adult and went as far as grabbing the adult's crop with its foot. The adult Gyrfalcon– in this instance the male – wrenched free of the chick's grip and flew off.

Cooperative feeding is rare, but it has been observed. Jenkins (1978) observed a brooding female. She flew from the nest, the male then arriving and starting to brood. The female returned with a food item, but the male did not leave the nest immediately upon her arrival. The female was seen standing on the food item, tearing a titbit from the carcass, and giving it to the male. The male then fed the titbit to the nestlings. The male ended this cooperative feeding behaviour by leaving the eyrie, and the female finished feeding the young.

Though feeding visits are unpredictable, their imminence can be inferred by typical actions of the chicks, which flap their wings and scream whenever an adult appears in view. Excess food items are removed from the nest by the adults until the young are developed enough to feed themselves. To remove the waste the adults pick the item up in their beaks, but then usually leap in the air, bringing their feet forward. The waste is then transferred to the feet for disposal.

REACTION TO HUMANS

Cade *et al.* (1998) summarised their studies by stating that the reaction of Gyrfalcons to humans varies greatly: some females and males do not show themselves at any period of the breeding cycle, whereas the boldest female may actually hit an observer. Generally, both sexes defend the nest, but the female seems to be more fearless. Observations by one of us (Potapov) of Kolyma Gyrfalcons lie in the mid-range on Cade's summary, though the reaction varied at different parts of the breeding period. On a sunny day in the Lower Kolyma, with crisp snow and an ice-bound river, the air temperature approaching -25°C (relatively warm compared to lower winter temperatures in this area) and a gentle breeze, the author approached a cliff on the riverbank and spotted a nest. He saw a Gyrfalcon quietly making a pass along the cliff and disappearing behind some larch trees at the top of the cliff. That was the only sighting of the male Gyr that day. The pass by the male is designed to inform the female at the nest that 'something is approaching, be alert' as the female, sitting deep in the nest, has a reduced view. The author climbed up to the nest. The female was glimpsed, making one call before departing to reveal four eggs which were incredibly warm compared to the deep cold of the surrounding cliff and the air. The author retreated immediately so that the eggs would not become chilled. Despite the remoteness of the site, which almost certainly meant that human visits were rare, and climbs to the nest site even rarer, the author was surprised that there was no attempt at an attack. By contrast, a similar approach to a Peregrine nest would be accompanied by noisy birds and even an attacking stoop – though such stoops do not involve close contact.

Langvatn and Moksnes (1979) reported that of 28 approaches they made to a nest the parent Gyrs were actually present only half the time. On most visits they saw only one parent: only on four occasions did they see both. The female was usually more aggressive, while the male often disappeared after a short while. As the observers approached the nest, the Gyrfalcon usually began with warning calls, and showed aggressive behaviour when the observers were at a distance of 100m or less. That females are more aggressive at nest sites was also mentioned by Cerely (1955).

Some of the nests Langvatn and Moksnes (1979) observed were located in a bird census study area. The censuses were performed by experienced bird observers who stayed for up to one month in the field during the time that the Gyrfalcons were rearing their young. Their workdays each year numbered between 95 and 188. However, only in three years out of six did they record any Gyrfalcons, with a single observation of one bird in one year and two observations of single birds in two other years. This indicates that the Gyrfalcons, even though they breed in the area, are very inconspicuous. Similar observations led Ødegaard (1969) to suggest that Gyrfalcons were not as rare as was generally believed.

In his study in Iceland Woodin (1980) reported that the reaction to humans varied as the breeding season progressed. Before the eggs had been laid the adults were shy, and it was difficult to assess one's effect on them. Normally a pair would tolerate an observer within 250–300m as long as the observer remained in the valley below the nest. If the observer took a more commanding position on a slope, about 300m from the nest ledge, the adults began periodic fly-overs, or otherwise indicated their agitation. One nest was abandoned during Woodin's study with its four chicks dying, after a photographer set a hide some 50m from the site. Eyrie defence showed a definite increase until hatching had occurred, then levelled off for a few weeks, then fell. As the time of hatching neared, the brooding female sat tighter upon the observer's approach. Finally she allowed the observer to come within about 3m before flying, though she would return immediately after the observer had left the ledge.

At the stage when the nest contained hatching eggs the birds screamed at the observer when he was at the nest: just after hatching, both parents stooped at the observer. Thereafter the birds' aggressiveness slowly declined: two weeks after hatching the female Gyrfalcon still stooped at the observer; when the chicks were three weeks old the female merely flew back and forth above the eyrie screaming. However, females at two other nests were more aggressive. One female struck the observer, while the other dived repeatedly within less than 1m of the observer. The aggressiveness of the female at one of Woodin's nests increased as the incubation progressed, and did not decrease after hatching. At any time the presence of more than one person made the attacks of both the observed females less aggressive and, if the observer happened to arrive when the females were away, the attacks upon their return were less vigorous. At one nest, where the chicks were less than one week from fledging, the female Gyr attacked Woodin when he was collecting prey remains from the nest site, even though the young Gyrs were at the time in the lava field below. Strangely she then ignored him when he attempted to catch the young. Interestingly, Woodin concluded that the eyries with more aggressive females were also more successful in fledging young.

Also in Iceland, Wayre and Jolly (1958) stated that both parent birds would attack an observer, one after the other, screaming their 'cakking' cries. However, the birds always passed several metres away. At another nest, the birds flew around once without calling while the observers were entering the gorge where the nest site was situated, but then disappeared and did not return. Later their nest was found to be empty.

When humans approach, the male Gyrfalcon seldom stays nearby but circles high overhead and drifts away. Some females may be also very shy, but others, with much calling, may circle for a while before leaving or may even make passes over the intruder. Mishenko (1981) reported that at a nest in southern Yamal, Russia, the adults attacked humans, approaching them in a dive to a distance of 7m at the time when one chick had fledged and another was about to fledge. Kalyakin and Vinogradov (1981) reported that the reaction of adult Gyrs becomes more nervous when the chicks approached fledging. The alarm calls started when an observer approached to within 100–200m of the nest. The adults flew to a distance of some tens of metres and often sat on surrounding trees. Such behaviour continued up to the period when the brood broke up and dispersed.

The differences noted above indicate that alarm behaviour in Gyrs varies from pair to pair. In one pair the adults might be very hostile, but in another they might remain very quiet.

DAILY ROUTINE

On Russia's Kola Peninsula Kishinskiy (1958) stated that the male Gyr woke at 03:50 hrs. During the polar day it is possible to see some Gyr activity at any time, but normally the adults rest in the vicinity of nest during the 'night'. The female Gyr usually departs for the morning hunt very early, at about 04:00–05:00 hrs. During the middle of the day the birds have a 'siesta', the male resting on his outlook post, the female at the nest.

Voronin (1984) recorded the activities of Gyrfalcons in Russia's Bolshezemelsakya tundra. He reported the onset of activity between 03:00 and 04:00hrs. The male Gyr spent 4 to 5 hours sleeping each day, the sleep consisting of continuous sleep (with both eyes closed) which lasted from only 22 to 122 seconds (with an average of 68 seconds) with short periods of observation between the sleeps. Mishenko (1981) stated that Gyrfalcons are active from 05:00 to 23:00hrs, with the maximum activity shown between 06:00 and 12:00hrs. Such observations indicate that Gyrfalcons maintain a circadian rhythm even during the polar day, but also that they are capable, in certain circumstances, of hunting around the clock.

POST-FLEDGING LIFE

Woodin (1980) reported that young Gyrs spend two to three weeks learning to fly and following their parents to the hunting grounds. After fledging the young normally spend about three weeks around the nest site (Kishinskiy 1958), sometimes coming back to the nest itself. At the beginning of August the young disappear from the breeding site.

Fledging was reported on 7 July in the Russia's southern Yamal in a year with an early spring and little snow cover in winter, and on 10 August in a year with a late spring and high snow cover in winter (Kalyakin and Vinogradov 1981). In the Lower Kolyma the young leave the nest from about 25 June at the timberline to 7–10 July for nests on nearby tundra, and 10 August in nests far from the timberline and outside areas of high grouse density. Kalyakin and Vinogradov reported that the broods stay together well into the autumn and consider late brood break-up as a peculiar characteristic of the species. They also reported that the adults deliver food to prematurely fledged young. Known as jumpers, these youngsters leave the nest too early and may sit on the local tundra.

Kalyakin and Vinogradov considered that Gyrfalcon chicks gained their flight abilities slower than Peregrines. According to their observations it took about a week after the first flight to master the process. Interestingly there were observations of chicks having their first flight across a river, and then remaining on the ground for a few days being fed by parents until they were able to take off again.

Jenkins (1978) reported that before nestlings fledged the adults appeared to be delivering food to the nest rather than to the chicks. Even if the nestlings were standing only a few metres away from the nest on nearby ledges, screaming and flapping their wings, the adults landed on the nest. After the first nestling fledged, the adults still delivered food to the nest rather than to the fledgling. Hence the first-fledged young was forced to return to the nest to be fed eight times after it had fledged, before its nest-mate fledged two days later.

Bengtson (1972) reported that of 13 chicks fledged, 12 remained in the vicinity of the nest after one week, and 10 remained after two weeks. In Norway young Gyrs were reported to leave the nest over a period of five days, and then to remain within 200–300m of the nest. However, after one week the birds were able to fly up to 1km away (Langvatn and Moksnes 1979, Poole and Bromley 1988a). During the sixth week the chicks begin to hunt for themselves (Woodin 1980).

Kalyakin (1989) considers that after fledging there are two types of social behaviour in a pair depending on the age of the male bird. If the male is young and inexperienced, it spends an increasing amount of time hunting grouse for the brood against a background of a depleting grouse population. As a result, after fledging the adult male stays largely out of touch with the brood. More experienced males switch to alternative quarry when grouse numbers decline, and after their broods have fledged they guard and feed them, so the female has more time for hunting for herself (Kalyakin 1994). In optimal conditions, such broods stay on the home territory for up to three months. By contrast Hagen and Barth (1952) state that the young Gyrfalcons remained as a group in the vicinity of the nest for at least one week and were frequently fed by their parents. It is likely that in years of poor food supply the brood disperses earlier, and this, perhaps, decreases its survival rate.

The young learn to hunt slowly. In the first six weeks after fledging they rely almost entirely on food supplied by the adults. The young only occasionally catch fledglings of small birds, and small mammals.

SURVIVAL OF ADULTS

Survival of adult Gyrs was measured in Iceland, where in 32 territory-years there were two replacements. This means that 90% of adults survived (Cade *et al.* 1998). The survival in the first year was thought likely to be 50%.

In one territory occupied for at least 15 years in northern Sweden one female Gyrfalcon bred for seven years, the second female at the site breeding for another seven years. The same male is thought to have bred in all 15 years (Lind and Nordin 1995). However, this record has to be treated with caution as it refers to unmarked individuals. The oldest ringed bird known is a 12-year-old male reported by Cade *et al.* (1998).

CHAPTER 8

Dispersal, Seasonal Movements and Winter Distribution

There are several ways to study the migration patterns of a species. The simplest is to record birds at breeding and wintering locations and then to compare these with possible migration routes. This method could be extended by making use of the large number of properly tagged specimens in museums across the world. Another way, one traditionally used in ornithology, is through ringing. However ringing requires there to be a reasonably large number of marked individuals, together with several trapping stations to record these individuals along their migration route. If the species in question is rare then this method provides few data. However, despite this reservation, the ringing of Gyrfalcon chicks and adults has taken place successfully in Iceland, Scandinavia, Yamal (Russia), Alaska (USA), Canada and Greenland.

Satellite telemetry (Fuller *et al.* 1995) has also been used, a technique that enables the monitoring of movements in an accurate way, though the sample size is necessarily small. In this technique a small transmitter is attached to a bird, the transmitted signal being picked up by the Argos satellite system orbiting the earth. By measuring the Doppler shift of the emitted signal the system can measure the exact distance between the transmitter and the satellite: knowing the parameters of the satellite orbit, the system can also calculate the exact coordinates of the transmitter. The method is expensive, but the data it provides are, to date, the best available in describing the movements of migratory birds. So far, satellite telemetry has been used on Gyrfalcons in Alaska and Greenland.

Gyrfalcon studies have shown that after fledging, young birds can wander over vast areas of the sub-Arctic. Indeed, the autumnal dispersal of young Gyrfalcons has often been treated as a migration, though in reality it is more a search for territory. There have been no specific studies on the dispersal of Gyrfalcons other than that of Nielsen (1991) in Iceland which suggested that Gyrs were, generally, fairly sedentary. However, it has to be borne in mind that Iceland is a relatively small island, and there is reason to believe that young Gyrs from continental parts of Eurasia and North America disperse over significant distances.

Cade (1960) noticed the extreme rarity of immature and first-year birds within the breeding range during summer and autumn. In six years he saw only one individual, which he identified as a one-year-old bird. The sighting was off Pitt Point on the Arctic coast of Alaska in late July: this location is a coastal plain well outside the Gyr breeding habitat.

Generally, adult Gyrfalcons stay at the breeding grounds all year round, though high-Arctic birds do come south to avoid the polar night. However, loyalty to the breeding area is significantly affected by fluctuations in the numbers of Willow Grouse and Ptarmigan. If food is scarce, the adults may shift location towards an area with a better source.

Dementiev (1941) was the first author to state clearly that the Gyrfalcon is both a migratory and a sedentary species. Cade (1960) found what appeared to be winter perches near Gyrfalcon nesting cliffs on the Colville River in Alaska and suggested that the birds probably wintered on their breeding grounds. However, Sutton (1960) discounted Cade's idea that Gyrfalcons could winter at Colville River latitudes (68°) and stated that there were few, if any, valid records of high-latitude Gyrfalcons in midwinter. Beebe (1974) maintained that only a few Gyrfalcons remained north of the timberline during winter and that they survived only by feeding on sea ducks. Kalyakin (1989) agreed with Cade (1960) when he found the fresh remains of a Willow Grouse at a nesting site in southern Yamal.

Platt (1976, 1977) was perhaps the first ornithologist who worked specifically with wintering Gyrs, his studies showing beyond doubt that the birds winter near their nest sites, and that it is the males who are more likely to do so. It is now clear that where possible Gyrs prefer to be resident, the dispersal of young birds being a variable, migratory movement, and the entire pattern of movement for all ages being affected by an unstable or seasonally varying food supply (Palmer 1988).

In most cases birds found outside the breeding range are immatures and subadults (Clum and Cade 1994), an observation which holds true in both the New and Old Worlds. Nevertheless the world's museum collections contain adult birds from places well outside the breeding range, including Ireland, Scotland and southern Russia.

In this chapter we shall endeavour to compile wintering records of the Gyrfalcon based on ringing data, museum specimens and a selection of reliable sightings of the species. The latter are sometimes difficult to find in the literature, especially for the Asian part of the Gyr's range, the most frequent problem being that even well-trained ornithologists sometimes misidentify light morphs of the Saker Falcon, which breed and winter in southern Siberia, Mongolia and China, as Gyrfalcons. This problem is exacerbated by the lack of good telescopes available for researchers in the area. Consequently, almost all Saker light morphs in this region in winter are recorded as Gyrfalcons. References where we suspect misidentification is highly probable are noted in the text. We have also avoided the citations of numerous birdwatchers, as to include them would make the reference list grow out of proportion to its value, and would skew the wintering range towards those countries with a strong tradition of birdwatching, making some regions of central Canada and the USA, as well as Siberia, under-represented. In addition, the strong tradition of falconry in Europe, Canada and the USA means some escaped birds may be misidentified as wintering birds, biasing the data. Apart from data obtained by satellite telemetry, the data we use is more or less equally spread across the wintering range.

Due to the cyclic nature of Ptarmigan/Willow Grouse populations, the appearance of the Gyrfalcons in southern areas is irruptive. The link between the cyclicity of grouse in northern latitudes and the irregular occurrences of Gyrs south of the breeding range was first noted by Palmer (1988) on the basis of an analysis of records of Gyrfalcons in the 'lower 48' states. One can speculate why records from a particular location may be separated by many years. This could be due to an uneven observation effort in a particular region in winter, or to weather fluctuations which make wintering birds shift somewhat within the breeding range. Alternatively the Gyrs might opt to stay within the breeding range at the timberline, feeding on wintering flocks of grouse. In fact, one can predict the best wintering conditions for Gyrfalcons in years after a high population year and after a depression. In such years the numbers of wintering grouse flocks at the timberline is high. One of the authors (Potapov) witnessed a huge concentration of Willow Grouse in Eastern Chukotka (Siberia) at the timberline in the years 1987 and 1988. In 1987 broods of local grouse were 100m apart, whereas in 1988 there was an equal concentration of non-breeding grouse which did not disperse into the normally occupied northern flat tundras. The local reindeer herdsman told the author that when a helicopter had visited their camp, on landing it had raised a dense flock of grouse nearly 1km long. The sound of the grouse wings exceeded that of the aircraft – a huge MI8 helicopter. Gyrfalcons were doing very well in these years, and equally well in 1989, a year of deep depression in grouse numbers. The author did not hear of any winter records of Gyrs during the winter of 1989/90, presumably because they had migrated elsewhere. However, there were many reports of wintering Gyrs in 1987/88.

Our data are plotted in Figures 8.1 and 8.2 (see colour section). It can be concluded that, in general, the wintering range of Gyrfalcons is merely an extension of the breeding range, with the presence of longitudal movements. Migrations outside the continents where Gyrs are breeding are unheard of. Lack of resistance to high ambient temperatures makes it virtually impossible to imagine that Gyrs would fly of their own accord to the tropics or subtropics. Thus climatic limits consign Gyrfalcons to the countries of the species' breeding range, as well as northern Europe, Kazakhstan, Russia, Mongolia, northern China, Canada and the USA. There are no reliable records of Gyrs in Mexico or North Africa.

RINGING DATA

Ringing has been carried out on a limited scale in Greenland (Mattox 1970, Burnham and Mattox 1984), the latter study having no recoveries. In a ringing effort in 1965 Mattox ringed 51 mostly young birds. Of these, five were re-covered later, all in Greenland. In 1967 a total of ten females and four juvenile birds were ringed in autumn at Disko, two females later being recovered in south Greenland. One was found 390km south-west of the ringing station, another was shot by a hunter 160km from the ringing station. In Iceland ringing has been carried out on a relatively large scale (Nielsen 1991). However, the Icelandic birds are believed not to migrate off the island, so in this case ringing in effect provides data on dispersal rather than on migration. The mean dispersal range of young Gyrs recovered in August and September was 16km (range 9–23km) for males and 12km (range 1–25km) for females. In October the distance increased, reaching 58km (14–109km) for males and 142km (24–384km) for females. Juveniles were mostly found in coastal areas. All recoveries from birds ringed in Iceland have come from within the island. There has been no confirmed record of emigration (Cade *et al.* 1998).

Seventeen recoveries of birds ringed in Scandinavia (1936–83) ranged from 17km to 707km from the ringing site (Tømmeraas 1993). Two-thirds of the birds were found during their first autumn, the oldest two and a half years later. A total of 14 recoveries were made on the Norwegian coast. One bird ringed in Scandinavia crossed the Baltic Sea and was found in Mamony, Pskov District, near the Estonian and Latvian borders (56°N 28°E), the southernmost recovery of a ringed example of the species (Tømmeraas 1993). In Finland there were six recoveries from 155 birds ringed up to 1966 (Saurola 1997). One of the one-and-a-half-year-old birds was recovered in Lofoten, Norway in winter (Cade *et al.* 1998).

Schmutz *et al.* (1991) analysed and ringed Gyrfalcons in Canada. Out of 301 birds ringed there had been six recoveries (one trapped alive, the other five dead or injured). Four birds were recovered between September and January, between 900km and 2,400km south or west of their nesting area. Two Gyrs were recovered near their nests. A bird found dead in Courtenay, British Columbia on 4 April 1986 was ringed as a nestling near Whitehorse, Southern Yukon, on 21 June 1984 (Campbell *et al.* 1990).

WINTER SIGHTINGS AND WINTERING RANGE

EUROPEAN RECORDS

There have been several records in Svalbard of non-breeding and wintering Gyrs (Kristoffersen 1931). Summer records are also known from Franz Josef Land (Guker Island), but there are no confirmed breeding records (Pleshak 2003).

The first known scientific depiction of the Gyrfalcon was made of a bird from Uppsala, Sweden, on 4 February 1698 (Rüdbeck 1693–1710: see Chapter 1). This is perhaps the first documented wintering record of the species. Wintering Gyrfalcons were noted in Stockholm during the winter of 1970–71 (Jenning and Friedzen 1972). Late-autumn sightings of Gyrs were made on Öland Island, Sweden (Forsman 1993). Overall for Sweden about 10 to 20 Gyrs are recorded annually in Sweden, south of the bird's breeding range. Some Gyrs seem to return to the same wintering grounds, even if the area is far away from their breeding grounds, an example being a bird which was sighted in Stockholm over several winters (Jenning and Friedzen 1972).

In Finland there are 59 records south of the Gyr breeding range: 66% in autumn (16 September to 9 November), 8% in winter and 26% in spring (8 April to 12 May). Of these birds 85% were juveniles (*i.e.* only nine adult birds were sighted) (Cade *et al.* 1998). Gyrs occasionally cross the strait from northern Scandinavia to Denmark: between one and four birds have been recorded annually in recent years (Gensbøl and Koskimies 1995), adding to the subadult Gyrs seen in Copenhagen (Tømmeraas 1988) and other areas (Rasmussen 1999) in earlier years. In Germany wintering Gyrfalcons were noted at Westerhever Sand, Eiderstedt (Schmidt 1958). A female Gyrfalcon was collected at Větrušic, 10km from Prague in the Czech Republic in 1926 (Urbanek and Jupa 1961). The specimen is kept at the Prague Natural History Museum. BMNH also has a specimen collected on the Faeroe Islands (BMNH 2066).

The status of the Gyrfalcon in the UK and Ireland is 'occasional winter visitor'. Cadbury (1980) reported one juvenile Gyrfalcon dying after feeding on alpha-chloralose-loaded rabbit bait and a poisoned gull at Islay, UK. Gyrs have also been seen at more southerly points (off Lizard Point in southern England for example). Museum collections have specimens from Argyle, Scotland (BMNH 1934-3-10-2,1) and Pembrokeshire (BMNH 55-12-19.1). In Ireland there have been 50+ winter records 'in apparently natural state' since 1950 according to an unpublished Irish Birds check-list of 2003. Gyrs have also been noted as early spring visitors to Owey Island and Clare Island in the Republic of Ireland (Williams 1905). A wintering specimen from Shannon was part of the famous Rothschild Collection (AMNH 537078). Sightings of Gyrfalcons in both the UK and Ireland can be found in regional bird reports and newsletters.

In Russia's Kola Peninsula Gyrfalcons tend to remain year-round: they are known to winter at Kharlov Island, a breeding location off the Murmansk coast, part of the Seven Islands Nature Reserve (Dementiev and Gortchakovskaya 1945, Schklyarevich and Krasnov 1980). Kokhanov (1970) reported wintering birds at the Bolshoi Ainov island, off the northern coast of western Kola (69°50'N 31°35'E) and the Litskiy Islands of the Seven Islands Nature Reserve (60°41'N 36°E).

There are vagrant records for Vaygach. On Novaya Zemlya there are numerous records of Gyrs, but no proven breeding records (Dementiev 1951). Dementiev (1951) refers to personal communications with S. Uspenskiy, who observed Gyrfalcons feeding on guillemots from the seabird colonies at the Gribova Guba Bay. Kuznetsov (1990) reported a wintering Gyrfalcon at Lake Shihi in Russia's Kostroma District.

ASIAN RECORDS

Kalyakin and Vinogradov (1981) reported sightings of Gyrfalcons, together with Goshawks in winter 1976 at the Laborovaya trading post, southern Yamal. They also noted that the concentrations of wintering Willow Grouse/Ptarmigan were quite high.

In Kazakhstan, Gyrs were recorded only twice in a 12-year period of monitoring. There are winter records for Gyrs from Kokchetav, near Ust'-Kammennogorsk and in Almaty (Pfeffer 1991, 1996, Gavrilov 1999). In autumn birds were sighted in Irtish, and at Pavlodarskoe settlement (Solomatin, in Gavrilov 1999).

In Tatarstan Gyrs are recorded irregularly in winter, mostly in October and November (As'keev and As'keev 1999). However, here it is possible that the observations are actually of Saker Falcons. In Krasnoyarsk a Gyrfalcon was noted in November in the city centre, and in October in the Yenisey River valley at 63°40'N (Yudin 1952). Wintering Gyrs were noted for the Putorana Plateau by Dorogov (1988). In the Tuva Republic the Gyrfalcon was noted as a wintering bird (Baranov 1991), but in this area the Gyr probably overlaps with wintering Sakers: the record is said to be based on an obtained specimen, but there is no indication of where the skin is kept for confirmation of the species, so the record must be viewed with caution. Gyrs have been recorded in the Khudun Mountain Range of western Transbaikalia (Esheev 1989) and in the Baikal Region, and have even been observed in Irkutsk (Ryabtsev 1997). However, here again many of the records may be of Saker Falcons, which also occur in the area during the winter season: investigations suggest that any whitish Saker in this area is automatically recorded as a Gyr.

In the Altai, wintering Gyrfalcons are mentioned by Sushkin (1938). However Sushkin treated the Altai Saker as a separate species, and could therefore be misidentifying a Saker as a Gyrfalcon. No specimens of Gyrfalcon from Altai are to be found in Sushkin's collection, which is currently kept in the Zoological Institute, St Petersburg. In Mongolia two records exist for November visits by Gyrfalcons (Bold and Boldbaatar 1999). However, having discussed these observations with the authors, we are convinced that both were of Saker Falcons.

Alexander Andreev (Krechmar *et al.* 1991) observed a Gyrfalcon eating a Willow Grouse by the Kolyma River on 23 February 1980 at the river's confluence with the Omolon River. Wintering Gyrfalcons were also reported in the Kolyma-Alaseya lowlands between the Cherskiy and Andrushkino settlements (van Orden and Paklina 2000).

Portenko (1972) reported documented sightings of Gyrs at Cape Schmidt, Chukotka on 22 February 1915. In autumn Gyrfalcons have been seen on the coast of Chukotka on a number of occasions. There have also been several reports of sightings of Gyrs on Wrangel Island in autumn and spring (Stishov *et al.* 1991).

Gyrs winter all over the Kamchatka Peninsula, from the northern limit of the peninsula to Lopaka Cape at the southern end (Dementiev 1951, Lobkov 1986, 1999). Gyrs were also seen migrating from the Cape towards the Kuril Islands by Lobkov (1997).

Gyrfalcons are regularly seen in winter on the Commander Islands. In the 1950s there was at least 20–25 individuals recorded during the winter (Marakov 1965), the Gyrs appearing in October and leaving in April. Currently the species is listed as a wintering and rare summer visitor on the islands (Artukin 1998). Eleven autumn/winter Gyr specimens are kept in the American Museum of Natural History (AMNH), New York, five in the Smithsonian, five in the Zoological Institute, St Petersburg, and there is a further one in the Natural History Museum, Stockholm. This number suggests that the Commander Islands have been a regular winter destination for wintering Gyrfalcons for a long time.

There was a winter sighting of a Gyr on the Shantar Islands (Dulkeit and Shulpin 1937) in February. There were no confirmed records of the Gyrfalcon in Ussuriland according to Vorobiev (1954). However, he mentioned a skin from the Khabarovsk Museum of a male shot near the source of the Tunguska River, and a skin from the Harbin Museum in Manchuria, China. The latter was from an immature bird shot on 15 November 1923 at the

Ilyinskiy railway station, 420km east of Harbin. There is also the skin of a male Gyrfalcon shot near Harbin in February 1909 (ZIN 0/2/1909). A sighting was also made in February 1947 in the Kedrovaya Pad Nature Reserve in Primorye (Vorobiev 1954).

There are very few wintering records of Gyrfalcons in the Sakhalin and Kuril Islands (Gizenko 1955, Nechaev 1991), these records mostly relating to the northern part of the islands. Nechaev (1991) noted Gyrfalcons as a wintering species on Sakhalin Island. Nechaev states that Gyrs are not a rarity during October to December. There were observations from Terpenia Cape and Krilion Point (48°N 144°E) and the village of Ulianovka, while in Novoakersandrovsk a Gyr attacked a chicken on 30 October 1961 (Nechaev 1991). In Japan observations are rare, and almost all are made during the winter – 25 December to 15 March – in Hokkaido, where the Gyr seems to be a regular winter visitor (Brazil and Hanawa 1991).

NORTH AMERICAN RECORDS

Kessel (1989) reported sightings of Gyrfalcons on passage on the Seward Peninsula, Alaska starting from late August/early September. In 1974 such movements were very large in scale: juvenile Gyrs did not winter in their natal areas and were predominantly migratory. One bird ringed at a nest in Nome was recovered in central Kamchatka the following winter. Some of the Gyrfalcons spent the winter on the islands and sea ice of the northern Bering Sea, on the southern coast of St Lawrence Island near polynyas (areas of open water surrounded by ice), and on Big Diomede Island, where they hunted Long-tailed Ducks and guillemots.

Palmer (1988) summarised when Gyrs had been sighted, in notable numbers, in the 'lower 48' states of the USA: 1905–06, autumn 1934 (several in Pennsylvania), 1938–39, 1944–45, and 1981–82. In 1982 Gyrs were sighted from California to Pennsylvania, with 19 sightings in Idaho and three birds seen together in Pennsylvania (*American Birds* 36 (1982): 263, 278).

Gyrfalcons are rarely seen in the central USA (less than 1% of large falcons recorded on Christmas Bird Counts in 1981, for example). Gyrfalcons were observed at only 20 Christmas Count locations, all north of the 40th parallel. At 18 of these locations Gyrs were seen in only one year. The remaining two locations recorded the species in only two years (Root 1988).

Most of the USA records come from the states of Washington, Montana and Wyoming (Sloanaker 1926, Dobler 1989, Garber *et al.* 1993). Burr (1975) reported several winter Gyrfalcon sightings in Illinois. Winter records also exist for Massachusetts, Rhode Island, Connecticut, New York, Pennsylvania, Wisconsin, Minnesota, Montana, Idaho, North Dakota, Oregon, Maine, New Hampshire,

South Dakota, Washington, Michigan, Nebraska and Kansas (Snow 1974, Burr 1975, Knapton 1982). The extreme record is of a juvenile bird seen at about 37°N in San Jose, California (Balgooyen 1988).

Dobler (1989) studied the territory use of Gyrfalcons in winter in Washington state. He radio-tagged three Gyrfalcons in three different parts of the state. A tail-mounted transmitter (weighing 20g) was used on two birds and a backpack (weighing 29g) on the third. All three birds were females, one of them being an immature. The radio-tracking lasted 29 to 52 days. The immature bird roamed a range totalling 35,430ha of largely agricultural land bordering tidal marshes in a major estuary in Puget Sound. The second adult female occupied a home range of a more compact size: 5,753ha of primarily open and pasture land. The best habitat was occupied by the largest female, the bird's territory covering mostly irrigated cropland with ditches and wasteways totalling 27,012ha. All habitats within the home ranges were 'locally homogeneous'. Dobler also plotted the number of sightings of wintering Gyrfalcons in Washington state reported between 1896 and 1985. The maximum number of sightings came from the central areas of the state, the Columbia Basin and Puget Sound.

Palmer (1988) gives an example of possible winter range fidelity. One bird (although whether this was the same bird is not known) was seen in five consecutive winters in a locality in south-east Pennsylvania (*American Birds* (1983) 37: 285). Platt (1976) studied wintering Gyrfalcons in a study area south of the Beaufort Sea. The study area was located between 68°50' and 69°40'N, and 136°W and 140°W, and contained 31 territories in which Gyrfalcons bred successfully in the subsequent breeding season. Twenty-eight Gyr nest sites used before the observations were visited during January, with 14 of them showing signs activities by the birds. Thirteen of these 14 continued to show evidence of recent Gyrfalcon activity in February. Two further nests, which had shown no sign of being visited in January, showed abundant signs of activity during February. Of the three nests visited only in February one was being frequented by Gyrfalcons. Platt stated that most of the Gyrfalcons moving south were non-breeders, *i.e.* juveniles and subadults.

Platt (1976) presented a table in which he summarised sightings of wintering (October–March) Gyrfalcons in North America. Out of 31 sightings, 24 were juvenile birds, one was a second-year bird and six were adults. In cases when the birds were sexed, the sex ratio was 20 females to six males. There was also evidence of a sex-ratio imbalance in trapped Gyrs in the 'lower 48' states (Sutton 1974, Burr 1975). The juvenile Gyrfalcon reported by Balgooyen (1988) at San Jose International Airport, California on 20 November 1986 was seen with a young Peregrine Falcon, which was eventually struck by a landing aircraft. The Peregrine had been ringed as a young bird on 16 July the same year, near Anvik, Alaska. Cade (1960) found winter perches near Gyrfalcon nest cliffs on the Colville River, Alaska, and suggested that Gyrfalcons winter close to the nest sites. Irving (1960) noted sightings of Gyrfalcons at the Anaktuvuk Pass in central Alaska throughout the winter, and Sheldon (1909, cited by Platt 1976) reported seeing a single Gyrfalcon in the area around Mount McKinley in winter.

In Canada Gyrs winter, sometimes as casual visitors, in Montreal and southern parts of Quebec, in Ontario, along the Straits of Belle Isle and the St Lawrence, in Nova Scotia and on Vancouver Island in British Columbia (Todd and Friedmann 1947, Campbell *et al.* 1990, Gauthier and Aubry 1996). On the Canadian Arctic islands, the latest autumn Gyr records usually occur in September, though the birds have been seen well into November (Gray 1990). One midwinter record of a Gyrfalcon exists for Taylor Island (west of Victoria Island) where a bird was observed in January 1918 (Parmelee *et al.* 1967). On the Arctic mainland of Canada a proportion of Gyrs are believed to overwinter, though some birds definitely migrate south (Platt 1976). On the Labrador Peninsula at Indian House, over 40 Gyrs were identified between late August and November 1944, amongst them five immature, 13 grey-brown and 13 black (R. Clement, in Palmer 1988). The Gyrs are far more numerous in the north of Labrador during the period September–April, indicating an influx of birds from the north (Palmer 1988).

In winter surveys, females were less numerous than males in January, but almost as common in February. Platt (1976) suggested that females winter in the Arctic regions but may avoid competition by moving away from nest sites.

GREENLAND AND ICELAND

In Iceland the population is considered to be resident (see Figure 8.2 in colour section). Most Icelandic adults spend the winter within their breeding territories. Even some young stay in their natal areas for up to 12 weeks, eventually leaving in August or September (Nielsen and Cade 1990a). On the southern coast of Iceland the birds are mostly winter visitors, staying from August to April. Of 106 birds sighted in this area 74% were juveniles, 9% were subadults and 17% were adults. In northern Iceland the percentage of juveniles is 35% of all Gyrs (Nielsen and Cade 1990a). A total of 1.9% of sighted birds, on average, are white Gyrfalcons visiting Iceland in winter (September to May: Petursson *et al.* 1993). These birds are believed to come from Greenland, as white Gyrs do not breed in Iceland. They form part of the Icelandic winter population (Clausen and Gudmundsson 1981).

In Greenland Gyrfalcons move mainly south for the winter, a view supported by a vast number of skins kept in the Copenhagen Museum of Natural History, as well as by the skins the museum has sent as part of exchange to other museums worldwide. Since the Gyrs travel along the Greenland coast their movement is relatively easy to detect since the coastal region is the only inhabited part of the island. Some of the museum's skins are 'oiled', suggesting that the Gyrs were shot close to the carcasses of whales at whaling stations where they would be a relatively easy target. Freuchen and Salomonsen (1958) observed the migration of Gyrfalcons from September to early November in Greenland. They considered that white Gyrs migrated south to winter together with grey and dark birds. At Scoresby Sound Gyrfalcon migration was observed from a ship stuck in the ice (Glutz von Blotzheim *et al.* 1971). Between 30 August and 18 September 1937 some 200–300 white Gyrfalcons were seen flying south.

On the east coast of Greenland, north of Scoresby Sound, the Gyr migration starts in late August, reaching a peak in early September and finishing by the end of September. The latest known sighting was on 27 November (Palmer 1988). At Scoresby Sound, Gyr movements extend from mid-September through October, reaching a peak in mid-October. Migrants down both sides of Greenland are unwary, even curious, and they were shot in large numbers at the settlements. This slaughter, as judged by the number of skins in museums, ended in the 1930s.

When Ptarmigan are scarce, some 200–300 white Gyrs cross the Denmark Strait, mostly in the first three weeks of September, to winter in Iceland. A few, mostly 'grey' birds, probably from Greenland, reach the Faeroes and British Isles regularly, and may perhaps even reach Western Europe. It is probable that it is these migrant Greenland grey Gyrs that are responsible for most, if not all, the sightings in those areas. The spring return of Gyrs to northern Greenland occurs through April and into May, the only migrant birds that reach the area earlier being Ptarmigan and Snow Bunting (Salomonsen 1950–51).

Out of around 1,200 skins with proper geographical locations recorded on tags which the authors have examined in museums worldwide, two places are noted as the collection points for large numbers of Gyrs. Both sites are in Greenland: Godthåb (now called Nuuk: 61°06'N 51°21'W) with 220 skins, and Sukkertoppen (now called Maniitsoq: 65°15'N 52°32'W) with 107 skins. There are also a number of skins from east Greenland (e.g. Scoresby Sound with 22). No other location has more than 20 skins. Most of these skins were collected in autumn and winter.

RESULTS OF SATELLITE TELEMETRY

Scientists of the Alaska National Parks Service and the US Fish and Wildlife Service placed several satellite transmitters on nine juvenile Gyrfalcons from the Seward Peninsula (McIntyre *et al.* 1994). One young Gyr left the natal area about four weeks after fledging and went to the Anadyr River, Chukotka in mid-September. From there it moved back to south-west Alaska, to Kodiak Island, in early October. Another of the study Gyrs, a young female, moved south to the western coast of Alaska and was last located in December on Nunivak Island. The other seven marked Gyrfalcons showed up on the Shantar Islands.

Alaskan Gyrfalcons tracked by satellite transmitters attached in the Denali National Park were followed during their autumn migration as they followed a route across the Bering Sea and the Kamchatka Peninsula, then along the north-east coast of the Sea of Okhotsk to their wintering place at the Shantar Islands. These islands were known as a wintering site well before satellite tracking became available (Dulkeit and Shulpin 1937) and Gyrs traversing the Bering Sea were also well known: Everett *et al.* (1989) reported an individual Gyr, and two known specimens were obtained from ships in the Bering Sea. One specimen is kept at the BMNH, the other at MZM.

From these observations it seems that there are three possibilities open to Alaskan Gyrfalcons in winter (Cade 1960). Some individuals remain in the region of their breeding grounds throughout the winter, these individuals preying almost exclusively on *Lagopus* grouse. Others may shift to the Bering Sea coast and the outlying islands, where polynyas support a number of waterfowl. The third option is to migrate south, out of the breeding range.

Satellite telemetry was used to study movements of Gyrfalcons in Greenland by the Peregrine Fund (Burnham 2001). To date they have placed about 20 satellite transmitters on Greenlandic Gyrs. The results of the tracking effort have not yet been fully analysed as it is ongoing study, but the preliminary results have been reported in the Peregrine Fund annual reports (Peregrine Fund 1999–2002) and newsletters. So far there has been one round-the-year tracking of a female Gyrfalcon. The female was trapped on 13 October 2000 at a trapping station near Maniitsoq in west Greenland. This site was selected on the assumption that the Gyrs, while on migration, would follow the edges of glaciers. At this site the glaciers extend a long way west, making the strip of ice-free land very narrow. The site is a known source of skins in museums (see above). In the month after trapping the female Gyr proceeded 200km south and spent the winter in an area extending to about 60km around Narsaq in southern Greenland. In mid-March the bird flew 768km north, following the coast, and settled in an area north-west of Kangerlussuaq and east of Holsteinsborg. In June the Peregrine Fund's High Arctic Institute team located the female's nest, with four nearly grown chicks. The female Gyr was then recaptured and its transmitter was replaced.

OPEN-SEA OBSERVATIONS

As Gyrfalcons sometimes appear far away from their breeding range, even on islands, it is obvious to suggest that they have to migrate over the sea. This is confirmed by satellite tracking (see above) as well as by skin collections and direct observations. One specimen at BMNH (Tring 1969-40-79) was shot from a ship 6.5km off Reykjanes, Iceland. Another specimen in the AMNH (AMNH 448983) was taken '500 miles east of New York on a boat'. As noted above, two satellite-tracking records also exist for the Bering Sea. On 7 September 1990 a Gyr was observed above open water in the middle of the Sea of Okhotsk (*c.* 55°N 148°E) (Ogi and Miyashita 1991). On 11 March 1983 a Gyrfalcon was sighted at 60°04'N 172°32'W above the Bering Sea pack ice south of Saint Matthew Island (Everett *et al.* 1989). The observation was made on board the US Coast Guard icebreaker *Polar Sea*, which was conducting marine mammal counts well within the pack ice area. On the same day there were also three Peregrine sightings. During the surveys about 1,500km was covered, totalling 200 hours of observations. Everett *et al.* suggested that the Gyrfalcon might have followed flocks of prey birds (wagtails and buntings) which were also seen from the boat. Moreau (1930, cited in Dementiev 1947) reported a sighting of a Gyrfalcon from the British vessel *Tantalus* on 16 October 1935. The Gyr was recorded at 39°N while the ship was en route from Yokohama to Vancouver.

Two interesting records are an unconfirmed sighting of a Gyrfalcon with a Norwegian leg ring caught on a ship in the Atlantic to the west of Portugal in 1978, and the record of an exhausted white Gyrfalcon caught on the shore of the Azores (Engelmann 1928, cited by Tømmeraas 1993).

CHAPTER 9

Competitors, Commensals and Conspecifics

In many respects the Gyrfalcon is a special bird of prey. It is one of the earliest raptors to start breeding in the season and perhaps the earliest breeding bird in the Arctic and sub-Arctic. It is stenophagous in the spring, which is rare for raptors (and for birds in general). The Gyr also exists with several apparently competing species as near neighbours, some of these with overlapping breeding times. In Norway, for example, Sortland (1997) reported that Peregrine Falcons, White-tailed Eagles, Rough-legged Buzzards and Golden Eagles nested on the same cliff as Gyrfalcons, sometimes within a few hundred metres.

Gyrfalcons do not usually build nests for themselves and depend on other species to provide their nest material. It would be incorrect to declare the Gyrfalcon an obligate parasite nest-builder, because it also uses sites that have only a bare substrate of earth or rocky materials (Palmer 1988). Occasionally, a Gyrfalcon will lay a clutch on a simple scratch on a cliff ledge, pinnacle or in a cave. In the nests of eagles the Gyr sometimes makes a mere scrape in the eagle's nesting platform.

Gyrs also occupy vacant nests, although because of the Gyrs' early nesting this usually means the taking of nests before the nest builder has arrived. Ecologically such a phenomenon could be considered a form of behavioural parasitism. However, in contrast to well-known obligate brood parasites (also called nest parasites) such as cuckoos and cowbirds who use other species to incubate, or help to incubate, their eggs, Gyrfalcons take possession of the empty nests of several 'host' species or, occasionally, 'capture' the nest after a fierce fight. We consider it appropriate to describe this type of symbiotic interaction as facultative interspecific nest-commandeering parasitism, or facultative (in that Gyrs will sometimes do without nest material altogether) nest-usurpation parasitism.

For some host species, such as eagles, the relationship is not a true parasitism, but more a commensalism (a relationship between two organisms of different species whereby one (the commensal) benefits and the other (the host) remains unaffected), as there are no records of Gyrfalcons either harming the eagles or reducing their breeding rate to any extent. However, interactions between Ravens and Gyrfalcons are certainly not commensal, the two species appearing to be direct competitors, with the Ravens almost always pushed out of their nest site and forced to build another nest. At present it is not clear whether the close proximity of Gyrfalcons reduces, or affects in any other way, the breeding performance of Ravens. Further studies are required in this area.

An interesting feature of Gyr nest usurpation is that in the following year the nest can be occupied by another species, sometimes the original builders of the nest. Such observations are known from North America (Cade 1960, White and Cade 1971, Platt 1976). Platt (1976) reported that nests known to have been used by Gyrfalcons were later occupied by Peregrines, Ravens and Rough-legged Buzzards.

NEST BUILDERS

The hosts for nest-usurping Gyrfalcons are Ravens, White-tailed Eagles, Golden Eagles and Rough-legged Buzzards. The proportions of these hosts for nest-usurpation are given in Figure 9.1. The sample data for nest host is dominated by the data from Iceland (Cade *et al.* 1998), which represents 49% of the total. Removal of the Icelandic data increases the Raven proportion from 56% to 59%, and that of the Golden Eagle, which is not found in Iceland, from 6.9% to 14%. Out of 442 Gyrfalcon nests in Iceland reported by Nielsen in the period 1981–96 (Cade *et al.* 1998), 52% were provided by Ravens, which is the only stick-nest provider in northern Iceland. The close relationship of the

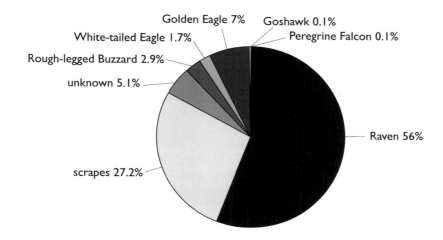

Figure 9.1 *Pie chart showing the main providers of nests for Gyrfalcons.*

Gyrfalcon and the Raven was noted in a paper by Tømmeraas (1978), who wrote that only one of 65 monitored sites in Norway lacked traces of a former nest construction. Twenty-four stick nests had been built by Ravens and three by Rough-legged Buzzards. The origin of 37 nests was unknown, and one nest had been placed directly on a cliff shelf in Peregrine fashion. In a later paper Tømmeraas (1990) reported a larger sample size: out of 136 nests, 134 were stick nests built by Ravens.

Morozov (2000) examined a total of 50 Gyrfalcon nests in north European Russia. A total of 18 of them (36%) had been built by Rough-legged Buzzards, 31 (62%) by Ravens, and one (2%) was placed on a ledge of a cliff in a similar fashion to that of Peregrines. In southern Yamal (Kalyakin and Vinogradov 1981) the majority of nests occupied by Gyrfalcons had been built by White-tailed Eagles and Rough-legged Buzzards. In this area the population density of Ravens was not very high, but was comparable to that of Gyrfalcons (about 1.5 Ravens per Gyrfalcon pair). This relatively low density might explain the fact that the Ravens were not the preferred host, though the comparable population densities do imply that the local Gyrs were opting for other hosts' nests. As a comparison, in northern Iceland the number of Raven territories was 75–89 in an area with 39–63 Gyrfalcon-occupied territories (Nielsen 1999a, Nielsen and Cade 1990a) giving, on average, 1.6 Raven pairs per Gyrfalcon pair. There are, however, very few White-tailed Eagles in Iceland (due to persecution by Common Eider farmers) and the usurpation of a White-tailed Eagle nest has not yet been recorded on the island.

Most of the Gyrfalcon nests in the central Canadian Arctic (*n* = 34) were built by Ravens (62%) or eagles (23%). Of the remainder, 6% were stick nests of uncertain origin and 9% were ledges with no stick substrate (Poole and Bromley 1988b). In the Denali National Park 64% of nests (or 23 nests) had originally been built by Golden Eagles, while 28% (or 10 nests) were on rock ledges with no sticks, and 8% (or three nests) had been built by Ravens (Swem *et al.* 1994).

THE RAVEN – A VERY SPECIAL NEIGHBOUR

Over the entire range of the Gyrfalcon, the number one nest provider is the Raven. This is followed by Golden and White-tailed Eagles, and then other species such as Rough-legged Buzzards.

The relationship by which the Raven supplies a stick nest that later becomes a Gyrfalcon eyrie has inspired a considerable literature. Kishinskiy (1988) even used the northern limits of Raven distribution to map the range of Gyrfalcon in Chukotka, north-east Siberia. Dementiev and Gortchakovskaya (1945) were perhaps the first to note the close relationship between Ravens and Gyrfalcons. Later, the relationship was described in Alaska (Cade 1960, White and Cade 1971). In their classic study of birds of prey on the Colville River, the authors drew attention to the species occupying the river cliffs. Among the four species of cliff-nesting birds the Gyrfalcons and Ravens were residents, whereas the Peregrines and Rough-legged Buzzards were migratory, arriving at Colville at a time when the Gyrfalcons and Ravens already had chicks or were in the later stages of incubation. Cade (1960) stated that both Gyrfalcons and Ravens begin nesting early, both require the same kind of habitat for breeding, and both are about the same body weight. He also observed that Gyrfalcons sometimes expelled Ravens and took over their nests. It was a Raven's nest that allowed Gyrfalcons famously to breed on an above-ground portion of the Trans-Alaska Oil Pipeline system (Ritchie 1991).

In Iceland and Finland (Cade *et al.* 1998) as well as in Russia's Kolyma region (our data) both species bred successfully several times within 200–500m of each other. In Canada Gyrfalcons and Ravens were reported to breed successfully as close as 65m from each other on the same cliff (Poole and Bromley 1988a). The nesting cliff parameters (height, position of the nest in the cliff) were found to be very similar for Ravens and Gyrfalcons, and the aspect angle of their nests did not differ statistically from an equal distribution among the eight directions examined (Poole and Bromley 1988b). Poole and Bromley found six cases of freshly built Raven nests usurped by Gyrfalcons. They also analysed the spatial distribution of Gyrfalcon nests and those of other raptors and found no statistical difference in Gyr breeding success when eagles nested closer than 2km away (*n* = 10) than when they nested further away (*n* = 54), or when Ravens nested closer than 1km (*n* = 14) than when they nested further away (*n* = 50). These data also support the idea that Ravens are not direct competitors of Gyrfalcons.

Woodin (1980) mentioned that the Gyrfalcons in Iceland normally bred in Raven-built nests. On one occasion he observed a pair of Gyrfalcons take over a Raven's nest at Selipdalur, near Myvatn in northern Iceland. However, not every such attempt was successful. Woodin writes:

> In late winter and early spring the Gyrfalcons lived on the western side of a canyon. This side of the canyon seemed to have an old Raven nest. In April a pair of Ravens began building a new nest near the old one. After the Ravens had laid eggs there was a series of spectacular fights between the Raven pair and the Gyrfalcons, which finally ended in the Ravens remaining where they were and the Gyrfalcons establishing control over a section of the cliffs with what appeared to be a suitable nest ledge above and further up the canyon from the Ravens.

Hagen (1952a, Hagen and Barth 1952), who studied Gyrfalcons in Norway's Dovrefjell, also gave a good description of the relationship between Ravens and Gyrs. He noted that the Dovrefjell Gyrfalcons depended on Ravens, whereas the Ravens did not depend on the Gyrs:

> Whether the predators, when nesting in close vicinity of each other, behave under the influence of some mutual benefit or not, is difficult to say. They may be nothing more than 'commensals', attracted by the more favourable topography or other advantages of the spot, though a scavenger like the Raven may also find some additional gain.

In Kishinskiy's (1958) study of Gyrs on Russia's Kola Peninsula all three Gyrfalcon pairs he observed were occupying nests built, he presumed, by Ravens. However, in one case (the nest on Muchka River), Kishinskiy claims that it was the Gyr which had built the nest, though this was an assumption as he had not seen the building. Kishinskiy noted that the lining of the Gyr nest was of vegetation and grass normally used in the nests of Ravens. All the plants were available in the cracks of the nest cliff.

Kishinskiy (1958) considered that the Gyrs preferred the use of Raven nests because the Ravens start to breed in the tundra zone as early as the second half of April when the tundra is covered by snow. By contrast Rough-legged Buzzards breed after the snow has melted. In early spring the Buzzard nests are therefore covered with snow which the Gyr is not capable of removing. Kishinskiy did not find any evidence that the Gyrs used a nest in successive years, but this conclusion might be a result of the limited timescale of his study, as it is known that if a nest site is good and alternatives are difficult to find Gyrs will occupy a site for many years. One of us (Sale) was told by local Inuit that a site on Bylot Island in the Canadian Arctic had been occupied for perhaps 50 years or more.

Ganusevich (1988) also reported the close relationship between Ravens and Gyrfalcons. However, he noted that if there were trees available the competition between the two species was less severe. In addition, Ganusevich reported that Ravens sometimes consumed Gyrfalcon food leftovers.

Ravens and Gyrfalcons usually occupy sites some distance apart and preferably out of each others' view (Palmer 1988). Close nesting is rare and quarrelling is frequent. On Alaska's Seward Peninsula aerial battles, usually initiated by the Gyrs, have been recorded (Roseneau 1972, cited by Palmer 1988). In many situations the Raven is clever enough to avoid or escape its assailant but, as we shall see below, Ravens do sometimes fall victim to Gyr attacks.

Occasionally Gyrfalcons will not only usurp a Raven nest but will also kill the owner (Nielsen and Cade 1990a, Cade *et al.* 1998). Ravens are also sometimes attacked and killed if they approach too closely to a Gyr nest (Platt 1977). Out of 60 observed attacks by Gyrfalcons in the Canadian Arctic four (6.6%) were against Ravens (Platt 1989). But Ravens sometimes reciprocate. Ravens in Iceland are known to take deserted Gyrfalcon eggs and to rob Gyr caches, and they are also potential predators of nestlings (Nielsen and Cade 1990a). However, Ravens were never seen to initiate an attack on a Gyrfalcon at an eyrie in Iceland, whereas the Gyrs were observed to chase Ravens until they sought shelter on the ground. Nielsen and Cade (1990a) reported four pairs of Gyrfalcons that would not tolerate Ravens at all. In 190 other cases, however, the Gyrs did not seem to make further attacks on the Ravens after having driven them away (Nielsen and Cade 1990a). Ravens sharing territories with Gyrfalcons had, on average, a lower breeding success than Raven pairs alone on their territories: 59% compared to 68%, but this difference was not statistically significant (Nielsen and Cade 1990a).

Jenkins (1978) reported the remains of a freshly killed Raven on one of two eyries he observed in Greenland. However, the second eyrie had a Raven's nest some 50m away with the Gyrs ignoring Ravens which flew directly beneath the site.

RELATIONSHIPS WITH EAGLES

Golden Eagles are the main providers of nests to the Gyrfalcons of Alaska's Denali National Park (Swem *et al.* 1994). The authors of this study also recorded a high number of nest switches in consecutive years between the Golden Eagles and the

Gyrfalcons, the highest number being 18. Three out of 13 Gyr nests in British Columbia were built by Golden Eagles, the other ten being scratched hollows in bare ground on a cliff ledge (Campbell *et al.* 1990). White and Nelson (1991) observed the hunting behaviour of a Gyrfalcon pair from a helicopter some 10km from the Dempster Highway, in Canada's Yukon Territory. On one occasion the female Gyr was observed to attack an intruding immature Golden Eagle.

Golden Eagles can be forced to abandon their eyries after persistent attacks by territorial Gyrs (Platt 1977). Platt (1989) reported 60 attacks of Gyrfalcons at nest sites, of which 24 (40%) involved an attack on Golden Eagles. A pair of Golden Eagles nested successfully about 800m from Gyrfalcons on the same cliff, but another nest about 450m from a Gyr site was abandoned after the laying of the first egg due to attacks by an unmated Gyrfalcon (Platt 1989).

The fact that the Gyr's severest and most persistent attacks seem to be against Golden Eagles (which, in some instances, seem to be attempting to visit old eyries of their own now occupied by Gyrs) might be explained by the suggestion that Golden Eagles prey on Gyr nestlings. This allegation is logical, but lacking in solid evidence, although a dead Gyrfalcon has been found in a Golden Eagle nest in Norway (Hagen 1952a). Poole and Bromley (1988a) reported that Golden Eagles do not have any significant effect on the breeding success of Gyrfalcons, although they observed that Gyrs often chased eagles for up to 2km.

Gyr breeding in a Golden Eagle tree nest was reported by Gorovenko (2003) in the northern part of Russia's Kamchatka Peninsula. The breeding of a pair of Golden Eagles within 3.5km of a Gyr nest was also noted by Gorovenko. On one occasion Gyrfalcons were breeding in a tree nest only some 800–1,000m from suitable nesting cliffs, on which Gyrs were known to have bred earlier. In the year of Gorovenko's study the cliff nest was occupied by Ravens. Vorobiev (1963) mentioned Gyrs occupying a tree nest built by Golden Eagles in northern Yakutia.

Danilov *et al.* (1984) reported three nests built by White-tailed Eagles but occupied by Gyrfalcons on Russia's Yamal Peninsula. Kalyakin (1989) supported these observations. In Kalyakin's study the Gyrfalcons were most often observed to occupy White-tailed Eagle nests (less often Raven nests and rarely the nests of Rough-legged Buzzards). The nest of the White-tailed Eagle is a large construction placed on the rather weak northern trees. Often the nests accumulate a lot of snow during winter, and subsequently collapse. Kalyakin observed that out of 21 nests occupied by Gyrfalcons, a total of 16 collapsed due to accumulated snow during the following winter. Thirteen replacement nests occupied by the Gyrs were built by White-tailed Eagles (9), Rough-legged Buzzards (2), Golden Eagles (1) and Ravens (1).

A. V. Kondratiev (Krechmar *et al.* 1991) found Gyrfalcons occupying an old White-tailed Eagle nest (two alternative sites) along the Rauchua River in Russia's eastern Chukotka, and one of us (Potapov) observed Gyrfalcons in an old

White-tailed Eagle nest in Russia's Lower Kolyma, some 6km away from an active Golden Eagle nest. Glotov (2000) reported Gyrfalcons occupying a White-tailed Eagle nest positioned on a triangulation tower in Russia's Pechora Delta.

In southern Yamal the majority of the Gyr nests had originally been built by White-tailed Eagles and Rough-legged Buzzards. In some years the nests were reoccupied by the White-tailed Eagles (Kalyakin and Vinogradov 1981), but in all such instances the reoccupied nests had originally been built by White-tailed Eagles.

RELATIONSHIPS WITH ROUGH-LEGGED BUZZARDS

Cade noted that Gyrfalcons were often seen attacking Rough-legged Buzzards breeding nearby at the time people were visiting the Gyrs, showing a perfect example of redirection behaviour (Cade 1960, White and Cade 1971). (Redirection anger is, for instance, when a Gyr is upset by human presence and vents its anger on a hapless passing bird.) Snow (1974) also noted that although Gyrs may breed close to Ravens without conflict, battles with Rough-legged Buzzards are frequent (Snow 1974). However, by contrast Hagen (1952a, Hagen and Barth 1952) mentioned that Rough-legged Buzzards in Norway bred within 60m of Gyrfalcons in three successive years. Hagen described the relationship between the two species as 'armed neutrality', as both maintained a limited nesting territory which was respected by the other pair. Hagen reported that the abandoned nests of Rough-legged Buzzards are sometimes occupied by Gyrfalcons, but are probably too exposed to wind and strong weather and too accessible for common usage. He wrote (1952a):

> It might be thought, perhaps, that the Rough-legged Buzzard would scavenge on remnants of Gyrfalcon meals, all the more so because analogous conditions are known from other birds of prey, but the writer's own experience makes it obvious that the Rough-legged Buzzard does not make a regular habit of this.

In Finland the proportion of Gyr nests built by Rough-legged Buzzards is higher than that in Norway (Cade *et al.* 1998), though the work of Morozov (1991) supports Hagen. He considers that Raven nests are tougher than those of Rough-legged Buzzards, the latter usually being completely destroyed by the Gyr chicks to the extent that on cliff ledges the chicks often find themselves on the bare ledge.

In Russia's Lower Kolyma area one of the authors (Potapov) noted that Rough-legged Buzzards bred in relatively close proximity to Gyrfalcons, on one occasion within 200m. It appeared that the Gyrs did not harass the buzzards, although the latter sat at the nest uncharacteristically tight in the presence of Gyrfalcons and were reluctant to fly away even when Potapov climbed to within 2m.

Mindell *et al.* (1987) stated that there were population fluctuations during the period 1971–85 for Rough-legged Buzzards and Gyrfalcons on Alaska's Colville River which were significantly correlated, the largest declines occurring synchronously. However, as a consequence of opposite population trends during the period from 1967 to 1969 there was no correlation between the numbers for the two species in 1967–85. It appears that the buzzards and Gyrfalcons were synchronised in the phase of declining numbers, but not during the peak phases. This might be expected as ideal conditions for the two species would not necessarily coincide.

Platt reported that if Rough-legged Buzzards approach Gyrfalcons they are sometimes killed (Platt 1977). He reported that out of 60 observed attacks by Gyrfalcons at nest sites the majority were against Rough-legged Buzzards – 29 cases (48.3%). Of the 60 attacks, one was against a Red-tailed Hawk and another against a Hen Harrier (*Circus cyaneus*) (these attacks each accounting for 1.7% of the total).

RELATIONSHIPS WITH PEREGRINE FALCONS

Voronin (1986) reported that in one case Gyrfalcons occupied a Peregrine nest in Russia's Bolshezemelskaya tundra, the Peregrines being forced to move some 400m from their old location. Despite the loss (or, perhaps, because of it), the Peregrines were very aggressive towards the Gyrfalcons, Voronin suspecting that the Peregrines killed one of two fledgling Gyrs.

In the Koryak District of north Kamchatka Gorovenko (2003) noted breeding Peregrines within 200–250m of a Gyrfalcon nest. One of us (Potapov) noted that in the Kolyma Delta Peregrines took over a nest which had been used by Gyrfalcons (depicted in photos in Vaughan 1992, p. 82) when the Gyrs disappeared, and used it for several successive years.

In Alaska, the two falcon species were found just 35m apart (White and Cade 1971) at the Colville River. However, Cade (1955a) observed that in the same study area the Peregrine Falcons were extremely aggressive toward any Gyrfalcon. Though Peregrines may harass a Gyr, the Gyr can easily outmanoeuvre it. Mindell *et al.* (1987) stated that for Peregrines breeding along the Colville River there was no correlation between numbers and the fluctuations in the population of local Gyrs.

Cade (1960) wrote that Peregrines have little effect on Gyrfalcons in the Arctic. Although the ecological plasticity of Peregrines allows them to gain temporary hold of nesting sites vacated by Gyrfalcons, it seems from the history of use by the two species of particular cliffs on the Colville River that such occupancy is contingent on the absence of Gyrs. Where the Gyrs have settled to breed, the Peregrines are not able to dislodge them.

Jenkins (1978) reported that on one nest he observed a Gyrfalcon–Peregrine conflict when an immature Peregrine 'buzzed' an adult male Gyr while the male was perched on the nesting cliff. The Gyrfalcon was visibly surprised by the attack, as evidenced by the rapid opening of his wings, but he remained on the cliff while the Peregrine soared away. On another occasion an adult Peregrine exchanged dives with a female Gyrfalcon.

In south-west Greenland, where prey is limited, Gyrfalcons and Peregrines share considerable dietary overlap and do not share the same cliff because of competition for food (Burnham and Mattox 1984), although some subsequent observations have confirmed that such sharing of nesting cliffs does occur on occasions (Cade *et al.* 1998). Cade (1960) described breeding Gyrfalcons and Peregrines on one cliff with sites about 500m apart. He also noted that in such instances of close nesting there were no examples of the nests actually being in view of each other.

RELATIONSHIPS WITH ACCIPITERS

Kalyakin (1994) mentioned attacks on a young Gyrfalcon by a Goshawk in autumn. In woodland any conspicuous call by an immature Gyrfalcon is known to attract the attention of Goshawks. One of us (Potapov) was training a young Gyrfalcon on a lure close to a forest patch. The flight of the Gyr immediately attracted a Goshawk which landed on the top of a tree and was almost certainly making ready to attack the inexperienced Gyr.

In Chukotka, north-east Siberia, the range of the Gyrfalcon overlaps with that of the white Goshawk. The latter breeds in a rather specialised habitat, namely strips of willow trees and shrubs alongside rivers (Krechmar and Probst 2003). Such habitats occur mostly along the Anadyr River, but also on the Omolon River system and the upper parts of rivers in southern Chukotka. The river valleys with these forest–shrub areas are surrounded by numerous lakes with plenty of waterfowl. The height of the bushes on the surrounding tundra, plus the occurrence of Siberian Dwarf Pine (*Pinus pumila*) makes it very difficult for Gyrfalcons to hunt in such areas in snow-free periods.

In such places Goshawks dominate, leaving the foothills of the mountains to the Gyrfalcons. Little is known of direct interactions between white Goshawks and Gyrfalcons, but it seems probable that the presence of Goshawks in the area, together with the different pattern of vegetation, makes life almost impossible for Gyrs. There is one reference to a Gyrfalcon occupying a nest on a cliff which had previously been occupied by a Goshawk in the Koryak District of north Kamchatka (Gorovenko 2003), but as this information came from local hunters it must be viewed as unreliable.

Ridge-hopping and low-altitude chasing are very widespread behaviour in parts of the Gyrfalcon's range. These hunting methods are similar to those used frequently by accipiters. The resemblance was especially striking in mid October 1963 at Eagle Summit, Alaska when Weeden (White and Weeden 1966) observed a Goshawk and a Gyrfalcon hunting Ptarmigan in the same area on four successive days. Both raptors visited one brushy slope frequently because Ptarmigan often fed there, and several times Weeden had to look closely to determine which raptor he was watching.

RELATIONSHIPS WITH SMALL FALCONS

Woodin (1980) describes the relationship of Gyrfalcons with Merlins in Iceland. Merlins there are strictly migratory, so the interactions between them and the sedentary Gyrfalcons occur only in late spring and summer. Woodin reported two aggressive encounters between the species. From these it appears that Merlins tend to attack any Gyr coming close to their breeding site. The Gyr was never tempted to attack the Merlin, the latter bird being highly manoeuvrable and capable of harassing the Gyr without fear of retaliation. In general it can be said that Merlin breeding areas do not often coincide with Gyrs, either in space or time, although one of us (Sale) found an occupied Merlin nest within 200–300m of an occupied Gyr nest in northern Iceland.

American Kestrels have been observed mobbing nesting Gyrfalcons in Canada's Yukon Territory (Platt 1989). Hagen (1952a, Hagen and Barth 1952) mentioned that Kestrels breed within Gyrfalcon habitat, but did not give specific details of their coexistence.

RELATIONSHIPS WITH OTHER SPECIES

In Iceland Woodin (1980) also describes attacks on Gyrs by Arctic Terns while the Gyrs were on perches close to a lake. The Gyrs would flinch, but did not take to the wing. Woodin noted that despite this the terns never seemed to gang up to drive the Gyrfalcons away. Also in Iceland, Suetens and Groenendael (1976) reported that Gyrfalcons protected their nests from Arctic Skua (*Stercorarius parasiticus*), and also attacked a Greylag Goose (*Anser anser*) which had blundered too close, while Galbraith and Thompson (1984) observed Gyrfalcons attacking Fulmars even though the Fulmar's oil-spitting behaviour poses a threat to the Gyr.

Kishinskiy (1980) saw both Long-tailed and Arctic Skuas attacking Gyrfalcons. Skuas may harass a Gyrfalcon, but the raptor can easily outmanoeuvre its tormentors. France (1992) reported a Gyrfalcon being mobbed by Glaucous

Gulls on Ellesmere Island. However, one of us (Sale) found a Glaucous Gull nest within 50m of a Gyrfalcon nest on Bylot Island, and observed no conflict between the species.

Gyrs were noted defending their nest furiously against Herring Gulls on Bolshoi Litskiy Island, off the Kola Peninsula (Shklyarevich and Krasnov 1980). One Herring Gull was killed and another almost certainly died after being hit by a Gyr and falling into the sea. Skuas were also attacked if they approached the Gyr nest. Arctic Skuas in turn attack Gyrs if they approach their nest or chicks. In one case an Arctic Skua forced a Gyr to flip over and extend its talons when it was attacked. Kittiwakes take off from their nesting cliff and fly onto the sea making loud calls when Gyrs approach. This behaviour is often used by large gulls that raid Kittiwake nests. Krasnov *et al.* (1995) reported that gulls would steal eggs and chicks from Kittiwakes when the latter were panicking after seeing a Gyr flying nearby. Gyrfalcon-induced gull predation was noted as the chief reason for Kittiwake mortality on the coast near Murmansk.

On the tundra of the Kola Peninsula Kishinskiy (1958) noted the following species breeding relatively close to nesting Gyrfalcons: Carrion Crow (Corvus corone), Common Redstart (*Phoenicurus phoenicurus*), Redwing (*Turdus iliacus*), Ring Ouzel (*Turdus torquatus*) and White Wagtail (*Motacilla alba*). On two occasions male Ring Ouzels successfully mobbed Gyrs, forcing them away from their nest. Hagen (1952a) reported the following species breeding in known Gyrfalcon territories: Willow Grouse, Ptarmigan, Bluethroat (*Luscinia svecica*), Ring Ouzel, Willow Warbler (*Phylloscopus trochilus*), Meadow Pipit, Golden Plover, Lapland Bunting, Northern Wheatear (*Oenanthe oenanthe*), Horned Lark (*Eremophila alpestris*), Dotterel (*Charadrius morinellus*)and Snow Bunting.

In the Kolyma lowlands the bird species in Gyrfalcon habitat on the tundra away from the timberline would usually include Willow Grouse, Northern Pintail, Scaup, Bewick's Swan (*Cygnus columbianus bewickii*), Peregrine, Rough-legged Buzzard, Ruff (*Philomachus pugnax*), Pectoral Sandpiper (*Caladris melanotos*), Red-throated Pipit (*Anthus cervinus*), Bluethroat, Snow bunting and Lapland Bunting. At the timberline this list is augmented by many other species such as Siberian Accentor (*Prunella montanella*), Ptarmigan and Dusky Thrush (*Turdus naumanni eunomus*), and, within forest patches, Siberian Jay (*Perisoreus infaustus*), Hazel Grouse (*Bonasa bonasia*), Great Spotted Woodpecker (*Dendrocopos major*), Siberian Tit (*Poecile cinctus*), Nuthatch (*Sitta europea*) and Nutcracker (*Nucifraga caryo-catactes*) (Potapov 1994b).

Of these various species Arctic Skua, Long-tailed Skua, Snow Bunting, Ring Ouzel and Carrion Crow have been noted to attack Gyrfalcons (Kishinskiy 1958, Shklyarevich and Krasnov 1980). In the New World American Robin (*Turdus migratorius*) has also been observed attacking Gyrs (Platt 1989). Amongst mammals Hagen (1952a) noted Reindeer, Red Fox and Mountain Hare, Norway Lemming and Root Vole in Norway. In the Gyrfalcon habitat of the Lower Kolyma one of us (Potapov) noted the following mammals: Arctic Hare, Collared and Siberian Lemming, Arctic Ground Squirrel and Black-capped Marmot (*Marmota camtschatica*). Though larger mammals are clearly not preyed upon by Gyrs and these same mammals are unlikely to offer much threat to nesting Gyrs (except in very specific circumstances) the falcon will attack mammals approaching their nests. Platt (1989) records attacks against Wolf (*Canis lupus*), Arctic Fox, Red Fox (*Vulpes vulpes*) and Wolverine (*Gulo gulo*).

COMMENSALISMS

Some commensal relationships between Gyrfalcons and other species have been mentioned in the literature. The commensal relationship between Arctic Peregrines and Red-breasted Geese (*Branta ruficollis*) is well known: on Russia's Taimyr Peninsula successful breeding of the geese is associated with nesting Peregrines which protect the local area from Arctic Foxes, against which the geese have little chance of defending themselves. Similar relationships have been observed for Gyrfalcons. In mid-Norway (Langvatn and Moksnes 1979) a Gyrfalcon nest was noted to be within 200m of a colony of Fieldfares. Normally such colonies experience predation by Hooded Crows and Stoats, but not at this site. The authors state that it is highly possible that the thrushes established their colony close to early-breeding Gyrfalcons specifically as a form of defence. In Yamal, Fieldfares have also been reported breeding in unoccupied Gyrfalcons' nests, while White Wagtails were noted to breed in the side 'walls' of the nests actually occupied by Gyrfalcons (Kalyakin and Vinogradov 1981).

A similar instance was noted for a Gyrfalcon nest at a triangulation tower in Russia's Pechora Delta (Glotov 2000). The nest has been monitored since 1996 when the territory became part of the newly created Nenetskiy State Nature Reserve. The researchers and rangers from the reserve noticed that a colony of Bean Geese (*Anser fabalis*) breeding around the triangulation tower had a higher breeding density, larger clutch sizes and a higher breeding success than geese breeding in the outer tundra. Ryabitsev (1986) reported the nest of a Bean Goose about 20m from a Gyr nest in southern Yamal.

Gyrfalcons breeding in close proximity to Herring Gulls and Glaucous Gulls were reported at Cape Shalaurova Izba, western Chukotka by Stishov and Marukhnich (1990) and breeding within colonies of seabirds has been reported on islands off the coast of the Kola Peninsula (Dementiev and Gortchakovskaya 1945, Shklyarevich and Krasnov (1980).

In Alaska White and Springer (1965) found a Canada Goose (*Branta canadensis*) nest some 4m below a Gyrfalcon nest. A White-fronted Goose (*Anser albifrons*), Common Eider and a Northern Pintail were also breeding within 36m of the eyrie, while a Teal (*Anas crecca*) nest was 180m away. None of these birds was molested by the Gyrs (White and Springer 1965, Clum and Cade 1994).

In Greenland Gyrs are known to breed within reach of a Little Auk colony (Peregrine Fund Report 1999), a situation not noted anywhere else in the Gyrfalcon's breeding range. Despite the fact that the Gyrs feed heavily on the Little Auks, their presence might be an overall benefit to the colony if it reduces predation by other species such as large gulls and Arctic Foxes.

REACTION TO CONSPECIFICS

Woodin (1980) mentioned that during the breeding period young Gyrfalcons are 'escorted' away from nearby cliffs by adult birds. Within their territories Gyrfalcons sometimes demonstrate aggressive behaviour towards conspecifics. Nielsen and Cade (1990a) observed the intrusion of two adult pairs, one adult male, one adult female, two juvenile males, three juvenile females and one male of uncertain age. Resident females usually protested loudly and followed the intruder or, in some cases, attacked an intruding female directly. Male Gyrs were present during several cases of intrusion: two single young females were followed without any overt aggression, but three single males and one pair were attacked repeatedly and chased for a distance of about 1km from the nesting cliffs. Attacks were especially aggressive against the trespassing pair, but these attacks were directed only at the male bird, the female being ignored. Previously Cade (1960) reported that he had not seen aggressive behaviour between Gyrs, but expressed no doubt that they will react antagonistically towards one another in certain circumstances. Of the 60 attacks reported by Platt (1989) only one (1.7%) was against another Gyrfalcon.

Poole and Bromley (1988b) analysed the spatial distribution of Gyrfalcon nests and found that the breeding success was significantly lower when conspecifics nested within 5km (n = 21) than when they nested further away (n = 43). On the other hand, breeding success was not associated with distance to the nearest neighbour of another species. For instance, as noted earlier, there was no significant difference in Gyrfalcon breeding success when Ravens nested closer than 1km (compared to those nesting further away) or when eagles nested closer than 2km (compared to those nesting further away).

CHAPTER 10

Man and Falcons

CULTS OF BIRDS OF PREY

The existence of cults of birds of prey was first identified in studies of ancient Egypt and Greece. The first attempt to summarise such cults was by Shternberg in his classic study *Cult of Eagles* (1925, 1936). Shternberg (1936) noted that:

> the cult of the eagle, as it is known, is one of most universal [cults]. We find it in peoples of various cultures, in people of various races, geographically remote from each other... Besides the common primitive psychology, this universality of the cult of the eagle could be easily explained by specific features of the bird which even now is acknowledged as the king of birds. In the eyes of a primitive man, the enormous strength of this bird of prey, which allows it to carry heavy prey, places it above terrestrial

predators and gives it the aura of a supernatural creature. The power of flight and the fearsome fire in the eagle's eyes, which could account for lightning, indicated to primitive man a link with the sun. However, perhaps most striking to primitive peoples was that the eagle was normally non-aggressive to humans ... it was 'human-minded'. Finally, in the cult of the eagle, as in the cult of migrating birds, the coincidence of the eagle's arrival in spring and departure in autumn allowed man to think of it as responsible for the seasons. All these features created a universal worshipping of eagles, linking them with the sun and a superior god. Though coincidences on the role of eagles in the spiritual sphere ... cannot be used as generic evidence for historical links between various peoples, in some details of the cult and myths characteristic features occur which are common for most known groups of peoples.

It should be noted that Shternberg, not being aware of the various species of birds of prey, ignores specific features of particular birds which were noted in some later works (e.g. Grossman and Hamlet 1964, Simakov 1998). Basically Shternberg is using 'eagle' as a generic name for any bird of prey.

According to Shternberg, the raptor could act as the owner and ruler of the sun: the ruler of fire; the god of fertility and, therefore, the propagator of nature; a totem; the ancestor and creator of shamans; and the link between this world and the heavens.

RAPTORS AS TOTEMS

Simakov (1998) noted that the Golden Eagle was the totem of the Turkic tribes of Siberia, including the Yakut, Teleut and Kachin people, where certain tribes consider themselves descendants of the eagle. The eagle was also a totem among the Turkmen people of Uzbekistan. An interesting old Hungarian saga tells of Almos, the child born to the goddess Emede after her relationship with a Gyrfalcon. Before their lovemaking the Gyrfalcon tells Emede that their offspring will be famous. The child goes on to found the Arpad dynasty and to this day many of the people call themselves *Turul*, the old name for the Altai Falcon. There is a similar legend amongst Oguz people (who lived to the west of the Caspian Sea) which includes the same reference to the Altai Falcon (Zhirmunskiy 1962):

> You, whose tent is pitched in the morning on a high place
> You, whose tent is decorated with good blue silk[1]
> You, whose horses are born in herds

You, whose rich purse, when it is full, is leaking as butter
The supporter of other dzhigit[2]
The hope for us poor
Son-in-law of Bayudyr-khan, son of the bird Tuulu[3]
Supporter of Turkestan, lion of the tribe and the clan
Tiger of the black mob, owner of the kaur-coloured horse[4]
Father of Uruz-khan, khan my Khazan
Listen to my voice, hear my speech

Interestingly, in some legends the spiritual fertility and lovemaking powers of birds of prey were transposed to those who kept such birds, in particular falconers, a fact which might go some way towards explaining the continuing importance attached to owning falcons in some societies. In a legend of the Kyrgyz people Obolbek was a famous *berkutchi* (a falconer with a Golden Eagle) of the Bugu clan. One day when he was hunting, Obolbek's eagle took no quarry and looked at his owner with distress. Obolbek was very concerned, but did not know what to do and was soon hunting again in the mountains, where he stayed at the home of a rich man from the Chirik tribe. Again the hunt was unsuccessful, and again the eagle behaved in the same mysterious, distressed way. The rich owner had to go away on business for a time, leaving his wife in charge of the house. The woman had been married for a long time, but had no children. Noticing that Obolbek was not in a good mood she asked what the matter was. When he told her about the strange behaviour of his eagle, the woman replied that she knew the reason of the eagle's despair, but would tell him only if he would agree to sleep with her. Obolbek agreed. In the morning the woman told Obolbek that this particular Golden Eagle was no ordinary bird, but a noble one. In order to stop the eagle's despair and to start it hunting successfully, Obolbek should dress well and ride his best horse for the hunt. Though surprised by the information, Obolbek followed the advice and things improved immediately, the eagle soon bringing great glory to him. The woman gave birth to a son who grew up to become a famous judge (Simakov 1998).

Another characteristic feature of totem animals is the taboo against harming them. Falcons were protected by law in medieval England. Anyone caught destroying a falcon's eggs could be imprisoned for a year, and anyone poaching a falcon from the wild risked losing an eye as punishment (Tennesen 1992).

Simakov (1998) questioned different Asian peoples (in Kazakhstan, Turkmenistan, Kyrgyzstan and Karakalpakia) whether it was acceptable to kill a bird of prey. The answers were unanimous: it was a sin to kill one, a similar crime to that of killing a person. Berezovikov (1986) noted that the killing of an eagle was not

---

[1] In the shaman world, fine blue silk was a symbol of Upper Heaven – Tengri – to which only the Gods and falcons could travel. [2] Brave horsemen. [3] The Altai Falcon, the same as *Turul*. [4] Silver-brown.

only considered a sin, but that if it happened near a village it was considered to be a humiliation for the village dwellers. Dementiev (1935b) mentioned that this taboo also extended to falconers: '... the people of Middle Asia consider sinful any attempt to humiliate or harm a person holding a bird of prey on the fist'.

It was an even greater sin to kill a white bird of prey. To the nomads of Middle Asia and Kazakhstan such a killing was a great taboo, as white falcons or Goshawks were sacred birds. The taboo can hold elsewhere: an ancient Danish law prohibited the killing of Gyrfalcons in Iceland. The selling of falcons was also frowned on, with numerous euphemisms being employed to cover the shameful deed. These usually revolved around the exchange of presents: a Persian treatise on falconry written by Husam d-Dawlah Taymur Mirza (1868) notes that 'a hawk catcher obtained a fine falcon and carried it as a *pishkas* to the Pasha of Baghdad'. The Persian word *pishkas*, though in this context meaning 'present', is actually a polite word for 'sale'. In Kyrgyzstan and Kazakhstan trained birds of prey were allowed to be given only to members of the same clan: giving them to elsewhere was thought to diminish the powers of the clan and was treated as a crime. This rule was extended to information on nest locations, which were considered the property of the clan, many of the sites being marked with clan signs (Simakov 1998). Simakov adds that in many tribes giving away your falcon was the equivalent of giving away your soul.

In fact the equality of soul and falcon was a common belief in pre-Christian and pre-Islamic Eurasia. In medieval times falcons were priceless diplomatic gifts, the equivalent of presenting your soul. Chinghis Khan received Gyrfalcons as gifts from chiefs of various clans: if he was not presented with a falcon he took it as a declaration of war. Throughout Asia the seizing of someone's falcon meant a victory over them, while a falcon presented to an enemy meant surrender. This underlies a true story from the time of the Third Crusade, even though by this time the Christian world had decoupled the falcon and the soul. The Crusade was led by Philip I of France, the Holy Roman Emperor Frederick I (Barbarossa) and Richard I of England. In 1190 their armies besieged Acre, which was defended by Saladin. It was a long siege and the kings distracted themselves by hawking. One day, Philip's finest Gyrfalcon broke its leash and flew to the top of city walls. Despite being offered the most succulent of lures, the falcon refused to return. Furious and desperate, the king sent envoys to Saladin who refused to return the bird. Philip offered the enormous sum of one thousand gold crowns for the return of the bird, but in vain. Both men, it seems, saw a deep meaning in the incident (it is worth noting however, that at the time Gyrfalcons were unknown in the Middle East).

Falcons also crop up in other stories from the Crusades: when the Christian forces of King Sigismund were defeated by the Turks under the command of Sultan Bayazid I (Bajazet) at Nicopolis in 1396, Jean de Nevers, the future Duke of Burgundy, was taken prisoner. His father offered fabulous sums for his freedom, but all his offers were refused. Jean languished in captivity until Sigismund offered twelve white Gyrfalcons for his freedom. This offer was accepted immediately.

Ritual sacrifice of birds of prey supports the role of raptors as totem birds. Such killings among the Ainu people of Japan were described by Shternberg (1936). The people sacrificed and buried a Steller's Sea Eagle (*Haliaeetus pelagicus*) to ask for good fishing. Similarly in Kyrgyzstan it was permitted to kill a wounded eagle, but only after it had been fed. In his treatise on falconry (1868) Husam d-Dawlah Taymur Mirza mentions that during falconry it was acceptable to kill Imperial Eagles (*Aquila heliaca*), but not to eat them. Ritual consumption of the meat of a totem animal, for healing, fertility or spiritual purposes, was another characteristic of the totem.

There are many examples of the use of the meat of birds of prey for healing. Zarudniy (1915) noted that boiled Egyptian Vulture (*Neophron percnopterus*) meat was eaten by infertile women as a potential cure. The same meat was also used to treat stomach problems. Simakov (1998) reports a current tradition among the Kazakh people that if a Golden Eagle is fed with the meat of an Eagle Owl for a week, then Black Vulture (*Aegypius monachus*) for another week, then swan for a further week and then killed, whoever eats the eagle will live long and never contract cancer. All the species mentioned in this 'treatment' are ancient totem birds.

There are also traditions of burying birds of prey which are consistent with the totem role of raptors. Numerous burial places of falcons are known in Egypt and there is a widespread tradition of burying eagles in Kazakhstan and Kyrgyzstan (Simakov 1998). Apart from burials, the bird could also be placed on the roof of a house with the wings spread, a tradition which has survived until recent times. The people believed that the bird's spirit then continued its journey to the sky. Often, Golden Eagles trained as falconry birds were buried in the same way as humans, the dead bird being wrapped in a shroud and placed in the ground during a funeral that was attended by people who wept and grieved just as they might for a dead relative. There are even instances of the anointing of the burial shroud with oil, and of feasts following the funeral (Simakov 1998).

These funereal rites are more easily understood when it is remembered that there was a widespread belief in the ancient world that after death, a man's soul became a falcon. In many regions of Asian people still say *shunkar boldy* of a dead person – he has become a Gyrfalcon – rather than the more common Western euphemisms such as 'passed away'. Ancient Turkish gravestones often included an image of a warrior with a bird on his fist, even if the grave was not that of a falconer (Sher 1963), while in Kazakhstan it was traditional to decorate the graves of men with sticks or spears surmounted by wooden models of falcons (Nazarov 1821). There are also examples of funereal art, from Scandinavia to eastern Asia, depicting falcons leaving the graves of the deceased.

There is a deep belief among Russians that when a man dies his soul enters heaven on the 40th day. Interestingly, Indian falconers believed that if a bird could not be trained in 40 days, it would never be trained (Mirza 1868). Dawlah Taymur Mirza also mentions a popular superstition that anyone killing a Lammergeier

(*Gypaetus barbatus*) will die within 40 days. He claims a personal story of hawking with a man who was intent on shooting a Lammergeier they found. Mirza attempted to stop the man, but was dismissed as repeating an old woman's story. The man shot the Lammergeier and duly died on the 40 day.

The most prominent display of totemism was seen in the ceremonial dances of native American tribes in which eagles were the most commonly represented animals. Eagle feathers – which often decorated the dancers – were also used in war costumes as there was a general belief that eagle feathers protected the wearer by diverting enemy arrows. The totem poles of south-eastern Alaskan tribes also frequently include an eagle in their carving. Though this is the most obvious and well-known example, relics of totemism can be found among indigenous peoples of all continents: for example one of the principal clan totems of native Australians is the eagle-hawk (Grossman and Hamlet 1964). Totemism has even survived the centuries of dominance of Buddhism in Mongolia: the winner of traditional Mongolian wrestling matches still performs an Eagle Dance.

BIRDS OF PREY IN SHAMANISM

Primitive religions were polytheistic, man investing god-like qualities to natural forces over which he had no control and whose appearance (thunder and lightning for example) or absence (the sun and seasons for example) had a dramatic influence on his life. From these polytheistic beliefs a mythology of the creation of the world and man's place in it arose. Though the mythologies of the ancient Greeks and the Romans (among others) have been passed down to us and now appear as appealing and entertaining stories, they developed from a religion that both preceded and outlasted them, a religion known by the collective term shamanism.

Though there were many versions of shamanism among the peoples of Eurasia and the Americas, several features were common to all forms. There was a spirit world, usually with several planes. On the upper plane lived the gods, while the shaman himself could travel to a lower plane in order to negotiate on behalf of his people. There was also a belief that it was not only man that had a spirit (the soul). All living things had a spirit, a concept of particular relevance to hunting peoples as the spirit of a prey animal had to be treated with respect so that it would allow its earthly body to be killed and eaten.

The ancient religions lacked written texts and shrines yet they are spread across all the inhabited continents. In all cases these religions had their own priests, the shamans (from *saman* – wise one – in the Tungusic language of the peoples of eastern Siberia), who inherited their status from a supernatural ancestor and were approved by the people at a special ceremony. Knowledge was passed from one generation to the next by the shamans, but also by the shaman's drum, a sacred object, often adorned with pictographs which held the people's cosmogony. The shaman's duty was to protect people from bad spirits, to heal diseases (healing being seen as the defeat of evil spirits) and to explain the structure of the universe and position of various gods and spirits within it. During their ceremonies shamans often posed as different animals and/or spirits, dressing up in special costumes and using their drum to beat a hypnotic rhythm. While his earthly body entered a trance-like state the shaman could travel to the lower regions of the heavens to act as intermediaries between the people and the gods.

Shamans made use of falcons and birds of prey as it was believed they could guide the shaman to the spirit world and because it was also believed that evil spirits were afraid of such birds. In Kyrgyzstan the evil spirit *al-basty* (usually identified as a yeti), was believed to be the cause of all diseases. But it was also believed that *al-basty* would not go anywhere near a Golden Eagle, Goshawk or Eagle Owl. One of these birds was often kept in the tent during childbirth to protect newborn children.

The Swedish traveller Swen Gedin noted a similar belief in Muslim Kashgar in the late 19th century:

> Shamans have falcons, of which bad spirits are afraid. The people say that a woman, when she is giving birth, can see the spirits trying to torture her. Other people cannot see the spirits, but the falcon can, so it is released into the room to scare them away.

The Altai people were never influenced by Buddhism or reached by either Islamic or Christian missionaries and maintain one of the purest forms of shamanism. The Altai epos (epic poem) *Maaday-Kara* describes the cosmological structure of nature and defines the place of birds of prey. In a place at the confluence of 70 rivers, there stood a 100-trunked, seven-junctioned poplar tree hung with gold and silver leaves. Under one branch of this tree a whole herd of horses could take cover. On top of the tree sat two cuckoos, their singing triggering flowers to bloom. On the middle branches sat two black Golden Eagles with diamond talons guarding the blue sky. At the base of the tree were two dogs, their eyes full of blood, each on an iron chain, and a great horse which can only be ridden by a famous hero (Evsukov 1988). In this legend the blue sky is *Tengri* – Upper Heaven – the place where the king of the gods dwelled. A shaman was not allowed to go that high, and it was the job of the eagles to guard the entrance.

During shamanistic acts, the shaman wore a costume which was invariably decorated with, or took the form of, totem animals such as raptors. Often the costume would include feathers, and occasionally bells similar to those used by falconers. In Asia the shaman's *yurt* (tent) would often be decorated with sculptures of falcons sat on poles, the poles sometimes being used in ceremonies. The shaman's drum would also be decorated with a falcon. The falcon was the favoured 'spirit helper', carrying the shaman's prayers and wishes to heaven. Shaman also wore costumes decorated with feathers (Prokofieva 1971). They were believed to have 'familiars' (helpers) living inside their bodies which could contact the spirit world directly. Carved images of these familiars were often grotesque, but frequently showed bird-like features. In the Inuit world such carvings were called *tupilaqs*. These are still produced, though now more as an art form for tourists, particularly in east Greenland: there is, in general, still a strong tradition of bird imagery in Inuit art.

In the time of Chinghis Khan, shamanism was a state religion. Shamans were part of the court of the Great Khan and accompanied him on all his military expeditions. There is indirect evidence that the shamans also participated in the Khan's falcon hunts, blessing the hunters and helping them with their drums. It possible that some shamans were also falconers, as Simakov (1998) noted a striking similarity between the initiation traditions of shamans and those of *berkutchi* in Kazakhstan and Kyrgyzstan, and even in the court of the Russian Tsar. Indeed, the profession of falconer was partially inherited, as was that of the shaman. Those who wished either position had to go through a process of approval before they were accepted.

THE CULT OF BIRDS OF PREY AND MONOTHEISTIC RELIGIONS

In general monotheistic, as well as the more dominant polytheistic, religions did not directly confront the cult of birds of prey (as they did with many other aspects of the religions they replaced), preferring to allow the evolution of society to (usually) transform the cult into sport. Nevertheless, the cult was at the very basis of the origin of the major religions. The fundamental difference between these religions and shamanism was that souls now 'belonged' to god, and therefore did not dwell in the skies in the form of birds of prey, although in some cases the birds were left the role of transporters of souls as, for instance, in the Mithraic religion of Zarathustra. Zarathustra (Zoroaster) was a sixth-century BC prophet who taught that fire, earth, water and wind were not gods, but sacred manifestations of a supreme god. Zoroastrianism became the state religion in Persia during the rule of Darius (522–486 BC). Later, followers were driven to India, where the religion survives. A characteristic feature of this religion is that the dead cannot be buried or burned, as such actions might defile the sacred elements. Instead corpses are displayed in 'towers of silence' and become food for vultures and kites. The birds are believed to be responsible for transporting the souls into the sky. They also act as cleaners, reducing the pollution of the sacred earth, air and water. This practice is echoed in the 'sky burials' of Tibet, but the analogy must not taken too far: although Tibetan practice does confer some status on the dead because their corpses enrich the living, the practice has as much to do with the lack of resources for alternative burials. Nevertheless the falcon is called *Cha* in Tibetan. The highest mountain in the world is known in Tibet as *Chomolungma*, Mother Goddess, though the name could also derive from 'the Peak of Falcons', since in the spiritual world of Tibetan monks the two are the same.

ORIENTAL RELIGIONS: HINDUISM, BUDDHISM AND SHINTO

Hinduism is a good example of a religion in which original animal gods have been anthropomorphised. 'The bird of life, destroyer of all, creator of all' appears in the *Mahabharata*, the creature being known in Central Asian countries as *Bidayuk, Humm, Humay* or *Humayun*. It has been suggested that the name Himalaya derives from the latter name, though most believe the origin to be Sanskrit for 'abode of snow'. The belief that there is a super-falcon which kills everything is not limited to Asia. Bö (1962) referred to the fact that in the medieval Norway there was a belief in the *hauk* (hawk) that 'kills everything'.

In India, the bird is more commonly called Garuda. With his human body, but raptor head and wings, Garuda is a familiar figure in temples throughout the subcontinent. Garuda is the servant and carrier of the god Vishnu and is often portrayed with red wings and a white face, the colours of the Brahminy Kite (*Haliastur indus*), which is sacred to Vishnu. The early spread of Hinduism carried the bird image to Indochina, Malaya and Indonesia where it was altered to suit the native taste for the frightening, grotesque and demonic. Despite these changes Garuda still stands, holding a snake in each hand (Garuda was the enemy of the half-snake, half-human Nagas, whose protector was Vajrapani) at the corners of the ruined temples of Angkor Wat (Grossman and Hamlet 1964).

In Mongolia, Buddhist tradition has eliminated most shamanism and totally changed the attitude of the local people to the natural world and to birds of prey in particular. However, ancient masks of Garuda in the museums of Ulanbataar depict the notched nostrils and beak of the Gyrfalcon. Some images even show the god as a falcon holding a snake in either its beak or feet.

Shinto, the traditional religion of Japan, is a typical monotheistic religion with monks, temples and a deep tradition. But even here ancient remnants of the cult of birds of prey can be found. The gates at the entrance to every Shinto temple are called *tori* (bird) and resemble a large perching site. In medieval times there was a belief that the bird involved was a cockerel, but recent studies have shown that in earlier times it was undoubtedly a raptor.

JUDAISM, CHRISTIANITY AND ISLAM

Though Judaism is not noted for references to the cult of birds of prey there are instances in the Old Testament that imply ancient totemism, often employing the eagle as a miraculous means of travel.

As Christianity spread it was required to tolerate, if not incorporate, traditional beliefs. Although the cult of birds of prey is notably absent, a reference in the New Testament – 'Wherever the body is, there the eagles will be gathered together' (*Matthew* 24.28; there is a similar reference in *Luke* 17.37) – might indicate a relic cult.

Also, the church encouraged falconry, perhaps channelling an ancient enthusiasm. The 11th-century frescoes which decorate the top part of the walls of the Orthodox St Sophia Cathedral in Kiev show two sides of a medallion, on each of which there is a Goshawk clutching a hare in its talons. In 12th-century France one of the jewels of Romanesque architecture, the church of Ste Foy de Conques, was dedicated to a saint who had performed one of her many miracles for a desperate falconer. In Denmark, the church of Skibby has frescos which include a procession of lords, wearing coronets, mounted on horses and carrying their falcons on their fists. In Sweden, a painting in the old church at Risinge (north-west of Norrköping) depicts a king riding a horse with a falcon on his left hand (Bö 1962).

Priests were allowed not only to hunt with birds of prey, but to take their birds into churches, temples and cathedrals: William of Wykeham (1324–1404), Bishop of Winchester, complained that the practice interfered with the service. In 1640 Le Curé d'Essy officiated in the Cathedral of Evreux, booted and spurred, to the sound of the drums, and with his falcon perched on the high altar, while Denis the Great, Bishop of Senlis, composed a scholarly treatise on falconry, and Giovanni de Medici, who became Pope Leo X, was an inveterate falconer, more interested in hunting than in church affairs.

Saint Bavon, the patron saint of falconers in western Europe, lived in the seventh century. He was a man of noble birth from Halle, in present-day Belgium, and in his youth was a keen hunter. He was accused of stealing a white Gyrfalcon, found guilty and condemned to death. As he was about to be executed, the missing falcon suddenly appeared in the sky, proving him innocent. The incident converted Bavon, who became a hermit, lived in a hollow tree and carried an enormous stone during church services as a penance.

Another falconer also became a saint. Triphon Patrikeev was a falconer at the court of Tsar Ivan I Kalita (1282–1340). One day on a hunt at Naprudnoe (then a village north of Moscow, but now part of the city) Triphon was flying a white Gyrfalcon, a favourite of the Tsar, but the bird disappeared. Ivan gave him three days to reclaim the Gyrfalcon or suffer death by beheading. On the third day the exhausted Triphon had a dream in which a man with a white Gyrfalcon on his right fist came to him on a white horse and told him that he would find the lost Gyrfalcon on the tallest pine of a nearby grove. Triphon woke and found the falcon just as the dream foretold. In thanks he built a wooden church at the site of the dream. Subsequently rebuilt in stone (in 1992 it celebrated its 500th anniversary) the church has survived Russia's troubled history. It once housed a famous icon (also known as an 'ambilance') of St Triphon holding a white Gyrfalcon, now in Moscow's Tretiakov Gallery.

There are striking similarities between these legends of the early Catholic and Russian Orthodox churches, and in both cases links with the old cults were removed as each faith became dominant. However, according to current 'official' legends neither St Bavon nor St Triphon had anything to do with falconry, Bavon converting when his sins as a husband filled him with remorse (though interestingly a statue to him in Ghent Cathedral where he is buried shows him with a falcon on his fist), while the Russian Orthodox Church claims that there is no link, other than coincidence, between St Triphon and Triphon Patrikeev (but fails to explain the famous icon or the persistence of the legend).

In contrast to Christianity, Islam incorporated the cult of birds of prey from its inception. There is a legend that some of the companions of the Holy Prophet took chicks from the nest of a bird called, in Arabic, *hammarah*. When the Prophet saw the mother bird hovering above in grief he ordered the men to return the fledglings to the nest (Masri 1992). In the story of the Lammergeier from Husam d-Dawlah Taymur the supernatural powers of the bird are clear. In the original the bird is called *humm* – close to the Russian *humanyun*, which, in folk tales, is a supernatural bird of prey which, unseen, 'takes everything'.

In Islam we see either a sceptical relationship between the ancient cults of birds of prey and falconry or a process of 'Islamicisation' of the legends which serviced the cults. Consider, for example, a famous Kazakh fairy-tale which recounts the story of Aleko Baatyr and his son Orak. Forty ravens flew at Orak, removing one eye. Orak lay under a tree, crying and thinking he would die. A large black bird of prey sat on the tree and the desperate Orak thought that the bird was waiting for him to die so it could eat his corpse. Orak cried even harder, thinking that his parents and sister would never see him again and never know what had happened. But then the bird – a *Kara Qush* (Imperial Eagle) – started to talk, telling Orak that it was actually Baba-Tokti-Tash-Tazy, a saint who had assumed the shape of an eagle in order to fly to his rescue (Potanin 1917, 1972). This is a perfect example of the combination of old cult legend and Islam, with a totem bird taking the form of a Muslim saint.

This blending of the pre-Islamic cult of raptors and Islam is perhaps most manifest in the famous text of the Koran carefully drawn in the shape of the falcon by Mohammed Fathiab. This text was produced at the end of the 17th century and can be seen in the Muséum National d'Histoire Naturelle, Paris. The falcon portrayed is a wild bird, without hood or jesses.

FALCONRY

Falconry is the ancient art of training birds of prey so that a human (the falconer) can utilise the natural ability of the bird to hunt. In this book we are not aiming to give a full account of falconry, but the subject cannot be ignored: the Gyrfalcon has played, and continues to play, a very important role in falconry, and it can be argued that the species' survival to an extent depends on falconry.

There is little information available on the origin of falconry. Flint and Sorokin (1999) thought that ancient humans may have taken a share of the quarry delivered by eagles or other birds of prey to the nest. Then, instead of slaughtering the chicks, they might have dreamed of having a raptor on hand at all times. As an example of this possible origin, we guarantee that a stay beside a Golden Eagle nest, say in Mongolia, will realise one marmot a day for the period of development of the chicks – about six weeks. Another idea on falconry's origin is suggested by Simakov's (1998, 1999) thoughts on the role of the cult of birds of prey in shamanistic tribes (see above), from which it might be hypothesised that the first falconer was a shaman. Whatever the origins, there are indications (from China and Persia) that falconry was widespread from the second century BC and there is no part of the ancient world without an indication of the presence of falconry.

FALCONRY AT ROYAL COURTS

A primary source on medieval falconry is the 13th-century treatise by Frederick II of Hohenstaufen (Wood and Fyfe 1943) (see Figure 10.1), which had a significant impact on falconry and the perception of birds of prey for centuries. The treatise (which can be seen as the first ornithological textbook) has a section on Gyrfalcons (indicating an in-depth knowledge of the species), as well as chapters on the keeping and training of birds of prey. The treatise introduced the concept of falconry as the sport of kings, a reflection of the fact that all European royal courts had falconries.

We believe that Frederick's manuscript influenced the famous traveller Marco Polo, a Venetian merchant born around 1254. It is our view, having studied the originals, that Marco Polo's book was compiled (perhaps plagiarised would be a better description, although at the time such practice was commonplace) from the accounts of others rather than from first-hand experience. The chief source was probably Rabbani Shawma (*c.* 1220–1294) whose text was discovered in 1887 in Tekhama, Iraq (Budge 1928). Rabbani Shawma was an Uygur Christian living in Khan Balik (now Beijing), who travelled to Rome to seek help from the Pope for the Christians of the East, who were threatened by the rise of Islam (thus making Marco Polo's journey in reverse). Rabbani Shawma did not mention the Great Wall of China (not wishing to suggest a divided country: Polo also failed to mention it, though he had no such motive). However, Rabbani Shawma did not mention falconry, which Polo certainly does. In part, Polo's description (and species names) was taken from Frederick II, but it does include famous accounts of the hunts of Kubilai Khan. Even the story of where the Gyrfalcons were caught ('the island off the shore of the northern ocean, 40 days of travel, where there are many Gyrfalcons, so that His Majesty can have as many as he wants') is very similar to the account given in Frederick's book (see below).

Figure 10.1 *Frederick II of Hohenstaufen, author of an important mediaeval treatise on falconry, prepares to release his Gyrfalcon.*

The supposed hunts began in March each year, when

> the Great Khan journeys north-east to within two days of the
> ocean, attended by ten thousand falconers, who carry with them
> a vast number of Gyrfalcons, Peregrine Falcons and Sakers, as well
> as many vultures, in order to pursue the game along the banks
> of the river.

Kubilai had four elephants, on top of which was a tent in which he kept his best 12 Gyrs. It is a very entertaining story, but there is no archaeological evidence or ancient texts to support such an array and Chinese chronicles do not verify the presence of such a number of birds (although it is possible that because of Taoist and Confucian theory hunting, like trade, was seen as a sin).

Later, when the land of the Great Khan was visited by Sir John Mandeville in the early 14th century (Mandeville 1910), the visitor recalled that:

> he [the Khan] hath of certain men as thought they were yeomen, that keep birds, as ostriches, gerfalcons, sparrowhawks, falcons gentle, lanyers, sakers, sakrets, popinjays well speaking, and birds singing, and also of wild beasts

Mandeville describes a hunt in which there were four elephants with a cabin mounted on top of them,

> and above the chamber of this chariot that the emperor sitteth in be set upon a perch four of five or six gerfalcons, to that intent, that when the emperor seeth any wildfowl, that he may take it at his own list, and have the disport and the play of the flight, first with one, and after with another

The account of Marco Polo is repeated once again.

Before Marco Polo's time we learn that Håkon of Norway sent 50 falcons to King Harald Bluetooth of Denmark (AD 910–940) (Bö 1962). For this reason Harald called Norway his *Haukøy* (Hawk Island). But the accounts of Marco Polo had a dramatic impact on the European perception of falconry in Asia. Although the first falconry in Russia dates from the ninth century, it was in medieval times that the sport reached its zenith, the signs of the sport still being evident in Moscow today (where the name Sokolniki Park descends from *sokol* – falcon). The Moscow mews employed as many as 300 men and housed Gyrfalcons in a variety of colours – *krechet krasniy* (white Gyr), *kraqpleni* (white with spots), *podkrasniye* (semi-white) and *tsvetnye* (coloured, *i.e.* grey). The favourite bird of the Tsar Alexei Michailovich was a speckled Siberian Gyrfalcon nicknamed *Gumayun* (*cf. Humayun*, the bird which takes everything, as noted above). The hunts of the kings in Russia's neighbour Georgia were lavish and ceremonial (Allen 1970). They were also important, the Master of Falconers being outranked only by the Grand Equerry. In 1656 the Russian Tsar had 70 Gyrfalcons and 29 falcons (Peregrines) (Dementiev 1951). Falconry was also widespread across Western Europe, although here Gyrfalcons were limited to kings and a very few of the aristocracy. Dementiev (1951, 1960) notes the number of falconry birds (of all species) in the royal courts of Elizabeth I of England (in 1596) – 96 birds; Louis XIII of France (1634) – 99; Louis XIV of France (1684) – 83; and Louis XVI of France (1777) – 82.

There are numerous accounts of falconry by the monarchs of Europe which are quite diverse in detail. What is clear is that Gyrfalcons were the birds flown at large quarry such as swans, kites, herons and even cranes.

Figure 10.2 *The gift of a Gyrfalcon was a powerful diplomatic tool throughout mediaeval Europe and Central Asia.*

Diplomacy

In medieval Norway one letter of the *Diplomaticum Norvegicum* (a collection compiled between 1050 and 1590) is from the Pope thanking the Norwegian King for the falcons he had received as gift (Bö 1962). It is just one of many acts of diplomacy in which a falcon (and often a Gyrfalcon) was used as diplomatic cement (see Figure 10.2). As noted in the Preface, so important were the birds to the Danish royal court as diplomatic gifts that a special house was built in Reykjavik to store them before transfer to Denmark.

The gift of a Gyrfalcon was seen almost as the signing of an alliance between two states: subject states of the empire of Chinghis Khan routinely sent Gyrfalcons to him to stop his armies coming the other way. The famous Russian traveller Afanasiy Nikitin, together with the ambassador Vasiliy Papin, was sent to the Mongol Horde in 1475 with a gift of Gyrfalcons. The Georgian King Alexander was 'more interested in the Gyrfalcon' than in any of the other sacred and luxurious gifts which had been sent to him by Russian Tsar Fedor Ivanovich as the finest Gyrfalcons were regarded as the equal of the splendid *argamak* horses which it was the custom of the Georgian Kings to send as gifts to the Russian court

(Allen 1970). So important were the birds that Russian diplomatic missions were given special instructions telling them how to care for the Gyrs – two pigeons or one hen each day, and as much ice as possible to keep the birds cool (Veselovskiy 1890). As an example of the diplomatic power of the Gyr, when Stephan Bathoriy, King of Poland, demanded white Gyrs from Tsar Ivan III the refusal – the Tsar said 'I did have some, but they have almost died out' – was a considerable slight (Dementiev 1951, 1960). Luckier rulers who did receive Russian Gyrfalcons included Sultan Ibraghim of Constantinople, the Shah of Iran (28 Gyrs and two Goshawks from Tsar Boris Godunov) and the Chinese Emperor. Sadly, on some of these very long journeys, though travelling in padded boxes and with every care taken for their welfare, the Gyrs often died. In that event, the mission was required to present the feathers of the deceased birds so that, in diplomatic terms, the gift was made (Dementiev 1951, 1960).

The gift of Gyrs to non-Christian countries is interesting. In about 1350 King Magnus Eiriksson of Norway applied to the Pope for permission to sell some falcons to an Arabian Sultan. He pleaded that he was deeply in debt and needed the money he could only obtain with the sale. The Pope granted him this, but only on condition that the Sultan, an enemy of Christendom, 'did not receive prohibited goods' (Bö 1962).

The Gyrfalcon as a falconry bird

Nothing is better than a good Gyrfalcon (Jack 1996)

In this section we shall endeavour to sketch the Gyr as a falconry bird. However, we cannot hope to compete with the numerous specialised falconry titles, nor is our aim the encouragement of experiments with Gyrfalcons without proper supervision. We would also draw attention to the comment of Nelson (1956), who wrote: 'So much has been written on the potential of the Gyrfalcons in speed, footing, temper etc. that it is difficult to make a scientific observation without being influenced by something read or heard'. The comment is even more correct now than when made half a century ago.

Frederick II (Wood and Fyfe 1943) wrote that 'the gerfalcon shall be given first place in our treatise', and ever since falconers all over the world have considered the Gyr to be the top hunting bird. No other bird used for falconry carries the same reputation as the Gyrfalcon: every falconer has at some time dreamed of owning a beautiful white Gyrfalcon (or indeed any Gyr). To some it has become an obsession, yet in reality there are limited numbers of people who ever hunt with Gyrfalcons, most falconers opting for other species despite the fact that the Gyrfalcon is considered to be one of the easiest birds to train.

The Gyr has no innate fear of man and starts training willingly and without hesitation (Durman-Walters 1994). In comparison to other raptors, the Gyr often appears remarkably tame when being handled for the first time. This may well be because their natural habitat is well away from human habitation, so they have not evolved a fear of man (Durman-Walters 1994). But despite these attributes falconers are warned not to use a Gyr as a first bird. The experienced falconer Jemima Parry-Jones (1994) wrote: 'Forget about Gyrs as a beginner, as I very much doubt if you will want to spend that much on a bird that you are fairly likely to lose. They can be very temperamental and throw pretty good tantrums'. Such warnings have a long pedigree, an old Portuguese account stating that Gyrfalcons take great offence if they are not treated in the correct way (Jack 1996).

Gyrs are very sensitive to heat coupled with humidity – even more so than high temperatures coupled with a dry atmosphere. Beebe and Webster (1994) noted that:

> Of all falcons the Gyr seems to falls out of condition the most rapidly and, despite its great strength, loses stamina if not flown and exercised daily... A few weeks of total inactivity can have such a devastating effect that the Gyr will almost fall from the air in sheer exhaustion after only a few easy passes at the lure.

Lascelles (1892) also believed that it was extremely difficult to keep the Gyrfalcons in good health until they had become thoroughly acclimatised to their surroundings.

The disease *frounce* (which attacks the throat and tongue) was once the number-one killer of Gyrfalcons, so much so that many falconers refused to use pigeons (which carry this, and other, diseases) in any form as falcon feed (Beebe and Webster 1994). However, the wealth of falconers in the Middle East as well as the general growth of veterinary knowledge has significantly advanced the speed and success of the treatment of birds of prey in cases of sickness. Twenty years ago diseases that were considered to be lethal (e.g. trichomoniasis, staphylococcus infection, bumblefoot: Webster 1959) are now curable by routine treatment. In countries where there is large-scale falconry, such as Saudi Arabia and the UAE, there are sophisticated falcon hospitals (some of which are also open to the public). For current advances in falcon medicine it is best to read recently published works such as Heidenreich (1997), Samour (2000) and Lumeij *et al.* (2000).

With good care, Gyrfalcons can live for many years. In 1615 Symon Latham wrote: 'I have known a gyrfalcon of excellent survival, and to continue her goodness very near twenty years, or full out of time' (Latham 1615). Similar views were expressed by Stevens (1956): 'Not only is it possible to keep these Arctic falcons in health, but they can be flown with an equal, if not with a greater, degree of control than can the Peregrine'.

For general falconry, whether for game hawking or for flights at crows, it is common knowledge that the Gyr jerkin or tiercel (*i.e.* a male bird) is preferred. He is large enough to take duck, pheasant or crow while the only reasonably common species with which a female Gyr could be fairly matched would be Raven, Sage Grouse (for North America), Black Grouse (*Tetrao tetrix*) or Willow Grouse. Diana Durman-Walters (1994), an expert on grouse hawking in the UK, wrote that the complaint that Gyrs were too powerful for quarry available in the UK was not correct, noting that 'in their natural habitat they spend a great deal of time pursuing birds parallel to the requirements of the Peregrine' and that, consequently, 'Red Grouse is a suitable quarry. Pheasants are well within the remit of the male, but would ideally fit the female.'

Most Gyrfalcons are good-tempered and playful. They recognise the falconer by face, so there is no need to always wear the same clothes as one has to do for some nervous Peregrines. Stevens (1956) notes that the 'Gyr has nothing to hide and is capable of dog-like devotion to its human partner' but also that 'the Gyr has changing moods and is easily upset.' Stevens goes on to note that the bird is intelligent:

> They love a bit of fun. They love a game with a ball at the block. I throw them a small rubber one which they catch and foot it around like a football... the Gyr nearly always retrieves it to my feet, which is an invitation for me to throw it to her again, and when she tires of the game she pretends that it is an egg and sits on it.

However, Gyrs are also possessed by what Stevens describes as 'senseless hysteria'. They are easily upset by potential dangers which another hawk would ignore or fail to notice. Frequently the falconer is momentarily at a loss to understand why his Gyr, riding relaxed one moment, is spinning upside down on the fist the next, panicking and stressed (Ford 1999). At the discipline of waiting on, the Gyr needs encouragement: it is more difficult for a Gyr than for a Peregrine. Some falconers state that, as a general rule, if a Gyr has not taken a pigeon or grouse on the first half dozen stoops they will give up the chase, but others claim that once started they will never give up until the quarry has reached cover or is taken (Nelson 1956).

Gyrfalcons can climb and maintain flying speed at a steeper angle than any other bird. This ability to climb was very precious to Russian falconers, who had a saying that Gyrs climb 'on the tail' (*i.e.* vertically up). This performance is displayed in the attack only: when merely flying, Gyrs are slow. Smaller falcons are superior to Gyrs in agility, but this is only relevant when dealing with quarry smaller than partridge (Nelson 1956). In courage they have no equal: Gyrs will attack into a stiff wind even when the quarry is 3km or more away. Their range of attack is two to three times that of smaller falcons under ordinary conditions (Nelson 1956).

In regions where the Gyrfalcon is not a wild bird, such as the Middle East, but where a strong falconry tradition exists, Gyrfalcons are considered to be a good addition to a collection. The relatively recent arrival of oil wealth to the Middle East, together with the hawking tradition, is thought by many to have driven up the demand for Gyrfalcons, as well as for other species (Allen 1980). Interestingly, in the Gulf states the Gyrfalcon was called *sunqur*. The name is based on the Mongolian *shonkhor*, which is given to any large falcon, Saker or Gyrfalcon alike, Gulf State birds initially being imported from Pakistan. It is not clear whether real Gyrs were traded, or if these were the Altai variation of the Saker. However, 'the Gyrfalcon's weight and delicate health makes them hard birds to fly well in Arabia and they generally remain *tuyur al majlis* (drawing-room falcons) condemned to lend elegance and exotic cachet to their master's entourage for the time they survive' (Allen 1980) – a change from the perspective of user value to one of symbolic value. This change is of a great importance in the UAE, Kuwait and Saudi Arabia, as it brings the falcon to another level where the falcon is no longer a provider of food but a symbol of status, and a declaration of allegiance to Arabic traditions (Mortensen 1998). Today falconers with white Gyrs in use as active falconry birds in overheated desert conditions are rare, but the handful that do exist are true masters of the art.

CHAPTER 11

Threats and Conservation

In general, the Gyrfalcon is rather a lucky bird. It breeds in areas unsuitable for arable farming so direct exposure to agricultural chemicals is not generally a problem. Gyrfalcons do not migrate long distances (as Peregrine Falcons do) and consequently do not pick up contamination in wintering grounds. Gyrs were not directly affected during the DDT era when that chemical was applied in huge quantities to control insect pests. Today, however, it is difficult for any animal species (including man) to avoid airborne pollution.

In Russia, excessive airborne pollution releases from the nickel–copper smelting complexes at Monchegorsk (on the Kola Peninsula) and Norilsk (on the Taimyr Peninsula) have created 'dead' zones of 20km radius around them, inside which virtually all plants and animals have been killed. There is also a nuclear power plant at Bilibino in Chukotka. In North America the only large industrial complex within the Gyrfalcon's range is the Alaska pipeline. While an oil spillage from the pipeline could be ecologically disastrous, there is some evidence (Ritchie 1991) that the overall effect of the pipeline has been beneficial for Gyrfalcons, the structure having offered convenient nesting sites for Ravens and, hence, to Gyrs. The controversial project to develop oilfields in the Arctic National Wildlife Refuge in Alaska has sparked considerable protest. Despite this the project will probably go ahead (as of early 2005) and might well have a negative impact on the local Gyrs.

Much more significant for the Gyrfalcon is indirect mortality caused by Arctic fur trappers and the effect of illegal trafficking in the birds. The former has become much less of an issue since the collapse of the international fur market. It is to be hoped that the trade will never recover, though the recent decision by the fashion industry to rehabilitate fur could signal a worrying increase. The second issue is a particular problem in states where the economic incentives of illegal trade exceed the danger of dealing with law enforcement agencies. Sadly, at present the number of cases of illegal trafficking shows no signs of decreasing.

NATURAL ENEMIES

Dementiev and Gortchakovskaya (1945) noted that eggs were disappearing from a Gyrfalcon nest during the final stages of incubation. They suspected that Herring Gulls, which were breeding nearby, were taking not only eggs but also newly hatched chicks when the falcon nest was unattended. Other species may also be responsible for nest-robbing, while several raptors may be enemies of adult birds – eagles and Eagle Owls for example – though the literature has no direct references to predation by them. Falkdalen (1997) reported a case of a Pine Marten (*Martes martes*) taking an entire Gyrfalcon brood of three.

The Brown Bear (*Ursus arctos*) was noted in Russia's southern Yamal by Morozov (2001). There, a bear was reported as having eaten two chicks from a nest in 1996 and chicks from another nest in 1997. As well as noting the bear predation, Morozov mentions that the early nesting of the Gyrfalcon was another reason to consider the species lucky, as Gyrs raise their chicks before the mass hatching of mosquitoes and midges. As a result Gyrfalcon chicks do not have the problems with blood-sucking insects that are experienced by chicks of the Peregrine Falcon, which may occasionally die as a result of attacks by these insects.

In Iceland Ravens are known to take deserted Gyrfalcon eggs and rob falcon caches, and they are also potential predators of nestlings (Nielsen and Cade 1990a). Steen (1999) reported that two Gyr chicks fell from a nest located on a very narrow cliff ledge in east Hardangervidda, south Norway. One was killed by a Stoat. The other broke a leg in the fall and had to be put down. Classifying the objective dangers of the environment as well as predators as a natural enemy, it should be noted that Cade *et al.* (1998) reported sliding rocks and mud as a cause of Gyrfalcon clutch loss.

PARASITES

Gyrfalcon chicks are known to be infested with ticks. In Alaska *Ixodus howelli* was reported (White and Springer 1965). Voronin *et al.* (1983) mention one Gyr male from north-eastern European Russia as being infected by nematodes. In a study in Iceland (Clausen and Gudmundsson 1981) 36 native Gyrfalcons – but not two Greenlandic visitors – were found to be infected with the nematode *Capillaria contorta*, which is usually observed in the pharynx and oesophagus. Large quantities of *Capillaria* and other parasite eggs were located, and the infestation caused the death of 13 birds. In addition 13 falcons had lesions in their respiratory system. One had acute pneumonia with a fibrinous pericarditis. *Corynebacterium murium* was isolated from the pericardium and liver of this bird. Seven birds had pneumonia, with seizure of the lung tissue and inflammation of the air sacs. The air sacs were covered with thick cheese-like membranes, often almost 1mm thick. One of these birds also had a superperitoneal abscess under the right kidney from which *Corynebacterium pyogenes* was isolated. Various Gram-negative bacteria, together with alpha-streptococci, were isolated from the pharynx, lungs, air sacs and livers of the diseased birds. Small numbers of parasites other than *Capillaria* were found in the intestines of 12 Gyrfalcons. *Plagiorchis elegans* (a trematoda worm) was found in two birds and the tapeworms *Cladotaenia cylindracae* in two others, with *Hymenolepis* in seven birds and *Mesocestoides* in a single bird.

Supporting the (relative) health of Greenlandic Gyrs, Taft *et al.* (1998) reported that 23 adult Gyrfalcons from Greenland were free of haematozoa. Arterial hepatitis was named as a cause of death of a Gyrfalcon caught as an immature female in Illinois (Burr 1975). In captive Gyrfalcons *Salmonella typhimurium* has been isolated from liver, spleen and small intestine. Captive birds have also contracted Chlamydia infection. It is believed that dual infection is usually fatal (Wernery *et al.* 1998). Captive Gyrfalcons can also be infected by an array of other parasites. Pavlik *et al.* (1998) reported infestation of the coccidia *Caryospora kutzeri* in a captive Gyrfalcon.

CHEMICAL POLLUTION

In the 1970s Snow (1974) suggested that the reproductive success of Gyrfalcons was not affected by pesticide residues, which had accumulated at low levels. In 1970–71 material collected on Alaska's Seward Peninsula showed that the local Gyrfalcons exhibited low levels of industrial pollutants, apparently as a result of eating migratory birds, but did not appear to be endangered by organochlorine contamination. There was no significant thinning of Gyr eggshells (Walker 1977). In the study of Clausen and Gudmundsson (1981) in Iceland, one out of 38 examined dead birds was poisoned with dimethoate, indicating that it probably died of alkylphosphate poisoning. Dimethoate is used mainly against flies in equestrian stables, though alkylphosphate poisoning was occasionally seen in Danish birds of prey when the insecticide was used illegally to kill gulls and crows.

Direct organochlorine contamination in Gyrfalcons has been measured in Iceland (Ólafsdottir *et al.* 1995), the levels reported not being dangerously high as they were, for instance, in Peregrine Falcons in Britain during the DDT era. Jarman *et al.* (1994) analysed the levels of organochlorine compounds in the blood plasma of nesting adult and nestling Gyrfalcons in western Greenland in 1989 and 1990. They found only DDE – a derivative of DDT – in contrast to the residues of DDT in Greenland Peregrines. The Greenland Gyrs had levels below 20μg/kg. Peregrines from the same area had levels of 220μg/kg of DDE in addition to other contaminants. As Peregrines are migratory and have a higher proportion of migratory birds in their diet, they are more exposed to contaminants.

In Alaska the DDE levels in Gyrfalcons (measured by biopsy) were 51ppm (parts per million). The range of measurements was 0.72–210 (n = 8) all in lipids in adult females, 5.6ppm and 210ppm in two adult males, 170ppm in one subadult female and 36ppm in an immature male (Walker 1977). In the eggs of Alaskan Gyrs there were 23ppm of DDE (range 3.9–53, n = 14). These data may be compared to the levels of DDE found in Siberian Peregrines during the episode of DDT contamination on the wintering grounds in the period from the end of the 1980s to the early 1990s, which were 6.19–22.44ppm wet weight (range 181.8–400.96ppm in lipid) (Potapov 1994a). In the United Kingdom the levels of DDE in Peregrine eggs during the DDT era was 0.1–70ppm wet weight (Ratcliffe 1980). In Alaskan *Lagopus* grouse and Arctic Ground Squirrels, the main food of Gyrfalcons, the DDE levels were found to be 0.5ppm lipid, *i.e.* at the edge of the resolution of the measuring technique (Walker 1977).

Iceland has had airborne DDT and PCB pollution, though by comparison with Europe and America it has not been seriously affected. Nevertheless, 37 Gyrfalcons collected in Iceland between 1966 and 1973 showed higher levels of organochlorines than birds from Norway (Helleberg *et al.* 1979). For comparison, the levels of organochlorines in Icelandic seabirds were lower than those from industrialised countries and areas, but comparable to those of Scottish birds. This confirms the insidious nature of the chemicals, and also suggests that organochlorines are ubiquitous in Iceland and, therefore, in Icelandic Gyrfalcons.

Langvatn and Moskenes (1979) wrote that the Gyrfalcon population in Norway had not decreased to the same extent as the Peregrines during the DDT period. The latter is thought to be more exposed to the toxic effects of biocides, which may partially explain the assumed difference in population changes.

There are no data on contamination from the Siberian part of the Gyr's range, except those of Kalyakin and Vinogradov (1981), who analysed the corpse of a young Gyrfalcon found in southern Yamal. The dead Gyrfalcon chick (450g in weight) was retrieved from a nest. Its crop and stomach contained the remains of a Velvet Scoter (*Melanitta fusca*). The other chick from the same nest fledged successfully. The authors suspect chemical poison as the cause of death since they found a high concentration of DDE in the chick's liver.

Another indirect indication of DDT/DDE contamination is eggshell thickness. It is usually measured by the Ratcliffe Index (R_i):

$$R_i = \text{Weight (eggshell)}/(\text{Length} \times \text{Breadth})$$

Anderson and Hickey (1972) reported work on the Ratcliffe Index of Gyrfalcon eggs collected across North America and Greenland. They noted a shell thickness of 0.432 ± 0.010mm ($n = 59$) for the pre-1947 period, whereas during the DDT era the thickness reduced to 0.410 ± 0.010mm ($n = 7$), *i.e.* it was thinned by 5%. Such a change could however be the result of a rather small and skewed sample size. The eggshells gathered in the period 1968–69 from the Seward Peninsula, Alaska had an R_i=2.21 (range 1.89–2.60, $n = 12$), which does not differ statistically from the pre-DDT index (Cade *et al.* 1971).

Due to the increased usage of cars over the last decades there was a fear that some elements from catalytic converters could enter the food chain and contaminate various birds, including Ptarmigan and Willow Grouse, and that these could in turn contaminate Gyrfalcons. The elements which are emitted from those cars with catalytic converters are Platinum Group Elements (PGE), Palladium (Pd) and Rhodium (Rd), these being traceable in airborne pollution, road dust and roadside soil. Particles of these elements have even been found in samples of Greenlandic snow. A study addressing this issue has been carried out in Sweden (Jensen *et al.* 2002). The authors measured the level of PGE, Pd and Rd in the feathers of various raptors and their prey. As with many other pollutants, Gyrfalcons were the least contaminated raptors, showing almost half the levels of the three contaminants compared to urban Sparrowhawks and captive-bred Peregrines. The levels in Gyrfalcons were slightly higher than those measured in Peregrine Falcons before 1986 (*i.e.* before catalytic converts were introduced in Sweden). The levels of the elements in the feathers of grouse species were comparable to those in the Gyrfalcons. In the past 60 years the levels of PGE in Peregrines have more than doubled, following the trend of usage of catalytic converters in cars: converters have been mandatory in Sweden since 1989. It looks, therefore, as though the upward trend will continue, with a rise in levels of PGE, Pd and Rd in Gyrfalcons as well.

There is, however, nothing to suggest at this stage that the presence of these elements at the measured doses is harmful to the raptors. We suggest that since a major expansion of road systems and urbanisation in the Arctic and sub-Arctic is unlikely (at least in the short- to medium-term), lethal levels of PGE, Pd and Rd will not be reached in the foreseeable future.

PERSECUTION AS VERMIN

In most Gyrfalcon range countries the Gyr, together with other birds of prey, was once considered a pest (particularly by sportsmen who saw raptors as competitors), and bounties were set for its extermination. Hunters were paid either cash or some other incentive for presenting the feet of the raptorial birds of prey to the authorities. Such bonuses were paid in Iceland (where bounties were paid, mostly by Eider farmers, from the mid 1800s until 1905), Norway, Russia (where the birds were mostly shot on their wintering grounds) and Sweden. Some vagrant Gyrfalcons were also killed in the UK (McGhie 1999). Although this barbaric practice largely ceased in the 1960s, occasional stories still surface of gamekeepers and hunters shooting raptors.

The situation is now very different in Iceland, where commercial eiderdown harvesting has ceased. The Gyrfalcon was eventually given full protection and its export was prohibited. During discussions at the Icelandic Parliament some MPs opposed the export prohibition on the grounds that 'there is a demand ... we have a supply ... let's make some money'. This view was defeated by a counter-argument which suggested that the same logic applied to the export of virgin daughters. The latter view closed the session: in the vote there was overwhelming support for a total ban on exports (O. Nielsen, pers. comm.).

Centuries of farming in Iceland have created a favourable landscape for Ptarmigan by converting birch forests into heathland (Cade *et al.* 1998). Local farmers, perhaps the descendants of some who persecuted the Gyrs, now have a very different attitude to the bird, seeing it as a tourist attraction as well as one of the great features of their landscape. Consequently, farmers are now among the Gyrfalcons' best friends, routinely informing the police if strangers seem interested in the whereabouts of Gyr nest sites.

Though the Icelandic situation is good news for the Gyrfalcon, a major conflict of interest has recently been reported from Sweden. In the mid-1990s the government allowed general hunting for grouse, an activity which had previously been restricted solely to landowners. In poor years Gyrfalcons consume 20% of the grouse population (but only 7.3% in good years); the birds now find themselves in conflict with hunting humans, who shoot 20–30% of the grouse population (Holmberg and Falkdalen 1996). This conflict for a finite resource is believed to have forced some Gyrfalcon pairs to give up breeding and abandon their territories.

There is some evidence of persecution in Greenland, but the most intense persecution has undoubtedly been in Europe. McGhie (1999) analysed persecution levels in Britain by examining records in the taxidermy books. In the period 1912–69 eight Gyrfalcons were shot and stuffed, a small number compared to other birds of prey, but significant in terms of the numbers reaching Britain. The majority of the birds were shot in the Outer Hebrides.

Clausen and Gudmundsson (1981) analysed the causes of death of 40 Gyrs (38 native Icelandic and two vagrants from Greenland). Twelve of the birds (32%) had been shot by small-calibre rifles or shotguns, eight (20%) had died as a result of trauma (most often a fractured wing after a collision with overhead wires), with one tangled in a net. One bird died from ingesting the femur of a ptarmigan which had penetrated its gizzard and damaged the liver. Two birds died from oil pollution, one after landing on a ship, the other after being covered with 'train grease'. Autopsies revealed that 84% of birds were young.

GYRFALCONS AS FOOD OR BAIT

Gyrfalcons are known to have been eaten by the Vikings. Excavations of a Viking homestead at Hope Island, close to Nuuk (Godthåb), Greenland (Vaughan 1992) unearthed two Gyr bone fragments from the floor depositions of the dwelling house. In comparison to the more than 150 bone fragments of various shorebirds, the Gyr bones appear insignificant, but the fragments included only one Ptarmigan bone, although it is known that Ptarmigan were a favoured food source. The excavated fragments do not appear to be wholly indicative of the Viking menu, though they do clearly show that the Gyrfalcon was not a taboo bird for the Norse settlers.

Chuvashov (1989) reported that the meat of Rough-legged Buzzards, Snowy Owls and falcons (Peregrines and Gyrfalcons) is considered a delicacy amongst nomadic peoples, particularly on Russia's Gydan Peninsula where the Nenets shoot the birds during the spring as they return to the area to breed. Chuvashov estimates that in winter hunters in the area set up to 3,000 traps to catch Arctic Foxes. Chuvashov estimated that around 100 hunters could, and would, shoot rare raptors for both food and trap bait during their outings, a considerable fraction of the total number. Gorovenko (2003) gives details on the population of Gyrs in Koryakia, Kamchatka. Out of eight nests monitored at least one was robbed by trappers.

HUMAN DISTURBANCE

Woodin (1980) observed a breeding pair of Gyrfalcons in which the female was a one-year-old juvenile. A photographer had set a hide some 50m from the nest. The feeding rate of the brood was too low, and the female tended to feed herself on the nest rather than her brood. A few days later the hide was dismantled, but by then one chick had disappeared while another was apparently dying. The remaining two chicks were somewhat lethargic. Two days later all four chicks were dead. Woodin concluded that the nest had been abandoned because of the hide, and that the young had starved. While this is an extreme case (and rare as photographers do not often work close to Gyr nests, and most are more sensitive to their impact on the birds), human-caused mortality is a significant threat to Gyrs. The threat is not only limited to areas where the birds and man normally overlap.

Direct human approach does not seem to alarm the birds excessively (unless, of course, it results in an attempt at capture or egg-robbing). Kishinskiy (1958) reported that when he approached a Gyr nest for the first time, the parent birds demonstrated a high state of alarm, but that when they had become used to daily nest-visits the female would slip off the nest calmly and without calling, returning after his visit. Our own personal experience confirms this. Indeed, during an approach to one egg-sitting female the bird at first seemed more surprised than alarmed, and then curious rather than concerned, though again the fact that the approach was not aggressive or very close may have contributed to this reaction.

A local decrease in the Gyr population in Scandinavia has been attributed to habitat deterioration from overgrazing by Reindeer, reduced numbers of *Lagopus* grouse, and human disturbances of various forms (snowmobiles, urbanisation, road and powerline building, etc.) (Tømmeraas 1993, Cade *et al.* 1998).

Indirect human disturbance – the building of dams for reservoirs, road building, snow scooter routes and other tourist activities – was mentioned as a factor limiting the spread of Gyrfalcons in Scandinavia (Cade *et al.* 1998). The same authors also noted that in Fennoscandia overhunting of Willow Grouse and overgrazing by Reindeer had a negative effect on Gyrfalcons.

Kalyakin (1989) suspected Reindeer herders of destroying three or four Gyrfalcon nests during his study in Russia's Yamal, and illegal shooting by Reindeer herders was also noted by Morozov (1991) as a probable cause of Gyr death in the Arctic Urals. Human disturbance is almost certainly the reason for the low breeding density around the Vorkuta industrial zone (Morozov 1991). Kalyakin and Vinogradov (1981) also reported direct persecution of a Gyrfalcon nest in southern Yamal in 1979 and 1980.

Also in Russia, especially on the Yamal Peninsula, oil exploration was considered a significant threat to the local Gyrs by Morozov (1991). However, the recent completion of the only road in southern Yamal (linking the town of Labytnangi to tundra oil rigs) and the consequent increase in human activity seems not to have affected Gyr numbers in the area, the population being more or less stable (Rupasov 2001, S. Rupasov pers. comm.). There are fears that controversial oilfield developments in the Arctic National Wildlife Refuge, Alaska, might harm Gyrfalcons. In 1989, the Refuge (the Sadlerochit and Shublik Mountains and the north side of the Franklin, Romanzof and British Mountains) had 42 occupied territories in an area of about 7,600km^2, a density of 5.5 pairs per 1,000km^2 (Swem *et al.* 1994).

As described in Chapter 5, White and Nelson (1991) found that it was possible to approach Gyrfalcons by helicopter. Generally, however, Gyrfalcons are less tolerant of helicopters than Peregrines. Gyrfalcons on the North Slope of Alaska and in Canada's Yukon Territory flew rapidly away from helicopters travelling at high speeds, while the aircraft was still several hundred metres distant (Platt 1977). Platt also made several experimental flights by helicopter above the nests of Gyrfalcons in Canada's Yukon Territory. Although there was no significant difference in breeding success between nests which were disturbed (Platt has subgroups of nests disturbed by humans (hides nearby) and by helicopter; only by helicopter; and only by humans) and undisturbed nest sites, the occupancies of the same territories in the following year was significantly less in disturbed sites. None of the five disturbed nests was occupied, whereas re-occupancy of undisturbed sites was six out of eight, or 75%. This suggests that if moderate disturbance occurs while breeding is in progress, the Gyrfalcons tolerate it without significant reduction in the breeding rate. However they are apt to change the nest location next year.

In some situations the Gyrfalcons vigorously attacked fixed-wing aircraft (Roseneau, cited by White and Nelson 1991), and Mossop (cited by White and Nelson 1991), while surveying Gyrfalcon nests, reported a number of Gyr attacks against a (predominantly white) helicopter.

THE EFFECT OF ARCTIC FOX TRAPPING

Arctic Fox trapping was once a traditional trade of local people all over the Eurasian Arctic. Trapping also occurred in the Canadian and Alaskan Arctic, but the fur trade there never reached the scale and ecological impact demonstrated in Eurasia. From the time the first Cossack teams penetrated Siberia, fur was the major attraction of the area. Initially, pelts were gathered close to villages set beside the principal rivers flowing into the Arctic Ocean. Mangazeya was the first and most famous of these, but settlements such as Kolymskoye, Pokhosk, Anadyr, Tiksi and Dickson were all important fur trading centres, an apparently insatiable demand for furs keeping the settlements busy. Later, the creation of the USSR pushed fur hunting (and indirectly the welfare of Gyrfalcons) to new extremes. As the communist regime maintained a monopoly on currency exchange and the rouble rate was artificially frozen, the government was continuously short of the valuable exportable commodities required to maintain the trade balance. Such commodities included gold (as well as other precious metals), oil and furs. The fur trade was centralised in the USSR, with special policing groups being set up in Arctic areas to combat 'illegal' (*i.e.* local) trade: all good fur was required for the export market. The fur was traded from a fur auction house located at Moscovskiy Prospect in Leningrad (a city which has now reverted to its historic name of St Petersburg), the house being one of the most important fiscal instruments of the communist empire. Each summer the house sold vast quantities of fur, all trapped in the world's largest forest or on the world's largest stretches of tundra. Although the most expensive fur at the time was Siberian Sable (*Martes zibellina*) and Beaver (*Castor fiber*), the champion fur, by quantity, was that of the winter-clad white Arctic Fox. The local market for fox fur was somewhat limited, the fur being considered insufficiently durable for the Siberian winter, but to the fashion industry of the 1970s and 1980s white fox was indispensable. The commercial harvest of Arctic Fox was at its highest at that time.

The technology of the fur trappers was rather simple. Local people fished all summer, storing some of the fish for bait and, importantly, as food for their dog teams, in large pits excavated in the permafrost. The importance of fish explains why settlements were largely set beside the rivers, though the harsh nature of the terrain also meant that rivers provided the only realistic way form of transport, furs being taken down to the Arctic Ocean and then along the coast. The trappers lived in log cabins setting these at least one day's rowing apart. A fish storage pit would be excavated close to each cabin. The remains of cabins, and even of entire, now-deserted, villages are still visible along the Kolyma, Lena and Indigirka rivers.

During the winter the trappers would bait their *pasti* – traditional traps made of logs – and the better-known leg traps. The latter were usually placed on natural or artificial tussocks, so that they were exposed to the wind to allow the bait scent to disperse, and were also highly visible to the quarry. At first the traps could only be set over limited ranges, but when helicopters, snowmobiles and outboard motors became available it was possible to penetrate any part of the tundra. By 1980 every square kilometre of tundra had been assigned to the state fur company (*Promkhos* – organised along the same lines as the infamous *colhoz*, or collective farms), with an individual trapper being allocated a particular territory. Annual and five-year plans were assigned to particular territories and individual trappers. In some cases these plans ignored the three- to four-year natural cycle in the fox population as the foxes respond to the cyclicity of lemmings. The Special Institute of Extreme North Agriculture located in Norilsk did maintain a monitoring programme of the lemming population, though this was largely to allow the Fur Auction House to establish a pricing policy.

Using modern transport, it is estimated that there was no area of the Russian Arctic greater than 10km^2 which did not have a fox trap. The trapping season began with the first snow and lasted until 1 April, the date at which Arctic Fox fur became commercially useless as the foxes were moulting to their summer coat. The vehicle of choice for Russia's trappers was the Russian-built *Buran* (Blizzard) 30hp snowmobile.

At the end of the hunting season the trappers returned to the larger settlements, surrendering their fur catch to the state authorities and going into 'hibernation' until the rivers became free of ice. This pattern of fox exploitation, with no traps set during the springtime, and no possibility or need to travel (except during the occasional goose hunt) saved the Gyrfalcon from disturbance and, probably, shooting during a critical period. However, during the winter trapping season the toll on the birds was significant. Attracted by the carrion bait, or occasionally using the traps (which are generally placed at a relatively high level) as perches, the Gyrs would land and become trapped. Although some inadvertent trappings were reported there is little doubt that these were the exception. In general the trapped Gyr would simply be used as bait in the reset trap.

However some reports of Gyr trappings were made. They come from the period when the foreign currency monopoly in the USSR had ceased to exist and the fur market had collapsed, contributing to the fall of the USSR in 1991: the infamous Fur Auction house in what is now St Petersburg became empty.

During their visit to the Cherskiy area and the Andruskino settlement in the Kolyma–Alaseya lowlands in the winters of 1998 and 1999, van Orden and Paklina (2000) found that trappers setting snares to catch Willow Grouse would occasionally catch Gyrfalcons: a single trapper could catch 1–3 Gyrs each year. However, over the same period no Gyrfalcons were caught in leg traps set for Arctic Fox because of the reduction in demand for fur (N. Paklina, pers. comm.).

Gyrfalcon deaths occasioned by Arctic Fox trappers were mentioned by Kalyakin (1989) in his studies in southern Yamal. He noted that during the winter of 1984/85 an unusually low snowfall allowed the Willow Grouse to remain in the bush tundra subzone, their spring/summer habitat, where, normally, the short bushes were engulfed by snow and the grouse could not maintain access. Heavy trapping occurred in this region, the trappers using traditional leg traps, and local reports said that many Gyrfalcons, attracted to the area by the density of Willow Grouse, were caught during the trapping season. This anecdotal information was backed up by Kalyakin's observation that in 1985 only one breeding pair of Gyrfalcons was noted, rather than the five pairs which had been the norm for the region. It is likely that the sole pair were first-time breeders. In the following year, when snow conditions were more normal, there were two breeding pairs in the region.

Morozov (1991) reported severe winter Gyr mortality caused by Arctic Fox trappers, and similar data are given by Chuvashov (1989) for Russia's Gydan Peninsula. Over a four-month period of the winter of 1986/87 (a year of high grouse and lemming numbers), the trap line of 710 leg traps set over a distance of 200km in the tundras of southern Gydan caught nine Gyrfalcons and five Snowy Owls. This catch rate equates to one Gyr killed for every 50 traps or 14km of trap line. Such a death rate is very significant given the population density of Gyrfalcons. In the following winter (1987/88, a period of low lemming and grouse numbers) Chuvashov examined data from 110km of trap line with 190 set traps. During a three-month period the line yielded six Gyrfalcons (and an additional three Snowy Owls). This means that during this period of low prey density the mortality rate for the Gyrfalcon had increased to one death for every 21 traps or 12km.

Deaths in Arctic Fox traps in the Commander Islands were also mentioned by Artukhin (1991). Arctic Foxes are quite numerous there and fox trapping was intensive. Gyrfalcons wintering at the islands prey on the abundant seabirds and Ptarmigan, but are also often caught in traps baited with meat. Belkovskiy (1998) estimated that one or two Gyrs die in fox traps on Bering Island, one of the Commander Islands, each year. On St Lawrence Island in the Bering Strait the death of a Gyrfalcon in a leg trap was mentioned by Portenko (1972).

Ellis (1993) extrapolated data on the deaths of Gyrfalcons in Russia's northern Yakutia (mostly the Indigirka River valley) and suggested that about 2,000 Gyrfalcons (and 100,000 Snowy Owls) die every year in Arctic Fox traps in Yakutia alone. We are highly sceptical of this estimate, but accept the point that death in fox traps is a significant cause of Gyr mortality.

The direct influence of Arctic Fox trapping on Gyrfalcons has also been monitored in Russia's Nenetskiy Nature Reserve (Glotov 2000). The only monitored nest in the Pechora Delta (1996–2000) was occupied in 1998 by a single adult male Gyr, the female having died, it was believed, in a fox trap set nearby. The rangers of the Reserve recovered two dead birds from these traps (A. Glotov, pers. comm.).

The deliberate use of leg traps to persecute birds of prey such as Gyrfalcons and Goshawks was reported in northern Yakutia (Vorobiev 1963). The hunters of the region had become increasingly annoyed that raptors wintering in the area were stealing Willow Grouse from their snares. Similar reports had been noted earlier by Mikheev (1941), who stated that Gyrfalcons took live grouse from snare nooses, dead birds quickly becoming frozen and therefore difficult to eat. Though these are isolated reports there is no reason to believe that any human population in which grouse snaring represented a significant food resource would not have individuals who would react in the same way: an almost identical problem was noted by Kalyakin and Vinogradov (1981) in the southern Yamal.

In Taimyr (Dorogov 1985, Rogacheva 1988) Gyrfalcons were reported to die in numbers in Arctic Fox leg traps. In two hunting territories allocated to trappers with a total area of 2,000km^2 12 Gyr trap deaths occurred between November and December 1980. The problem was considered to be so serious that the Norilsk Extreme North Agricultural Institute was asked to develop a solution. There were many suggestions as to how this might be achieved. One was to return to the use of the traditional trap, the *pasti*, which is constructed of large logs (one of which falls to crush the fox) and has no parts which would endanger a bird sitting on it. Another, much simpler idea, was to set a vertical pole above the trap, so that the bird does not perch on that deadly, first dark object it sees protruding from a tussock (Chuvashov 1989, Glenn 1993). However, the real decrease in Gyr death toll came with the dramatic collapse of the fur trade which reduced trapping almost 100-fold.

From these studies, and others that had preceded them, it is apparent that Gyrfalcon mortality in fox leg traps was highly significant. Indeed, it was mentioned in the *Red Data Book* of the USSR as a factor limiting the Gyrfalcon in

Russia (Borodin 1984). It is estimated that Russian trappers reduced the Arctic Fox population to about 1% of its original size. This decline in numbers led to a decline in traps as the catch reduced. That, and the reduction of the fur trade as tastes changed and other, cheaper, materials became available to ward off winter's chills meant that the mortality of Gyrs declined sharply.

The effect of Arctic Fox trapping has been less devastating in other parts of the Arctic, the overlap of the Gyrfalcon's range and that of fur trappers being less pronounced. However, Cade *et al.* (1998) noted that fox hunting was to blame for some significant Gyrfalcon casualties in Iceland during the period 1958–64, when the birds died after consuming poisoned bait laid out for the foxes. Instances in other countries have also been noted, though at much lower frequencies: a Gyrfalcon was observed eating a trapped Arctic Fox on Svalbard (Kristoffersen 1931), and when snare trapping of Willow Grouse took place in the vicinity of two Gyr nests in Norway local Gyrfalcons took food from the snares, but, on this occasion, without deadly effect (Langvatn and Moksnes 1979).

THE EFFECT OF ARCTIC WHALING

After abortive attempts to access the riches of Cathay through the North-East and North-West Passages in 1607, the British Muscovy Company sent Henry Hudson on another search for a route. Hudson's plan was audacious. Reasoning that near the Pole the sun, being 'a manufacturer of salt rather than ice', would make the sea ice-free, he decided to sail over the Pole. To us this seems nonsense, but at the time the idea of an ice-free polar sea did not seem so strange - if the sun shone 24 hours each day then surely that would melt the ice? Sadly, Hudson was to find that this was not so (though many continued to claim that he had merely failed to pick a way through the ice ring that surrounded the open polar sea). What Hudson did discover, in the bays of Svalbard, were whales – vast in both number and size.

Unaccountably, the British merchants waited two years before sending another expedition to check Hudson's findings. Jonas Poole, the new captain, confirmed the abundance whales, and the race to exploit them was on. The trade was primarily British and Dutch. At first the whales were killed and hauled to shore stations, such as Smeerenberg (Blubber Town) on Svalbard's Amsterdamøya and another station on Jan Mayen, for cutting up. Eventually the killing exterminated the inshore whales. The animals (Right and Bowhead Whales) then had to be sought further out and rendered on board the ships. One of the better stretches of whaling water was the sea off Greenland's east coast. Although no whaling stations of the size or sophistication of Smeerenberg were established, whales would occasionally be towed ashore for rendering, as flaying a dead whale in the water and hauling the blubber onto the ship's deck was both messy and far from straightforward. The whale carcass would be abandoned on shore, or cut loose from the ship to which it had been tied. Either way, the intestines and meat clinging to the skeleton attracted birds. In some reports it is said that men would be stationed at each end of the whalers to shoo the birds away. The majority of these avian freeloaders would be seabirds, but Gyrs might also raid the carcasses on shore. Oiled Gyrs would die, but as the falcons were highly prized by collectors they would be shot, this explaining the high percentage of heavily oiled birds in the museums of Europe. Thankfully whaling has now virtually ceased. Gyrfalcon mortality through oiling following the consumption of waste products is unlikely to return to 19th-century levels.

GENETIC POLLUTION

There was panic in Sweden in 1999 when an escaped male Gyrfalcon x Peregrine Falcon hybrid from Denmark paired with a native Peregrine female in Bohuslan, the male bird being identified by its leg ring. The pairing made the headlines of Swedish newspapers (e.g. *Sydsvenska Dagbladen* 10 October 1999, A38). Falconry is, in general, prohibited in Finland, Sweden and Norway, and so the public reaction to this event was negative because of the potential for genetic pollution of the native species. The case was termed the 'birds of prey scandal' by the Swedish Ornithological Society (Wirdheim 1999). Officials from Naturvårdsverket (the Swedish Ministry of the Environment) killed the chicks produced by the pair and shot the hybrid. They also wished to kill the female as her willingness to mate with a non-pure bird caused concern that should another escape happen the bird might be equally willing a second time. However the female escaped and remained at large (Lindberg 1999a, 1999b).

Captive breeding now supplies virtually all the demand for Gyrfalcons for falconry in the West (Cade *et al.* 1998). This seems better than the use of wild birds at first glance, but there are drawbacks. Because of the difficulty of breeding pure-bred Gyrfalcons in Middle Eastern countries, where falconry remains popular, hybrids are bred elsewhere and sold to these countries. As the birds are used for outdoor hunting escapes are almost inevitable. The fate of such birds is unknown, as are the implications for wild populations of falcons (though there is no suggestion that such hybrid birds represent a genetic hazard to wild Gyrfalcons).

HOMOSEXUALITY

Though not strictly a form of genetic pollution a report from coastal Norway is of interest. Gjershaug *et al.* (1998) reported a female–female pairing between a Peregrine and Gyrfalcon at the seabird colony island of Runde. The two females each laid eggs on one nest and participated equally in incubation. On one occasion a food delivery by the Gyr was recorded. The authors report an unusually long (90-day) incubation period and a clutch of five (1989). They consider this the first record of homosexuality in falcons. They authors consider that it is possible that Peregrines and Gyrfalcons hybridise naturally where isolation between the species is weak and conspecific mates are rare. Scratching was observed on 17 April by the two females together. The eggs did not, of course, hatch but the pairing was repeated the following year (1990) when a total of six eggs were laid.

EGG AND MUSEUM COLLECTIONS

In the past some populations of Gyrfalcons have suffered from continuous nest robbing by egg collectors. One Swedish collector is known to have taken 70 eggs in one season from an area close to the Konkamaeno River (Sjölander 1946), while it is estimated that hundreds of eggs were taken from northern Finland in the late 1800s and early 1900s (Cade *et al.* 1998).

In the 19th and early 20th centuries there was considerable trade in Gyrfalcon specimens, the rarity of the species in Europe creating a demand which was readily met by taxidermists. The majority of birds on which the taxidermists worked came from Greenland and Iceland, with the the specimens being seen in good numbers in collections all over the world (see Table 1.1). In total we have examined more than 1,800 specimens in the museums of the world, 1,210 of which had the country of origin on their tags. From these data we can say that the dominant country of supply has been Greenland, closely followed by Iceland.

To summarise, we can say that the world population of Gyrfalcons had to withstand the selective pressure of specimen collectors for more than a century, with an annual documented (*i.e.* the skin is present in the museum) removal of at least 100–150 individuals. In all probability the total number of birds shot or otherwise procured during this period was much higher.

THE TRAPPING OF FALCONS: PAST AND PRESENT

Since the publication of Frederick II's treatise, European falconers had known that Gyrfalcons bred on 'a certain island lying between Norway and Gallandia (Greenland), called in Teutonic speech Yslandia' (Wood and Fyfe 1943).

But Iceland was a difficult country to reach. Ferriera, who in 1616 published a treatise on falconry in Portugal (Jack 1996), wrote that Gyrfalcons nest in Norway and Sweden. Scandinavia was much easier to reach, and around this time Norway became a leading supplier of Gyrs to European courts (Bö 1962): the craft of the falcon trapper became established. The trappers were not falconers, although it is believed that they knew the basics of falconry. Their social status prohibited them from owning or hunting with large falcons. In practice the ban was chiefly cosmetic as the trappers had neither the resources to support the falcons, nor easy access to hunting grounds. What the trappers did know well was the biology of the species and, consequently, they developed sophisticated traps to catch the birds. When falconry ceased to be the preserve of kings alone, trading houses were set up across Europe to profit from the falcon trade.

As early as 1378 there was a trading house in Lübeck, northern Germany, which trained Norwegian falcons and delivered them for sale in Nuremberg, Venice and even Alexandria. Another famous trading house was in Falkensvaard, northern Brabant, Holland. Here migrant birds were caught and sold by local trappers, some of whom also travelled to Norway. A good Dutch trapper expected to catch 12–15 good birds per year. As well as trappers, there were many famous falconers at Falkensvaard. They mastered the art of taming wild-caught birds, in contrast to the English school of training which was focused on birds taken from the nest as fledglings. Though sought-after, Gyrs were rarely caught at Falkensvaard. Lascelles (1892) mentions just three migrant Norwegian Gyrs taken during a period of 50 years.

Some of the places used by Scandinavian trappers were visited by Linnaeus during his visit to Dalarna (Linnaeus 1953). He noted that trappers were mostly Dutch or French (at that time most trappers in Norway were Dutch, while it was mostly Germans who trapped in Sweden), used pigeons as lures and built huts to house the captured birds. In 1960 it was still possible to see some of the trapping stations viewed by Linnaeus (Bö 1962). Some of the trappers settled in Norway. Bö mentions the well-known Adrian Robertson Falkener (1515–1595) who became a Mayor of Trondheim before 1547 and whose descendants took the surname Falck.

Despite Falkener's success it appears that the attitude of local people to falcon trappers varied from tolerance to disapproval, the latter resulting in occasional conflict. We have not discovered any case where the local population was enthusiastic about trapping efforts or directly benefited from the harvest. The trappers usually operated in great secrecy. They sometimes rented their trapping huts and it was said that 'no matter how well local people know the man, they still never manage to set foot in their hut. The falcon trappers insisted on that even if the use of arms was imminent' (Bö 1962). Local farmers also alleged that *ratesyke* (syphilis) was introduced by Dutch trappers and 'ravages so much some years that a country doctor was called in to treat the numerous sufferers.' In another incident a parish priest was accused of having called a farmer a falcon trapper because he wore a grey hat (Bö 1962). This all suggests that trappers were not popular figures in Norway.

Though Norway was easy to reach, the Gyrs from there were grey birds. The great desire of every falconer was a white Gyr, and these, at first, were only available from Iceland which, until the mid-20th century, was under the rule of Denmark. In the 1760s a Falkenergaarden was established in Copenhagen by Crown Prince Christian (later King Christian V) (Tillisch 1949, Vaughan 1992, Nielsen and Petursson 1995). The main purpose of the falconry house was to receive and distribute Icelandic-caught Gyrfalcons as diplomatic gifts among the courts of Europe. All the trappers employed in Iceland were locals, these men being responsible for the export of almost 5,000 Gyrs during the period 1731–1793. Though most of these birds were native Icelandic grey Gyrs, there were also 315 prized white Gyrfalcons. While the official export of Gyrs stopped in the early 19th century, it is known that small numbers of birds were still taken from the island. In 1869 John and James Barr were sent to Iceland by the Maharajah Dhuleep Singh for the purpose of obtaining Gyrs. They trapped and took to India not less than 33 birds, at least one of which lived many years (Lascelles 1892).

The Icelandic trade was not without cost to the birds. As a result of the trade the number of Gyrs in Iceland decreased, although it is thought that trapping had less of an impact on numbers than the collectors of eggs and mounted birds who came in the late 19th and early 20th centuries. It is now illegal to catch birds or collect eggs in Iceland, though stories of attempts to steal eggs or chicks and even to trap adult Gyrs are still occasionally heard.

In Russia Gyrfalcon trapping was a monopoly of the Tsar. Initially the Novgorod Principality dominated the trade, as they controlled most of the trade routes to the Urals and the White Sea. Later, when the Principality lost its independence, falcon trapping became one of the duties of sovereign subjects (Dementiev 1951, 1960). Teams of falcon trappers (*promyshlenniky*) – sometimes working as fur trappers as well – went to remote areas of Russia's north. The trappers were prohibited from selling Gyrfalcons since the Tsar had a monopoly of Gyr ownership and their entire catch had to be taken to Moscow. The falcons were brought by sleigh, trappers being granted a food allowance of two kopeks per day for each bird (Dementiev 1951). The trappers themselves were entitled to receive food and accommodation free from the villages through which they travelled on production of their authority from the Tsar. In the 16th century, falcon trappers and the falconers at the Tsar's court were covered by special legislation, the Uryadnik (Legislation) of the Falconry Path (*Uryadnik* 1788). This defined both their duties and their behaviour: 'Falconers (*sokolniki*) of the Royal Mews found drunken, quarrelsome, intriguing or merely stupid are to be transported in chains to the Lena.'

By the end of the 17th century the demand for Gyrfalcons started to decline – a note from the time tells the Governor of the Upper Tura region of Siberia not to supply any more Gyrs to Moscow – though trapping itself continued. In the 1730s the Arkhangelsk and Rostov falcon trappers were given permission to catch Gyrfalcons for themselves on condition that they supplied 20 female Gyrs and 30 males to the Royal Mews (Dementiev 1951). The Rostov falcon trappers ceased to exist in 1787: other groups stopped in the early 1800s.

In the New World there was no tradition of exporting Gyrfalcons, mostly due to falconry already being in decline as colonisation took place. Today, the harvesting of Gyrfalcons in the USA is permitted in Alaska. Trade is restricted to Alaska residents and the annual harvest is fewer than ten nestlings. Gyrfalcon numbers in Alaska are thought to be stable at present, and the birds are not in imminent danger (Swem *et al.* 1994). In Canada there have been removal experiments, but no large-scale Gyr harvest is permitted.

In Scandinavia (including Greenland) no commercial removal of Gyrs is permitted (CITES 2000). The last Gyrfalcon harvesting expedition of a significant scale was one organised by the German Falkenordern in the 1930s to Iceland and Greenland. The expedition was due mainly to the efforts of the Falkenordern's leader at the time, the infamous Hermann Goring, whose plan, apart from using the birds for falconry, was to introduce Gyrfalcons to the European Alps. Some of the Greenlandic Gyrs were released in the German Alps in 1938. The result of the introduction was not properly monitored, but it clearly failed, as there has never been a record of an Alpine Gyr.

The problem of how many Gyrfalcons can be removed from the wild population has been addressed in Canada, where an experiment was carried out by government agencies to assess the impact of bird harvesting on the wild population (Mossop and Hayes 1981). The experiment took place across an area of 17,500km^2 of Arctic Slope in the Yukon Territory during 1974–80. The area was the same as that used for Platt's (1977) study on the influence of aircraft on Gyrfalcons. The area held about 95 Gyrfalcon nests, 30 of which were visited regularly. In different years the occupancy of the territories fluctuated from 59% to 80%. The density of the Gyrfalcons was therefore about one breeding territory per 180km^2. Each successful nest produced 3.0–3.4 young, giving between 116 and 206 (185 ± 33) young per year for the whole harvesting experiment territory. A three-year monitoring programme (1974–76) preceded the harvest experiment, during which the Ptarmigan numbers peaked and declined.

Over a three-year period (1977–79) ten young birds (representing about 5% of annual productivity) were harvested by government officials when they were about 21 days old. The results of this experiment were:

1. Removal of 5% of the annual young production had no effect on the wild population.
2. A minimum of 40% of known territories must be productive to allow the safe harvesting of an area.
3. There were no instances of an occupied territory from which a young Gyr was harvested being completely unoccupied in the following year. There

were minor instances of lack of occupancy in the subsequent year at harvested nests, at a rate similar to that at unharvested nests.

4. There was no evidence to suggest that the adults were aware of the 'theft'.
5. The single most important variable in the study was adult mortality. Very small adjustments in this parameter caused drastic declines in population levels. Under most regimes an increase of 5% in adult mortality would result in the extirpation of the population within 50 years.

At the time of the experiment the Yukon Territory Government (through an agency named the Yukon Wildlife Branch) was receiving from 30 to 50 applications per year for the taking of a Gyrfalcon chick. There was also an unknown (but, it is assumed, substantial) number of illegal 'demands' made on the resource through poaching. The harvesting experiment was implemented as it was believed that any human access to the raptor population might pose a threat to the species.

Despite the findings (of minimal impact on the population through limited harvesting of chicks), public opinion is substantially against the harvesting of falcons. A lobby (vocal but of unknown size) feels that falcons should not be held in captivity: wild birds should be left wild. To be successful the harvesting experiment therefore had to show that it was taking 'surplus' individuals and was not in conflict with the idea of the non-consumptive use of resources. The Yukon Government rejected so-called 'open harvest' schemes – those which operate with defined open seasons during which licensed people are allowed to take birds according to a set of given regulations. Earlier experiences with such open harvests had clearly illustrated that all the established prerequisites were violated, a summary of the open harvest experiences showing that:

1. Permittees cannot be controlled acceptably without a huge manpower expenditure.
2. Nests and areas visited are in conflict with non-consumptive uses.
3. Nest site information can be passed from one person to another or retained for future reference. The permanence of Gyrfalcon nest sites is one of the most vulnerable links in the bird's ecology and in itself completely jeopardises the philosophy of open harvest.
4. Illicit export cannot be adequately controlled.
5. Interference with other management schemes and research programmes is inevitable when a harvest occurs in summer.

The birds taken were mostly used in captive-breeding programmes, but some entered the international market.

To allow, or not allow, the keeping the Gyrfalcons as pets or falconry birds was a major problem for the Canadian government (Mossop 1982). Despite the harvesting experiment this issue has yet to be resolved.

Today, the demand for falcons in Western countries is mostly satisfied by captive-breeding programmes. However, pure breeding stock is prone to inbreeding which results in serious physical deterioration. Falconers suggest a legal infusion of wild birds into breeding programmes to maintain the health of the captive stock. The falconers note that such a controlled introduction of wild stock would reduce the likelihood of poaching (Heidenreich *et al.* 1993).

Both poaching and illegal egg collection has been reported to be a problem for both Iceland and Norway (Cade *et al.* 1998). For example, in 1992 more than 35 Gyrfalcons, all collected in Scandinavia, were confiscated by police in Germany (Forslund 1993). In Sweden, apart from occasional raids by (mostly German) illegal trappers, a problem does not exist, since falconry is illegal.

In Russia, the illegal taking of wild Gyrfalcons has been a problem since the beginning of the 1980s (Flint 1993, Lobkov 1999, 2000). The problem was first identified in Kamchatka in 1984–85 in the village of Tilichiki in the Olutorskiy region (Lobkov 2000). Based on information from local people, Lobkov estimated that between 1988 and 1991 chicks had been removed from at least 15–20 nests in the Koryak Mountains. In 1992 he revisited six nest sites which were known to be occupied in 1990 and found all of them empty. Lobkov expressed concern that selective pressure on the white birds of Kamchatka might shift the genetic balance of the Gyrfalcon population. In total Lobkov had 173 descriptions of the coloration of Kamchatka Gyrfalcons made between 1972 and 1999 (96 field descriptions, 17 museum specimens, 13 photographs and 47 confiscated birds). The proportion of white birds was 39.3% in 1981–90 and 20% in 1991–99. Lobkov (2000) considered that, based on the winter counts, the Kamchatka Gyr population had been halved in the previous 15 years, and that illegal trapping was to blame.

Further details on the illegal trapping of Gyrfalcons in Kamchatka were given by Gordienko and Nechitailov (2000). They stated that in the early 1990s there were only isolated incidents of illegal trapping, but by the end of the decade illegal trapping had become a widespread business. The authors estimated that in Kamchatka a total of 40–50 female Gyrfalcons, 50 Goshawks (mostly white) and 15–20 Peregrine Falcons were being trapped and exported from the Peninsula each year.

Around one-quarter of these movements were stopped by law-enforcement organisations. Gordienko and Nechitailov reported that in one period between November 1999 and March 2000 a total of 21 Gyrfalcons were confiscated during attempts to smuggle the birds out of Kamchatka. These birds were confiscated from aircraft – the Gyrs had already been loaded, bypassing airport security channels. Thirteen of these Gyrfalcons were released back into the wild and five were placed in rehabilitation centres. The remaining three birds died due to the barbaric conditions of transportation. In another case in Russia a Syrian citizen was detained at Ekaterinburg International airport in the southern Urals in 2000, carrying a sedated Gyrfalcon to a plane destined for Dubai, UAE. The incident was reported on Russian national Channel 4 TV news. The largest recorded fine for Gyrfalcon smuggling was imposed on a Saudi Arabian prince, who in 1986 paid $150,000 to the US Fish and Wildlife Service in an out-of-court settlement for illegally trafficking Gyrs from the USA (Shor 1988, Ford 1999).

Today, the Russian Ministry (currently the Ministry of Natural Resources) permits only removal of wild falcons for selected falcon propagation centres under special licence. No commercial trade officially exists but there are numerous stories of the illegal removal of Gyrfalcons from traditional breeding places. Not all such stories are hearsay: in autumn 1994 the then Prime Minister of the Russian Federation, Victor Stepanovich Chernomyrdin, decided that during a visit to a Middle Eastern country he would present the ruler with a pair of Russian Gyrfalcons. He hired two falconers who went to Magadan (where Alaskan and Chukotkan Gyrs can be seen in autumn–winter) and, assisted by the Russian secret police of the FSB (formerly the KGB), trapped two Gyrs (P. Dudin, pers. comm.). The falconers were each given four-wheel-drive cars as presents, but the public outcry prevented the export of the birds, which are still at a centre in Moscow.

THE FUTURE

The Gyrfalcon is a protected species in all the countries of its range, and is listed in Appendix I of the Convention of International Trade in Endangered Species of Wild Fauna and Flora (CITES). All Gyrfalcon range countries are CITES signatories, and all traffic in Gyrs is monitored. In most countries it is illegal to remove birds from the wild. In some it is possible to take chicks for captive breeding purposes, or for scientific research. Data on Gyrfalcon traffic can be obtained from Traffic International, an organisation which monitors all trade within the CITES framework. Unfortunately there is currently a fundamental glitch in the system, which does not allow the separation of hybrid Gyrfalcons from pure birds so that all we can say is that the total number of wild Gyrs that have crossed borders legally during the period 1976–2002 is just 20.

Gyrfalcon has enjoyed the legal protection of CITES as an Appendix I species (*i.e.* no commercial trade) since 1979, but in 1981 North American Gyrfalcons were transferred to Appendix II, making trade in them legal. In 1985 there was a heated debate at a CITES conference over whether American Gyrfalcons should be returned to Appendix I, on the basis that it was impossible to distinguish Nearctic and Palearctic birds. The motion was opposed by some range countries (Parrish and White 1987) but Gyrs were again listed in Appendix I. However, at a conference of CITES member countries in Nairobi, Kenya, in 2000 a proposal by the USA (Proposal 11.32) suggested that all Gyrfalcons be moved to Appendix II, legalising trade with a zero quota for wild birds. The proposal was rejected, not least because of the position of the Scandinavian countries, particularly Iceland. Currently, therefore, all Gyrfalcons have the maximum protection international law can provide.

However, CITES solely monitors and regulates international trade. The major problem the Gyrfalcon faces is at the national level, and this is particularly problematic in Russia. While most Gyrfalcon range countries strictly enforce their wildlife legislation, Russia has little desire or available finance to control illicit wildlife trade in general or to protect Gyrfalcons in particular.

That said, maintaining Gyrs in Appendix I serves the bird well, especially if the legislation in range countries is equally effective and management practices are transparent. Let us hope that the remote breeding grounds of the species will be as productive as ever, and that although the numbers of Gyrfalcons will fluctuate naturally, as they always have, populations of this most majestic falcon will remain steady, so that those willing to share the rigours of its habitat can continue to be enthralled by it.

Scientific names of plants and animals mentioned in the text

The text uses European names for mammal and bird species. In the list below the North American names, where these differ, are given in parentheses except for those species found only (except as vagrants) in North America.

PLANTS

Arctic White Birch	*Betula pubescens tortuosa*
Arctic Willow	*Salix arctica*
Balsam Poplar	*Populus balsamifera*
Cloudberry	*Rubus chamaemorus*
Creeping Pine	*Pinus pumila*
Crowberry	*Empetrum nigrum*
Dwarf Birch	*Betula nana, Betula glandulosa, Betula middendorffi*
Dwarf Willow	*Salix polaris, Salix glauca, Salix pulchra, Salix kolymensis)*
Korean Willow	*Chosenia arbutifolia*
Larch	*Larix sibirica*
Stone Birch	*Betula tortuosa*
White Birch	*Betula pubescens pubescens*
White Spruce	*Picea glauca*

INVERTEBRATES AND FISH

Brown Trout	*Salmo trutta*
Cod	*Gadus morhua*
Common Mussel	*Mytilus edulis*

INVERTEBRATES AND FISH *CONT.*

Grayling	*Thymallus arcticus*
Pike	*Esox* spp.

MAMMALS

American Beaver	*Castor canadensis*
Arctic Fox	*Alopex lagopus*
Arctic Ground Squirrel (Long-tailed Souslik)	*Citellus parryi*
Arctic Hare	*Lepus arcticus*
Asian Bison	*Bison priscus*
Black-capped Marmot	*Marmota camtschatica*
Bowhead Whale	*Balaena mysticetus*
Brown Bear	*Ursus arctos*
Brown Lemming	*Lemmus sibiricus*
Collared Lemming	*Dicrostonyx torquatus, Dicrostonyx groenlandicus*
Elk (Moose)	*Alces alces*
European Beaver	*Castor fiber*
Mammoth	*Mammuthus primigenius*
Mountain Hare	*Lepus timidus*
Musk Ox	*Ovibos moschatus*
Narrow-skulled Vole	*Microtus gregalis*
Northern Water Vole	*Arvicola terrestris*
Norway Lemming	*Lemmus lemmus*
Pine Marten	*Martes martes*
Polar Bear	*Ursus maritimus*
Przewalski's Horse	*Equus przewalskii*
Red-backed Vole	*Clethrionomys rutilus*
Red Fox	*Vulpes vulpes*
Reindeer	*Rangifer tarandus*
Right Whale	*Balaena glacialis*
Root Vole (Tundra Vole)	*Microtus oeconomus*
Sable	*Martes zibellina*
Saiga Antelope	*Saiga borealis*
Siberian Lemming	*Lemmus sibiricus*
Stoat (Short-tailed Weasel)	*Mustela erminea*
Wolf	*Canis lupus*

Mammals *cont.*

Wolverine	*Gulo gulo*
Wood Mouse	*Apodemus sylvaticus*
Woolly Rhinoceros	*Coelodonta antiquitatis*

Birds

American Golden Plover	*Pluvialis dominica*
American Kestrel	*Falco sparverius*
American Robin	*Turdus migratorius*
American Tree Sparrow	*Spizella arborea*
American Wigeon	*Anas americana*
Arctic Skua (Parasitic Jaeger)	*Stercorarius parasiticus*
Arctic Tern	*Sterna paradisaea*
Bald Eagle	*Haliaeetus leucocephalus*
Barbary Falcon	*Falco pelegrinoides*
Barn Owl	*Tyto alba*
Barnacle Goose	*Branta leucopsis*
Bean Goose	*Anser fabalis*
Bewick's Swan	*Cygnus bewickii*
Black Grouse	*Lyrurus tetrix*
Black Vulture	*Aegypius monachus*
Black-headed Gull	*Larus ridibundus*
Black-throated Diver (Arctic Loon)	*Gavia arctica*
Bluethroat	*Luscinia svecica*
Brahminy Kite	*Haliastur indus*
Brambling	*Fringilla montifringilla*
Brent Goose	*Branta bernicla*
Brünnich's Guillemot (Thick-billed Murre)	*Uria lomvia*
Buzzard	*Buteo buteo*
Canada Goose	*Branta canadensis*
Capercaillie	*Tetrao urogallus*
Carrion Crow	*Corvus corone corone*
Common Eider	*Somateria mollissima*
Common Redstart	*Phoenicurus phoenicurus*
Eurasian Curlew	*Numenius arquata*
Dotterel	*Eudromias morinellus*
Dusky Thrush	*Turdus naumanni eunomus*

BIRDS *CONT.*

Eagle Owl	*Bubo bubo*
Egyptian Vulture	*Neophron percnopterus*
Eurasian Curlew	*Numenius arquata*
Eurasian Teal	*Anas crecca*
Fieldfare	*Turdus pilaris*
Fulmar (Northern Fulmar)	*Fulmarus glacialis*
Glaucous Gull	*Larus hyperboreus*
Golden Eagle	*Aquila chrysaetos*
Golden Plover	*Pluvialis apricaria*
(Eurasian Golden Plover)	
Goshawk	*Accipiter gentilis*
(Northern Goshawk)	
Great Spotted Woodpecker	*Dendrocopos major*
Green-winged Teal	*Anas carolinensis*
Grey Partridge	*Perdix perdix*
Greylag Goose	*Anser anser*
Guillemot (Common Murre)	*Uria aalge*
Gyrfalcon	*Falco gyrfalco, Falco rusticolus*
Hazel Grouse	*Bonasa bonasia*
Hen Harrier	*Circus cyaneus*
(Northern Harrier)	
Herring Gull	*Larus argentatus*
Hobby	*Falco subbuteo*
Hooded Crow	*Corvus corone cornix*
House Sparrow	*Passer domesticus*
Hudsonian Godwit	*Limosa haemastica*
Imperial Eagle	*Aquila heliaca*
Kestrel	*Falco tinnunculus*
(Eurasian Kestrel)	
Kittiwake	*Rissa tridactyla*
(Black-legged Kittiwake)	
Knot (Red Knot)	*Calidris canutus*
Laggar Falcon	*Falco jugger*
Lammergeier	*Gypaetus barbatus*
Lanner Falcon	*Falco biarmicus*
Lapland Bunting	*Calcarius lapponicus*
(Lapland Longspur)	
Lesser Snow Goose	*Anser caerulescens*
Little Auk (Dovekie)	*Alle alle*
Long-tailed Duck	*Clangula hyemalis*

BIRDS *CONT.*

Long-tailed Skua (Long-tailed Jaeger)	*Stercorarius longicaudus*
Mallard	*Anas platyrhynchos*
Meadow Pipit	*Anthus pratensis*
Merlin	*Falco columbarius*
Mongolian Plover (Lesser Sand Plover)	*Charadrius mongolus*
Naumann's Thrush	*Turdus naumanni naumanni*
Northern Pintail	*Anas acuta*
Northern Wheatear	*Oenanthe oenanthe*
Nutcracker	*Nucifraga caryocatactes*
Nuthatch	*Sitta europaea*
Pacific Golden Plover	*Pluvialis fulva*
Pectoral Sandpiper	*Calidris melanotos*
Peregrine Falcon	*Falco peregrinus*
Pygmy Owl	*Glaucidium passerinum*
Pheasant (Common Pheasant)	*Phasianus colchicus*
Prairie Falcon	*Falco mexicanus*
Ptarmigan (Rock Ptarmigan)	*Lagopus mutus*
Puffin (Atlantic Puffin)	*Fratercula arctica*
Pygmy Owl	*Glaucidium passerinum*
Raven	*Corvus corax*
Red-breasted Goose	*Branta ruficollis*
Red-footed Falcon	*Falco vespertinus*
Redpoll (Common Redpoll)	*Carduelis flammea*
Red Grouse	*Lagopus lagopus scoticus*
Redshank	*Tringa totanus*
Red-tailed Hawk	*Buteo jamaicensis*
Red-throated Pipit	*Anthus cervinus*
Redwing	*Turdus iliacus*
Ring Ouzel	*Turdus torquatus*
Rock Dove	*Columba livia*
rosy finch	*Leucosticte* spp.
Rough-legged Buzzard	*Buteo lagopus*
Ruff	*Philomachus pugnax*
Sage Grouse	*Centrocercus urophasianus*
Saker Falcon	*Falco cherrug*
Sandhill Crane	*Grus canadensis*
Savannah Sparrow	*Passerculus sandwichensis*
Scaup (Greater Scaup)	*Aythya marila*

B<small>IRDS</small> *CONT.*

Shag	*Phalacrocorax aristotelis*
Shore Lark (Horned Lark)	*Eremophila alpestris*
Short-eared Owl	*Asio flammeus*
Siberian Accentor	*Prunella modularis*
Siberian Jay	*Perisoreus infaustus*
Siberian Tit	*Parus cinctus*
Snow Bunting	*Plectrophenax nivalis*
Snowy Owl	*Nyctea scandiaca*
Sparrowhawk	*Accipiter nisus*
Steller's Sea Eagle	*Haliaeetus pelagicus*
Tengmalm's Owl	*Aegolius funereus*
Tufted Duck	*Aythya fuligula*
Turnstone	*Arenaria interpres*
(Ruddy Turnstone)	
Velvet Scoter	*Melanitta fusca*
(White-winged Scoter)	
Whimbrel	*Numenius phaeopus*
White Wagtail	*Motacilla alba*
White-fronted Goose	*Anser albifrons*
(Greater White-fronted Goose)	
White-tailed Eagle	*Haliaeetus albicilla*
White-tailed Ptarmigan	*Lagopus leucurus*
Willow Grouse	*Lagopus lagopus*
Willow Tit	*Parus montanus*
Willow Warbler	*Phylloscopus trochilus*
Woodcock	*Scolopax rusticola*

Glossary

Aff.   abbreviation of *affinis*, related to but not entirely identical to the species given. Sometimes used by palaeontologists in cases where the lack of fossil material prevents definite species identification.

allele   any of the alternative forms of a gene that may occur at a given gene locus on the chromosome.

allopatric   the formation of a new species following geographical separation of two populations is termed allopatric speciation.

Arctic zone   region north of the Arctic Circle or of the timberline. The Arctic zone includes several biomes (habitat types): arctic deserts (sometimes called the High Arctic) and the sub-Arctic, which includes the typical tundra subzone and the forest-tundra subzone.

artificial nest   a nest structure constructed by humans that imitates nests built by birds. In the case of Gyrfalcons, such structures are usually erected in places where the birds are thought to be nest-site limited.

breeding rate   in this book we use breeding rate to mean the total number of nestlings produced by a pair or population. This parameter already includes the survival of chicks and hatching success of eggs.

cladistics   branch of biology that aims to erect classification groups for all organisms, based solely on their evolutionary relationships. Cladistics differs from the morphological approach, which groups organisms based on overall similarity, and from more traditional approaches based on 'key characters'. In cladistics, key characters or overall similarity are seen as useful only in so far as they point towards the correct evolutionary history. Thus subjective criteria, such as the relative importance for classification of various types of characters, are discarded in favour of a single objective (but inferred) historical criterion – the shared-derived character, also known as the synapomorphy. Thus, a cladistic group must contain both a common ancestor as well as all of its descendants, regardless of the evolutionary changes they may have undergone.

colour morph   a colour that is shared by some members of a species and is significantly different from that of other members of the same species.

commensalism   a relationship between two kinds of living organisms whereby one (the commensal) benefits and the other (the host) is unaffected.

conventional radiotelemetry (radiotracking)   a method of determining the position of a bird using a small transmitter, locating its signal using a receiver with a directional (Yagi) antenna. The position of the bird is determined either by triangulation (*i. e.* taking several bearings from different locations at one time), or by using a single bearing and approaching the bird to 'eyeballing distance' and subsequently determining the coordinates from a map.

cyclicity   periodic repetition of biological events with a more or less constant period between similar events, *i.e.* they re-occur at regular intervals.

cytochromes   membrane-bound proteins that contain heme groups (iron/protein complexes) and carry out electron transport. They are found in the inner membrane of mitochondria, in the chloroplasts of plants, and in bacteria. In genetic studies, the term usually refers to cytochrome *b*. Mitochondria have their own DNA; their genes are separate from the main (nuclear) DNA. Because eggs destroy the mitochondria of the sperm that fertilises them, the mitochondrial DNA of an individual derives exclusively from the mother (individuals inherit their nuclear DNA from both parents, half from each). Population geneticists and evolutionary biologists often use data from mitochondrial DNA sequences to draw conclusions about genealogy and evolution.

diagonal tarsus length   measurement from the lower part of the tarsus joint to the metatarsus joint.

dichromatism/trichromatism   having two (white and dark) or three (white, grey and dark) colour forms.

DNA–DNA hybridisation   technique used to determine the similarity of DNA sequences of different origin. The DNA is heated to temperatures just high enough to cause the protein within to denature (lose its structure). This causes the double helix to separate, yielding a pair of separate strands. The sample is then gently cooled so the helices reform at regions of sequence complementarity. The higher the degree of linkage between DNA samples of different origins, the closer the relationship between the organisms that provided the original samples.

DNA fingerprinting   method of analysing relatedness of organisms. It is usually used to investigate closely-related individuals (e.g. parent and offspring) by providing an inbreeding index, but it is less commonly used for comparing higher-level taxa such as genera or families. The fingerprinting begins by extracting a DNA sample, then performing restriction fragment length polymorphism (RFLP) analysis. In this process, a restriction enzyme cuts the DNA into fragments, which are separated into bands during gel electrophoresis. The position and similarity of these bands provide the band-sharing index. One modern and widely accepted use of DNA fingerprinting is in criminal cases involving the theft of birds of prey and false claims of their captive origins.

falconry terms:

block	smooth, rounded piece of wood attached to a stake, which is driven into the ground. This serves as a perch for a falcon.
cast off	the release of a bird from the fist.
eyass	a young falcon, usually fledgling.
hood	cap placed over the head of a falcon, covering the eyes. It is held in position by leather straps called braces.
jerkin	a male Gyrfalcon.
jesses	leather straps attached to each leg of a falcon to keep it captive. The jesses are attached to a leash by means of a swivel, a pair of rotating rings. The jesses are threaded through one ring, the leash through the other.
leash	a leather strap used to secure a falcon to its perch.
lure	artificial prey used to entice a falcon back to the falconer (the imitation quarry is swung on a line).
tiercel	a male falcon (originally a male Peregrine Falcon).
waiting on	circling in the air close to falconer awaiting prey to appear or to be flushed.

GIS   the Geographical Information System, a system of hardware and software that allows the mapping, and analysis of spatial data distributions.

haplotype   a set of closely linked alleles that are inherited as a unit.

hybrid   the product of successful mating between individuals of two different varieties or of two different species. Alternatively, the offspring of two parents that differ in one or more genetic characteristics.

Laurentide Glaciation   the period from *c.* 15,000 to 13,000 years BP when northeast North America was covered by the Laurentide Ice Sheet, which had advanced to its maximum.

minimum convex polygon (MCP)   a method used to calculate the home range of an animal. The polygon's angles are all less than, or equal to, 180°, and the number of sides is minimal.

monotypic   a species that is not differentiated into one or more subspecies.

natural pair   a term used in the captive propogation of falcons; a pair of birds that breed in a pen without artificial insemination, *i. e.* 'naturally'.

oligonucleotide probe   a short sequence of nucleotides (chemicals that form the genetic code within a DNA molecule) that are synthesised to accurately match a region on a DNA molecule where a mutation is known to occur. This is then used as a molecular probe to detect the mutation in other samples.

principal component analysis (PCA)   statistical method used to rearrange a dataset with many variables into a set with a smaller number of composite variables (called components or axes). These components represent most of the information in the original data set. The strongest covariation among the variables emerges in a few axes, hence 'principal components'.

permafrost   soil or rock that remains permanently frozen for the whole year round (strictly speaking, permafrost remains at temperatures below freezing for at least two years), except for the uppermost 'active' layer, which melts annually in summer. The depth of the active layer varies in different locations.

phenotype   the observable characteristics produced by an individual's genes.

phylogenetic events   evolutionary events that give rise to systematic differences between species with a common ancestry.

Pleistocene   geological period from *c.* 1 million (early Pleistocene) to *c.* 10,000 (late Pleistocene) years BP.

polymorphism   existence of a certain trait in many forms; also, the coexistence in the same locality of two or more distinct forms that are not connected by clines or intermediate gradations. In genetic linkage analysis., sequence variations that occur in more than 1% of a sampled population would be considered a polymorphism.

polytypic   a species that has two or more subspecies.

remote sensing   the science of acquiring, processing and interpreting images by remote means. The common application of remote sensing is the use of satellite-borne instruments to determine the location and number of objects of interest on the surface.

satellite DNA   DNA sequences are repeated in patterns of 10 to 2,000 base pairs. Because of the size variation, a DNA block is sometimes divided into microsatellite and minisatellite DNA. Microsatellite DNA is of 100–2,000 base pairs, minisatellite DNA is of 10–100 base pairs. Satellite DNA with few variations (and subsequently low mutation frequency) are used for analysis of related species, while those with a few more variations are used to identify discrete populations within a single species.

Satellite telemetry   a method of determining the coordinates of a bird using a small transmitter placed on the bird. The transmitter, known as a PTT (platform terminal transmitter) emits a signal that is picked up by the *Argos* array of satellites orbiting the earth. By measuring the Doppler shift of the signal, the system can determine the exact distance between the Earth and the satellite, and then, knowing the parameters of the orbit, calculate the exact coordinates of the transmitter. The method is expensive, but the data it brings are superlative for describing the movements of migratory birds.

scrape   a small hollow in the sand, turf or gravel scratched by a bird in order to lay eggs.

Shannon-Weaver Index   sometimes shortened to the Shannon Index, this index is derived from Information Theory. The index provides a measure of order (or disorder) within a particular system. In ecological studies it is characterised by the number of individuals observed for each subspecies in a sample plot.

social parasitism   coexistence of two species, one of which is dependent as a parasite on the society of the other.

speciation   the process of the formation of new species.

spline smoothing a method of fitting a curve to a number of points. Cubic spline smoothing is a non-parametric regression technique that fits a function to data (usually a polynomial function) while penalizing the size of its second derivative.

stenophagous species that specialises by hunting one species of prey; this limits both the range and breeding cycle of the predator

sympatric the formation of new species despite the absence of geographical separation is termed sympatric speciation; the process occurs through ecological (niche) separation. .

thermoregulate the ability to control body temperature. Hatchlings are unable to thermoregulate but they develop the ability over time.

timberline the northern border of boreal forests and the upper limit of the forests in the mountains. The timberline usually forms a line, or a mosaic of tundra habitat with patches of forests.

tor a natural structure, a spire of rock on top of a mountain ridge. Also known as 'kekur' in some Russian literature.

wing length the distance between the tip of the longest primary and the wrist. All feathers should be flattened along the ruler (hence 'flattened' wing length).

References

ABRAMSON, N. I. 1993. Evolution trends in the dentition of true lemmings (Lemmini, Cricetidae, Rodenti): functional-adaptive analysis. *Journal of Zoology* 230: 687–699.

ALERSTAM, T. 1987. Radar observations of the stoop of the Peregrine Falcon *Falco peregrinus* and the Goshawk *Accipiter gentilis*. *Ibis* 129: 267–273.

ALLEN, J. 1905. Report on the birds collected in Northeastern Siberia by the Jesop North Pacific Expedition, with field notes by collectors. *Bulletin of the American Museum of Natural History* 21: 219–254.

ALLEN, M. 1980. *Falconry in Arabia*. The Stephen Greene Press, Brattleboro, Vermont.

ALLEN, W. 1970. (ed.) *Russian Embassies to the Georgian Kings*. Cambridge University Press, Cambridge.

ANDERSON, D. & HICKEY, J. 1972. Eggshell changes in certain North American birds. *In* K. H. Voos (ed.), *Proceedings of the 15ᵗʰ International Ornithological Congress, 1979*, 514–554. The Hague.

ANDREEV, A. 1988. The ten-year cycle of the Willow Grouse of the Lower Kolyma. *Oecologia* 76: 261–267.

ANOKHIN, A. V. 1924. [*Shamanism in Altay People.*] Collection of Papers of the Museum of Anthropology and Ethnography, Russian Academy of Sciences, Leningrad. [In Russian.]

ANON. 2002. Eggs seized in Quebec. *Legal Eagle* 34: 7.

ARTUKHIN, YU. B. 1991. [Nesting aviafauna of the Commander Islands and influence of man on its condition.] *In* V. E. Sokolov (ed.), [*Natural resources of* 99–137. Moscow University Press, Moscow. [In Russian.]

ARTUKHIN, YU. B. 1998. [Rare birds of the Commander Islands.] *In* Yu. Blokhin & L. N. Mazin, [*The Problems of Conservation of the Poorly Studied Fauna of the North*], 71–75. TSNIL Glavokhota, Moscow. [In Russian.]

ARTUKHOV, A. 1986. [On characteristics of the ornithofauna of the Maliy and Bolshoy Anuy River Basins (Western Chukotka)]. *In* R. L. Potapov (ed.), [*Studies of Birds of the USSR, Their Conservation and Rational Use.*], 42–43. Academy of Sciences of the USSR Zoological Institute, Leningrad. [In Russian.]

AS'KEEV, I. & AS'KEEV, O. 1999. [*Ornithofauna of the Tatarstan Republic.*] Olitekh, Kazan. [In Russian.]

AVERIN, YU. V. 1948. [Terrestrial vertebrates of Eastern Kamchatka.] *Proceedings of the Kronoki Reserve* 1: 3–222. [In Russian.]

BALDAEV, KH. F. 1983. [Gyrfalcon and Osprey in the Mari ASSR.] *In* V. M. Galushin (ed.), [*Conservation of Birds of Prey; Proceedings of the First All-Union Symposium of Ecology and Conservation of Birds of Prey, Moscow, 16–18 February 1983*], 89–91. Nauka, Moscow. [In Russian.]

BALGOOYEN, T. 1988. A unique encounter among a Gyrfalcon, Peregrine Falcon, Prairie Falcon and American Kestrel. *Journal of Raptor Research* 22: 71.

BANNERMAN, D. A. 1956. *The Birds of the British Isles.* Oliver and Boyd, Edinburgh.

BARANOV, A. A. 1991. *Rare and Little-studied Birds of the Tuva.* Krasnoyarsk University Publishers, Krasnoyarsk. [In Russian.]

BARICHELLO, N. 1983. *Selection of Nest Sites by Gyrfalcons (*Falco rusticolus*).* Unpublished M.S. thesis. University of British Columbia, Vancouver.

BASILOV, V. N. 1984. *Chosen by Spirits.* Political Publishing House, Moscow.

BASILOV, V. N. 1992. [*Shamansism of the Peoples of the Middle Asia and Kazakhstan.*] Nauka, Moscow. [In Russian.]

BASKIRIAN E. 1977. [*The Black Pacer.*] Ufa Books, Ufa. [In Russian.]

BAUMGARDT, W. 2001. Reflections of Kleinshmidt's raptor work. *Falco* 18: 4–6.

BEEBE, F. L. 1974. Field studies of the Falconiformes of British Columbia. British Columbia Provincial Museum, Victoria.

BEEBE, F. L. & WEBSTER, H. M. 1994. *North American Falconry and Hunting Hawks.* Privately published, Denver, Colorado.

BELKOVSKIY, A. N. 1998. [Birds of Prey of the Bering Islands.] In [Proceedings of the 3rd Birds of Prey Conference of Eastern Europe and North Asia, Stavropol 15–18 Septermber 1998.], 8. Stavropol State University Publishers, Stavropol. [In Russian.]

BENGTSON, S–A. 1971. Hunting methods and choice of prey of Gyrfalcons *Falco rusticolus* at Myvatn in Northeast Iceland. *Ibis* 113: 468–476.

BENGTSON, S–A. 1972. Athunganir á varpháttum fálka (*Falco rusticolus*) í Myvatnssveit 1960–1969. *Náturufrædingurinn* 42: 67–74.

BENNETT, A. T. D. & CUTHILL I. C. 1994 Ultraviolet vision in birds: what is its function? *Vision Research* 34, 1471–1478.

BENNETT, A., T. D., CUTHILL, I. C., PARTRIDGE, J. C. & LUNAU, K. 1997. Ultraviolet plumage colours predict mate preferences in starlings. *Proceedings of the National Academy of Sciences* 94, 8618–8621.

BENT, A. C. 1938. Life histories of North American Birds of Prey: II: Orders Falconiformes and Strigiformes. *Bulletin of the United States National Museum ((Smithsonian Institute)* 170.

BEREZOVIKOV, N. 1986. [*Berkut*]. Ilim Publishers, Almaty. [In Russian.]

BERGMAN, S. 1935. *Zur kenntnis Nordostasiatischer vögel: eub beutrag zyr Systematik, Biologie und Verbreitung der Vögel Kamtschatkas unde der Kurilien.* Albert Bonniers Förlag, Stockholm.

BERTELSTEN, A. 1932. Meddeleser om nogle af de i Vestrgønlands distrikter mellem

60° og 77° n. br. Almindeligerre forekommende fugle, sælig am dereres udbredelsesomraade, deres yngleomraade og deres traæk. *Meddeleser om Grønland* 91: 29.

BILALIEV, A. 1967. [*Kyrgyz–Russian dictionary of professional hunting terminology.*] Frunze Publishing House, Frunze. [In Russian.]

BÖ, O. 1962. *Falcon Catching in Norway, with the Emphasis on the Post–reformation Period.* Universitetslaget, Oslo.

BOCHENSKI, Z., HUHTALA, K., JUSSILA, P. TORNBERG, R. & TUKKARI, P. 1998. Damage to bird bones in pellets of Gyrfalcon *Falco rusticolus*. *Journal of Archaeological Science* 25: 425–433.

BOLD, A. & BOLDBAATAR SH. 1999. [The rarest birds of prey species of Mongolia.] *Proceedings of the Biological Institute, Ulanbataar* 1: 129–138. [In Mongolian.]

BOOMS, T. L. & FULLER, M. R. 2003a. Gyrfalcon feeding behaviour during the nestling period in central west Greenland. *Arctic* 56: 341–348.

BOOMS, T. L. & FULLER, M. R. 2003b. Time-lapse video system used to study nesting Gyrfalcons. *Journal of Field Ornithology* 74: 416–422.

BOOMS, T. L. & FULLER, M. R. 2003c. Gyrfalcon diet in central and west Greenland during the nesting period. *Condor* 105: 528–537.

BORODIN, A. M. 1984. (ed.) *Red Data Book of the USSR*. Lesnaya Promyshlennost, Moscow.

BRANDT, I. F. 1853. [*Vertebrates of the Northern European Part of Russia, particularly the North Urals: Materials for Understanding the Zoogeography of North–eastern Europe. Volume 2: Travels in the North Urals.*] Imperial Academy of Sciences, St. Petersburg. [In Russian.]

BRAZIL, M. & HANAWA, S. 1991. The status and distribution of diurnal raptors in Japan. *Birds of Prey Bulletin* 4: 175–238.

BRODEUR, S., MORNEAU, F., DECARIE, R., DESGRANGES, J. & NEGRO, J. 1995. Southern extension of the breeding range of the Gyrfalcon, *Falco rusticolus*, in Eastern North America. *Arctic* 48: 94–95.

BROWN, L. & AMADON, D. 1968. *Eagles, Hawks and Falcons of the World*. McGraw-Hill, New York.

BUDGE, E. A. W. 1928. *The Monks of Kublai Khan, Emperor of China*. Religious Tract Society, London.

BURCHAK-ABRAMOVICH, N. I. & BURCHAK, D. H. 1998. The birds of the Late Quaternary of the Altai Mountains. *Acta Zoologica Cracoviensia* 41:51–60.

BURNHAM, K. 2001. Gyrfalcon tracking provides valuable information. *Peregrine Fund Newsletter* 32: 6–7.

BURNHAM, W. A. 1975. *Breeding biology and ecology of the Peregrine Falcon (*Falco peregrinus*) in west Greenland*. Unpublished M.Sc thesis, Brigham Young University, Provo, Utah.

BURNHAM, W. A & MATTOX, W. G 1984. Biology of the Peregrine and Gyrfalcon in Greenland. *Meddeleser om Grønland* 14: 1–25.

BURR, B. M. 1975. Status of Gyrfalcon in Illinois. *Wilson Bulletin* 87: 280–281.

BURTON, P. 1989. *Birds of Prey of the World*. Dragons World, Limpsfield.

CADBURY, C. J. 1980. *Silent Death*. RSPB, Sandy.

CADE, T. J. 1953. Behaviour of a young Gyrfalcon. *Wilson Bulletin* 6: 26–31.

CADE, T. J. 1955a. The predatory habits of Peregrines and Gyrfalcons in Alaska. *Journal of the Falconry Club of America* 1: 251–266.

CADE, T. J. 1955b. Variation of the common Rough-legged Hawk in North America. *Condor* 57: 313–346.

CADE, T. J. 1960. The ecology of the Peregrine and Gyrfalcon population in Alaska. *University of California Publications in Zoology* 63: 151–290.

CADE, T. J. 1982. *The Falcons of the World*. Cornell University Press, Ithaca, New York.

CADE, T. J., KOSKIMIES, P., NIELSEN O. 1998. *Falco rusticolus* Gyrfalcon. *Birds of the Western Palearctic Update* 2: 1–25.

CADE, T. J., LINCER, J. L., WHITE, C. M, ROSENEAU, D. G., & SWARTZ, L. G. 1971. DDE residues and eggshell changes in Alaskan falcons and hawks. *Science* 172: 955–957.

CALEF, G. W. & HEARD, D. C. 1979. Reproductive success of Peregrine Falcons and other raptors at Wager Bay and Melville Peninsula, Northwest Territories. *Auk* 96: 662–674.

CAMPBELL, R. W., DAWE, N. K., McTAGGART-COWAN, I., COOPER, J. M., KAISER, G. W. & McNALL, M. C. E. 1990. *The Birds of British Columbia. Volume 2: Non–passerines*. University of British Columbia Press, Vancouver

CASACCHIA, R., LAUTA, F., SALVATORI, R., CAGNATI, A., VALT, M. & ØRBÆK, J. B. 2001. Radiometric investigation of different snow covers in Svalbard. *Polar Research* 20: 13–22.

CERELY, S. 1955. *The Gyrfalcon Adventure*. Collins, London.

CHERESHNEV, I. A. 1996. [*Vertebrates of the Russian North-East.*] Dalnauka, Vladivostok. [In Russian.]

CHERNICHENKO, I. I., SYROECHKOVSKIY, E. E., CHERNICHENKO, R. N, VOLOKH, A. M. & ANDRUSHENKO, YU. A. 1994. Materials on fauna and bird populations on the Gydan peninsula. *In* E.V.Rogacheva (ed.), [*Arctic Tundras of Taimyr and Islands of the Kara Sea: Nature, Animals and Problems of Conservation*], 1: 223–260. [In Russian.]

CHUVASHOV, G. I. 1989. [Deaths of rare species of falcons and other rare birds on the Gydan peninsula.] *In* V. A. Kuzyakin (ed.), [Proceedings of Surveyed Characteristics, Results of Counts and Surveys on Non–commercial Birds, Reptiles, Amphibians and Fish.], 246–248. Bashkir Books, Ufa. [In Russian.]

CITES 2000. Transfer the North American populations of *Falco rusticolus* from Appendix I to Appendix II, with a zero quota for export of wild birds. *Eleventh Meeting of the Conference of the Parties, Nairobi (Kenya), April 10–20, 2000* (proposal 11.32).

CLARK, W. S. 1995. How fast is the fastest bird? *WildBird* 9: 42–43.

CLARK, W. S. & YOSEF, R. 1998. *Raptor In-hand Identification Guide*. IBCE, Eilat.

CLAUSEN, B. & GUDMUNDSSON, E. 1981. Causes of mortality among free–ranging Gyrfalcons in Iceland. *Journal of Wildlife Diseases* 17: 105–109.

CLUM, N. J. & CADE, T. J. 1994. Gyrfalcon *Falco rusticolus*. *In* A. Poole & F. Gill (eds), *The Birds of North America*. The American Ornithologists Union, Washington D.C.

COBLENTZ, C. 1943. The Greenland Falcon in History. *The American Falconer* 2: 9–11.

CODE OF ZOOLOGICAL NOMENCLATURE 2000. *Fourth Edition compiled by the International Commission on Zoological Nomenclature*. International Trust for Zoological Nomenclature, London.

COTTER, R. C., BOAG, D. A. & SHANK, C. C. 1992. Raptor predation on Rock Ptarmigan (*Lagopus mutus*) in the central Canadian Arctic. *Journal of Raptor Research* 26: 146–151.

COURT, G. 1999. Edmonton's Year of the Gyr. *Edmonton Naturalist* 27: 29–30.

CRAMP, S. & SIMMONS, K. E. L. (eds) 1980. *The Birds of the Western Palearctic*, volume 2. Oxford University Press, Oxford.

CUTHILL, I. C., PARTRIDGE, J. C., BENNETT, A. T. D., CHURCH, S. C., HART, N. S. & HUNT, S. 2000. Ultraviolet vision in birds. *Advances in the Study of Behaviour* 29: 159–214.

DANILOV, N. N., RYZHANOVSKIY, V. N. & RYABTSEV, V. K. 1977. [Distribution of rare birds in Yamal.] *In Proceedings of the 7th All-Union Ornithological Conference, Kiev.* [In Russian.]

DANILOV N. N., RYZHANOVSKIY, V. N. & RYABTSEV, V. K. 1984. [Birds of Yamal]. Nauka, Moscow. [In Russian.]

DE CHAMERLAT, C.A. 1987. *Falconry and Art*. Sotheby's Publications, London.

DEKKER, D. & COURT, G. 2003. Gyrfalcon predation on Mallards and the interaction of Bald Eagles wintering in Central Alberta. *Journal of Raptor Research* 37: 161–163.

DEKKER, D. & LANGE, J. 2001. Hunting methods and success rates of Gyrfalcons, *Falco rusticolus*, and Prairie Falcons, *Falco mexicanus*, preying on feral pigeons (Rock Doves), *Columba livia*, in Edmonton, Alberta. *The Canadian Field-Naturalist* 115: 395–401.

DEMENTIEV, G. P. 1935a. Sur des cas d'asymetrie de coloration chez les gerfauts *Falco gyrfalco*. *Alauda* 7: 480–485.

DEMENTIEV, G. P. 1935b. [*Hunting with birds of prey*]. KOIZ Publishers, Moscow. [In Russian.]

DEMENTIEV, G. P. 1941. [To the ecology of falcons in the Arctic.] *In* N. N. Fillipov (ed.), [*Proceedings of the State Zoological Museum of the Moscow State University*], 145–150. Moscow. [In Russian.]

DEMENTIEV, G. P. 1947. [Seasonal distribution and migrations of Gyrfalcon *Falco gyrfalco* Linnaeus. *Proceedings of the Central Bureau of Ringing* 6: 68–75. [In Russian.]

DEMENTIEV G. P. 1951. [Falcons; Gyrfalcons]. *Proceedings of the MOIP (Moscow Society of Naturalists) Department of Zoology* N29. [In Russian.]

DEMENTIEV, G. P. 1960. *Der Gerfalcke (*Falcon gyrfalco *L.* = Falco rusticolus *L.). Die Neue Brehm–Bucheriei.* A. Ziemsen Verlag, Witthenberg Lutherstadt

DEMENTIEV G. P. & GLADKOV N. A. 1951. [*Birds of the USSR. Volume 1: Birds of Prey.*] Sovetskaya Nauka, Moscow. [In Russian.]

DEMENTIEV, G. P & GORTCHAKOVSKAYA, N. N. 1945. On the biology of the Norwegian Gyrfalcon. *Ibis* 87: 559–565.

DEMENTIEV, G. P. & SHAGDARSUREN, O. 1964. [On the Mongolian Saker Falcon and the taxonomic position of the Altay Gyrfalcon.] *Archives of the Zoological Museum* 9: 9–37. [In Russian.]

DESBROSSE R. & MOURER-CHAUVIRÉ C. 1973. Les oiseaux magdaleniensis de Pierre–Chatel (Ain). *Qartar* 23-24, 149–164.

DIRECTORATE FOR NATURE MANAGEMENT, NORWAY. 1999. Norwegian Red List 1998. *Directorate for Nature Report* 3: 1–161.

DMOKHOVSKIY A. B. 1933. [Birds of mid– and Lower Pechora]. *Bulletin of the MOIP (Moscow Society of Naturalists) Department of Biology* 13: 214–242. [In Russian.]

DOBLER, F. 1989. Wintering Gyrfalcon *Falco rusticolus* habitat utilisation in Washington. *In* B-U. Meyburg & R. D. Chancellor (eds), *Raptors in the Modern World,* 61–70. World Working Group for Birds of Prey, Berlin, London and Paris.

DOROGOI, I. V. 1991. [On the fauna and distribution of birds in North-East Chukotka]. *Ornitologia* 25: 102–109. [In Russian.]

DOROGOV, V. F. 1985. [Gyrfalcon in the north of Siberia.] *Technical Bulletin of the Siberian Branch of the Agricultural Academy of the USSR* 23: 45–54. [In Russian.]

DOROGOV, V. F. 1988. [Birds of prey.] *In* N. S. Vodopyianova (ed.), [*Wildlife of the Putorana plateau, its rational usage and conservation.*], 72–88. Scientific Institute of the Agriculuture in the Extreme North, Novosibirsk. [In Russian.]

DOROGOV, V. F., BORZHONOV, B. B., ZYRYANOV, V. A., KOKOREV, YZ. I. KOLPASHIKOV, L. A. PAVLOV, B. M. & YAKUSHKIN, G. D. 1988. [Rare birds of the north of the Krasnoyarsk District.] *In* Yu. G. Shvetsov (ed.), [Rare terrestrial vertebrates of Siberia.]. Nauka, Novosibirsk. [In Russian.]

DULKEIT, G. D. & SHULPIN, L. M. 1937. [Birds of the Shantar Islands.] *Proceedings of the Biological Institute, Tomsk* 4: 116–136. [In Russian.]

DURMAN-WALTERS, D. 1994. *The Modern Falconer.* Swan-Hill Press, Shrewsbury.

DYBOWSKI, B. 1883. Remarques sur les oiseaux du Kamtschatka et des îles Comandores. *Bulletin de la Societie Zoologique de France* 8: 351–370.

EASTHAM, C. 1999. Species concepts and their relevance to the taxonomy of the Desert Falcons. *Falco* 13: 18–20.

EASTHAM, C. 2000. *Morphological studies of taxonomy of the Saker (*Falco cherrug – Gray 1833*) and closely allied species.* Unpublished Ph.D thesis. University of Kent, Canterbury.

EGOROV, O. 1958. [Materials on the ecology of Peregrine Falcon in the Upper Yana River.] *In* N. Salomonov (ed.), [*Scientific correspondence of the Yakutian Branch of the Siberian Division of the Academy of Sciences of the USSR*], 149–154. Institute of Biology of the Yakutian Branch of Siberian Division of the Academy of Sciences of the USSR, Novosibirsk. [In Russian.]

EKENSTEDT, J. 2001. *Projekt Jaktfalk Norrbotten, Projektrapport 2001.* http://www.jaktfalk.nu/rapport/jaktfalk2001.pdf

EKENSTEDT, J. 2002. *Projekt Jaktfalk Norrbotten, Projektrapport 2002.* http://www.jaktfalk.nu/rapport/projrapport2002.pdf

EKENSTEDT, J. 2003. *Projekt Jaktfalk Norrbotten, Projektrapport 2003.* http://www.jaktfalk.nu/rapport/projrapport2003.pdf

ELLIS, D. H. 1993. Preliminary report of extensive Gyrfalcon and Snowy Owl mortality in Northern Siberia. *Raptor Link* 1: 3–4.

ELLIS, D. H. 1995. What is *Falco altaicus* Mezbier? *Journal of Raptor Research* 29: 15–25.

ELLIS, D. H. , ELLIS, C. H., PENDLETON, G. W., PANTELEEV, A. V., REBROVA, I. V. & MARKIN, YU. M. 1992. Distribution and color variation of Gyrfalcons in Russia. *Journal of Raptor Research* 26: 81–88.

EMSLIE, S. D. 1985. The late Pleistocene (Rancholabrean) avifauna of Little Box Elder Cave, Wyoming. *Contributions to Geology* 23: 63–82.

ENDERSON, J. H., TEMPLE, S. A. & SWARTZ, L. G. 1973. Time-lapse photographic records of nesting Peregrine Falcons. *Living Bird* 11: 113–128.

ENDLER, J. A. 1990. On the measurement and classification of colour in studies of animal colour patterns. *Biological Journal of the Linnean Society* 41: 315–352.

ENGELMANN, F. 1928. *Die Raubvogel Europas: Naturgeschichet, Kulturgeeschichte und Falknerei.* J. Neumann, Neudamm.

ESHEEV, V. E. 1989. [Gyrfalcon.] *In* A. M. Amirkhanov (ed.), [*Rare and endangered animals: materials for the Red Data Book*], 66. TSNIL Glavokhota, Moscow. [In Russian.]

ESTAFIEV, A. A. 1980. [Data on the distribution, numbers and breeding of rare birds of prey in the taiga zone of the European North–East of the USSR.] *In* O. A. Kibalchich (ed.), [*Seasonal pace of rare and vanishing species of plants and animals*], 17–19. Russian Geographical Society, Moscow. [In Russian.]

ESTAFIEV, A. A (ed.) 1999. [*Fauna of the European North-East of Russia. Volume 1: Birds.*] Nauka, St Petersburg. [In Russian.]

EVERETT, W., WARD, M. & BRUEGGEMANN, J. J. 1989. Birds observed in the Central Bering sea pack-ice in February and March 1983. *Le Gerfaut* 79: 159–165.

EVSUKOV, V. V. 1988. [*Myths of the Universe.*] Nauka, Novosibirsk. [In Russian.]

FALKDALEN, U. 1997. Project Jaktfalk 1997: Rapport från Jämtland–Härjedalen. *Blåfoten* 3: 2–3.

FALKDALEN, U. & HOLMBERG, T. 1997. Project Jaktfalk – resultat Jämtland-Härdalen 1994–1996. *Blåfoten* 1: 2–3.

FERGUSON-LEES, J. & CHRISTIE, D. A. 2001. *Raptors of the World.* Christopher Helm, London.

FISHER D. C. & BELD S. 2002. Whole-tusk growth records of Late Pleistocene Woolly Mammoth from the Taimyr Peninsula, Siberia. *Journal of Vertebrate Paleontology*, 22: 53A.

FLANN, I. 2003. Gyrfalcon color variation. *Journal of Raptor Research* 37: 173–174.

FLETCHER, D. J. & WEBBY, K. 1977. Observations on Gyr Falcons *Falco rusticolus* in Northeast Greenland. *Dansk Ornithologisk Forenings Tidsskrift* 71: 29–35.

FLINT, V. E. 1993. Russian birds of prey are protected by law, but the maximum penalty does not exceed 61 cents. *Raptor Link* 1 (2): 1–2.

FLINT, V. E. & SOROKIN, A. G. 1999. [*Falcon on a Glove.*] Egmont, Moscow. [In Russian.]

FORD, E. 1999. *Gyrfalcon.* John Murray Press, London.

FORSLUND, M. 1993. Fågelvakten. Arbetet mot fauna-kriminaliteten sprids. *Vår Fågelvärd* 52: 17–19.

FORSMAN, D. 1993. Identification of large falcons. *Birding World* 6: 66–72.

FORSMAN, D. 1999. *The Raptors of Europe and the Middle East: A Handbook of Identification.* T & AD Poyser, London.

FOX, N. & POTAPOV, E. 2001. Altai Falcon: subspecies, hybrid or colour morph? *Proceedings of 4th Eurasian Congress on Raptors, Seville, Spain, 25–29 September 2001, Abstracts* 66–67.

FRANCE, R. 1992. Aerial mobbing of a Gyrfalcon by Glaucous Gulls. *Journal of Raptor Research* 26: 269.

FRANTZEN, B. F., DRANSFELD, H. & HUNSDAL, O. 1991. *Fugleatlas for Finmark.* Fylkesmannen I Finmark & Norwegian Ornithological Society, Vadso.

FREUCHEN, P. & SALOMONSEN, F. 1958. *The Arctic Year.* Jonathan Cape, London.

FRIEDMAN, H. 1950. *The Birds of North and Middle America (part XI). US Natural History Museum Bulletin* 50.

FULLER, M. R., SEEGAR, W. S. & HOWEY, P. W. 1995. The use of satellite systems for the study of bird migration. *Israel Journal of Zoology* 41: 243–252.

GALBRAITH, C. A & THOMPSON, P. 1984. Nest-defence by female Gyrfalcon. *British Birds* 77: 483.

GANUSEVICH, S. A. 1983. [On the status and distribution of birds of prey of the Kola Peninsula.] *In* V. M. Galushin (ed.), [*Proceedings of the First Symposium on Birds of Prey of the USSR*], 117–118. Nauka, Moscow. [In Russian.]

GANUSEVICH, S. A. 1988. [Birds of prey of the Kola Peninsula.] *Ornitologia* 23: 73–78. [In Russian.]

GANUSEVICH, S. A. 1991. [Interspecific relationships in a community of birds of prey.] In *Proceedings of the 10ᵗʰ All-Union Ornithological Conference, Minsk*, 59–60. Navuka i tekhnika, Minsk. [In Russian.]

GANUSEVICH, S. A. 1992. Results of long-term studies of raptor populations in the Kola Peninsula (NW Russia). In *Abstracts of the 4ᵗʰ World Conference on Birds of Prey*, 7–8. World Working Group on Birds of Prey, Berlin.

GANUSEVICH, S. A. 2001. [Gyrfalcon.] *In* D. S. Pavlov, L. N. Mazin, V. V. Rozhnov & V. E. Flint (eds), [*Red Data Book of the Russian Federation (Animals)*], 454–455. AST, Aginskoye: Astrel', Balashikha. [In Russian.]

GARBER, C. S., MUTCH, B. D. & PLATT, S. 1993. Obeservations of wintering Gyrfalcons (*Falco rusticolus*) hunting Sage Grouse (*Centrocercus urophasianus*) in Wyoming and Montana, USA. *Journal of Raptor Research* 27, 169–171.

GÄRDENFORS, U. (ed.) 2000. *Rödlistade arter I Swerige*. ArtDatabanken, SLU, Uppsala.

GAVRILOV, E. I. 1999. [*Fauna and distribution of birds in Kazakhstan*.] Nauka, Alma-Aty. [In Russian.]

GENSBØL, B. & KOSKIMIES, P. 1995. Suomen ja Euroopan Päiväpetolinnut. WSOY, Helsinki.

GIZENKO, A. I. 1955. [*Birds of the Sakhalin District*.] Academy of Sciences of the USSR, Moscow. [In Russian.]

GJERSHAUG, J. O., THINGSTAD, P. G., ELDØY, S. & BYRKJELAND, S. 1994. *Norsk Fugleatlas*. Norsk Ornitologisk Forening, Klæbu.

GJERSHAUG, J. O., FOLKESTAD, A. O. & GOKSØYR, L. O. 1998. Female–female pairing between a Peregrine Falcon *Falco peregrinus* and a Gyrfalcon *Falco rusticolus* in two successive years. *Fauna Norvegica Series C Cinclus*. 21: 87–91.

GLADKOV, N. A. 1951. [Birds of the Timan tundra.] *Proceedings of the Zoological Museum of Moscow University* 7: 15–89. [In Russian.]

GLADKOV, N. A. & ZALETAEV, V. S. 1962. [New data on the distribution and biology of birds in north-western Yakutia (Anabar River).] *Ornitologia* 5: 31–34. [In Russian.]

GLENN, T. 1993. Suggestions for curbing Snowy Owl depletion in the Russian Arctic. *Raptor Link* 1: 4.

GLIG, O., SITTLER, B. & SABARD, B. 1997. Numerical and functional response of Gyrfalcon (*Falco rusticolus*) to lemming (*Dicrostonyx groenlandicus*) fluctuations in Norh–East Greenland. *In* T. B. Berg, M. C. Forchhammer & E. Skytte (eds), *Arktisk Biologisk Forskermode VI*, 5–6. Danish Polar Centre, Copenhagen.

GLOTOV, A. S. 2000. Gyrfalcon. *Diaries of the "Nenetskiy" Nature Reserve* 1: 45–47. [In Russian.]

GLUTZ VON BLOTZHEIM, U. N., BAUER, K. M. & BEZZEL, E. 1971. *Handbuch der Vogel Mitteleuropas*. Volume 4. Akademische Verlagsgesellschaft, Frankfurt.

GODFREY, W. E. 1986. *Birds of Canada*. National Museum of Natural Sciences, Ottawa.

GORDIENKO, T. A. & NECHITAILOV, YU. I. 2000. [Problems of birds of prey conservation in the Kamchatka District.] *In* R. S. Moiseev (ed.), [*Abstracts of the 1st Conference on Conservation of biodiversity in Kamchatka and its coastal waters, 11-12 April 2000*], 111–113. KamchatskNIRO, Petropavlosk-Kamchatskiy. [In Russian.]

GOROVENKO, A. V. 2002. [Distribution and numbers of Gyrfalcon *Falco rusticolus grebenitskii* in the North of the Kamchatka Peninsula]. *In* A. M. Torkanov (ed.), [*Abstracts of the 3rd Conference on Conservation of biodiversity in Kamchatka and its coastal waters, 26–27 November 2002*], 30–31. KamchatskNIRO, Petropavlosk-Kamchatskiy. [In Russian.]

GRAY, D. 1990. Winter studies of birds and mammals in the Canadian Arctic Islands. *In* C. R. Harington (ed.), *Canada's Missing Dimension: Science and History in the Canadian Arctic Islands*, 568–589. Canadian Museum of Nature, Ottawa.

GRIFFITHS, C. S. 1999. Phylogeny of the Falconidae inferred from molecular and morphological data. *Auk* 116: 116–130.

GRIFFITHS, R., DOUBLE, M. C., ORR, K. & DOWSON, R. J. 1998. A DNA test to sex most birds. *Molecular Biology* 7: 1071–1075.

GROSSMAN, M. L. & HAMLET, J. 1964. *Birds of Prey of the World*. C. N. Potter, Inc., New York.

GUDMUNDSSON, F. 1972. The predator–prey relationship of Gyrfalcon (*Falco rusticolus*) and Rock Ptarmigan (*Lagopus mutus*). *In* K. H. Voous, (ed.), *Proceedings of the 15th International Ornithological Congress, 30 August-5 September 1979* (abstracts), 649. The Hague.

HAFTORN, S. 1971. *Norges Fugler*. Universitetsforlaget, Oslo.

HAGEN, Y. 1952a. The Gyrfalcon (*Falco r. rusticolus* L.) in Dovre, Norway: Some breeding records and food studies. *Skrifter utgitt av Det Norske Videnskaps-Akademi i Oslo* 4: 5–37.

HAGEN, Y. 1952b. *Rovguglene og viltpleinen*. Gyldendal Norsk Forlag, Oslo.

HAGEN, Y. 1969. Norwegian studies on the reproduction of birds of prey and owls in relation to micro–rodent population fluctuations. *Fauna* 22: 73–126.

HAGEN, Y. & BARTH, E. 1952. Jaktfalken (*Falco rusticolus*): Noen iaktagelser fra Dovre I Norge. *Vår Fågelvärd* 11: 116–125.

HAMILTON, W. D. 1990. Mate choice near or far. *American Zoologist* 30: 341–352.

HARRIS, J. T. 1981. *The Peregrine Falcon in Greenland*. University of Missouri Press, Columbia, Missouri.

HART, H. C. 1880. Notes on the ornithology of the British Polar Expedition, 1875–6. *The Zoologist* 1–18.

HARTERT, E. 1912–1921. *Die Vögel der paläarktischen Fauna*. Erganzungsband, Berlin.

HARTING, J. E. 1883. *Essays on Sport and Natural History*. Horace Cox, London.

HARTING, J. E. 1891. *Bibliotheca Accipitraria. A Catalogue of Books Ancient and*

Modern Relating to Falconry. Facsimile published 2000: Martino Publishing, Mansfield, Connecticut.

HEIDENREICH, M. 1997. *Birds of Prey: Medicine and Management*. Blackwell, Oxford.

HEIDENREICH, M., KUSPERT, M., KUSPERT, H. J. & HUSSONG, R. 1993. Falkenhybriden. Die Zucht, zum Verwandschaftsgrad verschiedener Falkenarten sowie zum Thema der Faunenverfälschung durch Hybridfalken. *Beitrage zur Vogelkunde* 39: 205–206.

HELBIG, A. J., SEIBOLD, I., BEDNAREK, W., BRÜNING, H., GAUCHER, P., RISTOW, D., SCHARLAU, W., SCHMIDL, D. & WINK, M. 1994. Phylogenetic relationships among falcon species (genus *Falco)* according to DNA sequence variation of the cytochrome b gene. *In* B-U. Meyburg & R. Chancellor (eds), *Raptor Conservation Today*, 593–599. Pica Press, Robertsbridge.

HELLEBERG, A., KRAUL, I. & DALGAARD-MIKKELSEN, S. 1979. *Mercury, DDT and PCB in Gyrfalcons from Iceland*. Unpublished report.

HENDERSON, D. & BIRD, D. 1996. Gyrfalcon. *In* J. Gauthier & Y. Aubry (eds), *The Breeding Birds of Quebec*, 1123–1125. Province of Quebec Society for the Protection of Birds, Montreal.

HERDEMERTEN, K. 1939. *Jakunguaq*. Georg Westermann, Braunshweig.

HOLMBERG, T. & FALKDALEN, U. 1996. Jaktfalken och ripjaketn – forslag till en ekologisk uthållig jakt. *Vår Fågelvärld* 55: 19–23.

HOU, L. 1993. Avian fossils of Pleistocene from Zhoukoudian. *Memories of the Institute of Vertebrate Palaeontology and Palaeornithology, Academia Sinica* 19: 165–297.

HUHTALA, K., PULLIAINEN, E., JUSSUIA, P. & TUNKKARI, P. S. 1996. Food niche of the Gyrfalcon *Falco rusticolus* nesting in the far north of Finland as compared with other choices of the species. *Ornis Fennica* 73: 78–87.

HUNT, S., CUTHILL, I. C., BENNETT, A. T. D. & PARTRIDGE, J. C. 1999. Preference for ultraviolet partners in the Blue Tit. *Animal Behaviour* 58, 809–815.

HYYTIÄ, K., KELLOMÄKI, E. & KOISTENEN, J. (eds) 1983. *Suomen Lintuatlas*. SLY:n Lintutieto, Helsinki.

IRVING, L. 1960. Birds of Anaktuvuk Pass, Kobuk and Old Crow. *US National Museum Bulletin* 217.

IVANOV, A. I. 1976. [*Catalogue of the Birds of the USSR*.] Nauka, Leningrad. [In Russian.]

IVANOV, S. V. 1970. [*Sculpture of the peoples of North Siberia*.] Nauka, Leningrad. [In Russian.]

IVANOV, S. V. 1979. [*Sculpture of the Alay, Khakass and Siberian Tatars*.] Nauka, Leningrad. [In Russian.]

JACK, A. 1996. *Ferreira's Falconry*. Privately published.

JACOBS, G. H. FENWICK, J. A. & WILLIAMS, G. A. 2001. Cone-based vision of rats for ultraviolet and visible lights. *Journal of Experimental Biology* 204: 2439–2446.

JANOSSY, D. 1972. Die mittelpleistozane Vogelfauna der Stranska Skala. *Anthropos*

20: 35–64.

JANOSSY, D. 1986. *Pleistocene Vertebrate Faunas of Hungary*. Elsevier, Oxford.

JARMAN, W. M., BURNS, S. A., MATTOX, W. G. & SEEGAR, W. S. 1994. Organochlorine compounds in the plasma of Peregrine Falcons and Gyrfalcons nestling in Greenland. *Arctic* 47: 334.–340.

JENKINS, M. A. 1978. Gyrfalcon nesting behaviour from hatching to fledging. *Auk*: 95: 122–127.

JENNING, W. & FRIEDZEN, K-E. 1972. Iakttagelser rörande en övervintrande jaktfalk. *Vår Fågelvärd* 31: 1–8.

JENSEN, K. H., RAUCH, S., MORRISON, G. M. & LINDBERG, P. 2002. Platinum group elements in the feathers of raptors and their prey. *Archives of Environmental Contamination and Toxicology* 42: 338–347.

JOHNSGARD, P. A. 1990. *Hawks, Eagles, and Falcons of North America*. Smithsonian Institution Press, Washington D. C.

KAHLKE, R-D. 1999. *The History of the Origin, Evolution and Dispersal of the Late Pleistocene Mammuthus/Coelodonta Faunal Complex in Eurasia (Large Mammals)*. The Mammoth Site of Hot Springs, South Dakota Publishers, Inc., Hot Springs.

KALYAKIN, V. N. 1983. [Birds of Prey Faunas and Status of Populations of rare species in the Southern Yamal.] *In* V. E. Galushin (ed.) *Ecology of Birds of Prey: Proceedings of the 1st USSR Conference on Ecology and Conservation of Birds of Prey, Moscow*, 120–124. Nauka, Moscow. [In Russian.]

KALYAKIN, V. N. 1988. [Rare animal species in extreme northwest Siberia.] *In* Yu. Shvetsov (ed.), [Rare terrestrial vertebrates of Siberia.], 97–107. Nauka, Novosibirsk. [In Russian.]

KALYAKIN, V. N. 1989. [Birds of Prey in Ecosystems of the Extreme North.] *In* Yu. I. Chernov, Yu.I. (ed.), [*Birds in the Natural Communities of the Tundra Zone*], 51–112. Nauka, Moscow. [In Russian.]

KALYAKIN, V. N. 1993. [Birds and mammals of the Novaya Zemlya Islands and an Estimate of its Status.] *Proceedings of the Arctic Sea Complex Expedition* 2: 23–90. [In Russian.]

KALYAKIN, V. N. 1994. [Gyrfalcon hunting]. *Priroda I Okhota* 1: 42–43. [In Russian.]

KALYAKIN, V. N. & VINOGRADOV, V. G. 1981. [Breeding Gyrfalcons in the south of the Yamal Peninsula]. *Bulletin of the MOIP (Moscow Society of Naturalist) Department of Biology* 86: 42–51. [In Russian.]

KESSEL, B. 1989. *Birds of the Seward Peninsula, Alaska*. University of Alaska Press, Fairbanks, Alaska.

KIRIKOV, S. V. 1952. *Birds and Mammals in the Landscape of the Southern Urals*. Academy of Sciences of the USSR, Moscow. [In Russian.]

KISHINSKIY A. A. 1958. [The biology of Gyrfalcon *Falco gyrfalco gyrfalco* in the Kola Peninsula]. *Scientific Notes of Moscow State University*, 197: 61–75. [In Russian.]

KISHINSKIY, A. A. 1968. [*Birds of the Kolyma Highlands.*] Nauka, Moscow. [In Russian.]

KISHINSKIY, A. A. 1980. [*Birds of the Koryak Mountains.*] Nauka, Moscow. [In Russian.]

KISHINSKIY, A. A. 1988. [*Ornithofauna of Northeast Asia.*] Nauka, Moscow. [In Russian.]

KLEINSCHMIDT, O. 1901. Der Formenkreis *Falco hierofalco* und die stellung der ungarischhen wurgfalcen in demselben. *Aquila* 8: 1–49.

KLEINSCHMIDT, O. 1923–1937. Falco hierfalco *(Kl).* Beriajah Zoogeograhia infinita, Halle.

KLUGMAN, S. S., FULLER, M. R., HOWEY, P. W., YATES, M. A., OAR, J. J., SEEGAR, J. M., SEEGAR, W. S., MATTOX, W. G. & MAECHTLE, T. L. 1993. Use of satellite telemetry for study of a Gyrfalcon in Greenland. *Journal of Raptor Research* 27: 75–76.

KNAPTON, R. 1982. The Changing Seasons. *American Birds* 36: 261–265.

KOKHANOV, V. D. 1970. [On the winter diet of the Gyrfalcon]. *Proceedings of the Kandalaksha Nature Reserve, Murmansk* 8: 233–235. [In Russian.]

KOLOSOV, A. M. (ed.) 1983. *Krasnaya Kniga RSFSR.* Rossyelkhozizdat, Moscow.

KOON, D. W. 1998. Is Polar Bear hair fiber optic? *Applied Optics* 37: 3198–3200.

KOSKIMIES, P. 1989. [Distribution and numbers of Finnish breeding birds.] *In* K. Hyytiä, E. Kellomäki & J. Koistenen (eds), *Suomen Lintuatlas*, Appendix. SLY:n Lintutieto, Helsinki. [In Finnish with English summary.]

KOSKIMIES, P. 1995. Tunturihaukat tarkkailussa. *Linnut* 30: 4.

KOSKIMIES, P. 1998. Gyrfalcon studies in Finland in 1997. *Blåfoten* 5: 2.

KOSKIMIES, P. 1999. *Gyrfalcon (*Falco rusticolus*) International Action Plan.* Birdlife International and EU.

KOSKIMIES, P. & SULKAVA, S. 2002. Tunturiahaukka elaa riekolla ja kiirunalla. *Linnut* 37: 6–10.

KOTS, A. F. 1948. [The Russian Gyrfalcon from a Darwinian point of view]. *Okhrana Prirody* 5: 66–79. [In Russian.]

KOZLOV, A. M. (ed.) 1983. [*Red Data Book of the RSFSR: Animals.*] Rosselkosizdat, Moscow. [In Russian.]

KOZLOVA, E. V. 1969. [The relationship between Saker Falcon and Gyrfalcon and a possible history of their distribution.] *Zoologicheskij Zhurnal* 58: 1838–1851. [In Russian.]

KOZLOVA, E. V. 1975. [*Birds of the zonal steppes and deserts of Central Asia.*] Nauka, Leningrad. [In Russian.]

KRASNOV, YU. V., MATISHOV, G. G., GALAKTIONOV, K. V. & SAVINOVA, T. N. 1995. [*Colonial seabirds of the Murman.*] Nauka, St Petersburg. [In Russian.]

KRECHMAR, A. V., ANDREEV, A. V. & KONDRATIEV, A. YA. 1991. [*Birds of the Northern Plains.*] Nauka, Leningrad. [In Russian.]

KRECHMAR, A.V. & NAZARENKO, A.A. 1989. Gyrfalcon. *In* V. A. Kostenko, P. A.

Ler, V. A. Nechaev & Yu. V. Shibaev (eds), [*Rare vertebrates of the Soviet Far East and their protection*], 96. Nauka, Leningrad. [In Russian.]

KRECHMAR, A. V. & PROBST, R. 2003. Der weise Habich *Accipiter gentilis albidus* in Nordost-Sibirien – porträt eines Mythos. *Limicola* 17: 289–305.

KRISTOFFERSEN, S. 1931. Fugle–observasjoner fra Sydkapp p Svalbard, (76°30' n.br. 16°30' øst.l), 1929–1930. *Norsk Ornithologisk Forenings Tidsskrift III* 248–257.

KUCHERUK, V. V., KOVALEVSKIY, YU. L. & SURLINOV, A. G. 1975. [Changes to Southern Yamal bird populations over the last 100 years]. *Bulletin of the MOIP (Moscow Society of Naturalists) Department of Biology* 80. [In Russian.]

KUYT, E. 1962. A record of a tree-nesting Gyrfalcon. *Condor* 64: 508–510.

KUYT, E. 1980. Distribution and breeding biology of raptors in the Thelon River area, Northwest Territories, 1957–1969. *Canadian Field Naturalist* 94: 121–130.

KUZNETSOV, A. V. 1990. [Rare birds of the Kostroma District.] *In* A. M. Amirkhanov (ed.), [*Results of studies of Rare Animals: Proceedings of the Central Laboratory of the Glavokhota.*], 42–46. Moscow. [In Russian.]

LANGVATN, R. 1977. Characteristics and relative occurrence of remnants of prey found at nesting places of Gyrfalcon *Falco rusticolus*. *Ornis Scandinavica* 8: 113–125.

LANGVATN, R. & MOKSNES, A. 1979. On the breeding ecology of the Gyrfalcon *Falco rusticolus* in central Norway. *Fauna Norvegica Series C Cinclus* 2: 27–39.

LASCELLES, G. 1892. *The Art of Falconry*. Reprinted 1985 by C. W. Daniel Co, Saffron Waldon.

LATHAM, S. 1615. *Falconry: or the Faulcon's Lure and Cure*. Roger Jackson, London.

LIFJELD, J. T., BJØRNSTGAD, G., STEEN, O. F. & NESJE, M. 2002. Reduced genetic variation in Norwegian Peregrine Falcons *Falco peregrinus* indicated by minisatellite DNA fingerprinting. *Ibis* 144 (online): E19–E26.

LIND, G. & NORDIN, A. 1995. Indum – ett productivt jaktfalk – revir. *Fåglar i Jämtland Harjedalen* 2, 2–4.

LINDBERG, P. 1983. *Relations between the diet of Fennoscandian Peregrines (*Falco peregrinus*) and organochlorines and mercury in their eggs and feathers, with comparison to the Gyrfalcon* Falco rusticolus. Unpublished Ph.D thesis. University of Goteborg, Sweden.

LINDBERG, P. 1999a. Falkenerfalk häckande I Bohuslän. *Vår Fågelvärd* 2: 25.

LINDBERG, P. 1999b. Förrymda falkenerarfalkar hächar I Bohuslän. *Vår Fågelvärd* 8: 22–23.

LINDBERG, P. 2002. *Faktablad:* Falco rusticolus – *Jaktfalk*. Sveriges lantbruks-universitet, Uppsala.

LINDER, U. & TJERNBERG. M. 1997. Jaktfalkeninveneringar I Norrbotten 1996. *Blåfoten* 1: 4.

LINNAEUS, C. 1746. *Fauna Svecica*. Stockholm.

LINNAEUS, C. 1758. *Systema Naturae*. Holmiae.

LINNAEUS, C. 1761. *Fauna Svecica*. Stockholm.

LINNAEUS, C. 1788. *Systema naturae*. Leipzig.

LINNAEUS, C. 1953. *Linne's Daleresa, iter Dalecarlicum*. Hugo Gebers Ferlag/ Svenska Linneskllskapet och Nordiska Museet, Stockholm.

LITVINOV, YU. N. & CHUPIN, I. I. 1983. [Studies and conservation of terrestrial vertebrates in the forest–tundra part of the Taymir reserve.] *In* Yu. P. Yazan (ed.), [*Conservation of living nature: Proceedings of the Conference of Young Scientists, November 1983*], 127–128. Central Management Committee for Nature Reserves, Nature Conservation, Forestry and Game, Moscow. [In Russian.]

LOBKOV, E. G. 1986. *Breeding Birds of Kamchatka*. Academy of Sciences (Far Eastern Scientific Centre), Vladivostok. [In Russian.]

LOBKOV, E. G. 1997. *Die Vogelwelt Kamtschatkas*. Acta Ornithoecologica. Band 3, Heft 4, 319–451.

LOBKOV, E. G. 2000. [Illegal trapping and export of Gyrfalcons from Kamchatka is a threat to the very existence of the Kamchatka population]. *In* R. S. Moiseev (ed.), [*Abstracts of the 1ˢᵗ Conference on Conservation of biodiversity in Kamchatka and its coastal waters, 11-12 April 2000*], 115–119. KamchatskNIRO, Petropavlosk-Kamchatskiy. [In Russian.]

LÖNNBERG, E. 1930. *Festskrift*. Transactions of Uppsala University, Uppsala.

LÖNNBERG, E. 1931. Olof Rudbeck Jr., the first Swedish ornithologist. *Ibis* 13: 302–307.

LUMEIJ, J. T., REMPLE, J. D., REDIG, P. T., LIERZ, M. & COOPER, J. E. 2000. *Raptor Biomedicine III*. Zoological Education Network.

MacDONALD, G. M., VELICHKO, A. A., KREMENETSKI, C. V., BORISOVA,O. K., GOLEVA, A. A., ADREEEV, A. A., CWYNAR, L. C., RIDING, R. T., FORMAN, S. L., EDWARDS, T. W. D., ARAVENA, R., HAMMARLUND, D., SZEICZ, J. M. & GATTAULIN, V. N. 2000. Holocene treeline history and climate change across Northern Eurasia. *Quaternary Research* 53: 302–311.

McDONALD, S .D. 1976. Gyr! *Audubon* 78: 76–79.

McGHIE, H. 1999. Persecution of birds of prey in north Scotland 1912–69 as evidenced by taxidermists' stuffing books. *Scottish Birds* 20: 98–110.

McINTYRE, C. L., ADAMS, L. G. & AMBROSE, R. E. 1994. Using satellite telemetry to monitor movements of Gyrfalcon in northern Alaska and the Russian Far East. *Journal of Raptor Research* 28: 61.

MANDEVILLE, J. 1910. Travelles of John Mandeville. In *Catholic Encyclopaedia 1910,* volume 9. Robert Appleton Company, New York.

MANNICHE, A. L. 1910. The terrestrial mammals and birds of North-east Greenland. *Meddeleser om Grønland* 45: 183–187.

MARAKOV, S. V. 1965. [Birds of prey and owls of the Commander Islands]. *In* [*Proceedings of the 4ᵗʰ Onithological Conference of the USSR*], 228–229. Nauka, Alma–Aty. [In Russian.]

MARKOVA, A. K., SMIRNOV, N. G., KOZHARINOV, A. V., KAZANTSEVA, N. E., SIMAKOVA, A. N. & KITAEV, L.M. 1995. Late Pleistocene distribution and diversity of mammals in northern Eurasia. *Paleontologia I Evolucio* 28–29: 5–143.

MASRI, AL–HAFIZ B. A. 1992. *Islam and Ecology. In* F. Khalid & J. O'Brien (eds), Islam and Ecology. Cassell Publishers, London.

MATTOX, W. G. 1969. The white Gyrfalcon: Field studies of *Falco rusticolus* in Greenland. *Polar Notes* 9: 46–62.

MATTOX, W. G. 1970. Banding Gyrfalcons (*Falco rusticolus*) in Greenland, 1967. *Bird Banding* 41: 31–37.

MEINERTZHAGEN, R. 1954. *Birds of Arabia.* Oliver and Boyd, Edinburgh.

MENZBIER, M. A. 1891. *Ornitologie du Turkestan et des pays adjacents.* Privately published, Moscow.

MENZBIER, M. A. 1900. [Birds of the Pacific seacoast of Siberia: on the material collected by Dr. N. V. Slunin. *In* N. V. Slunin, [*Okhotsko–Kamtchatskiy region: Natural History Description*], volume 1, 341–353. [In Russian.]

MENZBIER, M. A. 1916. [Fauna of Russia.] *Birds* 6: 165–169. [In Russian.]

MERKEL, F. R., MOSBECH, A., BOERTMANN, D. & GRØNDHAL, L. 2002. Winter seabird distribution and abundance off southwestern Greenland, 1999. *Polar Research* 21: 17–36.

MILLER, A. H. 1941. The significance of moult centers among the secondary remiges in the Falconiformes. *Condor* 43: 113–115.

MILLER, L. 1927. The falcons of the McKittrick Pleistocene. *Condor* 19: 150–152.

MIKHEEV, A.V. 1941. [Some information of Gyrfalcons in the Timan Tundra]. *Nature and Socialist Economy* 8: 455–457; reprinted in 2002 in *Russian Journal of Ornithology (Express)* 199: 905–907. [In Russian.]

MIKKOLA, H. & SULKAVA, S. 1972. Mitä syö tunturihauka. *Suomen Luonto* 5: 183–185.

MINDELL, D. P., ALBUQUERQUE, J. L. B. & WHITE, C. M. 1987. Breeding population fluctuations in some raptors. *Oecologia* 72: 328–388.

MINDELL, D. P., SORENSON, M. D. & DIMCHEFF, D. E. 1998. Multiple independent origins of mitochondrial gene order in birds. *Proceedings of the National Academy of Sciences* 95: 10693–10697.

MINDELL, D. P. & WHITE, C. M. 1988. Fluctuations of observed breeding Rough-legged Hawks and Gyrfalcons: regularity reconsidered. *Oecologia* 77: 14–18.

MINEYEV, YU. N. 1994 [Birds of the Nenetskiy State Reserve (northeast of the Malozemelskaya tundra).] *Russian Journal of Ornithology.* 3: 319–336. [In Russian.]

MIRSKY, J. (ed.) 1964. *The Great Chinese Travellers.* Pantheon Books, New York.

MIRZA, H. D-D. T. 1868. *A Persian Treatise on Falconry.* Translated edition (2002) by D. C. Phillott, Erye Press, London.

MISHENKO, A. L. 1981. [Observations of a Gyrfalcon nest in the Southern Yamal]. *Ornitologia* 16: 175–176. [In Russian.]

MONTGOMERY, R., LYON, B. & HOLDER K. 2001. Dirty Ptarmigan: Behavioural modification of conspicuous male plumage. *Behavioural Ecology* 12: 429–438.

MOROZOV, V. V. 1991. [Peregrine and Gyrfalcon in the extreme northeast of Europe.] *Bulletin of the MOIP (Moscow Society of Naturalists) Department of Biology* 96, 57–65. [In Russian.]

MOROZOV, V. V. 2000. [Distribution of Gyrfalcon *Falco rusticolus* on the tundras of European Russia]. *Russian Journal of Ornithology (Express)* 95: 3–11. [In Russian.]

MOROZOV, V. V. 2001. [Influence of some predators and parasites on the breeding rate of rare raptor populations.] In *Proceedings of the 9th Ornithological Conference, Kazan.* 440–441. Matbugat yourty, Kazan. [In Russian.]

MORTENSEN, O. 1998. *An Anthropological Study of Falconry in the UAE.* Unpublished Report. Museum of Anthropology, Oslo University, Norway.

MOSSOP, D. H. 1982. Domestic Gyrfalcons – a uniquely northern enterprise or a monumental headache? In *Transactions of the 46th Federal-Provincial Wildlife Conference,* 130–136. Canadian Wildlife Service, Ottawa.

MOSSOP, D. H. & HAYES, R. D. 1981. The Yukon Territory Gyrfalcon harvest experiment (1974–1980). In W. N. Ladd & P. F. Schemph (eds), *Proceedings of a symposium and workshop: Raptor management and biology in Alaska and Western Canada, Anchorage, 1981,* 263–280. United States Department of the Interior & United States Fisheries and Wildlife Service, Anchorage.

MOSSOP, D. H. & HAYES, R.D. 1994. Long–term trends in the breeding density and productivity of Gyrfalcon *Falco rusticolus* in the Yukon territory, Canada. In B-U. Meyburg & R. Chancellor (eds), *Raptor Conservation Today,* 403–413. Pica Press, Robertsbridge.

MOURER-CHAUVIRÉ, C. 1975. Les oiseaux du Pleistocene Moyen et Superieur de France. *Documents des Laboratorie de Geologie de la Faculte des Sciences de Lyon* 64: 1–624.

MOURER-CHAUVIRÉ, C. 1983. Les oiseaux dans les habitats paleolithiques: Gibier des hommes ou proies des rapaces? *British Archaeological Research (International Series 2: Animals and Archeology)* 183, 111–124.

MUIR, D. & BIRD, D. M. 1983. Food of Gyrfalcons at a nest on Ellesmere Island. *Wilson Bulletin* 96: 464–467.

NAZAROV, F. 1821. [*Records of some rare findings in peoples and lands of the Middle Asia by Philip Nazarov,.an interpretor of the Siberian Corps, sent to Kokant in 1813 and 1814*]. St. Petersburg. [In Russian.]

NECHAEV, V. A. 1991. *Birds of the Sakhalin Island.* Academy of Sciences (Far-Eastern Branch), Vladivostok. [In Russian.]

NEGRO, J. J. & TORRES, M. J. 1999. Genetic variability and differentiation of two Bearded Vulture *Gypaetus barbatus* populations and implications for reintroduction projects. *Biological Conservation* 87: 249–254.

NEGRO, J. J., VILLARROEL, M., TELLA, J. L., KUHNLEIN, U., HIRALDO, E., DONAZAR,

J. A. & BIRD, D. M. 1996. DNA fingerprinting reveals a low incidence of extra-pair fertilizations in the Lesser Kestrel. *Animal Behaviour* 51: 935–943.

NELSON, M. 1956. Observations of Gyrfalcon in training and hunting. *Journal of the Falconry Club of America* 2: 21–25.

NESJE, M. & RØED, K. H. 2000. Sex identification in falcons using microsatellite DNA markers. *Hereditas* 132: 261–263.

NESJE, M., RØED, K. H., LIFJELD, J. T., LINDBERG, P. & STEENS, O. F. 2000. Genetic relationships in the Peregrine Falcon (*Falco peregrinus*) analysed by microsatellite DNA markers. *Molecular Ecology* 9: 53–60.

NEWTON, I. 1979. *Population Ecology of Raptors.* T & AD Poyser, Berkhamsted.

NIELSEN. Ó. K. 1986. *Population ecology of the Gyrfalcon in Iceland, with comparative notes on the Merlin and Raven.* Unpublished Ph.D thesis. Cornell University, New York.

NIELSEN, Ó. K. 1991. Kynproskaaldur og átthagatryggd fálka. *Náttúrfrædis-tofnunar* 60: 135–143.

NIELSEN, Ó. K. 1999a. Gyrfalcon predation on Ptarmigan: numerical and functional responses. *Journal of Animal Ecology* 68: 1034–1050.

NIELSEN, Ó. K. 1999b. [Monitoring of the ptarmigan population in Iceland 1963–1998]. *Fjölrit Natturufraedistofnunar* 39. [In Icelandic.]

NIELSEN, Ó. K. 2002. Falki kostgangari [Observations on carrion feeding by Gyrfalcons in Iceland.] *Natturufraedingurinn* 71: 4–7. [In Icelandic.]

NIELSEN, Ó. K. & CADE, T. J. 1990a. Annual cycle of the Gyrfalcon in Iceland. *National Geographic Research* 6: 41–62.

NIELSEN, Ó. K. & CADE, T. J. 1990b. Seasonal changes of food habits of Gyrfalcons in NE Iceland. *Ornis Scandinavica* 21: 202–211.

NIELSEN, Ó. K. & PÉTURSSON, G. 1995. Population fluctuations of Gyrfalcon and Rock Ptarmigan: Analysis of export figures from Iceland. *Wildlife Biology*: 1: 65–71.

NORMENT, C. J. 1985. Observations on the annual chronology for the birds in the Warden's Grove Area, Thelon River, Northwest Territories, 1977–1978. *Canadian Field Naturalist* 99: 471–483.

NORMENT, C. J., HALL, A. & HENDRICKS, P. 1999. Important bird and mammal records in the Thelon River valley, Northwest territories: Range expansions and possible causes. *Canadian Field Naturalist* 113: 373–385.

OBST, J. 1994. Tree-nesting by the Gyrfalcon (*Falco rusticolus*) in the western Canadian Arctic. *Journal of Raptor Research* 28: 4–8.

OGI, H. & MIYASHITA, T. 1991. Sighting of Gyrfalcon in the Sea of Okhotsk. *Journal of the Yamasina Institute of Ornithology* 23: 20–21.

OKLADNIKOV, A. P. & ZAPOROZHSKAYA V. A. 1970. [*Petroglyphs of Trans-Baikalia.*] Nauka, Leningrad. [In Russian.]

ÓLAFSDÓTTIR, K., PETERSEN, Æ., THÓRDARDÓTTIR, S. & JÓHANNESSON, T. 1995. Organochlorine residues in Gyrfalcons (*Falco rusticolus*) in Iceland. *Bulletin of*

Environmental Contamination and Toxicology 55: 382–389.

OVODOV, N. & MARTYNOVICH, N. 1992. [New data on mammals and birds of the Dvuglazka cave in Khakassia]. *In* A. M. Borovskiy (ed.) [*Problems of archaeology, ethnography, history and regional studies of the Krasnoyarsk District*], 78–83. Krasnoyarsk University Publishers, Krasnoyarsk. [In Russian.]

OVODOV, N. & MARTYNOVICH N. 2000. [Vertebrates of caves of Biruysinskiy region, environs of Krasnoyarsk]. In E. A. Vaganov, M. A. Grachev & A. P. Derevyanko [*Problems of climatic and environmental reconstructions of the Holocene and Pleistocene of Siberia*], 375–382. Institute of Anthropology and Ethnography, Russian Academy of Sciences Publishers, Novosibirsk. [In Russian.]

ØDERGAARD, H. 1969. Noen nyere hekkefunn av jaktfalk. *Sterna* 8: 360–368.

PALMER, R. S. (ed.) 1988. *Handbook of North American Birds,* volume 5. Yale University Press, New Haven, Connecticut.

PARKIN, D. & MAY, C. 1993. DNA fingerprinting of young falcons in the nest. *In* M. Nicholls & R. Clarke (eds), *Biology and Conservation of Small Falcons,* 45–50. The Hawk and Owl Trust, London.

PARMALEE, D. F., STEPHENS, H. A. & SCHMIDT, R. H. 1967. The birds of southeastern Victoria Island and adjacent islands. *Bulletin of the National Museum of Canada* 222: 1–229.

PARRISH, J. R. & WHITE, C.M. 1987. CITES classification of the Gyrfalcon. *Journal of Raptor Research* 21: 40.

PARRY–JONES, J. 1994. *Training Birds of Prey.* David and Charles, Newton Abbott.

PAVLIK, I. CERNIK, J, BARTA, J., KUNDERA, J., & PECKA, Z. 1998. Occurrence of coccidia (*Caryospora neofalconis* and *Caryospora kutzeri*) in birds of prey in the Falcon Breeding Facility in Milotice in the Czech Republic. *Veterinarni Medicina (Praha)* 43: 301–306.

PAVLOV, D. S., MAZIN, L. N., ROZHNOV, V. V. & FLINT V. E. (eds) 2001. *Krasnaya kniga Rossiyskoy Federatsii (Zhivotnye)* [*Red Data Book of the Russian Federation (Animals).*] AST, Aginskoye: Astrel', Balashikha. [In Russian.]

PEARSON, H. 1899. *Beyond Petsora Eastward: Two summer voyages to Novaya Zemlya and the islands of the Barents Sea.* R. H. Porter, London.

PENNYCUICK, C. J. 1989. *Bird Flight Performance: A practical calculation manual.* Oxford Universtiy Press, Oxford.

PENNYCUICK, C. J., FULLER, M. R., OAR, J. O. & KIRKPATRICK, S. J. 1994. Falcon versus grouse: Flight adaptations of a predator and its prey. *Journal of Avian Biology* 25: 39–49.

PEREGRINE FUND 1999–2002. *Peregrine Fund Annual Report.* Peregrine Fund Inc., Boise, Idaho.

PERERVA, V. I., GUSAKOV, E. S. & OSTAPENKO, V. A. 1987. [Birds of prey of the north of Penzhina District (Penzina River basin)]. *Bulletin of the MOIP (Moscow Society of Naturalists) Department of Biology* 92, 1–10. [In Russian.]

PETER, D. & KESTENHOLTZ, M. 1998. Sturzfluge von Wanderfalke *Falco peregrinus* und Westenfalke *F. peregridoides*. *Ornithologische Beobachter* 95: 107–112.

PETERS, J. 1931. *Check-list of birds of the world,* volume 1. Harvard University Press, Cambridge.

PÉTURSSON, G., PRAINSSON, G. & OLAFSSON, E. 1991. Sjadlgæfir fuglar a Islandi. *Bliki* 13: 11–44.

PFEFFER, R. 1991. [Gyrfalcon.] *In* A. F. Kovshar' (ed.), [*Red Data Book of Kazakhstan. Volume 1: Animals*] . Gylim Publishers, Alma-Aty. [In Russian.]

PFEFFER, R. 1996. [Gyrfalcon.] *In* [Red Data Book of Kazakhstan.], 150–151. National Academy of Sciences, Almaty. [In Russian.]

PHANDER, P. V. 1994. [On the Altay Gyrfalcon again.] *Selevinia* 2: 5–9. [In Russian.]

PLATT, J. N. 1976. Gyrfalcon nest-site selection and winter activity in the western Canadian Arctic. *Canadian Field Naturalist* 90: 338–345.

PLATT, J. N. 1977. *The breeding behaviour of wild and captive Gyrfalcons in relation to their environments and human disturbance.* Unpublished Ph.D thesis. Cornell University, New York.

PLATT, J. N. 1989. Gyrfalcon courtship and early breeding behaviour on the Yukon North Slope. *Sociobiology* 15: 43–69.

PLESHAK, T. V. 2003. [Birds of Franz Josef Land]. *Russian Journal of Ornithology (Express)* 232: 881–885. [In Russian.]

POLO, M. 1324. *Travels of Marco Polo.* English translation (1930) by Garden City Publishing, New York.

POOLE, K. G. 1987. Aspects of the ecology, food habits and foraging characteristics of Gyrfalcons in the central Canadian Arctic. *Journal of Raptor Research* 21: 80.

POOLE, K. G. 1988. Feeding responses by Gyrfalcon to brood size manipulation. *Journal of Raptor Research* 22(2): 67–70.

POOLE, K. G. 1989. Determining age and sex of nestling Gyrfalcons. *Journal of Raptor Research* 23: 45–47.

POOLE, K. G. 1991. A replacement clutch in wild gyrfalcons (*Falco rusticolus*) in Northwest Territories. *Canadian Field Naturalist* 202: 62–64.

POOLE, K. G. & BOAG, D. A. 1988. Ecology of Gyrfalcons (*Falco rusticolus*) in the central Canadian Arctic: Diet and feeding behaviour. *Canadian Journal of Zoology* 66: 334–344.

POOLE, K. G. & BROMLEY, R. G. 1988a. Natural history of the Gyrfalcon in the central Canadian Arctic. *Arctic* 41: 31–38.

POOLE, K. G. & BROMLEY, R. G. 1988b. Interrelationships within a raptor guild in the central Canadian Arctic. *Canadian Journal of Zoology* 66: 2275–2282.

PORDARSON, B. 1957. *Islenzkir fälkar. Safn til sögu íslands og íslenzkra bókmennta, annar flokkur. I. 5.* Hid Islendzka Bokmenntafelag, Reykjavik.

PORTENKO, L. A. 1937. [*Birds of the non-polar parts of the Northern Urals.*] Academy of Sciences, Leningrad. [In Russian.]

PORTENKO, L. A. 1972. [*Birds of the Chukotka Peninsula and Wrangel Island.*]

Nauka, Leningrad. [In Russian.]

POTANIN, G. N. 1917. [*Kazakh-Kyrghis and Altay Sagas, Legends and Fairy Tales.*] Published privately, Petrograd. [In Russian.]

POTANIN, G. N. 1972. [Kazakh folklore in the materials of G. N. Potanin.] Ilym, Almaty. [In Russian.]

POTAPOV, E. 1993. *Ecology and energetics of Rough-legged Buzzard in the Kolyma River Lowlands.* Unpublished D.Phil thesis. Oxford University, Oxford.

POTAPOV, E. 1994a. Time budget, organochlorines and productivity in Peregrine Falcon *Falco peregrinus* in the Kolyma Lowlands (Northeast Siberia). *In* B-U. Meyburg & R. Chancellor (eds), *Raptor Conservation Today*, 195–201. Pica Press, Robertsbridge.

POTAPOV, E. 1994b. Birds in the lower Kolyma River (Northeast Siberia). *Bulletin of the British Ornithological Club* 114: 66–73.

POTAPOV, E. & BENNETT, A. T. D. 1999. Gyrfalcon (*Falco rusticolus*) colours. *Proceedings of the 2nd European Conference of the Raptor Research Foundation, Mikulov, Czech Republic, November 1999: Buteo supplement* 61.

POTAPOV, E. BENNETT, A. T. D. & SALE, R. in Press. UV/UV+ reflectance in whitewash at nesting cliffs of the Saker Falcon *Falco cherrug* (a diurnal raptor). *Biology Letters.*

POTAPOV, E., SUMYA, D., GOMBOBAATAR, B. & FOX, N. C. 2002. Migration studies of the Saker Falcon. *Falco* 19: 3–4.

POTAPOVA, O. 2001. Snowy Owl *Nyctea scandiaca* (Aves: Strigiformes) in the Pleistocene of the Ural Mountains with notes on its ecology and distribution in the Northern Palearctic. *Deisea* 8: 103–126.

PROKOFIEVA, E. D. 1971. [Shamanic costumes of the Siberian peoples.] *In* L. P. Potapov & S. V. Ivanov (eds), [*Religious Views and Ceremonies of the Siberian Peoples*]. Nauka, Leningrad. [In Russian.]

PULLIAINEN, E. 1975. Choice of prey by a pair of Gyrfalcons (*Falco rusticolus*) during the nesting period in Forest-Lapland. *Ornis Fennica* 52: 19–22.

PULLIAINEN, E., IIVAINEN, J., KORHONEN, K., OVASKAINEN, P. & TOLONEN, A. 1973. Southern nesting of the Gyrfalcon. *Luntumies* 8: 30.

PUNTILA, M. 2004 Pictures of a tree-nesting Gyrfalcon in Finland. In J. Ekenstedt (ed.), *Proceedings from the workshop on Gyrfalcons, Umeå 28 September 2004,* 42.

RAKHILIN, V. K. 1997. [*Ornithogeography of Russia.*] Institute of History of Natural Science and Techniques, Russian Academy of Sciences, Moscow. [In Russian.]

RASMUSSEN, P. 1999. Rare birds in Denmark and Greenland. *Dansk Ornithologisk Forenings Tidsskrift* 93: 127–140.

RATCIFFE, D. 1980. *The Peregrine Falcon.* T & AD Poyser, London.

REID, D. G., KREBS, C. J. & KENNEY, A. J. 1997. Patterns of predation on noncyclic lemmings. *Ecological Monographs* 67: 89–108.

RICKLEFS, R. 1983. Avian postnatal development. *In* D. Farner, J. King & K. Parkes (eds), *Avian Biology*, volume 7, 2–83. Academic Press, New York.

RITCHIE, R. J. 1991. Effects of oil development on providing nesting opportunities for Gyrfalcons and Rough-legged Hawks in northern Alaska. *Condor* 93: 180–184.

ROGACHEVA, E. V. 1988. [*Birds of Middle Siberia.*] Nauka, Moscow. [In Russian.]

ROGACHEVA, E. V., LAPPO E. G. & VOLKOV A. E. 1995. [Fauna and zoogeography of Eurasian Arctic birds.] *In* E. Grönlund & O. Melander (eds), *Swedish–Russian Tundra Ecology: Expedition 94 – A Cruise Report*, 156–164. Swedish Polar Research Secretariat, Stockholm. [In Russian.]

ROGACHEVA, E. V., SIROECHKOVSKIY, E. E, BURSKIY, O. V., MOROZ, A. A. & SEFTEL, B. I. 1988. [Birds of the Central Siberian Biosphere Reserve.] *In* E. V. Rogacheva (ed.) [Conservation and Rational Use of the Fauna and Ecosystems of the Yenisei North.], 42–96. Severtsev Institute of Evolutionary Morphology and Ecology of Animals of the Central Siberian Nature Reserve, Moscow. [In Russian.]

ROGACHEVA H. 1992. [*Birds of Central Siberia.*] Husum Druck – u. Verlagsges, Husum. [In Russian.]

ROMANOV, A.A. 1998. [Rare birds of the Putoran Plateau.] *In* Yu. Yu. Blokhin & L. N. Mazin (eds), [*The Problems of Conservation of the Poorly Studied Fauna of the North*], 67–71. TSNIL Glavokhota, Moscow [In Russian.]

ROOT, T. 1988. *Atlas of Wintering North American Birds.* The University of Chicago Press, Chicago.

ROSENEAU, D. G. 1972. *Summer distribution, numbers, and food habits of the Gyrfalcon (*Falco rusticolus *L.), on the Seward Peninsula, Alaska.* Unpublished MS Thesis. University of Alaska, Anchorage.

ROSLYAKOV, G. YE. & ROSLYAKOV, A. G. 1991. [Role of zakazniks in the conservation of rare birds in the Khabarovsk region]. *In* [*Proceedings of the 10th All-Union Ornithological Conference, Minsk*], part 2, 184. Navuka i tekhnika, Minsk. [In Russian.]

ROULIN, A. 1999. Nonrandom pairing by male Barn Owl (*Tyto alba*) with respect to female plumage trait. *Behavioural Ecology* 10: 688–695.

ROULIN, A., JUNGI, T. W., PFISTER, H. & DIJKSTRA, C. 2000. Female barn owls (*Tyto alba*) advertise good genes. *Proceedings of the Royal Society of London B* 267: 937–941.

ROULIN, A., RIOLS, C., DIJKSTRA, C. & DUCREST, A-L. 2001. Female plumage spottiness signals parasite resistance in Barn Owl (*Tyto alba*). *Behavioural Ecology* 12: 103–110.

ROWE, M. P. 1999. UV-visible reflectance patterns of raptor feathers and the potential arms race between stealthy raptors and their sub-aerial prey. *Investigative Ophthalmology and Visual Science* 40: 750.

RÜDBECK O, 1693–1710. *Book of Birds.* Cited in B. Lowendahl (1986), *Facsimile of the Original Watercolours of the Leufsta Collection of the Uppsala University Library.* Bjork and Brojesson, Stockholm,

RUPASOV, S. V. 2001. [Data on breeding birds of prey in the Southern Yamal in 2001.] *Russian Journal of Ornithology (Express)* 166: 968–971. [In Russian.]

RUPASOV, S. V. 2003. [Territorial dependencies of Falconiformes of the forest–tundra and southern tundra of the Yamal Peninsula.] *In* V. M. Galushin (ed.), [*Proceedings of the 4th Conference on Birds of Prey of Northern Eurasia, Penza 1–3 February 2003*], 82–84. [In Russian.]

RYABTSEV, V. K. 1986. [*Birds of the Tundra.*] Sverdlovsk Books, Sverdlovsk. [In Russian.]

RYABTSEV, V. K. 1997. [Gyrfalcon *Falco rusticolus* in the Baikal Region.] *Russian Journal of Ornithology (Express)* 27: 2–5. [In Russian.]

RYCHLIK, I., KUBICEK, O., HOLCAK, V., BARTA, J & PAVLIK, I. 1994. DNA fingerprinting in Falconidae. *Veterinarni Medicina (Praha)* 39: 111–116.

SABANEEV, L. P. 1871. [Catalogue of mammals, birds, reptilia and fishes of the Middle Urals.] *Bulletin of the MOIP (Moscow Society of Naturalists) Department of Biology* 2: 210–278. [In Russian.]

SABANEEV, L. P. 1874. [*Vertebrates of the Middle Urals and their geographical distribution in the Perm and Orenburg Disricts.*] St Petersburg. [In Russian.]

SALOMONSEN, F. 1950–1951. *Grønlands Fugle*, volumes 1–3. Enjar Munksgard, København.

SALOMONSEN, F. 1967. *Fuglene på Grønland*. Rhodos, København.

SALTER, R. E., GOLLOP, M. A., JOHNSON, S. R., KOSKI, W. R. & TULL, C. E. 1980. Distribution and abundance of birds on the Arctic coastal plain of northern Yukon and adjacent Northwest Territories, 1971–1976. *Canadian Field Naturalist* 94: 219–238.

SAMOUR, J. H. (ed.) 2000. *Avian Medicine*. Harcourt Publishers Ltd., London.

SAUROLA, P. 1997. Rengastusvuosi 1996. *Linnut-vuosikirja 1996* 64–69.

SCHMIDT, G. 1958. Gerfalke am Westehever Sand. *Die Heimat (Kiel)* 65: 127–128.

SCHMUTZ, J. K., FYFE, R. W., BANASCH, U. & ARMBRUSTER, H. 1991. Routes and timing of migration of falcons in Canada. *Wilson Bulletin* 103: 44–58.

SEIFERT, V. 1982. Captive breeding of a passage Gyrfalcon (*Falco rusticolus*): An example of an approach to breeding. *In* W. N. Ladd & P .F. Schempf (eds), *Raptor Management and Biology in Alaska and Western Canada*, 281–294. United States Department of the Interior & United States Fisheries and Wildlife Service, Anchorage.

SEMENOV-TYAN-SHANSKIY, O. I. 1959. [*Ecology of the Tetraonidae.*] Lapland State Reserve, Moscow. [In Russian.]

SEMENOV-TJAN-SHANSKIY, O. I. & GILYAZOV, A. S. 1991. [*Birds of Lapland.*] Nauka, Moscow. [In Russian.]

SHANK, C. C. & POOLE, K. G. 1994. Status of Gyrfalcon *Falco rusticolus*: Populations in the Northwest Territories, Canada. *In* B-U. Meyburg & R. Chancellor (eds), *Raptor Conservation Today*, 421–436. Pica Press, Robertsbridge.

SHAPAREV, YU. P. 1998. [Rare birds of the Yenisey taiga.] In: *In* Yu. Blokhin & L. N. Mazin, [*The Problems of Conservation of the Poorly Studied Fauna of the North*], 57–67. TSNIL Glavokhota, Moscow. [In Russian.]

SHELDON, C. 1909. List of birds observed on the Upper Toklat river near Mount McKinley, Alaska, 1907–1908. *Auk* 26: 66–70.

SHER, A. V. 1997. [Environmental restructuring at the Pleistocene/Holocene boundary in the east Siberian Arctic and its role in mammalian extinction and establishment of modern ecosystems.] *Cryosphere of the Earth* 1: 21–29. [In Russian.]

SHER, A. YA. 1963. [Stone sculptures of the Seven-rivers.] Nauka, Moscow and Leningrad. [In Russian.]

SHKLYAREVICH, F. & KRASNOV, YU. 1980. [The biology of the Gyrfalcon (*Falco gyrfalco gyrfalco* L.) in the Kola Peninsula.] *In* V. A. Zabrodin (ed.), [*Ecology of the birds of the sea coasts*], 17–26.TSNIL Glavokhota, Moscow. [In Russian.]

SHOR, W. 1988. Operation falcon and the Peregrine. *In* T. J. Cade, J. H. Enderson, C. G. Thelander & C. M. White (eds), *Peregrine Falcon Populations: Their Management and Recovery,* 831–842. The Peregrine Fund, Inc., Boise, Idaho.

SHTEGMAN, B. K. 1937. [*Fauna of the USSR: Birds. Volume 1: Birds of Prey.*] Zoological Institute, Academy of Sciences of the USSR, New Series 14, Moscow. [In Russian.]

SHTERNBERG, L. YA. 1925. [Cult of Eagles in Siberian People.] *Collections of Papers of the Museum of Anthropology and Ethnography* 5: 717–740. [In Russian.]

SHTERNBERG, L. YA. 1936. [*Prehistoric religion in the light of anthropology.*] Smiridovich Institute of the Peoples of the North, Leningrad. [In Russian.]

SIBLEY, C. G. & AHLQUIST, J. E. 1990. *Phylogeny and classification of birds: A study in molecular evolution.* Yale University Press, New Haven, Connecticut.

SIMAKOV, G. N. 1998. [*Falconry and the Cult of Birds of Prey in Central Asia (Ritual and Practical Aspects).*] Peterburgskoe Vostokovedenie, St Petersburg. [In Russian.]

SIMAKOV, G. N. 1999. [*Falconry in Central Asia in the 19th and 20th centuries.*] Mektep. Bishkek. [In Russian.]

SIMMONS, R. 1986. Food provisioning, nestling growth and experimental manipulation of brood size in the African Redbreasted Sparrowhawk *Accipiter rufiventris. Ornis Scandinavica* 17: 31–40.

SJÖLANDER, D. 1946. Zoologiska lapplandsminnen. Sverges Natur Årsbok 37: 95–107.

SLOANAKER, J. I.. 1926. The grey Gyrfalcon in Washington. *Condor* 28: 172.

SNOW, C. 1974. Gyrfalcon, *Falco rusticolus.* Habitat management series for unique or endangered species. *US Department of the Interior (Bureau of Land Management) report N9, technical note 6601.*

SOLOMONOV, N. G. (ed.) 1987. [*Red Data Book of the Yakut ASSR: Rare and endangered species of animals.*] Nauka, Novosibirsk. [In Russian.]

SORTLAND, F. 1997. Erfarenheter av ett rovfageproject pa Lofoten. *Blåfoten* 2: 3–4.

SPANGENBERG, E. P. & LEONOVICH V. V. 1958. [Ecology of predatory birds on the Kanin Peninsula]. *Scientific Reports of Moscow University* 197: 49–60. [In Russian.]

STABLER, R. M. 1942. Observations on molting in captive falcons. *American Falconer* 1: 6–12.

STEEN, O. F. 1998. Jaktfalken på Harrdangervidda. *Blåfoten* 5: 1–2.

STEEN, O. F. 1999a. Jaktfalk i Norge – fylkesvis oversikt over hekkeplasser og anslag pa hekkende par. *Vandrefalken* 4: 48–51.

STEEN, O. F. 1999b. Jaktfalkens *Falco rusticolus* valg av reirplass pa Østre Hardangervidda, Sør–Norge. *Ornis Norvegica* 22: 53–59.

STEJNEGER, L. 1885. Results of ornithological explorations in the Commander Islands and in Kamtschatka. *Bulletin of the United States National Museum, Washington* N29: 1–382.

STEPANYAN, L. S. 1975. [*Composition and distribution of birds of the USSR: Non-passerines.*] Nauka, Moscow. [In Russian.]

STEPANYAN, L. S. 1990. [*The ornithological fauna of the USSR.*] Nauka, Moscow. [In Russian.]

STEVENS, R. 1953. *Laggard*. Faber & Faber, London.

STEVENS, R. 1956. The Gyrfalcon. *Journal of the Falconry Club of America* 1: 18–22.

STEWART, J. R. 1999. Intraspecific variation in modern and Quaternary European *Lagopus*. *Smithsonian Contributions to Paleobiology* 89: 159–168.

STISHOV, M. S & MARUKHNICH, A. M. 1990. [Rare birds of the Arctic coast of Western Chukotka.] *In* A. M. Amirkhanov (ed.), [*Rare and Endangered animals: Materials for the Red Data Book*], 45–50. TSNIL Glavokhota, Moscow. [In Russian.]

STISHOV, M. S., PRIDATKO, V. I. & BARANYK, V. V. 1991. [*Birds of Wrangel Island.*] Nauka, Novosibirsk. [In Russian.]

SUETENS, W. & GROENENDAEL, P. V. 1976. Observations au nid du Faucon Gerfaut (*Falco rusticulus*) en Islande. *Le Gerfaut* 66: 44–61.

SUMMERS, R. W. & GREEN, G. H. 1974. Notes on the food of the Gyrfalcon *Falco rusticolus* in northeast Greenland in 1972. *Dansk Ornithologisk Forenings Tidsskrift* 68: 87–90.

SUSHKIN, P. P. 1925. [*List and distribution of birds of the Russian Altay and adjoining parts of north-western Mongolia.*] Academy of Sciences, Leningrad. [In Russian.]

SUSHKIN, P. P. 1938. [*Birds of the Soviet Altay and adjacent parts of Northwestern Mongolia, volume 1.*] USSR Academy of Sciences, Moscow/Leningrad. [In Russian.]

SUTTON, G. M. 1960. Review of "*The Ecology of the Peregrine and Gyrfalcon population in Alaska*", Tom Cade, University of California Press, Berkley. 1960." *Science* 132, 1832–1833.

SUTTON, G. M. 1974. *A Check-list of Oklahoma Birds*. University of Oklahoma

Press, Norman, Oklahoma.

SWEM, T., MCINTYRE, C., RITCHIE, R., BENTE P. & ROSENEAU, D. 1994. Distribution, abundance and notes on the breeding biology of Gyrfalcons *Falco rusticolus* in Alaska. *In* B-U. Meyburg & R. Chancellor (eds), *Raptor Conservation Today*, 437–444. Pica Press, Robertsbridge.

SYROECHKOVSKIY, E. E. & ROGACHEVA, E. V. 1995. [*Red Data Book of the Krasnoyarsk District.*] Krasnoyarsk University Publishers, Krasnoyarsk. [In Russian.]

TABACHNIK, B. & FIDELL, L 1989. *Using Multivariate Statistics.* Harper and Row Publishers, New York.

TAFT, S. J., ROSENFIELD, R. N., SEEGAR, W. S. & MAECHTLE, T. L. 1998. Paucity of hematozoa in Peregrine Falcons (*Falco peregrinus*) in west Greenland and coastal Texas. *Journal of the Helminthological Society of Washington* 65: 111–113.

TENNESEN, M. 1992. *The flight of the falcon.* Swan Hill Press, Shrewsbury.

TER BRAAK, C. J. F. 1996. Canonical correspondence analysis: A new eigenvector technique for multivatiate direct gradient analysis. *Ecology* 67: 1167–1179.

TER BRAAK, C. J. F. & SMILAUER, P. 1998. *Canoco Reference Manual and Users Guide to Canoco for Windows: Software for Canonical Community Ordination.* Microcomputer Power, New York.

TILLISCH, C. J. 1949. *Falkejagten og dens historie.* P. Haase & Søns Forlag, København.

TINBERGEN, L. 1940. Beobachtungen uber due Arbeitsteilung des Turmfalken (*Falco tinnunculus* L.) wahrend der Fortplanzungszeit. *Ardea* 29: 63–98.

TJERNBERG, M. 1997. 1997 års jaktfalkenvintering I Norrbotten. *Blåfoten* 3: 1–2.

TJERNBERG, M. 1998. *Jaktfalcenvintering i Norbotten 1997.* Sveriges Ornithologiska Forening, Stockholm.

TJERNBERG, M. 2000. Fåglar på den nya rödlistan. *Vår Fågelvard* 4: 27–27.

TKACHENKO, M. I. 1937. [*Birds of the lower River Tunguska.*] [*Proceedings of the Society of the Studies of the Eastern Siberia*] 2: 152–161. [In Russian.]

TODD, W. E. C. 1963. *Birds of the Labrado Peninsula and adjacent areas.* Toronto University Press, Toronto.

TODD, W. E. C. & FRIEDMANN, H. 1947. A study of the Gyrfalcons with particular reference to North America. *Wilson Bulletin* 59: 139–150.

TOLMACHEV A. I. 1928. [*The aviafauna of Kolguev Island.*] *Proceedings of the Zoological Museum* 28: 335–365. [In Russian.]

TOMKOVICH, P. A. & VRONSKIY N. V. 1988. [Fauna and bird populations of the Arctic tundras of the Khariton Laptev coast, north-western Taimyr]. *In* E. V. Rogacheva (ed.), [*Papers on the fauna of Central Siberia and adjacent regions of Mongolia.*] IEMEZh, Moscow. [In Russian.]

TOMKOVICH, P. A. & VRONSKIY, N. V. 1994. [Birds of the lower Uboynaya River (NW Taymir)]. In E. V. Rogacheva (ed.), [*Arctic tundras of Taimyr and the islands of the Kara Sea: Nature, animals and problems of conservation.*], volume 1,

161–206. Severtsev Institute of Evolutionary Morphology and Ecology of Animals of the Central Siberian Nature Reserve, Moscow. [In Russian.]

TØMMERAAS, P. J. 1978. Artificial nest sites for the Gyrfalcon and Peregrine. *Vår Fuglefauna* 1: 142–151. [In Norwegian, English summary.]

TØMMERAAS, P. J. 1988. Gyrfalcon *Falco rusticolus* predation on poultry and domestic animals: A review. *Dansk Ornithologisk Forenings Tidsskrift* 82: 109–116.

TØMMERAAS, P. J. 1989a. A time-lapse nest study of a pair of Gyrfalcons *Falco rusticolus* from their arrival at the nest ledge to the completion of egg laying. *Fauna Norvegica Series C Cinclus* 12: 52–63.

TØMMERAAS, P. J. 1989b. Carrion feeding in the Gyrfalcon *Falco rusticolus*: A review. *Fauna Norvegica Series C Cinclus* 12: 65–77.

TØMMERAAS, P. J. 1990. Falkenes reirbyggere. Utdag fra rovfuglstudiene ved Alta-Kaukokeino-og Reisavassdragene. *Vår Fuglefauna* 13: 205–214.

TØMMERAAS, P. J. 1993. The status of Gyrfalcon (*Falco rusticolus*) research in northern Scandinavia. *Fauna Norvegica Series C Cinclus* 16: 75–82.

TØMMERAAS, P. J. 1994a. Jaktfalk *Falco rusticolus*. *In* J. O. Gjershaug, P. G. Thingstad, S. Eldøy & S. Byrkjeland (eds), *Norsk Fuglreatlas*, 134–135. Norsk Ornithologisk Forening, Klæbu.

TØMMERAAS, P. J. 1994b. Jaktfalken. Ripjägare på vikande front. *Vår Fågelvärd* 53: 20–23.

TREVOR-BATTYE, A. 1895. *Ice-bound on Kolguev: A Chapter in the Exploration of Arctic Europe to which is added a Record of the Natural History of the Island.* Archibald Constable and Co., London.

TUCKER, V. A. 1998. Gliding flight: Speed and acceleration of ideal falcons during diving and pull out. *Journal of Experimental Biology* 201: 403–414.

TUCKER, V. A. 1999. The stoop of a falcon: How fast, how steep and how high? *Hawk Chalk* 38: 58–63.

TUCKER, V. A. 2000a. The deep fovea, sideways vision and spiral flight paths in raptors. *Journal of Experimental Biology* 203: 3745–3754.

TUCKER, V. A. 2000b. Gliding flight: drag and torque of a hawk and a falcon with straight and turned heads, and a lower value for the parasite drag coefficient. *Journal of Experimental Biology* 203: 3733–3744.

TUCKER, V. A., CADE, T. J. & TUCKER, A. E. 1998. Diving speeds and angles of a Gyrfalcon (*Falco rusticolus*). *Journal of Experimental Biology* 201: 2061–2070.

TUGARINOV, A. YA. & BUTURLIN, S. A. 1911. [Birds of the Yeniseyskaya District]. Proceedings of the Krasnoyarsk Subdepartment of the Russian Geographical Society, Krasnoyarsk. [In Russian.]

TYRBERG, T. 1995. Paleobiogeography of the genus *Lagopus* in the West Palearctic. *Courier Forshungsinstitut Senkenberg* 181: 275–291.

URBANEK, B. & JUPA, K. 1961. *Falco gyrfalco* – novy druh pro avifaunu Cezskoslovenska: Vrestnik Ceskoskovenske splecnosti zoologicke. *Acta Societatis*

Zoologicae Bohemicae 25: 369–371.

URYADNIK [legislation] 1788. [On the Tzar Alexis Michailivich. The book on the law: new rules and regulations for the practices of falconry and trapping, 1668, volume 3]. Published by N. Novikov (2nd ed.). [In Old Russian.]

USPENSKIY, S. M. 1965. [Birds of eastern Bolshezemelsakya tundra, Yugor peninsula and Vaigach island]. *Proceedings of the Institute of Biology, Ural Academy of Sciences, Sverdlovsk* 38: 65–102. [In Russian.]

USPENSKIY, S. M. 1984. *Life in High Latitudes: A Study of Bird Life.* A. A. Balkema, Rotterdam.

VÄISÄNEN, R. A., LAMMI, E. & KOSKIMIES, P. 1998. *Muuttuva pesimalinnusto [Distribution, numbers and population changes of Finnish breeding birds].* Otava, Helsinki. [In Finnish.]

VAN ORDEN, C. & PAKLINA, N. 2000. The mortal link between Willow Grouse *Lagopus lagopus* and Gyrfalcon *Falco rusticolus* in Eastern Siberia. *De Takkeling* 8: 36–139.

VARTANYAN, S. L., GARUTT, V. E. & SHER, A. V. 1993. Holocene dwarf mammoths from Wrangel Island in the Siberian Arctic. *Nature* 362: 337–340.

VAUGHAN, R. 1992. *In Search of Arctic Birds.* T & AD Poyser, London.

VAURIE, C. 1961. *The Birds of the Palearctic Fauna. Volume 2 – Non-Passeriformes.* H. F. & G. Witherby, London.

VESELOVSKIY, N. K. 1890. [Memories of the diplomatic and trade links of Russia with Persia during the rein of Fedor Ioanovich.] *Proceedings of the Oriental Department of the Russian Imperial Archeological Society, St. Petersburg* 20: 246. [In Russian.]

VITALA, J., KORPIMÄKI, E., POLOKANGAS, P. & KOIVULA, M. 1995. Attraction of kestrels to vole scent marks visible in ultraviolet light. *Nature* 373: 425–427.

VLADIMIRSKAYA, M. I. 1948. [Birds of the Lapland Nature Reserve]. *Proceedings of the Lapland Nature Reserve* 3: 171–245. [In Russian.]

VOLKOV, A. E. 1988. [About the fauna and bird population of the Kotuy River basin and the environs of the Tura settlement.] *In* E. V. Rogacheva (ed.), [*Conservation and rational use of the fauna and ecosystems of the Yenisey North*], 97–113. Severtsev Institute of Evolutionary Morphology and Ecology of Animals of the Central Siberian Nature Reserve, Moscow. [In Russian.]

VOLKOV, A. E., STEPANITSKIY, V. B. & TAKHOV, S. V. 1998. [The nesting of Gyrfalcon in Putorana Nature Reserve.] *In* [*Materials for the Red Data Book*], 190–191. Ministry of Agriculture and Central Science Laboratory of Game Management and Nature Reserves., Moscow. [In Russian.]

VOROBIEV, K. A. 1954. [*Birds of the Ussuri Region.*] Academy of Sciences, Moscow. [In Russian.]

VOROBIEV, K. A. 1963. [*Birds of Yakutia.*] Academy of Sciences, Moscow. [In Russian.]

VORONIN, R. N. 1977. [The biology of Peregrines and Gyrfalcons in the

Bolshezemelsakya Tundra]. *In* M. A. Voinstvenskiy (ed.), [*Proceedings of the 7th All-Union Ornithological Conference, Kiev*], 203–204. Naukova Dumka, Kiev. [In Russian.]

VORONIN, R. N. 1983. [Influence of Gyrfalcon on the population structure of Willow Grouse in the Bolshezemelsakya tundra]. *Proceedings of the Komi Branch of the Academy of Sciences, Syktyvkar* 62: 17–20. [In Russian.]

VORONIN, R. N. 1984. [Daily activity of Gyrfalcons during the chick-rearing period in the Bolshezemelsakya tundra]. *In* M. I. Braude (ed.), [*Fauna of the Urals and adjoining territories*], 72–75. Ural University Publishers, Sverdlovsk. [In Russian.]

VORONIN, R. N. 1986. [Breeding of Gyrfalcon in the south of the Bolshezemelskaya Tundra.] *Ornitologia* 21: 130–131. [In Russian.]

VORONIN, R. N. 1987. [Biology of Gyrfalcon (*Falco gyrfalco* L.) in the south-east of the Bolshezemelsakya tundra.] *Bulletin of the MOIP (Moscow Society of Naturalists) Department of Biology* 92: 10–17. [In Russian.]

VORONIN, R. N., ESTAFIEV, A. A. & MINEEV, YU. N. 1983. [The biology of the Golden Eagle, Peregrine and Gyrfalcon in the European northwest of the USSR]. *In* V. M. Galushin (ed.), [Conservation of birds of prey], 108–114. Nauka, Moscow. [In Russian.]

VORONIN, R. N. & KOCHANOV, S. E. 1989. [New findings on the breeding sites of Peregrine and Gyrfalcon in the tundras of the NE European part of the USSR.] In: X. X. Kuzyakin (ed.), [*Proceedings of the Surveyed Characteristics, Results of Counts and Survey Materials of Non-commercial Birds, Reptiles, Amphibia and Fish*], 44–45. Bashkir Books, Ufa. [In Russian.]

WALKER, D. 1974. A Pleistocene Gyrfalcon. *Auk* 91: 820–821.

WALKER, W. 1977. Chlorinated hydrocarbon pollutants in Alaska Gyrfalcons and their prey. *Auk* 94: 442–447.

WAYRE, P. & JOLLY, G. 1958. Notes on the breeding of the Icelandic Gyr Falcon. *British Birds* 51: 285–290.

WEBSTER, H. 1959. Gyrfalcons – in sickness and in health. *Journal of the Falconry Club of America* 2: 25–27.

WERNERY, U., WERNERY, R., ZACHARIAH, R. & KINNE, J. 1998. Salmonellosis in relation to chlamydiosis and pox and Salmonella infections in captive falcons in the United Arab Emirates. *Journal of Veterinary Medicine Series B – Infectious Diseases and Veterinary Public Health* 45: 577–583.

WHITE, C. M. & CADE, T. J. 1971. Cliff-nesting raptors and ravens along Colville river in Arctic Alaska. *Living Birds* 10: 107–150.

WHITE, C. M. & NELSON, R. W. 1991. Hunting range and strategies in a tundra breeding peregrine and gyrfalcon observed from a helicopter. *Journal of Raptor Research* 25: 49–62.

WHITE, C. M., OLSEN, P. D. & KIFF, L. F. 1994. Family Falconidae (falcons and caracaras). *In* J. del Hoyo, A. Elliot & J. Sargatal (eds), *Handbook of the Birds of the World*, vol. 2: 216–275. Lynx Edicions, Barcelona.

WHITE, C. M. & ROSENEAU, D. G. 1970. Observations on food, nesting, and winter populations of large North American falcons. *Condor* 72: 113–115.

WHITE, C. M. & SPRINGER, H. K 1965. Notes on Gyrfalcon in western coastal Alaska. *Auk* 82: 104–105.

WHITE, C. M. & WEEDEN, R. B. 1966. Hunting methods of Gyrfalcons and behaviour of their prey. *Condor* 68: 517–519.

WILLIAMS, E. 1905. On the occurrence of the Greenland and Iceland falcons in Ireland during spring 1905. *Irish Naturalist* 14: 201–202.

WILLINGHBY, F. 1676. *Synopsis Methodica Avium*. London.

WINK, M. 1998. Application of DNA markers to study the ecology and evolution of raptors. *In* R. D. Chancellor, B-U. Meyburg & J. J. Ferrero (eds), *Holarctic Birds of Prey*, 49–71. ADENEX/World Working Group on Birds of Prey, Mérida and Berlin.

WINK, M., SEIBOLD, I., LITFIKHAH, F. & BEDNAREK, W. 1998. Molecular systematics of Holarctic raptors (Order Falconiformes). *In* R. D. Chancellor, B-U. Meyburg & J. J. Ferrero (eds), *Holarctic Birds of Prey*, 29–48. ADENEX/World Working Group on Birds of Prey, Mérida and Berlin.

WINTHER, J-G. 1991. Landsat TM derived and *in situ* summer reflectance of glaciers in Svalbard. *Polar Research* 12: 37–55.

WINTHER, J-G. 1993. *Snow and glacier ice characteristics measured using Landsat TM data*. Unpublished thesis (IVB Report B–2–1993–5), Norwegian Institute of Technology, University of Trondheim.

WIRDHEIM, A. 1999. Svenska rovfågelskandaler. *Vår Fågelvärd* 8: 5.

WITHERBY, H. F., JOURDAIN, F. C. R., TICEHURST, N. F. & TUCKER, B. F. 1943. *The Handbook of British Birds*. H. F. & G. Witherby. London.

WOLLEY, J. 1864. *Ootheca Wolleyana: an illustrated catalogue of the collection of birds' eggs begun by the late John Wolley, Jun., M.A., F. Z. S.* John van Voorst, London.

WOOD, C. & FYFE, F. 1943. *The Art of Falconry: "De arte venandi cum avibus of Fredereck II of Hohenstaufen"*. Stanford University Press, Stanford.

WOODIN, N. 1980. Observations on Gyrfalcon (*Falco rusticolus*) breeding near Lake Myvatn, Iceland, 1967. *Journal of Raptor Research* 14: 97–124.

WREGE, P. H. & CADE, T. J. 1977. Courtship behaviour of large falcons in captivity. *Raptor Research* 11: 1–46.

YAKHONTOV, V. D. 1979. [Birds of the Penzhina District.] *In* A. V. Krechmar (ed.), [*Birds of Northeast Asia*], 135–163. Institute of Biological Problems of the North, Vladivostok. [In Russian.]

YAMASHINA, Y. 1931. Die Vogel der Kurilen. *Journal für Ornithologie*, 79: 491–541.

YAMASHINA, Y. 1941 *A Natural History of Japanese Birds*. Iwanami, Tokyo.

YUDAKHIN, K. 1965. [*Kyrgyz–Russian Dictionary*.] Sovetskaya Publishers, Moscow. [In Russian.]

YUDIN, K. A. 1952. [Observations on the distribution and biology of birds of the Krasnoyarsk Region]. *Proceedings of the Zoological Institute, Academy of Sciences of the USSR* 9: 1029–1060. [In Russian.]

YURTSEV, B. A. 1966. [*The Hypoarctic Botanico–geographical Belt and the Origin of its Flora.*] Nauka, Moscow/Leningrad. [In Russian.]

YURTSEV, B. A. 1981. [*Relict Steppe Complexes of Northeast Asia.*] Nauka, Novosibirsk. [In Russian.]

ZAHAVI, A. & ZAHAVI, A. 1997. *The Handicap Principle.* Oxford University Press, Oxford.

ZARUDNIY A. N. 1915. [*A short account on hunting in the Syr–Darya district*]. Tashkent. [In Russian.]

ZHIRMUNSKIY, V. M. 1962. [*Book of my grandfather Korkut*]. Nauka, Moscow & Leningrad. [In Russian.]

Index

The scientific names of all species mentioned in the text are given in the Appendix.